ADVANCE PRAISE FOR *SOCIAL SCIENCE AND POWER IN INDONESIA*

"Western observers of Indonesia often wonder about the capacity of Indonesian social scientists to address issues of basic public importance. Here is a volume that answers that question with clarity and power. The essays address problems at the heart of Indonesia's future. They also bear witness to the sophistication and achievement of a new generation of Indonesian social scientists." – *Robert Hefner, Boston University*

"The book is very timely, because there are still many people in Indonesia who think that social science is neutral, especially after the Soeharto regime. I am sure this book will open up an interesting debate for the years to come." – *Arief Budiman, University of Melbourne*

"This book offers fresh and critical voices from a new generation of Indonesian social scientists. Familiar with western theory and Indonesian reality, these writers offer a kaleidoscope of views marked by cynicism and indignation, idealism and optimism." – *Robert Cribb, Australian National University*

"Intellectuals in Indonesia have always had high social status. They haven't always deserved this status, especially during the New Order when they allowed themselves to be used by the regime. By examining the varieties of 'usefulness', this book begins the process of redemption." – *Joel Rocamora, Institute of Popular Democracy, Manila*

"For those interested in exploring contemporary dynamics of social realities in the world's fourth largest nation, this is an exciting book written by Indonesian social scientists that applies the latest developments in social thought." – *Mayling Oey-Gardiner, Insan Hitswasana Sejahtera*

"This collection provides a very thoughtful and illuminating treatment of the connection between knowledge and power in Indonesia, bringing to bear both theoretical sophistication and empirical depth to a crucial topic in the country's political and social life." – *John Sidel, London School of Economics*

"This is an excellent and important book. It is exciting that Indonesian scholars have seized the moment to comment on the impact of New Order policies on the growth of social science in Indonesia over the past several decades. The myth-making, the distortion of research agendas for the benefit of 'development', old and new theoretical approaches, and concerns for the future are prominent themes. This adds timely critical analysis to the rapidly growing field of Southeast Asian studies in Southeast Asia." – *Laurie Sears, University of Washington*

"A pioneering collection of exciting, scholarly analyses of the politics of Indonesian social science, between state-authoritarianism and neo-liberalism. [This book is] an indispensable contribution to its intellectual integrity, academic quality and thus democratic potential." – *Olle Törnquist, Professor of Political Science and Development Research, University of Oslo*

The **Celebrating Indonesia** Series is a set of four books jointly
produced by the Ford Foundation and Equinox Publishing
to celebrate Ford's 50th anniversary in Indonesia.
Each volume will be available in both English and Indonesian.

The other titles in the series are:

Environmental Politics and Power in Indonesia

*Indonesian Arts since Independence:
Changing Contexts, Content, and Careers*

People, Population, and Policy in Indonesia

An accompanying volume,
Celebrating Indonesia: Fifty Years with the Ford Foundation 1953-2003,
was published in 2003 and is available for download on
http://www.fordfound.org/publications/
recent_articles/celebrating_indonesia.cfm.

Vedi R. Hadiz and Daniel Dhakidae, Editors

SOCIAL SCIENCE
AND
POWER
IN
INDONESIA

EQUINOX
PUBLISHING
JAKARTA SINGAPORE

ISEAS
INSTITUTE OF
SOUTHEAST ASIAN STUDIES
Singapore

First published in Jakarta and Singapore in 2005 by

Equinox Publishing (Asia) Pte. Ltd.
PO Box 6179 JKSGN
Jakarta 12062
Indonesia
www.equinoxpublishing.com

and

Institute of Southeast Asian Studies
30 Heng Mui Keng Terrace
Pasir Panjang
Singapore 119614
www.bookshop.iseas.edu.sg

ISEAS Library Cataloguing-in-Publication Data

Social science and power in Indonesia / edited by Vedi R. Hadiz and Daniel Dhakidae.
1. Social sciences-Indonesia.
2. Social sciences-Research-Indonesia.
3. Indonesia-Politics and government.
4. Indonesia-Social conditions.
I. Hadiz, Vedi R., 1964-
II. Dhakidae, Daniel, 1945-
H53 I5S67   2005

Equinox Publishing ISBN 979-3780-01-0
ISEAS ISBN 981-230-293-X
Printed in Indonesia.

The **Institute of Southeast Asian Studies** (ISEAS) was established as an autonomous organization in 1968. It is a regional centre dedicated to the study of socio-political, security and economic trends and developments in Southeast Asia and its wider geostrategic and economic environment.

The Institute's research programmes are the Regional Economic Studies (RES, including ASEAN and APEC), Regional Strategic and Political Studies (RSPS), and Regional Social and Cultural Studies (RSCS).

ISEAS Publications, an established academic press, has issued more than 1,000 books and journals. It is the largest scholarly publisher of research about Southeast Asia from within the region. ISEAS Publications works with many other academic and trade publishers and distributors to disseminate important research and analyses from and about Southeast Asia to the rest of the world.

TABLE OF CONTENTS

ABOUT THE CONTRIBUTORS

ROCHMAN ACHWAN is Chair of the Laboratory of Sociology and Senior Lecturer in the Department of Sociology, University of Indonesia. His Ph.D thesis "Weaving Business Networks among Textile Entrepreneurs in Indonesia" was submitted to the Faculty of Sociology, University of Bielefeld, Germany in 1998. Currently, he conducts research on peace and development in West Kalimantan, and on liberalization and Muslim entrepreneurs in Indonesia.

ASVI WARMAN ADAM is Research Professor at the Indonesian Institutes of Sciences. He received his Ph.D in 1990 from L'Ecole des Hautes Etudes en Sciences Sociales, Paris, for a thesis on relations between the Netherlands Indies and Indochina in the colonial era. He recently published *Pelurusan Sejarah Indonesia* (Rewriting Indonesian History), *TriDE* (2004) *and Soeharto, Sisi Gelap Sejarah Indonesia* (Soeharto, the Dark Side of Indonesian History), Ombak (2004).

ARIS ANANTA has been Senior Research Fellow at the Institute of Southeast Asian Studies in Singapore since 2001. He was Senior Fellow at the Department of Economics, National University of Singapore during 1999 and 2000. He has been Professor in Population Economics at the University of Indonesia since 1995 and was Associate Director of the Demographic Institute, University of Indonesia between 1995 and 1998. His recent publications include two books co-authored with Leo Suryadinata and Evi Nurvidya Arifin: *Indonesia's Population. Ethnicity and Religion in a Changing Political Landscape* (2003); and *Indonesian Electoral Behaviour.*

*A Statistical Perspective (*2004), both published by the Institute of Southeast Asian Studies, Singapore.

DANIEL DHAKIDAE is currently Head of *Kompas* Research and Development Department, Jakarta. He was formerly the Chairman of the Board of Editors of *Prisma*, a Jakarta-based social and economic journal published by the Institute for Social and Economic Research, Education and Information (LP3ES), where he served as vice director from 1982-84. He authored *Cendekiawan dan Kekuasaan dalam Negara Orde Baru* (Intellectuals and Power in the New Order State), Gramedia (2003) (soon to be published in English by Equinox Publishing), and has contributed chapters to *Southeast Asian Middle Classes, Prospects for Social Change and Democratisation* by Abdul Rahman Embong (ed.), National University of Malaysia Press (2001), and *Exploration of the Middle Classes in Southeast Asia*, Hsin-Huang Michael Hsiao (ed.), Taipei (2001).

HILMAR FARID is Researcher at the Institute for Social History in Jakarta, and a long-standing democracy activist. He studied history at the University of Indonesia, and has taught history at the National University and the Jakarta Arts Institute. He has written a number of articles and papers on violence and capitalist expansion, including the recent "The Struggle for Truth and Justice: A Survey of Transitional Justice Initiatives throughout Indonesia" (2004) and *Tahun yang Tak Pernah Berakhir* (The Year that Never Ends), ELSAM 2004. He is currently conducting research on working class formation in Indonesia.

MEUTHIA GANIE-ROCHMAN is Chief Sociologist for civil society and governance at the Laboratory of Sociology, and Senior Lecturer in the Department of Sociology, University of Indonesia. She received a Ph.D degree from the Faculty of Social Science, University of Nijmegen, the Netherlands, in 2002. Her latest book in English is *An Uphill Struggle, Advocacy NGOs under Soeharto's New Order*, LabSosio-University of Indonesia (2002).

VEDI HADIZ is Associate Professor at the Department of Sociology, National University of Singapore. He was previously a Research Fellow at the Asia Research Centre, Murdoch University. His other books include the authored *Workers and the State in New Order Indonesia*, Routledge (1997), the co-edited *Politics of Economic Development in Indonesia: Contending Perspectives*, Routledge (1997) and *Indonesian Politics and Society: A Reader*, RoutledgeCurzon (2003), and the co-authored *Reorganising Power In Indonesia: The Politics of Oligarchy in an Age of Markets*, RoutledgeCurzon (2004).

ARIEL HERYANTO is Senior Lecturer in Indonesian studies at the University of Melbourne in Australia. Previously he was Senior Lecturer at the National University of Singapore and Universitas Kristen Satya Wacana (Salatiga, Indonesia). Recent publications include "Can There be Southeast Asians in Southeast Asian Studies?", *Moussons* no. 5 (2002); "Public Intellectuals, Media and Democratization" in A. Heryanto and S.K. Mandal (eds*) Challenging Authoritarianism in Southeast Asia: Comparing Indonesia and Malaysia*, RoutledgeCurzon (2003), and "The Debris of Post-Authoritarianism in Indonesia" in F. Quadir and J. Lele (eds) *Democracy and Civil Society in Asia: Volume 2*, Palgrave and Macmillan (2004).

ALEXANDER IRWAN is currently Executive Director of Tifa Foundation (Jakarta), which provides grants to local governance, access to justice, pluralism, human rights, media, and capacity building programs. Previously he was advisor to the donor agency Partnership for Governance Reform, responsible for coordinating their Aceh and Papua program. He has written articles in domestic and foreign journals and newspapers such as *Journal of Contemporary Asia, Far Eastern Economic Review, South China Morning Post, Nikkei Weekly, Kompas*, and the *Jakarta Post*. He holds a Ph.D. in Sociology from the University of New York at Binghamton.

P.M. LAKSONO is Senior Lecturer at the Department of Anthropology, Gadjah Mada University. He holds a B.A. in anthropology from Gadjah Mada University and S1 at the University of Indonesia. His postgraduate training was at Leiden University, the University of Indonesia, and Cornell University. His books published in English include *Tradition in Javanese Social Structure: Kingdom and Countryside*, Gadjah Mada University Press (1985) and *The Common Ground in the Kei Islands, Eggs from One Fish and One Bird*, Galang Press (2002).

HERU NUGROHO is Lecturer in the Faculty of Sociology, Social Science and Politics at Gadjah Mada University. He is also Director of the Center for Critical Social Study. He graduated in 1993 from the University of Bielefeld, Germany with a degree in development sociology. He has published extensively on social sciences and universities in Indonesia, as well as several critiques of the neo-liberal global agenda.

BEN WHITE is Professor of Rural Sociology at the Institute of Social Studies in The Hague. He is currently Chair of the Editorial Board of the international development studies journal *Development and Change;* Chair of the ISS post-graduate program; and Director of the newly-established *International Centre for Child and*

Youth Studies. He studied philosophy and ancient history at Oxford University (B.A. 1968) and anthropology at Columbia University (Ph.D 1976). He spent five years (1975-1980) attached to the Agro-Economic Survey of Indonesia before moving to the Netherlands. Recent books and edited volumes include *Agrarian Transformations: Local Processes and the State in Southeast Asia,* University of California Press (1989); *Child Workers in Indonesia,* Akatiga (1998), *Forests: Nature, People, Power,* Blackwell (2000), *and Child Labour: Policy Options,* Aksent Academic Publications (2001).

GLOSSARY

AAEI	*Asosiasi Ahli Epigrafi Indonesia*; Association of Indonesian Epigraphists
AAI	*Asosiasi Antropologi Indonesia*; Association of Indonesian Anthropologists
ADC	The Agricultural Development Council
AMAN	*Aliansi Masyarakat Adat Nusantara*; Alliance of Customary Communities in Indonesia
API	*Asosiasi Prehistori Indonesia*; Association of Indonesian Pre-historians
Bakin	*Badan Koordinasi Intelijen Negara*; State Intelligence Coordination Agency
BAKN	*Badan Administrasi Kepegawaian Negara*; Institute of State Personnel Administration
BAPPENAS	*Badan Perencanaan Nasional*; National Planning Agency
BHMN	*Badan Hukum Milik Negara*; State Owned Legal Bodies
BKKBN	*Badan Koordinasi Keluarga Berencana Nasional*; National Family Planning Coordination Board
BPS	*Badan Pusat Stastik*; Central Bureau of Statistics
BTI	*Barisan Tani Indonesia*; Indonesian Peasant Front
CECA	Council on Economic and Cultural Affairs

CGI	Consultative Group on Indonesia
CSIS	Center for Strategic and International Studies
DPR	*Dewan Perwakilan Rakyat*; House of Representatives
FEUI	*Fakultas Ekonomi Universitas Indonesia*; Economics Faculty of the University of Indonesia
GBHN	*Garis-garis Besar Haluan Negara*; Broad Outlines of State Policy
HIPIIS	*Himpunan Indonesia untuk Pengembangan Ilmu-Ilmu Sosial*; Indonesian Association for the Development of Social Sciences
HISKI	*Himpunan Sarjana Kesusasteraan Indonesia*; Association of Indonesian Literary Scholars
IAAI	*Ikatan Ahli Arkeologi Indonesia*; Association of Indonesian Archeologists
ICMI	*Ikatan Cendekiawan Muslim Indonesia*; Indonesian Association of Muslim Intellectuals
IDEA	Institute of Development and Economic Analysis
INFID	International NGO Forum on Indonesian Development
ISEI	*Ikatan Sarjana Ekonomi Indonesia*; Indonesian Association of Economists
ISI	*Ikatan Sosiologi Indonesia*; Association of Indonesian Sociologists
JPS	*jaringan pengaman sosial*; social security net
KADIN	*Kamar Dagang dan Industri*; Indonesian Chamber of Commerce and Industry
KKN	*korupsi, kolusi dan nepotisme*; corruption, collusion, nepotism
Kopkamtib	*Komando Operasi Permulihan Keamanan dan Ketertiban*; Operational Command for the Restoration of Security and Order
LEKNAS	*Lembaga Ekonomi dan Kemasyarakatan Nasional*; National Social and Economic Institute
LEMLIT	*lembaga penelitian*; research institute
LIPI	*Lembaga Ilmu Pengetahuan Indonesia*; Indonesian Institute of Sciences
LP3ES	*Lembaga Penelitian, Pendidikan dan Penerangan Ekonomi dan Sosial*; Institute for Social and Economic Research, Education and Information
LPIST	*Lembaga Penelitian Ilmu Sosial Transformatif*; Institution of Social Transformation Research

MANIPOL	*Manifesto Politik*; Political Manifesto
MLI	*Masyarakat Linguistik Indonesia*; Indonesian Linguistics Community
MPR	*Majelis Permusyawaratan Rakyat*; People's Consultative Assembly
MSI	*Masyarakat Sejarawan Indonesia*; Indonesian Historians Community
MWA	*Majelis Wali Amanat*; University Senate
Nasakom	*nasionalis-agama-komunis*; nationalist-religious-communist
NKK	*Normalisasi Kehidupan Kampus*; Normalization of Campus Life
P4	*Pedoman Penghayatan dan Pengamalan Pancasila*; Upgrading Course on the Directives for the Realization and Implementation of Pancasila
PAU	*Pusat Antar Universitas*; Inter-University Center
PDI-P	*Partai Demokrasi Indonesia Perjuangan*; Indonesian Democratic Party of Struggle
Perekat Ombara	*Persekutuan Masyarakat Adat Lombok Utara*; North Lombok Traditional Communities Alliance
Permesta	*Perjuangan Semesta*; Universal Struggle
PKI	*Partai Komunis Indonesia*; Indonesian Communist Party
PLPIS	*Pusat Latihan Penelitian Ilmu-ilmu Sosial*; Training Center for Social Science Research
PPPB	*Pusat Pembinaan dan Pengembangan Bahasa*; National Center for Language Development
PRRI	*Pemerintah Revolusioner Republik Indonesia*; Revolutionary Government of the Republic of Indonesia
PSPB	*Pendidikan Sejarah Perjuangan Bangsa*; Education of History of the Nation's Struggle
SDKI	*Survai Demografi dan Kesehatan Indonesia*; Indonesian Health and Demography Survey
SEP	*Sistem Ekonomi Pancasila*; Pancasila Economic System
Seskoad	*Sekolah Staf dan Komando Angkatan Darat*; Army Staff and Command School
SOBSI	*Sentral Organisasi Buruh Seluruh Indonesia*; All-Indonesia Central Workers' Organization

SOKSI   *Sentral Organisasi Karyawan Seluruh Indonesia*; All-Indonesia
               Central Employees' Organization

Supersemar   *Surat Perintah 11 Maret*; 11 March Letter of Instruction

TNI   *Tentara Nasional Indonesia*; Indonesian National Army

WALHI   *Wahana Lingkungan Hidup*; Friends of the Earth Indonesia

WTO   World Trade Organization

YIF   *Yayasan Indonesia Forum*; Indonesian Forum Foundation

YIIS   *Yayasan Ilmu-ilmu Sosial*; Social Sciences Foundation

YLBHI   *Yayasan Lembaga Bantuan Hukum Indonesia*; Foundation of the
               Indonesian Legal Aid Institute

TRANSLATOR'S NOTE

The reason for writing this Translator's Note is not in order to explain any particular technical aspects relating to problems of translation in this project. Rather it is to point to some important issues raised by the effort of translation relating to the development of the social sciences in Indonesia and the issue of engagement between Indonesian social scientists and non-Indonesian Indonesianists.

Translating the Indonesian essays in this book did raise some specific issues relating to language, and these issues in turn relate directly to the state of social science and analysis in Indonesia. The strength of this collection is its theoretical engagement with Indonesian social reality, something that has long been missing as a general feature of foreign Indonesian studies. Post-modernist, structuralist, post-structuralist, Marxist and other critical theoretical approaches are all used by different authors in this book. And they are all pioneers. This means that the development of Indonesian language versions of the specific vocabulary for each school of analysis has not yet been fully developed and assimilated into a broadly read body of Indonesian language literature.

The other refreshing feature of this collection is their energy, responding as they do the immediate demands for analysis that can help solve urgent social, economic, political and cultural problems. The nature of current intellectual engagement in Indonesia also has implications for language. Indonesian intellectuals do not primarily write for refereed academic journals, i.e. for each other, as is the case for the majority of foreign Indonesianists. They are frequent participants in public forums with political actors, student activists and NGO advocates. They may appear on TV and radio and in a whole host of other dialogue oriented situations where there is an urgency to both explain to and convince an audience themselves deeply engaged with a tumultuous and challenging reality posed as a real problem for themselves and their society.

Thus the language and style of these articles is more varied than might be found in a collection of American or Australian papers. They are the product of a different reality. Indonesian academics often complain that it is difficult to get published in international academic journals. Sometimes I think this is not so much because they do not meet the so-called standards of refereed journals but because they haven't had the spirit and engagement squeezed out of them by refereed standardisation. In any case, I hope that the energy and urgency of these essays has been retained even after translation.

I hope too that more non-Indonesian Indonesianists will take on tasks of translating into English the works of Indonesian academics and intellectuals. Indonesian studies as an international endeavour seems to have become almost an imperial business dominated by non-Indonesians, despite the theoretical decline of foreign Indonesian studies since the late 1970s. This can only be rectified if more Indonesian works are translated into English and other international languages and enter into international circulation to be read by a wider body of scholars. New students of Indonesia in schools, universities and social movements also need access to these ideas.

Such a commitment by foreign Indonesianists to such translation work is essential if a genuine engagement with analysis and thinking deriving from within Indonesia is to occur. Such a commitment also makes sure that Indonesian thinking and analysis is not just seen as an object of study as part of Indonesiana but as a contribution to the collective effort to develop knowledge and understanding.

Max Lane
Asia Research Centre
Murdoch University
Perth, December 2004

PREFACE

The primary purpose of the social sciences is to explain the social world around us, making collective events intelligible by means of critical and detached analysis. The social sciences cannot predict social actions and should not attempt to justify them. However, ever since the social sciences emerged in Europe in the mid-19th century they have been employed for political purposes, either by those who sit in government or by those who wish to be there. The relationship between social science and power can be uneasy, as the state lures academics with access to influence and resources. Wary scholars must withstand those calls in order to remain autonomous and credible.

The Ford Foundation in Indonesia is celebrating its 50th anniversary. As part of this commemoration, we are publishing a series of books that take a critical look at fields in which our institution has invested over the past half century. Part of the early mandate of the Foundation's office in Jakarta was to build the higher education sector and support the development of research capacity in such disciplines as economics, public administration, sociology and anthropology. When Indonesia gained its independence in 1949, there were only a handful of trained economists in the country and hardly any planners, geographers or political scientists. Over the last half century, and especially during the 1955-1980 period, the Ford office contributed tens of million of dollars to universities and research centers around the country. Gadjah Mada, Nommensen, Udayana, Andalas and the University of Indonesia are among the many institutions that developed or expanded social science programs with this funding. In the 1970s, particular emphasis was placed on fieldwork-based disciplines, with support for social science research training stations in Aceh and Ujung Padang. During the past twenty years, university departments around the country have received support for research and dissemination of information within the fields of the Foundation's programmatic interest, including women's reproductive health and rights, agriculture and natural resources management, arts and culture, and governance. Recently, this targeted funding has been supplemented with general scholarship programs in the social sciences and humanities, both for post-graduate studies abroad and within Indonesia.

But there is also a very different story to tell about the social sciences in Indonesia, relating how the disciplines were used for nation- and regime-building purposes over several decades, and how critical thought was discouraged and higher education tightly controlled. Academics were encouraged to pursue studies that would build national character or otherwise support the government. Many of the academics trained abroad, including some supported by Ford, left the universities to join government. Indonesian intellectuals and social scientists stand out in Southeast Asia for their proximity to power. Intentionally or not, many became architects of the authoritarian Soeharto government. The interpretive power of the social sciences provided the material out of which a prescriptive national identity and a repressive political regime were constructed. For several decades, the main emphasis of the social sciences in Indonesia was not so much to explain, but to justify and predict, and the discipline suffered. As Clifford Geertz wrote in a Ford Foundation-funded assessment of the social sciences in 1971: "Indonesian intellectual life is centralized, over-organized, spasmodic, practical and strongly influenced by economists".

As we know, the authoritarian nation-building project failed. And the social sciences played a role in this as well. The growth of democracy is closely related to the capacity of those ruled to analyze social structures, power relations and state institutions. It is no coincidence that some of the most active participants in the student movement of 1998-99 (as well as the movement of 1966-67) were from social science faculties. Students had long chafed at the outdated curricula and the manipulative program promoting Pancasila. The discrepancy between what institutes of higher learning formally provided and what students and teachers wanted was glaring. Researchers and scholars began to challenge the system by asserting their right to independence from state ideology. They recognized that it is only from a position outside power relations that the social scientist can critically interrogate political, social, and economic relations and processes, and hence contribute to building a more open and diverse society.

Yet developing independent and critical social sciences in Indonesia entails a complex process of introspection and analysis. There is little hope for change until academics recognize that their disciplines are value-laden and subjective and have been used for purposes of national development – with or without their active acquiescence. Scholarship must be independent from nationalism, lest it lose its credibility. Thus, the social sciences in Indonesia cannot advance until they are freed from their close relationship with government policies and national ideologies.

This book is intended to contribute to this liberating process – an as-yet unfinished revolution – and to celebrate the renewed enthusiasm and vigor of contemporary social scientists. The volume explores the ideology and values that have determined priorities in building social science education and charts the road to regaining a responsive role for the social sciences within the political sphere.

We wish to express our gratitude to the individuals who have contributed to this book. Vedi Hadiz and Daniel Dhakidae have been engaged from the beginning of the project. They were our first choice to be editors, and we have been honored to work with them. Their knowledge and enthusiasm made the volume possible. The contributors were identified jointly by the editors and Foundation staff. We sought individuals from within the social sciences able to view them from a critical distance. Thus, some of the contributors have written on a discipline other than their own; others have taken a critical step back to reflect upon power relations and struggles that have shaped their field over the past decades. It is a difficult and sometimes unsettling task to reflect critically on one's own occupation, but we hope the reader can agree that the contributors have achieved this objective. Each author has been magnificent and it has truly been an honor to work with each of them. Finally to Max Lane, the translator; Carolyn Oei, the copyeditor; Jonathan Zilberg, the proofreader; and Mark Hanusz, the publisher. Their dedication, flexibility and capacity to work under pressure have made this book more readable and accessible.

Together, we dedicate this volume to the members of the social science community in Indonesia who endured the authoritarian regime, helped bring it to an end and are now furthering our understanding of a rapidly developing and democratizing Indonesia.

Hans Antlöv
Program Officer
Governance and Civil Society
Ford Foundation
Jakarta, December 2004

-1-

INTRODUCTION

Vedi R. Hadiz and Daniel Dhakidae[1]

O ver the years, there have been a few scattered attempts to document and trace the development of the social sciences in Indonesia, or some of its individual branches (Geertz 1970; Bachtiar 1974a; Koentjaraningrat 1975; Alfian 1979; Kleden 1986; Nordholt and Visser 1997; and other selected writings and articles on Indonesia). Many have been valuable endeavors in charting the changes in the orientation of the social sciences across many disciplines, providing useful data and identifying problems that hinder further development. Almost without exception, among the problems mentioned has been the lack of resources and institutional and/or infrastructural support for long-term, serious social science research or training that complies with internationally accepted standards. Today, it is generally regarded that Indonesian scholars have contributed much less to the international academic literature on their own country than scholars of the neighboring countries of Malaysia, Thailand, Singapore and the Philippines (Evers 2000).

Whilst this book recognizes the valuable contribution that previous "reflections" have had on the state of Indonesian social sciences, it employs a somewhat different approach to the assessment of Indonesian social science as we currently know it. Rather than concentrating on the "technical" aspects of social science development or underdevelopment, it assesses social science over a period of some fifty years by primarily looking at the interface between social science and power. It is argued

---

[1] The authors would like to thank Arya Wisesa and Kurniawan for their research assistance and all the participants of two workshops on the *Social Science and Power in Indonesia* (most of whom appear in this book as contributors), held at the Ford Foundation office in Jakarta in January and June 2003.

here that the development of Indonesian social science – its very nature and character – is inextricably linked to the shifting requirements of power over time. The problems that the Indonesian social science community has confronted and the challenges it continues to face, cannot be understood without an appreciation of this facet of power.

The following is the basic premise of this book in very simple terms: Indonesian social science issues – what is researched and what is not; which frameworks achieve paradigmatic status within particular disciplines and which are consigned to obscurity or marginalized; which disciplines achieve dominance and which ones wither away; and what type of social scientist becomes either "influential" or "ignored" – are all basically a matter of power. It might be worthwhile trying to understand this with the aid of the concept of "social capital" as used by Bourdieu (1986) – prestige, honor and privilege are embedded in and mobilised through social relationships expressed in networks of power – rather than with the now more conventional version associated with Putnam (1995; 2000) and his followers. In the case of the Indonesian social science community, one network of power – as embodied in the Indonesian Association of Economists (*Ikatan Sarjana Ekonomi Indonesia* – ISEI) – played a major part in advancing economics as the provider of all the major reference points or signs of "development" during the New Order. More than merely an association of academics specializing in the field of economics, ISEI was directly linked to the core of state bureaucracy itself. Its leadership typically consisted of government ministers, top bureaucrats, as well as politically connected businessmen (see Laksono, this volume). Indeed, it acted as a conduit to state power and therefore, not surprisingly, played a part in the reproduction of bureaucratic policies and requirements in the academic agenda, primarily via the discipline of economics. Other social science disciplines were pressed to adhere to the developmental reference points provided, which mainly stressed growth, stability and the non-disruption of the social order.

Whilst we are primarily interested in state power, we are also concerned with the changing requirements of capitalism, and, therefore, of capital and the agendas of society-based movements and groups. With regard to the former, the requirements of the press and television industries in particular since the 1970s, 80s and 90s, have arguably influenced the practice of social science and of social scientists in Indonesia. Today, the global market-driven agenda of "reform" in the tertiary education sector has already had a noticeable impact on social science practices in Indonesia, with the reduction of already limited state subsidies for universities (see Nugroho, this volume). With regard to the requirements of society-based movements and groups, from time to time, we have seen concrete attempts to develop alternative social science agendas that challenge dominant assumptions and concerns of the university-based social science community. Those involved in these endeavours seek to link social research with issues of democratization, rights and freedoms, rather than with the problems of technocratic governance, or the demands of the market. In this regard, the role of non-governmental organizations (NGO) during certain periods in the development of Indonesian social science has been notable.

The relationship between social science and power – or more generally, between "knowledge" and power – is by no means a novel proposition (Foucault 1980). Moreover, issues of power are anything but alien to the concerns of various branches of the social sciences. But, what we have in mind are the specific instrumental relationships between power holders, especially the state and the academic community, which influence social science programs. These also influence the relationship between the different social science branches – with some, for example, being in greater proximity to policy-making circles and others being relatively excluded, for better or for worse. Indeed, the exclusionary nature of state politics towards some branches of the social sciences during the New Order period was notorious.

For most of the contributors to this volume, inserting the factor of power into the analytical equation constitutes nothing more than the exercise of common sense. Whilst power has been a constant presence in the analytical frameworks of many branches of the social sciences, it has not been used as much in the analysis of the actual development of the social sciences. One reason for this is the lingering influence of the North American tradition of empiricism that claims to be very close to absolute objectivity and presupposes the ability to use methodology to overcome any hindrance to achieving that aim. To those heavily immersed in empiricism, "achieving" objectivity simply becomes a matter of technique. In this sense, the element of power is indeed alien to the usual self-reflections of the social scientist, though it is in reality indispensable to any exercise of a critical nature.

Power, of course, needs to be defined in an operational manner. On the one hand, power refers to a set of hierarchical relations between the "power holder" – a tautology of sorts – and the "powerless", where submission of the latter to the former is, quite simply, a logical consequence. On the other, power relations may, under certain conditions, elicit resistance. The submission of Indonesian historiography is the best example of the first case; the submission of social science associations is another example *par excellence*. The resistance of the "under-resourced" social science through the development of "socially transformative" and "socially empowering" plans is a good example of the second case (see Ganie-Rochman and Rochman, this volume). It is significant that the dissenting inclinations within some of the relatively under-resourced social sciences, however, were only possible because of the support of foreign donor organizations. As a consequence, the influence of foreign donor organizations has left an indelible mark on domestic research programs and constitutes a factor in any analysis of social science and power in Indonesia.

Indeed, foreign donors such as the Ford Foundation, USAID, the Asia Foundation, the Japan Foundation, the Friedrich Naumann Foundation and many others, have provided much support to both state and non-state social science activities in Indonesia and in the professional training of Indonesian social scientists. Whilst such support and training schemes have been highly valuable to the individuals who have personally benefited from them, they have not been able to alter the basic nature of Indonesian academia. By their very nature, these support and training schemes cannot offer a thorough understanding of the overall framework of power within which professional social science activity and development has had to take place. Nevertheless, there have been some notable exceptions. The Ford Foundation, for example, was highly instrumental in the development of resources at such institutions as Cornell University and the Massachusetts Institute of Technology (MIT) in the 1950s and 60s, which, as we shall see, left a clear legacy for social science orientations and practices in Indonesia. It also successfully helped to develop the Faculty of Economics at the University of Indonesia, which churned out a steady supply of New Order technocrats (Dye 1965; see also Irwan, this volume). But, these endeavors also cannot be understood in isolation from power, whether emanating from the United States, especially during the Cold War and other foreign countries, or domestically within Indonesia.

Over the years, the objectives of foreign donors – inextricably linked to the social and political issues and concerns in their countries of origin – have left an imprint, for better or for worse, on the type of research projects undertaken and supported in Indonesia. Gender and feminist studies in Indonesia, arguably, benefited a great deal from donor agencies in the mid-1980s. The same may be said about the issue of ecologically "sustainable development" (SPES 1994). More recently, the interest of foreign donors in certain areas of civil society, good governance and Putnamian "social capital" – linked to the rise in prominence of variants of neo-liberalism and neo-institutionalism in Western academia (Fine 2001; Harriss 2002) – has outlined the starting points and frameworks of Indonesian debates, especially with regard to economic and political reform.

At the same time, however, local research institutions also benefited materially in the 1970s, following the student riots of 1974 and 1978, when the New Order government invested funds in universities primarily to keep students and academics inside university campuses under the guise of a "back to campus" campaign. It is interesting to note that the importance of government funding of the social sciences was already highlighted as early as 1977 at a major social science gathering in Medan. According to one of the speakers, Soedjatmoko, a major intellectual figure during the New Order:

> On the one hand, funds provided to various governmental institutions for social research are immense and my guess is they have never been this much. However, it is clear that the expenses have significantly reduced the role of the universities in social science education while at the same time the funds do not guarantee the quality of research conducted. Furthermore, doubt has arisen as to whether the funds, provided for limited fields and areas of problems, have not taken research further away from the problems that have to be studied. There are so many commissioned studies that function only for the sake of image building of those policy lines that had been taken much earlier, or that function as instruments to hook up with future projects. Furthermore, since the results of the research are never published, they are deprived of the critique and reviews of peers. They also lack the incentive for quality maintenance, data and new knowledge provision, and the capacity to provide more scientific knowledge of our society, Lastly, they are insufficient to be used as university teaching material. The unavoidable disappointment in the decision makers at the contribution of the social sciences and the sneering at the low quality of research will ultimately backlash on the social sciences.
>
> Soedjatmoko 1977, as quoted in Dhakidae 2003: 311

One outcome of this increased expenditure was that universities found a new competitor in the field of social research. Though institutions like Gadjah Mada University's Center for Population Research thrived – paving the way for population studies which were important in many ways – government departments, bodies and agencies all built up their research and development sections, and established their authority over policy-related studies undertaken within their respective areas of jurisdiction. The State Ministry of the Environment, for example, took up responsibility for environmental impact assessments without which, industrial projects would not have begun.

HISTORICAL PRECEDENTS

Although this book devotes much attention to the New Order period, the legacy of the politics of pre-New Order Indonesia cannot be ignored. This is perhaps especially so in such areas as agrarian change (see White, this volume), history and anthropology. In these areas, the influence of the colonial historiography – and therefore, the requirements of colonial rule – has been particularly important. Thus, some of the contributions to this book will deal with the lingering influence of the colonial tradition of scholarship on the trajectories of some social science disciplines – their orientations, frameworks and research programs. But, an under-investigated, albeit related question, is whether there has been any influence on Indonesian social science that originates from the period of early independence. Insofar as this question has been addressed, the emphasis, rightly, has been on the influence of the Cold War era, namely, US-initiated programs of assistance for the social sciences. But, was there a contribution to any area of the social sciences made by the Indonesian pre-New Order Left, for example, in the area of agrarian or labor history or transformation (see White and Farid, this volume). Is there a lasting, albeit indirect, legacy on the concerns of more contemporary scholars of agrarian transformation, for instance, at a time of deeper capitalist penetration into the rural economy?

If the legacy of the early post-colonial Left on the social sciences in Indonesia remains contestable, this is certainly not the case for the preceding colonial-era scholarship. It was the army of Dutch administrators-advisors-scholars, Hurgronje perhaps being the most famous member, which established the foundations for the social scientific study of Indonesian society. However, the relationship between social science knowledge and the concrete requirements of the social and cultural engineering of colonial administration was very transparent, as in the case of Hurgronje's study of Islam (1906; 1916). The Dutch, of course, were not in any way unique in this regard. The British, too, produced some of the greatest colonial administrator-advisor-scholars of all time, including Furnivall who contributed important volumes on the "plural society" in the Dutch colony as well as a comparative study of the Netherlands Indies and Burma (1944; 1948). For better or for worse, the assumptions of the "plural society" framework have influenced the way in which ethnic relations and conflict have been construed and debated in Indonesia for decades (Coppell 1997).

Moreover, in the case of Indonesia, Bourchier (1999) has shown that the development of the field of *adat* law, which has influenced understandings of Indonesian culture and society beyond the strictly narrow confines of legal theory, had its origins in the concerns of colonial-era Dutch legal scholars and administrators. Scholars such as Van Vollenhoven were to influence many prominent Indonesian legal and political thinkers, Supomo being a very good example. It is significant, however, that the tradition of legal thinking that influenced the pioneers of *adat* law was that of European Romanticism, an anti-Enlightenment forerunner of German (and by consequence, Japanese) fascism. Thus, the way in which the New Order used the 1945 Constitution to legitimize its authoritarian rule (Simandjuntak 1994) was one with strong historical underpinnings.

MODERNITY, THE STATE AND SOCIAL SCIENCE

Bureaucratization of Social Science

This book addresses the development of social science in Indonesia over fifty years, but with an emphasis on the thirty-two years of New Order rule in Indonesia, during which the interface between social science and state power became especially prominent. It was during the New Order, for example, that social sciences and academia were geared towards fulfilling the requirements of the exercise of state power. This clearly shaped the orientation of social science research, activity and training. The harnessing of the social sciences – especially in fields such as economics – to fulfill the needs of centralized authoritarian rule meant that they became increasingly pragmatic and practical, lacking a theoretical orientation. Paradoxically, there has probably been more opportunity for disciplines that the New Order ignored to produce more theoretically- as well as critically-oriented work, while simultaneously being under-resourced and under-supported. It is important to note that while the institutions of centralized state power have largely unraveled today, the legacies of the New Order-era still remain as far as the social sciences are concerned.

One of these relates to a pivotal development during the New Order: the increasingly close intertwining of social science careers and state patronage. This went hand in hand with the regime's continuous attempt to legitimize its policies by making "scientific" and "objective" claims (Moertopo 1972).

It is perhaps relevant to highlight the technocratic aspects of the New Order rule as an example (MacDougall 1975). "Experts" from various disciplines were regularly recruited into state bureaucracies, whether as advisers – Soedjatmoko, Soelaiman Soemadardi, Harsja Bachtiar, amongst others – or as bureaucrats proper. Furthermore, armies of foreign "experts" were often employed as consultants in a number of technical and planning agencies and departments, including those from renowned universities such as Harvard. But, it must be understood that projecting the image of technocratic governance was part and parcel of the regime's strategy to contain internal as well as external criticism of its rabidly authoritarian and predatory nature.

The embedding of academia in bureaucracy clearly contributed to the bureaucratization of social science practices and orientations in Indonesia. This was reflected in the career paths of many academics. Social scientists could dominate their fields, not necessarily because of the quality of their publications and/or research, but as a direct result of their loyalty and proximity to the regime. An army of social scientists came to be well trained in the technique of developing research programs, project evaluations and the like, that essentially helped to legitimize state development policy. It perhaps did not help that the bestowing of honors, including professorial titles, was a Presidential prerogative (see Nugroho, this volume). That said, it is not suggested that all senior social scientists were beholden to the regime. In fact, criticism of the regime's practices emanated from sections of academia through newspaper articles, seminar presentations and media interviews. However, appearing to be staunchly and openly critical of the regime did place one's academic career in some jeopardy.

In spite of the presence of the social scientist-critic, one avenue for intertwining bureaucratic power and academic advancement was the state-sanctioned and approved social science association (see Laksono, this volume), which functioned in a highly corporatist manner rather than as a professional association. On the one hand, the association helped to ensure the co-opting of salient sections of the social sciences community. On the other, it assisted in furthering state control over academic programs and priorities in general.

The best example of this almost intimate connection between bureaucratic power and academic advancement concerns ISEI. On one significant occasion, President Soeharto asked ISEI leaders, all leading professional economists in their own right, to draw up a "blueprint" of "economic democracy" that was consistent with the New Order implementation of Pancasila, the state ideology. This was in response to accusations that Indonesia's "capitalist" economic development path had veered away from the egalitarian ideals of the National Revolution, which by then had attained near "mythical" status and yet the state continued to obstruct the workings of the free market. In particular, there was much public debate and gossiping about the growth of large business conglomerates during Soeharto's tenure, many of which were controlled by ethnic Chinese cronies and family members and other relatives of Soeharto. ISEI duly complied and developed a schematic framework that purported to describe the principles and workings of the Indonesian economy and demonstrated how economic democracy, as practiced under Pancasila, was in accordance with both the principles of the market and social egalitarian ideals. ISEI achieved this by resorting to intellectual acrobatics (ISEI 1990).

But, there were clear responses and reactions to such developments, which denoted that complete state hegemony over the social sciences was not achieved. Endeavors were frequently undertaken, for example, to develop the social sciences outside of the bureaucracy proper and outside of the universities. In 1971, with the support of the Friedrich Naumann Stiftung (FNS) of Germany, the Institute for Social and Economic Research, Education and Information (*Lembaga Penelitian, Pendidikan dan Penerangan Ekonomi dan Sosial* – LP3ES) was established. This private institute initiated the prestigious *Prisma*, a journal that specialized in the publication of social science research and also began a program of publishing social science and economics textbooks. It also developed several good quality research programs. In fact, LP3ES represents one of the rare cases in which commitment to social science research and publication was able to continue for a long period of time, at least for a decade or decade and a half. Its decline began in the early 1980s when FNS stopped its institutional support and LP3ES was forced to seek other sources of substantial funding. However, even today, there exist numerous smaller research institutions around the country that undertake research with little direct connection to formal academia – many of which must have been inspired by LP3ES's earlier successes. These typically combine social activists and academics seeking to channel their intellectual energies outside the university (see Ganie-Rochman and Rochman, this volume).

Also, with full support from the Ford Foundation, the Social Sciences Foundation (*Yayasan Ilmu-ilmu Sosial* – YIIS) was founded in 1977. The main objective of YIIS was to develop the social sciences through the training of social scientists. It was instrumental in the establishment of research stations in several regions to train social scientists. Ford Foundation also pioneered the first systematic efforts to translate books that marked key watersheds in the development of the social sciences.

Another major example of a research institute established outside of the bureaucracy and the university was the Center for Strategic and International Studies (CSIS) (see Irwan, this volume). As it was well connected to the center of state power and to major Chinese business groups, its "independent" status was, therefore, questionable. Although these strong state links have now largely been lost, CSIS remains a major site for debate and discussion of economic and political development strategies.

But the main inclination was still toward social science development that basically became part and parcel of the New Order's broader development agenda from the 1970s until its demise in the late 1990s. With state support, foreign and domestically trained social scientists convened seminars and workshops to consider how the social sciences could be made "relevant" to New Order development. The study and practice of social science in a theoretical and normative manner – a throwback to colonial traditions – warranted a change in orientation towards more empirical research. As such, research techniques had to be modified, which benefited quantitative methodologies, replete with their claims of rationality, objectivity and neutrality. The late Selo Soemardjan, for example, once the doyen of Indonesian sociology and a staff member in the office of the vice president in the 1950s, argued strongly in 1983 that science was objective and that social scientists must be neutral (Soemardjan 1983). He was one of the earliest Indonesian recipients of a social science scholarship, supported by the Ford Foundation, to Cornell University in the United States. Moreover, strategies for the pursuit of social science objectives were formulated in such a way that they resembled those espoused by the bureaucracy whose major policy stipulations, as formulated by the State Minister for Research, became a guideline of sorts for social scientists. At a conference on the "role" of social science in development, top Indonesian social scientists declared – in strikingly instrumentalist fashion – that in "formulating a social science research policy, the problem of values and beliefs should not be neglected. Taking these into account, the successful transmission of important messages in development can then be evaluated" (HIPIIS 1975: 11).

The entanglement of social science in bureaucratic objectives could be seen clearly in the establishment of regional research stations, the Banda Aceh station being the pilot project. Apart from training social scientists, these research stations would identify problems and seek technocratic solutions to various local development issues in a fairly technocratic fashion. For example, they were expected to make a meticulous and complete inventory and classification of regional "social symptoms" (HIPIIS 1975). There was close cooperation between social scientists and the bureaucrats in the setting up of the regional research stations. Not surprisingly, the opening ceremony of the Aceh station in 1974 resembled a festive political event more than a sedate meeting of social scientists. The list of attendees included a curious amalgam of low and high-level local authorities such as the governor and the Aceh Regional Military Commander. Notably, no less than the governor himself was to give key opening and closing addresses.

But, the link between social science practices and bureaucratic requirements extended far beyond events such as this. It is important to remember that much of the period of New Order rule coincided with the Cold War. In this context and, given the New Order's own political needs, tight controls by government agencies over research activity – especially, but not exclusively, by foreigners – was maintained for decades in the name of national security and interest. The agencies involved in the intricate system of controls included Indonesian Institute of Sciences (*Lembaga Ilmu Pengetahuan Indonesia* – LIPI) and security organizations such as the Operational Command for the Restoration of Security and Order (*Komando Operasi Permulihan Keamanan dan Ketertiban* – Kopkamtib) and the State Intelligence

Coordination Agency (*Badan Koordinasi Intelijen Negara* – Bakin). Under this system, research projects without the requisite permits from LIPI and endorsements by Bakin were disallowed. Arguably, this system discouraged a lot of social science research on Indonesia, especially in areas or subjects considered to be politically sensitive. In other words, it clearly helped to define what was *not* studied by Indonesian social scientists.

Social Science and the Cold War

Some observers trace the beginnings of the social sciences in Indonesia from the return to the country of the first students who studied overseas in the 1950s and 1960s (Kleden 1986), mostly in the West, especially the United States. Whilst this position probably ignores the pre-independence work carried out under the rubric of colonial historiography and, certainly the works of Indonesians such as the law scholar, Supomo, and of activist-scholars of the Hatta generation, there is more than a grain of truth in the assertion. These students were the first to introduce "Area Studies" to Indonesia. These were post-Cold War development oriented economics, sociology and political science; studies that shaped the social sciences in post-colonial Indonesia. Benedict Anderson wrote that American interest in Southeast Asia grew with the end of World War II (1998) and that in the context of the new Cold War, combined with the proliferation of newly independent nation-states in formerly colonized Asia and Africa, "Area Studies" gained prominence within US academia. "Southeast Asian Studies" thus emerged as an examination of the processes of social change, nation-building, economic development and political institutionalization in Southeast Asia. Cornell University was at the forefront of these efforts for many years, as was MIT, which sponsored the pioneering post-World War II "expedition" into Javanese culture in the 1950s and early 60s, in which Clifford Geertz emerged as the undisputed star.

The point to be emphasized, however, is that the rise of Southeast Asia as an area of academic concern was deeply indebted to Cold War era American geo-political interests. Here, the connection between social science and the requirements of power – in this case, an actual super-power – is obvious. As Dean Rusk, a former top State Department official, and then head of the Rockefeller Foundation was to suggest at the height of the Vietnam War, "communist aggression" in Asia needed to be confronted not only by the training of American combatants, but also by the opening up of US "training facilities" for "the increasing numbers" of America's Asian allies (Ransom 1970: 40). Given this history, it is probably not surprising that the post-Cold War period saw a dramatic reduction in the level of US commitment to Southeast Asian Studies.

As such, a number of American universities, other than Cornell and MIT, were to develop centers of education and research with an emphasis on Asia or Southeast Asia. Some notable ones include those at Wisconsin, Michigan, Yale and Ohio State. Many Indonesian academics were attracted to these universities in their pursuit of postgraduate qualifications, although of course many more were not involved in area studies per se. Nevertheless, they quickly grew intimate with a social science environment within which "modernization" theory had become ascendant in its various incarnations across numerous disciplines, perhaps more so in the fields of economics, political science and sociology.

Indonesian economics students, for example, were to be deeply influenced by the avowedly "anti-communist" theoretical framework famously advanced by Walt Whitman Rostow (1964) which proposed a linear conception of the "stages of growth" that societies universally go through. Those studying political science would be well acquainted with comparative politics as developed by Almond and Verba (1963), with an emphasis on the ideal secular and modern "civic culture", or with the Eastonian "political system" replete with "black boxes", "inputs" and "outputs" (Easton 1953; 1965a and b). Those studying sociology would be familiar with Parsonian structural functionalism, with university instruction typically veering towards emphasis on such notions as system maintenance and "equilibrium" (Parsons 1951; 1960) and therefore logically averse to system disruption. The combination of theories and concepts from the likes of Parsons, Easton, Almond and Verba distinctively influenced academic, intellectual, political and even day-to-day bureaucratic discourse, which was frequently characterized by the use of such tricky concepts as "systems", "systems analysis" and "systemic change".

In anthropology, a giant had emerged in the form of Clifford Geertz – whose work on religion, agricultural involution and traditional statecraft – deeply influenced anthropological work on Indonesia up to the present. But, in the area of anthropology, there was also a domestic giant: Koentjaraningrat. More than any other Indonesian anthropologist, it was he who established the parameters of anthropological concerns in Indonesia in the 1960s – which included "defining" the features of "an Indonesian culture" – and therefore played a major intellectual role in the state-led modernization and nation-building process (Koentjaraningrat 1975). Koentjaraningrat can also be credited for stressing quantitative research methodologies to generations of social scientists who studied a seminal textbook on social science research that he edited (Koentjaraningrat 1973). The textbook, originally published in 1973, on its eleventh print-run and third edition by 1993, must be seen in relation to the re-orientation of Indonesian social science towards North American empiricism. Among its contributors were a number of scholars who would become major New Order-era academics, including the sociologist-bureaucrats Harsja Bachtiar and Selo Soemardjan, future Minister of Education Fuad Hasan and Saparinah Sadli, married to noted technocrat, Mohammad Sadli.

It is of course commonplace now to criticize modernization perspectives as being a convenient façade for American political and economic global hegemony. In the context of the Cold War, the future of the developing world was often, directly or indirectly, portrayed as being the mirror image of contemporary America (Almond and Verba 1963). In other words, present time in 1950s America was to be the rest of the world's future. More important, however, the "ideal America" that was envisaged was one free of ideological and class conflict. Yet, the reality was that this ideal paid scant attention to the growing unrest amongst ethnic minorities, resulting in increasing tension in America's vast urban ghettoes, which sometimes exploded into race riots. As such, this reality set the context for the emergence of the civil rights and peace movements and major upheavals in American society in the 1960s and early 70s.

It was clearly important that the implicitly a-political, even anti-political, nature of North American modernization theory (see Heryanto 1999; Irwan, this volume) suited the New Order's need to portray itself as a technocratic regime governed by those who knew what was best for the country and who were not blinded by self-interest or ideological biases. But, in an ironic twist, the implantation of North American social science metastasized into something immensely political once "the system" produced its own political discourse. The ideas of "modernization" and "system" cut so deep into the dominant political and academic discourses that the system itself became the metonym for modernity. In a further twist, the system was deemed to be a closed one, with the consequence that dissent and conflict were seen primarily as disruptive, if not dysfunctional. Furthermore, once the system had been formalized as the bureaucracy itself, the political consequence was that everything "informal" was outside the system. As a result, the system became the state.

It is therefore not surprising that New Order technocracy went hand in hand with exclusionary politics. The New Order's top ideologue, Ali Moertopo, infamously borrowed from Rostownian terminology when he declared a blueprint for the "acceleration of 25 years' modernization" in Indonesia (Moertopo 1972).

Moreover, according to Moertopo, who, apart from Soeharto himself, was the man probably most responsible for the establishment of the New Order's party and corporatist representation system:

> As a developing country, Indonesia is still always confronted with the problem of having to decide how to shape its future development. The appropriate policy is what is generally called modernization, In order to achieve our goals as

efficiently as possible, modernization is nothing more than the process of using all available material, ethical, scientific and technical means to organize, structure and implement development based on one way of thinking.

Moertopo 1972[2]

The almost casual reference to the necessity of "one way of thinking" should be emphasized here for it points to a fatal mistake committed by some of the regime's earliest domestic and international supporters. Their error was to assume that a capitalist-friendly and anti-communist regime in Indonesia would usher in liberal market policies and/or liberal democratic political institutions. Most New Order state planners were in awe of Western technology and material wealth, but averse to liberal or social democratic values. Indeed, "Western", liberal or social democratic values were to be cast as being equally alien to Indonesia's allegedly indigenous culture as communism. In this sense, New Order Indonesia exhibited a case of what Jayasuriya has called "reactionary modernization" (Jayasuriya 1998). Rather than being the harbinger of liberal democratic values, economic technocracy, in the Indonesian case, became an integral part of the formation of increasingly powerful predatory alliances, cemented by the power of Soeharto himself and propped up by foreign assistance, oil booms and foreign investment. Thus, accusations about the dominance of an American-trained, essentially "comprador", community of economists – a "Berkeley Mafia" (Ransom 1970) – largely missed the point. These economic technocrats, although at times influential (see Irwan, this volume), were no more than junior partners within the broader framework of power. This was primarily characterized by the fusion of corporate, politico-bureaucratic and military interests, which was ultimately expressed in the ascendance of dominant, predatory, business and politico-bureaucratic families that secured their position through the instrumental possession of control over state institutions and resources (Robison and Hadiz 2004).

Having noted the importance of US influence on social science scholarship on and in Indonesia, it is perhaps useful to recall that there were other major sites of Indonesia-related research during the Cold War. A study conducted in 1987 showed that Dutch researchers made up the majority, some 56 percent, of European social science researchers who cited Indonesia as their country of interest (Directory of West European Indonesianists 1987). This was perhaps not surprising given the colonial connections. In a later study, conducted in 1998, 64 percent of 1,250

---

[2]   This is a translation of Ali Moertopo's, "Our National Development Strategy", as reprinted in Chalmers and Hadiz 1997: 75.

European Southeast Asianists polled cited Indonesia as their country of interest. On the basis of country of origin, Dutch scholars comprised 40 percent of the total number of European Southeast Asianists, followed by Germany at 14 percent and France and England at about 12 percent each. Although supporting data is difficult to find, it is reasonable to assume that considerable numbers of Indonesian students pursued their higher social science degrees in these same countries, thereby mitigating to some extent the influence of American institutions and traditions of scholarship.

TABLE 1: EUROPEAN SOUTHEAST ASIANISTS 1998					
	Degree of Researchers				
Country of Interest	MA	MSc	Ph.D/Dr	Others	Total
Brunei	-	-	2	1	3
Burma	2	-	22	8	32
Cambodia	5	-	24	10	39
Indonesia	202	18	509	76	805
Laos	-	-	13	6	19
Malaysia	6	1	44	14	65
Philippines	6	3	35	2	46
Singapore	-	-	10	2	12
Thailand	2	1	61	20	84
Vietnam	13	-	75	21	109
Others	7	-	25	4	36
Total	243	23	820	164	1250

Source: Kees van Dijk et al. 1998.

But, the major competing center for the study of Indonesia to have emerged was undoubtedly Australia, partly due to its close geographical proximity and to the growing intertwining of the Australian economy with that of its Asian neighbors. Developments at Cornell University – the "home" of scholarship on Indonesia in the US – hinted at the displacement of the US to a considerable degree by Australian research institutions. There, the Modern Indonesia Project building, the one with a "Bhinneka Tunggal Ika" sign over the door, was moved in 1992 to another, more modern building, known as the George McT Kahin Center for Advanced Research on Southeast Asia, dedicated to George Kahin who pioneered Cornell's Modern Indonesian studies in the 1950s. The new building marked a change of orientation in which Indonesian studies were subsumed under the broader Southeast Asian scholarship, although they did not necessarily become indistinct (www.news. cornell.edu/Chronicle/00/2.3.00/obits.html, accessed on 6 November 2004).

The key document that "declared" Australia's interest in Asia was probably a 1989 report sponsored by the Australian Department of Foreign Affairs and Trade, commonly known as "The Garnaut Report". In this report, Australia was encouraged to establish stronger economic and cultural relations with Asia (Garnaut 1989). In 1991, another report entitled, "Australia and North-East Asia in the 1990s: Accelerating Change", was produced to support similar objectives. Closer ties with Asia of course do not necessarily mean closer ties with Indonesia, since Japan and China are more important economically and culturally and the languages of both these nations are the more popular foreign languages taught and learned in Australia. However, the Indonesian language did become the most popular Southeast Asian language that was taught and learned by Australian high school students and academics (Dhakidae 1993; Australian Department of Foreign Affairs and Trade 1991; Asian Studies Association of Australia 1992). Unfortunately, the ascendance of Asian/Southeast Asian and Indonesian Studies in Australia was short-lived, as evidenced by neo-liberal "reforms" in the tertiary education sector which have reportedly exerted grave funding pressure on the relevant university departments (Hill 2003).

Cultural Essentialism and Development as the Foundations of Social Stability
Whatever the real or imagined level of influence of the economic technocrats, it was clear that the social sciences, including economics, were harnessed to support the needs of the New Order's developmentalist project from its inception. Thus, the role of political science was to chart the course of "political development" and institutionalization; sociology was about ensuring social integration; and anthropology was about identifying and defining the elements of an officially sanctioned "national culture". In the case of political science, it was significant that the revisionist modernization theory of Samuel Huntington was particularly influential.

According to Huntington, the future proponent, ironically, of both a thesis on a "Third Wave of Democratization in the 1980s" (Huntington 1991) and of a "Clash of Civilizations" (1993) – within which democracy is essentially rooted in Western culture – "modernity" was measured on the basis of the state's ability to maintain political stability and hence, pursue capitalist development. Thus, the institutionalization of the structures of power was paramount to avert a descent into chaos and anarchy. This idea fitted quite nicely with the New Order ideologues' assertion that the institutional framework of the regime was tailored to ensure the stability required in guaranteeing economic progress. It suited their idea that liberal democracy, with its potentially destabilizing characteristic, was not in accordance with development aims and also culturally un-Indonesian. The result was that political science in Indonesia, which began life as the colonial-era legalistic study of "statecraft" (Alfian 1979), essentially morphed into little more than the science of "political development", defined as the maintenance of social stability in the sense earlier elaborated by Lerner, among others (1958).

Ignas Kleden has provided a systematic assessment of the nature and functions of social science to the New Order up to the 1980s. According to Kleden, Indonesian social science during the New Order served the function of "engineering" – political, educational, cultural, legal and moral (Kleden 1986: 6-7). For Kleden, the result was an un-reflective, a-theoretical and bureaucratically-oriented social science culture that developed "techniques" such as "linguistic euphemism" and "tautological expression" in order to "survive" in an inhospitable political environment, when it should have focused on conceptual and logical clarity and precision, despite the risk of confrontation (Kleden 1986: 9-10). The pragmatic and instrumental nature of the bureaucratized social sciences, according to Kleden, goes a long way toward explaining the intellectual poverty of Indonesia's social sciences. It is not necessary to support his call for the "indigenization" of the social sciences as the remedy in order to agree with this view.

In spite of this "poverty", important works continued to be written by Indonesian scholars from time to time. Interesting enough, the discipline of history, perhaps the most under-resourced of the social sciences under the New Order, provides some of the best examples. Sartono Kartodirdjo (1972), Onghokham (1978) and Taufik Abdullah (1971), among others, produced works that remain enduring reference points in their respective areas of research. Kartodirdjo's work, in particular, gave an alternative insight to the subject that was potentially intellectually subversive. And the political scientist, Deliar Noer (1973), also authored a well-known study on the history of Islamic politics in Indonesia in the first half of the twentieth century.

It may not have been purely coincidental that these historical works were, almost without exception, either written overseas and/or before the New Order systematically manipulated history, using it as a tool to legitimize its claim to power. In fact, Soeharto himself became increasingly obsessed with securing his place in history through various means, including making appearances in movies such as *Janur Kuning*, which exaggerated the importance of Soeharto in the nationalist war against the Dutch and which was repeatedly aired on television until he fell from power. Indeed, in the annals of New Order history, Soeharto featured prominently in key events, even while he was still a relatively minor army officer. Soeharto's apparently growing obsession – for example, to be recognized as the Father of Development – recalled Milan Kundera's wry observation that "the only reason people want to be masters of the future is to change the past" (Kundera 1999).

Under the aegis of Nugroho Notususanto, the army general-historian-New Order government minister (1982-1985), the codification of an official narrative of Indonesian history was actively and vigorously pursued (see Adam, this volume) and dutifully reproduced in school textbooks. The function of this official narrative, it seemed, was to explain the linear progression of the Indonesian nation from Javanese Hindu/ Buddhist kingships, the spread of Islam, the rise of colonialism, capped by national independence movements and independence wars in which the military had a key role. The establishment of the New Order, in which the military was immensely powerful, was described as the culmination of this linear progression of history. The case of school textbooks on history is illuminating in this regard. The writing and rewriting of Indonesian history textbooks, from elementary to senior high school level, was under the tight control of a body that comprised bureaucrats from the Ministry of Education, the Ministry of Religion, the Ministry of Home Affairs, as well as members of the intelligence services (see Adam, this volume; Dhakidae 2003).

Moreover, students were inculcated with the notion that the New Order represented the recovery – or better yet – the resurrection of the indigenous cultural values that binds all Indonesians, male and female, of all ethnic groups, religions and classes, together as one nation. Thus, the New Order represented the continuation of a "national" project; one that was embarked upon as early as the Majapahit empire but rudely "interrupted" by the European colonialists. According to New Order "history", Soeharto's primordial dreams and aspirations of the "national" project were realized only after his rise to power. This manipulation of facts and history propagated the Soekarnoist myth of "350 years of colonialism in Indonesia". In the process, the reification of a "national culture" in official discourse was legitimized both by university teaching and socio-cultural research that implicitly assumed an a-historical, immutable and Indonesian cultural "authenticity".

ANTI-STATE DISCOURSES: NEW CONTRADICTIONS

It is significant for our purposes that Ignas Kleden also noted the expulsion of Marxist-oriented social science from official discourse (Kleden 1986). For a long time, the position of Marxist theory in academic teaching was at best ambiguous and Marxist academic and political literature was eventually officially banned. Of course, notions of class or class conflict were anathema to the New Order's discourse of harmony and co-operation under the aegis of a wise and benevolent state. The result is a great lacuna in Indonesian academic investigations; the absence of class in Indonesian analyses of Indonesian society belied the fact that social classes, as well as inequalities in wealth and power, were on the rise during most of the New Order as capitalism grew in Indonesia.

Thus, the suppression of any discourse on class in Indonesia occurred precisely at a time when the advancement of capitalism was radically transforming Indonesia's class structure, creating the bourgeoisie, an urban middle class and a growing industrial proletariat. With class largely outside the reach of social scientists (see Farid, this volume), studies of the various dimensions of social and economic inequality were partly subsumed under demography and statistics, disciplines with methodologies that could easily be deemed to be objective. The reality, however, was that statistics was an important tool for presenting the "successes" of the New Order in a particular fashion, especially in relation to socially-sensitive issues such as the eradication of poverty (see Ananta, this volume).

Even as the New Order claimed that Indonesia did not have social classes and therefore no class conflict, other forms of social conflict came to the fore, the most prevalent being ethno-religious ones. Like other regimes in the region, most notably Malaysia and Singapore, the New Order essentially asserted itself as the guardian of ethno-religious harmony (Hefner 2001). Raising issues of ethnicity and religion was forbidden and, if deemed provocative, was a crime. Paradoxically, the New Order's own policies tended to exacerbate ethno-religious differences, often crossing the border into racism and this served to emphasize the need for a "security and order" approach when addressing societal concerns.

At the same time, Papuans and Dayaks were regarded as "backward", as were many other ethnic minorities. The indirect product of this situation were studies that served *pembangunan* (development) by proposing how these cultures could be better "integrated" into the nation, or those that served government programs such as transmigration. These studies were sometimes startlingly technical, given their social ramifications and staunchly devoid of politics except the kind embodied in the New Order's own developmental politics. This encouraged the development of alternative studies of ethnic politics that were at odds with the official discourse (see Institut Dayakologi, www.dayakology.com).

Perhaps the thorniest issue relating to ethnicity and/or race was that of the Chinese Indonesians (Suryadinata 1978). New Order policy towards Chinese Indonesians involved the suppression of the markers of Chinese identity. Ironically, this policy came into force at a time when large ethnic Chinese-owned business conglomerates became an integral part of the New Order's ruling capitalist oligarchy.

It is frequently suggested that it was the strategy of the New Order to maintain the political vulnerability of the Chinese as an ethnic group, given common perceptions of their economic dominance, so that they would become convenient scapegoats for any social dissatisfaction with existing conditions. Significantly, while studies on Indonesians of Chinese descent have been frequently conducted abroad, few Indonesians have delved seriously into the subject matter. A rare exception is perhaps Mely G. Tan and her unpublished Masters thesis (1961) and Heryanto's insightful article on the representations of riots in Jakarta in May 1998 during which many Chinese, especially women, were victimized and attacked (Heryanto 1999). The fact that most of such works were written in a foreign language is, in itself, revealing.

It might be useful, at this juncture, to compare Chinese Indonesian studies and Arab Indonesian studies. In the last decade or so there has been no serious effort to study Arab Indonesians, the rare exception being an unpublished Ph.D dissertation by the Malaysian scholar, Sumit Mandal (1994). Other than that, no real example of studies by Indonesian scholars can be given. Here, the politics of ethnicity and religion have played out differently; the perception of social distance between *pribumi* (native) Indonesians and Arab Indonesians is shortened by religion, namely, Islam. However, it would be incorrect to conclude that studying Islam in Indonesia would automatically shed light on the Arab Indonesian community.

Another important development was the emergence of a discourse on state and civil society beginning in the 1980s. By this time, liberal-pluralists, emerging primarily from the growing urban middle class, came to be attracted to a brand of Marxism that notably lacked the element of class conflict. In articles once influential among some Indonesian liberal intellectuals, Hamza Alavi had argued that post-colonial states enjoyed relative autonomy from social classes because of the underdeveloped class structure that had been inherited. Post-colonial states, according to Alavi, were "overdeveloped" in relation to social classes (Alavi 1972; 1982). Showing the traces of a dependency perspective, the interests of metropolitan capital remained more powerful in Alavi's theoretical construction because of the underdevelopment of its domestic counterpart. Thus, while the post-colonial state had a dominant presence, it was structurally beholden to the interests of international capital. Alavi's work on Pakistan and Bangladesh was adapted to the Indonesian case by the late Farchan Bulkin (1984a and b), not to mention an array of Indonesian student and NGO activists, who in the 1980s, argued that the underdevelopment of the bourgeoisie and middle classes was the basis for state dominance over civil society. This kind of state dominance, it was concluded, was responsible for hindering the development of democracy.

Such intellectual developments were reflective of the new inclination among sections of the liberal intelligentsia to view the bureaucratic and authoritarian state as the main nemesis of democratic life. This was partly attributable to their declining influence within the regime and partly to the fact that any hope of the New Order developing into a democracy had been quashed by the mid-1970s, when student demonstrations were crushed and leading liberal activists imprisoned. Perhaps the most identifiable representative of this phenomenon was Arief Budiman, a sociologist, political activist and public intellectual who had been an early supporter of the New Order, but later switched loyalties to the dependency theory and neo-Marxism in a bid to criticize the regime (1982). But, then again, the emphasis on the state and, to varying degrees, the role of metropolitan capital, meant little or no acknowledgement of internal class conflicts and dynamics except to lament the absence of a dynamic and politically liberal middle class. Significantly, the neo-Marxist-inspired dependency theory was to be combined in Indonesia with populist, Islamic-oriented criticism of capitalism, the major exponents of which included the economist and NGO leader, Dawam Rahardjo (1987) and Adi Sasono (Arief and Sasono 1984), also an NGO activist. However, in an ironic twist, both were to become major figures in the New Order-spawned Indonesian Association of Muslim Intellectuals (*Ikatan Cendekiawan Muslim Indonesia* – ICMI).[3]

Another manner in which Marxism or variants of neo-Marxism made their way into Indonesian academic discourse was via a Frankfurt School-inspired critical theory. Habermas, for example, prominently appears in the work of many of Indonesia's leading social scientists such as Kleden (Kleden 1987). Like the dependency theory in the area of development studies, critical theory in the area of cultural studies provided an avenue to "smuggle in" Marxist analyses without appearing overtly Marxist.

The non-Marxist and state-centered approach to politics and society also grew in influence. For example, politically liberal scholars such as Mochtar Mas'oed (1989) and representatives of NGOs and student movements, began to borrow freely from the lexicon of literature on bureaucratic authoritarian regimes, as perhaps epitomized in the work of the Latin American specialist, Guillermo O'Donnell (1973). More so than ever, the rise of civil society, perceived to be representative of middle class resurgence, was put forward in Indonesian political discourse as the antithesis to an overbearing and stifling state.

A substantial urban middle class and bourgeoisie were indeed developing under the New Order (Robison 1986). But, unlike the assumptions of liberal political theory, these social forces were deeply conservative and inclined towards acceptance of the

---

[3]   This organization was set up in the early 1990s as Soeharto adopted the political strategy of courting the new Muslim urban middle class. It was initially headed by B.J. Habibie, Soeharto's long-time State Minister for Research and Technology, and of course, his immediate successor as President in May 1998.

political status quo. Benefiting materially from Indonesia's economic growth under the New Order, they feared instability and the threat to social order and property that typically accompanies a regime change.

Nevertheless, the 1980s and 90s saw a slew of writings on the almost "naturally" progressive nature of the middle class and/or bourgeoisie. The economist Sjahrir, for example, argued that economic liberalization and deregulation would strengthen the middle class and therefore the democratic impulse within Indonesian society because the power of the state would be compromised (1997). Not surprisingly, this kind of development coincided with an ascendance of a global neo-liberal agenda based on economic deregulation and free markets and the global resurgence of the modernization theory in the form of neo-institutionalism and rational choice theory.

Another noteworthy development was the popularity in some intellectual circles of post-modernism beginning in the 1990s. Contemptuous of grand narratives such as modernization and Marxism, post-modernism offered potentially subversive ideas to a variety of critics of the social order that Soeharto built. The idea of "deconstruction", for example, was heartily embraced by many. To Muslim scholars such as Komaruddin Hidayat, post-modernism presented the opportunity to engage in Islamic concerns about a just society with some of the critical aspects of contemporary social theory (1994). Others, however, while generally welcoming of post-modernism, lamented its superficial and sometimes frivolous usage (Sahal 1994), a position that contrasts with Heryanto's (see Heryanto, this volume) favorable appraisal of post-modernism's self-reflexive qualities.

DEMOCRATIZATION AND THE SOCIAL SCIENCES

What of *reformasi* and the social sciences? Will the great liberation of the social sciences ensue after the removal of the bureaucratic shackles of the New Order? It may seem logical to expect this, but, as discussed further below, there is nothing inevitable about such a possible course of development. Indeed, there has so far been little indication of a transformation. The reason for this is the possibility that Indonesian social science might graduate from the rule and tyranny of an authoritarian regime to that of the market. Indeed today, Indonesian educational and research institutions are being forced to seek their own sources of income and therefore have been engaged in developing market-friendly educational and research programs (see Nugroho, this volume).

Nevertheless, the newfound freedom of expression in post-New Order Indonesia has certainly contributed to a much less politically stifling, if not always intellectually stimulating, environment for social science discussion, debate and perhaps self-reflection. Fewer social scientists fear direct punishment, at least by the state, when airing their views publicly. Certainly, academics and intellectuals in general are more in demand now than ever before as public commentators, as is illustrated by their ubiquity in the print and electronic media. Moreover, the active participation of some sections of the academic community in the *reformasi* movement of 1998 indicated the degree to which many, relatively privileged, middle class academics had become frustrated with the New Order's rapacity and arbitrary rule. Half a decade on, post-modernism still retains its original allure of subversive potential, although a still-newer generation of students seems to have found something appealing in the previously tabooed Marxist theory: those involved in Islamic-based study groups who are interested in wide-ranging critiques of social injustice and inequality (*Kompas* 14 April 2000; 30 August 2000). All these, in many ways, hold a promise of the development of a more dynamic, socially relevant and less bureaucratically stifled social science community.

But, is it too early to make a fair judgment, either way, about post-New Order Indonesian social sciences? Whilst some might suggest so with some validity, it is nevertheless possible to make a well-informed preliminary assessment, especially while taking into account two factors to which we have already alluded.

First, there is the continuing legacy of the New Order on social science practices. Whilst there is a new, more open environment conducive to critical thinking, the institutions of education and research remain largely the same. It is highly unlikely that their bureaucratic culture, practices and orientations have changed overnight. In other words, the political reform of Indonesia's higher educational, as well as research institutions, has not taken place. There is a second factor of potentially greater long-term importance and that is prohibitive of the quality of social science research in a newly democratic Indonesia. This is the new onslaught of a dogmatic, narrow, neo-liberalism on Indonesia's institutions of education and research. Although the unleashing of dogmatic forms of neo-liberalism on education and research is creating havoc as well in many other countries, including advanced industrialized countries such as Australia and many in Western Europe, it might arguably cause greater damage in countries like Indonesia, where the culture and practice of social science has traditionally been weak. In short, the combination of the new tyranny of the market and the legacy of political authoritarianism at this particular juncture does not bode well for the growth of vital, theoretically informed, as well as socially and politically relevant social science in Indonesia. It might also pose a threat, as it already has in other countries with stronger social science traditions, to other disciplines such as history, philosophy and the like, which have little direct applicability.

In the case of Indonesia, the threat to the social sciences is not only represented by the predictably increasing importance of especially applied and market-oriented research – the kind, for example, that serves the immediate needs of industry. But, given the already weak material base of academia, social science talent will also, predictably, be lost to more lucrative options such as consulting and media commentating. Of course there is already a long history of public intellectualism in Indonesia that, for all its advantages in terms of bridging the gap between academia and society, does potentially consume a lot of the time of some of the most talented scholars. The effect, unfortunately, would be a consolidated social science world-view that is eminently instrumental and pragmatic, rather than critical and reflective.

What remains unclear is the impact of the neo-liberal intellectual ascendance on the types of social science research undertaken outside of the universities, for example, those conducted by NGOs, as they are heavily reliant on foreign donor support. When universities and "official" research institutions have been politically constrained, NGOs were sometimes able to fill the void with socially and politically relevant scholarship and research. Nevertheless, it has been apparent for a long time that even established institutions such as LP3ES has had to prioritize its consulting work and relegate its once highly respected social science research activity to a secondary status.

The purpose of this introduction has not been to paint an overly bleak picture of the state of the social sciences in Indonesia, although some might rightfully take exception to the generally critical nature of the preceding analysis. It has also not been the intention of the authors to suggest that Indonesian social science is at a standstill. Serious and useful works have been produced and, it is hoped, will continue to be produced by Indonesians. Having said that, such works invariably have been in the form of student Ph.D theses written in foreign universities. Indonesia now has more Ph.Ds across the social sciences. and social science experts, than it did at the start of the New Order, when the bureaucratization of the social sciences began in earnest. Harsja Bachtiar noted in 1974 that there were only two Indonesians with Ph.Ds in anthropology, five in political science, two in mass communications and seven in sociology. However, it is interesting to note that there were 30 in economics (Bachtiar 1974b). Today, at the University of Indonesia's Faculty of Social and Political Sciences alone, 51 of the 219 teaching staff, or close to a quarter, now have Ph.Ds, while another 112 have Masters degrees.[4] But, a worrying fact is that, as mentioned earlier, relatively few Indonesian social scientists, compared to their counterparts in neighboring countries, are represented in international social science literature.

---

[4] This data was provided by FISIP-UI.

Although this cannot be taken as conclusive "evidence" of the state of Indonesian social sciences, it should nevertheless be taken seriously as an indicator of an inability to raise the standards of domestic scholarship. From this point of view, developing the social sciences in Indonesia is not simply about building a critical mass of Ph.Ds. It also requires a conducive set of social, political and economic circumstances in which social science research has some degree of autonomy, independent of both the state and the growing global tyranny of the market over academic agendas.

BIBLIOGRAPHY

Abdullah, Taufik (1971) *School and Politics: The Kaum Muda Movement in West Sumatra (1927-1933)*, Ithaca (NY): Cornell University, Modern Indonesia Project.

Alavi, Hamza (1972) "The State in Post-Colonial Societies: Pakistan and Bangladesh", *New Left Review* 1(74): 59-81.

—— (1982) "The State and Class Under Peripheral Capitalism", in *Introduction to the Sociogy of Developing Societies*, Hamza Alavi and Teodor Shanin (eds), London: Macmillan, pp. 289-307.

Alfian (1979) *Political Science in Indonesia*, Yogyakarta: Gadjah Mada University Press.

Almond, Gabriel and Sidney Verba (1963) *The Civic Culture: Political Attitudes and Democracy in Five Nations*, Princeton: Princeton University Press.

Anderson, Benedict R. O'G. (1998) *The Spectre of Comparisons: Nationalism, Southeast Asia and the World*, London: Verso.

Arief, Sritua and Adi Sasono (1984) *Ketergantungan dan Keterbelakangan*, Jakarta: SII/ LSP.

Asian Studies Association of Australia Inc. (1992), "Guide to Asianists in Australia", Nathan (Qld).

Australian Department of Foreign Affairs and Trade (1991), "Australia and North-East Asia in the 1990s: Accelerating Change", Canberra: Government Publishing Service.

Bachtiar, Harsja Wardhana (1974a) "The Social Sciences in Indonesia", in *Masyarakat Indonesia*, I: 1-16.

—— (1974b) *Directory of Social Scientists in Indonesia*, Jakarta: Lembaga Ekonomi dan Kemasyarakatan Nasional.

Bourchier, D.M. (1999) "Romanticism and Positivism in Indonesian Legal Thought" in Timothy Lindsey (ed.) *Law and Society in Indonesia*, Melbourne: Federation Press, pp. 186-196.

Bourdieu, Pierre (1986) "The Forms of Capital", in J. Richardson (ed.), *Handbook of Theory and Research for the Sociology of Education*, New York: Greenwood Press, pp. 241-258.

Budiman, Arief (1982) "Sistem perekonomian pancasila, kapitalisme dan sosialisme", in *Prisma* 1(11): 14-25.

—— (1983) "Ilmu-ilmu sosial Indonesia a-historis" in *Prisma* 6(12): 74-90.

Bulkin, Farchan (1984a) "Kapitalisme, golongan menengah dan negara: sebuah catatan penelitia", in *Prisma* 2: 3-22.

—— (1984b) "Negara, masyarakat dan ekonomi", in *Prisma* 8: 3-17.

Chalmers, Ian and Vedi R. Hadiz (eds) (1997) *The Politics of Economic Development in Indonesia: Contending Perspectives*, London: Routledge.

Coppell, Charles (1997) "Revisiting Furnivall's 'Plural Society': Colonial Java as a Mestizo Society?", *Ethnic and Racial Studies* 20(3): 562-575.

Dhakidae, Daniel (1993) "Indonesia dan Australia berapa dekat jarak akademis", in *Kompas* 3-4 February.

—— (2003) *Cendekiawan dan kekuasaan dalam negara orde baru*, Jakarta: Gramedia Pustaka Utama.

Dijk, Kees van, et al (1998) *European Directory of South-East Asian Studies*, Leiden: KITLV Press.

Directory of West European Indonesianists (1987) Compiled by Documentation Centre for Modern Indonesia, Koninklijk Institute voor Taal-Land en Volkenkunde, Doordrecht-Holland/Providence (MA): Foris Publications.

Dye, Richard W. (1965) "The Jakarta Faculty of Economics", Jakarta: Ford Foundation (mimeographed manuscript).

Easton, David A. (1953) *The Political System*, New York: Alfred A. Knopf, Inc.

—— (1965a) *Framework for Political Analysis*, Englewood Cliffs (NJ): Prentice Hall.

—— (1965b) *System Analysis of Political Life*, New York: Wiley.

Evers, Hans-Dieter (2000) "Globalization, Local Knowledge, and the Growth of Ignorance", *Southeast Asian Journal of Social Science* 28 (1): 13-22.

Fine, Ben (2001) *Social Capital versus Social Theory, Political Economy and Social Science at the Turn of the Millennium*, London and New York: Routledge.

Foucault, Michel (1971) *The Archaelogy of Knowledge and the Discourse on Language*, New York: Pantheon Books.

—— (1980) *Power/Knowledge: Selected Interviews and Other Writings 1972-1977*, Colin Gordon (ed.), London: Harvester.

Furnivall, John Sydenham (1944) *Netherlands India: A Study of Plural Economy*, New York: The Macmillan Company.

—— (1948) *Colonial Policy and Practice: A Comparative Study of Burma and Netherlands India*, Cambridge: Cambridge University Press.

Garnaut Ross (1989) *Australia and the North East Asian Ascendancy*, Canberra: Australian Government Publishing Service.

Geertz, Clifford (1960) *The Religion of Java*, New York: The Free Press of Glencoe.

—— (1963) *Agricultural Involution: The Process of Ecological Change in Indonesia*, Berkeley, Los Angeles: The University of California Press.

—— (1970) "A Program for the Stimulation of the Social Sciences in Indonesia: A Report to the Ford Foundation", Jakarta: Ford Foundation (mimeographed manuscript).

Harriss, John (2002) *Depoliticizing Development: The World Bank and Social Capital*, London: Anthem Press.

Hefner, Robert (2001) *The Politics of Multiculturalism: Pluralism and Citizenship in Malaysia, Singapore, and Indonesia*, Honolulu: University of Hawai'i Press.

Heryanto, Ariel (1999) "Rape, Race, and Reporting", in *Reformasi: Crisis and Change in Indonesia?* Arief Budiman, Barbara Hatley, and Damien Kingsbury (eds), Clayton: Monash Asia Institute, pp. 299-334.

Heryanto, Ariel and Sumit K. Mandal (2003) *Challenging Authoritarianism in Southeast Asia: Comparing Indonesia and Malaysia*, London: RoutledgeCurzon.

Hidayat, Komaruddin (1994) *Melampaui nama-nama: islam dan postmodernisme* www.islampembebasan.virtualave.net/Komaruddin1.html.

Hill, David T. (2003) "Neglected Neighbour", *The Australian* (Higher Education Supplement) 13 August: 37.

HIPIIS (1975) "The Role of the Social Sciences in Development" Bukit Tinggi, 1-6 September.

Huntington, Samuel (1991) *The Third Wave: Democratization in the Late Twentieth Century*, Norman (OK): University of Oklahoma Press.

—— (1993) 'The Clash of Civilizations', *Foreign Affairs*, Summer: 23-49.

Hurgronje, C. Snouck (1906) *The Achenese,* trans. by A.W.S. Sullivan. Leiden: E.J. Brill (Vol.I-II).

—— (1916) *Mohammedanism*, New York and London: G.P. Putnam's Sons.

ISEI (1990) Penjabaran Demokrasi Ekonomi, Jakarta: ISEI.

Jayasuriya, Kanishka (1998) "Understanding Asian Values as a Form of Reactionary Modernisation", *Contemporary Politics*, 4(1): 77-91.

Kartodirdjo, Sartono (1972) "Agrarian Radicalism in Java: Its Setting and Development", in Claire Holt (ed.) *Culture and Politics in Indonesia*, Ithaca (NY) and London: Cornell University Press, pp. 71-125.

Kleden, Ignas (1986) "Alternative Social Science as an Indonesian Problematique", *New Asian Visions* 3(2): 6-22.

—— (1987) *Sikap ilmiah dan kritik kebudayaan*, Jakarta: LP3ES.

Koentjaraningrat (ed.) (1975) *The Social Sciences in Indonesia*, Jakarta: Indonesian Institute of Sciences (LIPI).

—— (1973) *Metodologi penelitian masjarakat*, Jakarta: Lembaga Ilmu Pengetahuan Indonesia.

—— (1974) *Kebudayaan, mentalitet dan pembangunan.* Jakarta: PT Gramedia.

Kundera, Milan (1999) *Book of Laughter and Forgetting*, trans. Aaron Asher, New York: HarperCollins.

Lerner, Daniel (1958) *The Passing of Traditional Society*, New York: The Free Press.

Mac Dougall, John (1975) "Technocrats as Modernizers: the Economists of Indonesia's New Order", Ph.D thesis, University of Michigan.

Mandal, Sumit K. (1994) "Finding Their Place: A History of Arabs in Java Under Dutch Rule, 1800-1924", Ph.D thesis, Columbia University.

Mas'oed, Mochtar (1989) *Ekonomi dan struktur politik orde baru, 1966-1971*, Jakarta: LP3ES.

Moertopo, Mayor Jenderal TNI/AD Ali (1972) *Dasar-dasar pemahaman tentang akselerasi modernisasi pembangunan 25 tahun*, Jakarta: Yayasan Proklamasi and Center for Strategic and International Studies.

Noer, Deliar (1973) *The Modernist Muslim Movement in Indonesia, 1900-1942*, Singapore, New York: Oxford University Press.

Nordholt, Nico Schulte and Leontine Visser (1997) *Ilmu sosial di Asia tenggara: dari partikularisme ke universalisme*, Jakarta: LP3ES.

O' Donnell, Guillermo A. (1973) *Modernization and Bureaucratic Authoritarianism*, Berkeley (CA): Institute of International Studies.

O'Donnell, Guillermo A. and Philippe C. Schmitter (1986) *Transitions from Authoritarian Rule: Tentative Conclusions about Uncertain Democracies*, Baltimore (MD): Johns Hopkins University Press.

Onghokham (1978) "The Inscrutable and the Paranoid: An Investigation into the Sources of the Brotodiningrat Affair", in Ruth McVey (ed.) *Southeast Asian Transitions*, New Haven: Yale University Press, pp. 112-157.

Parsons, Talcott (1960) *Structure and Process in Modern Societies*, Glencoe (IL): The Free Press.

—— (1951) *The Social System*, New York: The Free Press.

Putnam, Robert D. (1995) "Bowling Alone: America's Declining Social Capital", *The Journal of Democracy* 6(1): 65-78.

—— (2000) *Bowling Alone: The Collapse and Revival of American Community*, New York: Simon and Schuster.

Rahardjo, M. Dawam (ed.) (1987) *Kapitalisme dulu dan sekarang*, Jakarta: LP3ES.

Ransom, David (1970) "The Berkeley Mafia and the Indonesian Massacre", *Ramparts* 9(4): 27-29, 40-49.

Robison, Richard (1986) *Indonesia: The Rise of Capital*, Sydney: Allen and Unwin.

Robison, Richard and Vedi R. Hadiz (1993) "Privatization or the Reorganisation of Dirigism: Indonesian Economic Policy in the 1990s", *Canadian Journal of Development Studies*, Special Edition: 13-32.

—— (2004) *Reorganising Power in Indonesia: The Politics of Oligarchy in an Age of Markets*, London: RoutledgeCurzon.

Rostow, Walt Whitman (1964) *The Stages of Economic Growth*, Cambridge: Cambridge University Press.

Sahal, Ahmad (1994) "Kemudian, di manakah emansipasi? Tentang teori kritis, genealogi, dan dekonstruksi", *Kalam* 1: 12-22.

Simandjuntak, Marsillam (1994) *Pandangan negara integralistik*, Jakarta: PT Pustaka Utama Grafiti.

Sjahrir (1997) "The Struggle for Deregulation in Indonesia", in *The Politics of Economic Development in Indonesia: Contending Perspectives*, Ian Chalmers and Vedi R. Hadiz (eds), London: Routledge.

Soemardjan, Selo (1983) "Ilmu itu netral dan ilmuwan harus obyektif", *Prisma* 6(12): 73-80.

SPES (1994) *Economy and Ecology in Sustainable Development*, Jakarta: Gramedia Pustaka Utama.

Suryadinata, Leo (1978) *The Chinese Minority in Indonesia: Seven Papers*, Singapore: Chopmen Enterprises.

Tan, Mely G. (1961) "The Chinese Community in a Sundanese Town" M.A. thesis, Cornell University.

-2-

INSTITUTIONS, DISCOURSES, AND CONFLICTS IN ECONOMIC THOUGHT

Alexander Irwan

What are "institutions" and how important are they? In order to fully understand the struggle over access to resources and power in Indonesia, the concept of "institution" needs to be taken into account. This will help in identifying the factions that struggle over power, and that have developed and established a fully-fledged discourse, and the factions that still operate only at the level of language or idea. We are assuming here that a discourse wields more influence, and while battles at this level can indeed be tumultuous, this does not necessarily mean that they have a significant impact on the access to or utilization of resources.

In the mid-1980s, Chris Weedon (1987: 40-1) stressed that a discourse does not only operate at the level of language or idea. To be considered a discourse, it must also operate at the level of social processes and institutions, and even at the level of subjectivity. One indicator that a discourse is operating at the level of subjectivity is when a wide range of individuals is identified with that discourse. When liberalism, and later neo-liberalism, was on the rise, a wide and varied range of individuals were identified with this school of thought, including Friedrich van Hayek, Milton Friedman, Margaret Thatcher, Ronald Reagan, and Newt Gingrich. At the national level, and since the economic crisis of 1997, prominent individuals such as Sri Mulyani and Faisal Basri identified themselves with the neo-liberal current in Indonesia. Soon after, others such as Muhammad Ikhsan and Chatib Basri followed, and we can expect to see the rise of more and younger figures in the coming years.

If a discourse stops operating at the level of subjectivity, or when it disappears all together, this would indicate that it has degenerated to the level of operating only as a way of thinking. For example, at present there are no proponents of the "Indonesia Incorporated" approach that was represented by Panglaykim (1974; 1983), founder and first economist at the Center for Strategic and International Studies (CSIS), in the 1970s. Today, there are also no proponents of the dependency theory and the New Left in Indonesia, which in the past were identified with people like Dawam Rahardjo (1979; 1980) and Adi Sasono (1980; 1983), who provided many stimulating and critical ideas to students in the late 1970s and early 1980s.

With regard to institution, discourse operates at two levels. The first level is where a discourse operates to socialize a way of thinking. This first level of institution is identical with organization. For example, a group may gain control and make use of an economics faculty, or even a university, a research institute, or mass media in order to establish its presence as a current of thought. The second level does not relate to organization as such but rather to regulations issued by the state or by multilateral entities that provide the legal power to implement sanctions against those who violate norms. This second level of institution is what Hadi Susastro called "norms, principles and rules, and institutions which establish the rules of the game and ensure that those rules are not violated" (2002: 338). Of course, a discourse operating only at the first level will be weaker than that which operates at both levels. In the global context, neo-liberalism operates as a discourse at the second level. The World Trade Organization (WTO) is a good example. However, at the national level in Indonesia, neo-liberalism only operates at the first level. Even if there were indeed norms, principles, and regulations, and institutions that establish rules of the game, there is no consistency in the implementation of laws that could guard against the violation of those rules.

The strongest and most established economic discourse in Indonesia is still the state protection and intervention that was generated by the government in association with crony conglomerates when Indonesia was ruled by Soeharto. At present, the discourse continues to operate at the second level, controlling important decision making national institutions, thereby frustrating the course of neo-liberalism and sidelining critics who demand participation and a more equal distribution of income. At the level of language and idea, Indonesia in 2004 might look like a good neo-liberal country, but if we look at the level of institution in operation here, we see and understand the frustrations of neo-liberalism proponents.

TWO TENDENCIES IN ECONOMIC THOUGHT AT A TIME OF A WEAKENING STATE

It is possible to describe a landscape in order to appreciate its beauty. By describing the combination of colors, the geological contours, the spread of flora, and the aesthetics of the shape of the roofs of houses, one can open other people's eyes to this beauty. However, it is also possible to look at the landscape in order to understand power relations. For instance, the geographical features can be interpreted to reflect or represent the struggle over access to resources. Seen from this perspective, it is no longer the color of the earth on the hills that attracts attention but rather the railway line that runs parallel to the horizon; neither is it the beautiful roofs of the houses nor the winding river, but rather the bald forests over to the east, and the irrigation trenches that come out of the east and cut across to the southwest.

When I look across the landscape of economic thought during the three decades of the New Order and sharpen my senses to grasp the patterns of reasoning among the plurality of economic thoughts, I can sense the existence of two schools of thought. The first school of thought is that of the WTO, an institution operating across countries, which has been pressuring Indonesia to succumb to its rules and liberalize its economy. The WTO was born on 15 April 1994 in Marrakech, Morocco, as a result of the Uruguay Round. Indonesia hurriedly ratified the WTO agreement. The Indonesian House of Representatives ratified the agreement just a few months after the meeting on 13 October 1994, by passing Law 7, 1994 (Setiawan 2000: 93). Sri-Edi Swasono described the unseemly haste to succumb to the free market as "already saying yes, even before being asked" (Swasono 2001: 7). However, Law 7 has not been ratified; economic liberalization has not been implemented in Indonesia. Within the state and among big businesses, there is strong resistance to liberalization, and up until 2003 there were no signs that the supporters of neo-liberalism in Indonesia would succeed in enforcing the dictums of the free market upon institutions responsible for state policy.

Setiawan has depicted power relations in the WTO as an uneven boxing match between the heavyweights, the powerful industrial states, and the welterweights, the impoverished former colonies (Setiawan 2000: 27). This imbalance places poor countries in a disadvantaged position. While pressuring poor countries to reduce import tariffs on agricultural products, rich industrial countries continue to provide various subsidies to their farmers (Setiawan 2001). Furthermore, the Trade Related Aspect of Intellectual Property Rights (TRIPs), which has been ratified by the Indonesian government, gives multinational corporations (MNCs) an upper hand in the case of intellectual property rights. With their technological and capital strength, MNCs are in a more superior position than any Indonesian company or individual, or any community that possesses biological diversity. Using technological manipulation, bio-piracy takes place whereas MNCs patent many natural specificities, processed foods, and traditional Indonesian designs (Setiawan 2001: 39-40).

While the first school of thought, characterized by the ratification of the WTO agreement, strengthened during the peak of the Soeharto government, a second school of thought started to gain ground only after he fell from power and the state weakened because of a power fragmentation. The second school of thought is based not on the logic of the market, but on community sovereignty. This paradigm could only emerge when the New Order began to crumble. In fact, power had already started to fragment some time before the Soeharto government's demise.[1] After the fall of Soeharto, political and economic resources were divided among many different vested interest groups. Resource mobilization by these groups has made the state unable to protect the resources that should have been used to finance public services in general, and to increase the welfare of marginalized people in particular.

The inability of the state to protect its resources is clearly illustrated by the example involving the Indonesian Bank Liquidity Assistance (*Bantuan Likuiditas Bank Indonesia* – BLBI), a form of financial support given to troubled banks during the 1997-98 financial crisis. The government converted the BLBI into government bonds and took control of a majority share in those banks in trouble. As a consequence, the government has been taking approximately 40 trillion rupiah every year from the state budget to pay the interests of the bonds to the ailing banks. The state has also failed to protect the country's natural resources, which should rightly be used for the benefit of the people. Data collected by Kwik Kian Gie (2003), one of the leaders of the Indonesian Democratic Party of Struggle (*Partai Demokrasi Indonesia Perjuangan* – PDI-P) and until 2004 head of the National Planning Agency (*Badan Perencanaan Nasional* – BAPPENAS), and by *Kompas* (16 February, 2003: 25), reveal the size of the losses in natural resources due to official policy, corruption, and smuggling. The vested interest groups, sometimes working together with foreign interests, have been robbing Indonesia of its natural riches.

The data collected by Kwik Kian Gie is set out in Table 1. It shows that in the past few years, the total losses of resources amounted to 444 trillion rupiah a year. This is a result of rampant extraction of natural resources, tax evasion, subsidies to unhealthy banks and leaks in the national budget. The amount is considerably higher than the value of the national budget in 2003, which was only 370 trillion rupiah. Table 2 focuses on the smuggling of natural resources. But here, too, the figures are

---

[1]   As an illustration, in the first half of 1998, the fragmentation of power made the state unable to provide protection to its ethnic Chinese citizens during the May 1998 riots. As a consequence, many ethnic Chinese citizens, women in particular, became victims of (sexual) violence.

fantastic: 78 percent of the value of the 2003 national budget. Ironically, the 2003 national budget, like earlier national budgets, is a deficit budget.

Hal Hill (*Bisnis Indonesia*, 31 January 2003) said that the Indonesian government is a "lazy" one because it has chosen to balance its budget in the easiest way possible, namely by continuing to borrow more money from the Consultative Group on Indonesia (CGI) countries. The deficit should have been covered by improving budget efficiency and effectiveness, and by cutting back leakages due to corruption. The government has done none of these. The government of Indonesia is not lazy. It is the fragmentation of power that has prevented the government from protecting the public's interest.

When Abdurrahman Wahid's presidency was in the process of being destabilized, a senior National Awakening Party (*Partai Kebangkitan Bangsa* – PKB) figure, close to the Megawati Soekarnoputri camp, repeatedly advised PKB legislative members that if Wahid had shared "his plot of land" with other political forces, he would not have been forced to resign. The data below provides evidence that Megawati appears to have learned from the fall of Wahid. She allows power and resources to be divided among the fragmented elite groups. It should therefore be no surprise that the state under the Megawati government has been unable to protect resources required for the benefit of the public.

TABLE 1: ALLEGED CORRUPTION, 2003*

Natural resources: fish, sand, and timber	90
Tax: tax paid by taxpayers but not received by the state	240
Budget: subsidies to banks that will never return to a healthy state	40
Budget: 20% leakage from a total budget of Rp. 370,592 billion	<u>74</u>
TOTAL	**444**

* Estimated value in trillion of rupiah
Source: Kwik Kian Gie (2003)

TABLE 2: SMUGGLED NATURAL RESOURCES, 2003*

Sea sand	72
Oil	50
Timber	30
Ocean resources	36
Endangered animal species	<u>100</u>
TOTAL	**288**

* Estimated value in trillion of rupiah
Source: *Kompas* (16 January 2003: 25)

There are two important reasons for the strengthening of the second school of thought. First, power fragmentation caused the struggle over the control of resources to spin out of control, resulting in increased damage to the fabric of traditional or *adat* communities. This is because natural resources are to be found in areas that are home to these communities. Second, the implementation of the system of decentralization that started in 2001 provided local communities the chance to assert control over their own resources. Law 22/99 on Local Governance allows for the formation of village governments based on local customary law institutions (Antlöv 2003). While the central government and provincial, district and municipal governments have been busy rearranging the balance of power, traditional communities and civil society organizations have consolidated their efforts to rearrange the balance of power between regional government, at the district level, and the village (FPPM 2002). Natural resources are often located in areas inhabited by *adat* communities, and according to *adat* law, those resources are under the authority of the *adat* communities. However, according to the 1945 Constitution, all natural resources in Indonesia are under the control of the state. This and the continued exploitation of natural resources by the various fragmented groups wielding power over the country have pushed *adat* communities to strive harder to protect and control those natural resources.

One form that the second school of thought has taken is the establishment of the Alliance of Customary Communities in Indonesia (*Aliansi Masyarakat Adat Nusantara* – AMAN) in March 1999. AMAN was set up by and comprises 12 NGO networks and traditional community organizations from various parts of Indonesia. This network has spread and developed quickly, and by mid-2003, more than one thousand *adat* communities had joined AMAN. One of the main issues raised by AMAN is the drastic impact on the communities caused by a combination of the weakening state and the unseemly hastiness with which the government has given in to pressures from the WTO. As a result, natural resources at the community level have become more vulnerable to the interests of the different fragmented political forces and MNCs. AMAN's position is:

> Economic policy oriented to economic growth and the interests of capital has had extensive impacts on the environment. The first and foremost victims are traditional communities that live in and around the forest, mine, sea and coast.
>
> National Secretariat, AMAN manual: 4

The stance taken by the traditional communities in the protection of their natural resources can be seen in this excerpt from the AMAN vision, namely:

> ...the integration of the traditional community with their natural environment, including ensuring sustainability and the use of the natural resources in a way that causes no damages either now or in the future.
>
> National Secretariat, AMAN manual: 9

In 2001, I spoke with Karmadi, a village headman in Lombok and chairperson of the North Lombok Traditional Communities Alliance (*Persekutuan Masyarakat Adat Lombok Utara* – Perekat Ombara), a member organization of AMAN. He explained that the traditional Lombok culture of Sasak does not view forests as a resource to be cut down for economic gain. The North Lombok Sasak book of traditional wisdom, *Kitab Awig-awig*, asserts that forests are not a commodity to be used for capital accumulation. There are now attempts to revitalize and, at the same time, democratize traditional Sasak institutions. If those institutions could be made to function properly again, then anyone who needs to cut down a tree will have to convince the community council that they need funds for some major life cycle purpose, such as a marriage or funeral.

If Sasak communities had been able to participate in determining policy on the natural resources in the northern part of Lombok, no company would have received a license to fell trees at the foot of the Mt. Rinjani, the island's principal volcano. They would not have stripped the forests bare. This has given rise to floods during the rainy season and springs drying up in the dry season. Intensive logging of the forests might have resulted in impressive growth statistics at the province level and might have increased per capita income at the national level. However, the economic losses suffered by the people living in the area are enormous, causing their welfare and standard of living to decline. Therefore, there is a negative correlation between economic growth and the welfare and prosperity of local communities.

This negative correlation between economic growth and local prosperity is also seen in Grasberg, Papua, as a result of the activities of PT Freeport Indonesia. When Freeport dumped tailings from copper and gold mining, it severely damaged 133 square kilometers of fertile community land. According to Friends of the Earth Indonesia (*Wahana Lingkungan Hidup* – WALHI) (2003: 20), the total area of land contaminated by the tailings was 32,820 hectares. 84,158 hectares of ocean were also contaminated. These mining activities clearly contributed to macroeconomic growth, but at the same time, they caused the welfare of local communities to decline. The scale of the destruction can be seen from the air on a commercial flight between Timika and Jayapura. Another example of this negative correlation is described by Aditjondro (2003: 84-6), namely the clearing of forests by logging companies in Central Kalimantan. Their activities, while contributing to national economic growth, bring losses to the local communities due to major flooding of the Barito and Kapuas rivers. Licensed logging companies have also displaced the local Dayak people who have been dependent on those forests for their livelihoods for centuries.

Within the context of the increasing fragmentation of power and WTO pressures for liberalization, it is not surprising that the key word for the second school of thought is "community sovereignty", that is:

> Sovereignty of the political alliance of traditional communities to manage their cultural, legal, and socio-economic life, including sovereignty over the control and exploitation of land, natural resources, and other sources of livelihood.
>
> National Secretariat, AMAN manual: 10

AMAN does not stand alone. Efforts to develop bottom-up planning, village-level decentralization, and community autonomy are part of a wider effort to assert control over local resources. These efforts do sometimes also involve local government. For example, the *bupati* (regent) of the district of Fakfak in Papua allocated 350 million rupiah from the 2002-03 local budget to facilitate bottom-up planning, and the development of the village budget and village regulations in 78 villages. A joint effort by donor agencies (in this case, the Partnership for Governance Reform and the Civil Society Support and Strengthening Program), the *bupati* of Fakfak, the Institute for Popular Economic Empowerment (Elpera), and the local communities, the objective was to develop best practices in eight villages between 2003 and 2004. In the future, the villages will work as learning centers for other villages in Papua. The stakeholders involved are also planning to facilitate the development of a regional ordinance that could become a legal basis for the bottom-up planning exercises to develop autonomous communities.

The success of this economic school of thought depends on its ability to develop institutions. It is clear that, at the moment, the community sovereignty economic thought does not have a second-level institution with cross-country authority, such as the WTO, to assert and enforce rules. In fact, this economic thought has not even succeeded in developing such an institution at the national level. The proponents of this school of thought have only established the first level of institution in the form of a network of civil society organizations and communities, which acts to establish support and acceptance of their ideas. They have not been able to win the support of any renowned universities, research institutes, or the media to help them establish their economic thought as a public discourse.

In this section, we have made an overview of the landscape of economic thought in Indonesia from the perspective of the struggle over resources. One hopes that the economic perspective that considers the question of institution allows us to develop a more accurate picture of economic thought in Indonesia, one that correctly depicts the struggle over the control of resources. We have so far identified two schools of thought: One takes the form of neo-liberalism, and attempts to minimize government regulations in order to gain maximum access to natural resources through a free market mechanism, with the goal of producing high economic growth. The other, responding to a perceived negative correlation between economic growth and community welfare, attempts to develop community sovereignty to protect local resources and use them to increase people's welfare.

THE INSTITUTION DICTUM IN THE STRUGGLE OVER POWER

The power struggle over resources during the New Order period are reflected in the relations between the two schools of economic thought as described above. Differentiating between what is economics and what is not in the mapping of economic thinking during the New Order is misleading. Such a differentiation would, in itself, be a manifestation of power, and it would marginalize certain streams of economic thought thereby rendering them invisible. If efforts to develop community sovereignty do not form part of an economic agenda, then it could be argued that the struggle over economic power is confined to that between the supporters of the WTO and those of the neo-liberal economic school of thought, and those who support economic growth but want the state to play a real role in ensuring that economic development benefits the poor. However, if the agenda includes economic thinking that is not oriented to economic growth but to local community welfare, sustainable environment, and community control over local resources, the landscape of economic thought as it relates to the struggle over resources during the New Order will appear different.

My method of mapping out economic thought in Indonesia during the New Order period is not based on any categorization of the social sciences into sociology, politics, history, economics, anthropology and so on. The collapse of the boundaries between the social sciences has become more evident post-World War II (Wallerstein 1997). It is even more evident now in this third millennium with the consolidation of fields into various inter-disciplinary studies such as area studies (for example, Japanese

Studies, Chinese Studies, European Studies, Southeast Asian Studies), women's studies, peace and security studies, political economy, and so on. The current effort to examine the contours of economic thinking is not constrained by the tendency of economics to define traditional communities or society as culture and therefore part of the study of sociology, history, anthropology, or even archaeology. If studies are based on the old criteria, the efforts of traditional communities and their support networks in the struggle over economic resources would go unnoticed. This is because "community" is not recognized as an element of economic thought. Rather, it is seen either as a mere political factor, undermining the confidence of foreign investors, or a cultural factor, where foreign investors might not be sensitive to local values.

When this perspective is deployed to map the significance of the two schools of thought, we can see that both schools have gained a status as a discourse, but their discursive strengths differ. In Indonesia, the neo-liberal school of thought operates at the first level of institutionalization. In the global context, it operates at the second level of institutionalization. The community sovereignty school of thought is even weaker since it only operates at the first level of institutionalization in Indonesia. The transformation of economic thought into discourse starts with the success of its proponents to gain control over existing institutions, such as the economics faculty of a well-known university, which can then be used as a stepping stone to winning over prominent media and state decision-making institutions. The revival of economic liberalism began with the success of its thinkers to gain control of several prominent universities throughout the world and subsequently identifying them with neo-liberalism. I would argue that it was a conscious penetration and co-optation.

The rise of neo-liberalism to global prominence was a long struggle, waged by the supporters of liberalism and the free market – Adam Smith's term was "the invisible hand". Keynesianism – an economic approach of using state policy to stimulate economic initiatives – had been the dominant stream of economic thought from the end of the World War II until the 1970s. The neo-liberals built a base in three universities, namely the London School of Economics (LSE), University of Chicago (where two long-standing free market supporters taught: Friedrich von Hayek and Milton Friedman) and the Institute Universitaire de Haute Etudes Internationales in Geneva. Besides building these fortresses in the universities, they also established various institutions for research and lobbying such as the Societé du Mont-Pelerin, the Institute of Economic Affairs and the Centre for Policy Studies in Britain, as well as the Heritage Foundation, the International Center for Economic Policy Studies, the Institute for Public Policy and the Center for International Studies in the United States. They all worked to popularize their ideas in a climate dominated by Keynesianism, the preferred school of thought of policy makers. The results have been recorded in history. In 1974, Hayek won the Nobel Prize for Economics, followed by Friedman in 1976, and this opened the door to some control over government policy making. In the 1980s, this liberal stream gained prominence in two powerful countries, namely Britain and the United States, and neo-liberalism later became known as Thatcherism and Reaganomics respectively. The neo-liberals were in a much better position than their liberal predecessors in the early twentieth century because they had the backing of an international institution, namely the WTO, which could be used to enforce neo-liberal policies on all countries that had ratified the WTO agreements.

The path taken by the disciples of the free market to influence public decision-making in Indonesia was not as straightforward as the one taken by their counterparts in the West. In Indonesia, their efforts were preceded by two armed struggles between the proponents of socialism and capitalism. The first armed struggle took place in 1958, in which the proponents of capitalism were defeated. But, the capitalists eventually won the contest of power in 1965-67 when the army took over power from President Soekarno.

Sumitro Djojohadikusomo played an important role in laying the groundwork for the rise of future neo-liberal economics. It began when he became the Dean of the Faculty of Economics of the University of Indonesia (FEUI) in the early 1950s. The FEUI itself was established in 1950. Sumitro restructured the curriculum, organization, and staffing of the faculty which he considered to be Dutch-centric. Sumitro, a believer in capitalism, was hostile to Soekarno's politics (Anwar 2003: 219). But his thoughts were not even close to liberalism. In the early 1950s, he developed a detailed plan for state-led industrialization, and in the early years of the New Order, he supported the Keynesian approach (Chalmers and Hadiz 1997: 94). When he supported the Revolutionary Government of the Republic of Indonesia (*Pemerintah Revolusioner Republik Indonesia* – PRRI) rebellion in 1958, he did so in the name of capitalism. His actions were not unconnected to the Cold War and the battle between the capitalist and socialist blocks for influence in the former colonial countries. During this time, Indonesia was moving towards socialism, a process that climaxed in 1959 when Soekarno introduced the policies of Guided Democracy. There was a growing hostility towards foreign capital, which had led to the nationalization of Dutch companies in 1957. In addition, with the Indonesian Communist Party (*Partai Komunis Indonesia* – PKI) slowly gaining a stronghold in Indonesian politics, the state featured more prominently in economic planning. It was this political development that Sumitro and colleagues fought against.

Two days after the PRRI was established, the Permesta (*Perjuangan Semesta* – lit. Universal Struggle) forces that had rebelled in North Sulawesi declared that they had joined forces with the PRRI. Sumitro was the Minister for Trade and

Communications in the PRRI-Permesta government, which was headed by Sjafrudin Prawinegara, Prime Minister and Minister for Finance. However, the rebellion was crushed within a few months and Sumitro fled to Singapore. In 1956, however, while Sumitro was still in control, the Faculty received grants from the Ford Foundation to send some of its graduates to study at the University of California at Berkeley.

Given that anti-capitalist sentiment was growing at that time, foreign grants such as this could be viewed in two ways: David Ransom (1970) alleged the creation of the so-called "Berkeley Mafia" was linked to US policy to remove Soekarno and neutralize the PKI, which culminated in the massacres of 1965-67. On the other hand, the "Affiliation Program of the University of Indonesia with the University of California (Berkeley)" can be viewed as a program that aimed to increase the number and quality of teachers at the university and not an attempt to create a group of pro-American economists who would help steer Indonesia into the capitalist realm after the fall of Soekarno (Glassburner 1971: 33; Salim 2002: 5). All the FEUI graduates who were sent to Berkeley at the end of the 1950s and early 1960s, including Widjojo Nitisastro, Ali Wardhana, Johannes B. Sumarlin, Emil Salim, and Mohammad Sadli, had received funding from the Ford Foundation. By 1965, 47 FEUI graduates had been sent to the US; many of them to Berkeley and some to Chicago, the bastion of neo-liberal economics (Dye 1965: Appendix III).

One by one, starting with Sadli in 1957, they returned to Indonesia to face Soekarno's policies that were hostile towards Western capitalism and which gave the state a major role in managing economic resources. The process, which eventually led them to become the formulators of economic policy under Soeharto, began with them developing links with the military at the Army Staff College (*Sekolah Staf dan Komando Angkatan Darat* – SESKOAD) in Bandung. It was Sadli who, in 1958, was asked to lecture there by a former high school classmate, Colonel Suwarto, the SESKOAD Commandant at the time (Brooks 1997: 29). Widjojo Nitisastro, Subroto Ali Wardhana, and Emil Salim all lectured at SESKOAD. Their students at the time included Soeharto, Umar Wirahadikusumah, Sarbini and Mohamad Jusuf (Salim 2002: 5-6), who later became important military figures in the New Order government.

When Soeharto became president in 1967 he asked the Berkeley graduates to formulate Indonesia's economic policies. However, they only partly liberalized the economy, primarily by opening up the country to foreign investments. There were several factors that prevented the economic technocrats from pursuing more liberal economic policies. First, there was no external pressure to liberalize the economy further. Removing the PKI and opening up the Indonesian economy to foreign investment were considered as adequate measures by the US and its Cold War allies. Second, Keynesian policies were considered politically necessary to prevent popular discontent against the capitalist system. Third, within the development theory circle in the former colonies, which included scholars such as Alexander Gerschenkron and Hamza Alavi, the dominant perspective was to support state intervention in promoting economic growth. High economic growth being achieved in countries like Japan and South Korea added further support for state intervention in economic planning. Fourth, the military played a dual role in the country, both as a security and socio-political force. From as early as 1978, the Business International Research Division (1978: 57-61) reported that since the national budget only covered about thirty percent of Indonesian military expenditure, state-owned enterprises were treated as cash cows by the military, and certain businesses were provided with protection and facilities in return for financial contributions. In other words, privatization and free competition were not encouraged by the economic technocrats. As a consequence, "regulation and bureaucratization was rampant in this period and was accepted as a logical consequence of accelerated development" (Seda 1997: 243).

It was in 1982 that the economic technocrats saw a window of opportunity to pursue liberal economic policies. In the early 1980s, the oil boom that Indonesia had enjoyed since 1974 suddenly ended. The drastic drop in oil prices that began in 1983 provided the opportunity for the economic technocrats to pressure the state, which had lost its oil revenues, to liberalize the economy through deregulation. Investment by the government and government expenditures could no longer keep the wheels of the economy turning. At that point, the neo-liberal economists under Sumitro were able to establish a strategic partnership with the largest-circulation daily newspaper, *Kompas*. The *Kompas* economics discussion panel, which still exists to this day, was established in 1983. Its first chairperson was Mohammed Sadli. The owner of *Kompas*, Jakob Oetama, explained the aim of the economic panel as being "to contribute to a societal understanding of the process of change from *ekonomi etatisme* (state-directed economy) to a market economy and to help ensure that the consequences and implications of this change are understood by the government and its apparatus and also by actors in the private sector" (2002: 13-14).

The struggle between the support for state intervention and economic deregulation was also apparent within the main New Order economic think-tank, the Center for Strategic and International Studies (CSIS). CSIS was established in 1971 by military officers such as Benny Moerdani, Ali Moertopo and Sudjono Humardani, and obtained immediate funding, with Soeharto's blessings, from businessmen close to the president. The CSIS promoted economic nationalism and supported a strong state, which could gather and concentrate national capital (Chalmers and Hadiz 1997: 73). The first generation of CSIS economists included Panglaykim, one of the original 47 FEUI graduates sent to Berkeley. But Panglaykim's approach differed from that of the other Berkeley graduates who believed in the free market and in opening up the Indonesian economy to foreign capital. Panglaykim instead wanted the state to intervene in the market to promote the development of competitive national business groups in the way that the Japanese government had done after World War II. In order to compete with the MNCs in general and with Japanese business groups in particular, Panglaykim emphasized the need for close cooperation between government, businesses and technocrats in order to create an "Indonesia Incorporated" or "Indonesia, Inc." If the aim of neo-classical economics is to realize true prices through the market mechanism, then the aim of Indonesia Incorporated was, to borrow Alice Amsden's term (1989) in describing the South Korean economy, to deliberately get the "relative prices wrong" in order to develop business groups around the government banks which it was hoped would help create national competitiveness.

Panglaykim's case was undermined by the fact that supporting a strong role for the state in developing the economy did not in fact promote competitiveness. The military-bureaucrat-politician block in Indonesia did not use the boom in oil revenue for the state during 1974-82 to develop *zaibatsu* styled industrial groups capable of competing at the international level. Rather, they took Indonesia in the direction of ersatz capitalism, to borrow Yoshihara's term, which was not based on developing competitiveness but on KKN (*korupsi, kolusi dan nepotisme* – corruption, collusion, nepotism) to build individual and group economic fiefdoms. One tell-tale sign was the mismanagement of the state-owned oil company, Pertamina, when it was under the leadership of General Ibnu Sutowo. In 1975, it became public knowledge that Pertamina had defaulted on its US$10.5 billion loans due to inefficiencies, incompetence, and corruption (Robison 1986: 153-154).

Given this situation, once the oil boom ended in 1982, it was impossible to sustain the concept of Indonesia, Inc. any longer. It is not surprising then that the second generation of CSIS economists did not advocate state intervention, supporting economic liberalism instead. This second generation of economists included Hadi Susastro, Pande Raja Silalahi, Djisman Simandjuntak, and Panglaykim's daughter, Mari Pangestu. Together with other neo-liberal economists, they pressed the government in the mid-1980s to carry out the first batch of economic liberalization policies. Their view was that only a liberal economic system could create a strong economy and thereby bring benefits to society. The following quote sums up their annoyance with the political obstacles they faced:

...the failure to develop economic institutions has meant that the management of the economy has been dependent on the personal whim of some people who have authority because of political power, or because they possess weapons, or because they hold some strategic bureaucratic position. The economy was then managed in the interests of these people or their group and not in the interest of society. As a consequence, what emerged was a system of exploitation, and it was even worse because the exploitation was done by Indonesians.

Susastro 2002: 338

Although the neo-liberal agenda had been assisted by the drastic drop in oil prices, by the most dominant newspaper in the country, by an influential research institute returning to liberalism, and by pressure from multilateral institutions such as the World Bank, the supporters of the free market were still very disappointed with the results of their struggle against the military-bureaucrat-politician block. After a decade of struggle, they achieved little. Mari Pangestu (1997: 158) and Hadi Susastro bitterly described the results as "half-hearted" deregulation (2002: 338-339). This half-hearted deregulation represented a defeat for the supporters of the free market because, according to Susastro: "Economic liberalization is like pregnancy, it cannot go half-way." After a decade of reluctant deregulation, deregulation fatigue set in during the early 1990s. This was concomitant with an increasing role of Soeharto's family in national economic and political affairs; two Soeharto children were in Golkar's central committee and all had built powerful business-houses through protectionism and facilities provided by the state.

I would thus argue that Rizal Mallarangeng is mistaken when he argues that the reason for the deregulation fatigue in the early 1990s was the intellectual failure of liberalism's proponents to answer the legitimate questions of their critics, led by populist intellectuals and NGO activists (2002: 219-232). These people focused their criticism on the rise of economic conglomerates which were founded on nepotistic principles and contributed to the widening economic divide in the country. However, this challenge from the NGO activists and populist intellectuals never moved beyond the realm of language as they never met the institutionalization criterion. They did not have the same capacity to block deregulation as did the Soeharto family, high-ranking government officials, the military and the conglomerates who had grown strong under government protection and subsidy. According to Mari Pangestu, the main obstacle to deregulation in the 1990s was the absence of any political will on the part of the government (2003: 32).

It was only after the economic crisis of 1997 that the proponents of the free market communicated their frustration with the political obstacles to liberalization raised by the government. They used a variety of media, from print to student forums. For example, Pangestu (2003) was a contributor to Garuda's in-flight magazine, and Faisal Basri used student discussion forums in 1998 and 1999. Basri strongly rejected subsidies or protection for the businesses hit by the crisis arguing that such assistance would only be used to promote KKN principles again. Basri stated: "It is only in a very few cases that there is any theoretical proof that practices limiting trade between nations are superior to that of free trade as regards impact upon the economy" (1997: 242).

Although the liberal economic stream has still not been able to consolidate control over economic policy, it has been able to establish itself as an economic discourse in Indonesia. This line of thinking has support from multilateral institutions such as the International Monetary Fund (IMF) and the World Bank, as well as some foreign corporations. It controls university institutions, dominant media, significant research institutions, and some state institutions. This superior position is supplemented by its capacity to groom a steady pool of scholars, who uphold FEUI as a fortress of liberal economic thinking, and who supply the media with articles supporting liberalization. Some of FEUI's more prominent scholars include Sri Mulyani Indrawati (former IMF Executive Director and currently head of BAPPENAS), Faisal Basri, Muhammad Ikhsan and Chatib Basri. Compare this with the failure of people like Panglaykim to produce new cadres as proponents of Indonesia, Inc. or with Professor Mubyarto of Gadjah Mada University, who has been on a solo quest for establishment of Pancasila economics since the mid-1970s.

Although Indonesia is a signatory to WTO agreements, the politically unstable situation in the country makes it difficult for free marketeers to achieve full-blooded deregulation. In fact, those in power, the various vested interest groups, big businesses and so on, will do what they can to prevent deregulation. These groups have a common interest, and that is to maintain the status quo so that they can continue mobilizing resources for their own parties and groups through plunder and fraud. And the supporters of free market economics, a coalition comprising the international institutions such as the IMF and the World Bank, the technocrats, and the intellectual proponents of the free market stream, have not been able to beat them in the policy-making game.

However, free market proponents have developed a discourse with their own concepts, institutions and prominent individuals identifiable with their stream of thought. They may not have conquered the state, but they have won the public opinion to support Rostow's thesis (1971) that in order to catch up, the former colonized societies must follow the strategy of their former colonizers in the liberal West if they are to achieve maximum economic growth.

The idea of "catching up" with the liberal west through maximum economic growth has become so embedded in the public mindset that even the failure to "take off" in terms of development in 1994, as promised by the government and the Berkeley economists, did not rattle the legitimacy of the growth-oriented ideology. However, the successes of other Asian countries such as Japan, South Korea and Taiwan cannot be reproduced in Indonesia without disturbing the legitimacy of this ideology (Irwan et al 1993).

During the financial crisis of 1997, gross national product (GNP) per capita fell from US$1200 in 1997 to US$500 in 2002. But society still held fast to the idea that going for maximum growth and opening up the economy to foreign capital to the maximum extent was the solution. In reality, after thirty years of sacrificing its natural resources and environmental sustainability, Indonesia's GNP per capita remained constant.

FAILURE TO DEVELOP INSTITUTIONALIZATION

Developing a discourse is not an easy task. A dissenting thought would not be able to challenge a discourse if it fails to develop institutionalization. Professor Dorodjatun Kuntjoro-Jakti, the Coordination Minister for the Economy and Finance in the Megawati cabinet, is a good case in point. He has always been critical of many of the ideas of the Berkeley Mafia. Mallarangeng (2002: 219-232) described him as part of the "epistemological liberals", but when deregulation accelerated in the mid-1980s, he warned the public that this would result in Indonesia being trapped in a liberal capitalist economy. Since his Berkeley days, Dorodjatun has been espousing a variant of economic thought, different from that of his peers and predecessors at Berkeley. He chose a doctorate in political science over economics. Furthermore, his thesis (Kuntjoro-Jakti 1981) focused on the political economy of development in Indonesia between 1966 and 1978. When I invited him to speak at a forum organized by the Student Senate of the Faculty of Social Sciences at the University of Indonesia in 1980, he said in his presentation that FEUI had stopped sending its young economists to UC Berkeley when it saw that the last person to go there, referring to himself, had strayed from the neo-classical economic school.

When Hadi Susastro taught "An Introduction to Economics" at the Faculty of Social Sciences and Politics at UI in the early 1980s, he preferred Paul A. Samuelson's *Economics* (a neo-classical textbook) to Dorodjatun's choice of Michael P. Todaro's *Economic Development*. The latter expressed a more critical attitude on relations between the first and third worlds. Dorodjatun even made sure that the book was translated into Indonesian. That translation, entitled *Pembangunan Ekonomi di Dunia Ketiga* (Developmental Politics in the Third World), can still be found in bookshops throughout the country.

Subjectively speaking, his ideas stray from the neo-liberal path, but interestingly, Dorodjatun has never been able to give his ideas an institutional manifestation separate from that of the neo-liberal school. This has meant that, even as Coordinating Minister, his variant of thinking was overwhelmed and overshadowed by the agenda formed by the free market dynamic and the WTO. His speech to the influential Indonesian Association of Economists (*Ikatan Sarjana Ekonomi Indonesia* – ISEI) on 13 July 2003 in Malang entitled, "Economic Development Strategy in the Era of *Reformasi* and Globalisation", reflected this. Although he acknowledged a connection between environmental destruction, exploitation of labor, and increased poverty, he went on to say:

> The world trade system which appears to be increasingly stable in following the rules established by the WTO has brought significant benefits to the progress of the world economy. Levels of production and the volume of world trade continue to rise. In its journey, the implementation of this trade system has shown the many different results that different nations can achieve.

Let us now turn our attention to another of the five founders of the Berkeley Mafia, a very influential thinker of the New Order (and beyond), Emil Salim. He, too, strayed from the liberal discourse when he became Minister for Environment and Population between 1978 and 1993, and failed to institutionalize his support for environmental sustainability (Salim 1978; 1983; 1991). As a defender of environmental conservation, he directly confronted the power of the state and capital, which exploited nature in order to achieve maximum economic growth. One year after becoming minister, he launched a public campaign against the giant timber companies that were carrying out massive deforestation in East Kalimantan and were ignoring legal requirements regarding replanting and selective logging policies (Aditjondro 2003: 59-61). Several of these giant companies were joint ventures between foreign companies, the Indonesian military, and ethnic Chinese businessmen who were closely connected with those in power.

However, as minister, he was never able to develop the institutions necessary to support the popularization of environmental conservation. The mere existence of the Ministry for Environment was insufficient to develop and enforce regulations to stem, let alone reverse, deforestation in Indonesia, which had been a growing problem since the drop in oil prices in 1983. Data from Indonesia Forest Watch-

Global Forest Watch shows that deforestation increased from 1 million hectares per year in the 1980s to 1.7 million hectares in the early 1990s, rising to 2 million hectares in 1996.

There are many other examples of thinkers and scholars whose ideas failed to achieve institutionalization. As mentioned in the introduction, the ideas about dependent development, promoted by Adi Sasono and Dawam Rahardjo in the late 1970s and early 1980s, are today little more than distant memories. The same fate befell Sritua Arief (1982) who advocated a theoretical as well as mathematical calculation of the surplus extracted by the rich countries from the poor. Arief Budiman (1997: 123-127) argued that Indonesia's poverty was structural and therefore required a structural overhaul through socialism. Budiman's story is somewhat different. After completing his doctoral studies at Harvard in the 1980s, he returned to Indonesia to occupy a strategic position at Satya Wacana University in Salatiga. But it turned out that it was not easy to transform this university institution into a fortress from which to create a discourse. His critical stance towards New Order state-led economic policies and political actions contributed to the emergence of conflicts inside UKSW, and Budiman was pushed out of the university in 1996, exiled, so to speak. He now teaches at the University of Melbourne, which makes it even harder still for him to fulfill the criteria of institutionalization of a dominant discourse.

Even those who have control over leading research institutions have not been successful in transforming their views into an economic discourse with the national interest as a top priority. Rizal Ramli, long-time head of the independent Ekonit research institute, was a known critic of the IMF. But at the level of the struggle for control over power, he achieved no significant change, in spite of being Minister for Economic Affairs in the government of President Abdurrahman Wahid. Picking a fight with both the neo-liberals and the anti-deregulation forces at the same time did not get him anywhere. The same can be said of Didik Rachbini from the INDEF research institute. He is known as an economist who sides with the people and the national interest. His voice often resonates strongly in the mass media but he has nevertheless been unable to create an impact on the struggle over control of resources at the national level or gain any institutional support.

The economists at Gadjah Mada University perhaps have had more success in institutionalization of their ideas. Mubyarto, for example, struggling for Pancasila Economics since the 1970s, was able to eventually establish a Center for the Study of Pancasila Economics in September 2002 (Mubyarto 2002). Nonetheless, he is still a long way from making the Economics Faculty of Gadjah Mada University (FE UGM) carry the flag of Pancasila economics. It is therefore no coincidence, and certainly not a matter of choice, that Mubyarto's center is administered under the auspices of the vice-chancellor's office and not the economics faculty. One stumbling block in Mubyarto's way is the term "Pancasila" itself. It was the subject of manipulation and distortion during the Soeharto period, so much so that many people now are keen to avoid using it to describe a school of economic thought. Revrisond Baswir, a lecturer at the FE UGM and a defender of a pro-people economics, is one who avoids this term. On some issues, he takes sharper positions. He opposes foreign debts, the IMF, and privatization that favors only foreign capital. He also takes a very strong anti-corruption stance (Baswir 2002; 2003). Although he also rejects neo-liberalism, he has never used Pancasila economics as the framework for his thinking or his political stance. With regard to institutionalization, Revrisond has been more successful in establishing networks for his university with civil society organizations and the pro-democracy movement, of which, in fact, he is a core figure. He founded the Institute of Development and Economic Analysis (IDEA), a body that is not only popular with critically minded Gadjah Mada students but has also become part of the network of organizations opposed to government policies harming the interests of the people. He currently also sits on the executive board of the International NGO Forum for Indonesian Development (INFID). Because of the difficulties faced with developing a partnership with prominent media such as KOMPAS, Revrisond and IDEA use the Internet to spread their ideas. But as long as civil society organizations remain fragmented, people like Revrisond will find it difficult to institutionalize their ideas. Moreover, their opponents are strong and well organized.

In addition to Mubyarto and Revrisond, a prominent political economist and media contributor at FE UGM worthy of mention is Tony Prasetiantono (2000). While accepting that economic liberalization, in the context of the development of the WTO, APEC and AFTA, cannot be avoided, Prasetiantono has adopted a political economy approach arguing that Indonesia's competitiveness will not develop, and therefore will not benefit from economic liberalization, until it can democratize its political infrastructure and make its economic infrastructure more equitable. His emphasis on democracy and justice provides a clear basis for connecting with the approaches of Mubyarto and Revrisond.

CONCLUSION: THE DEVELOPMENT OF A DISCOURSE BY DESIGN

As stated in the introduction to this chapter, a school of thought can become a discourse by achieving a specific level of institutionalization. If a school of thought does not develop into a discourse, it will not have sufficient clout to succeed in any struggle over power. A discourse operates at two levels of institutionalization. The first level is where the discourse operates to spread or embed a school or stream of thinking in society. The second level of institutionalization does not take the form of an organization but rather that of state or cross-state regulations that have legal authority and are backed by the power to impose sanctions for violation. A discourse operating only at the first level is obviously weaker than one that operates at both levels.

Table 3 sets out a summary of the strengths and weaknesses of the different schools of economic thought in Indonesia over the past 40 years: neo-liberalism, state intervention, and community sovereignty. The table also highlights the agendas of each school of thought. The opponents of the neo-liberals are the government institutions that are the basis of the bureaucratic-military-conglomerate-politician alliance. Strategic alliances are built with multilateral agencies and international financial institutions. They seldom will be able to obtain grassroots support, because they are seen as responsible for unpopular policies such as the reduction in government subsidies for a range of basic needs.

TABLE 3. MAP OF STRENGTHS AND WEAKNESSES BY LEVEL OF INSTITUTIONALIZATION

| | Economic School of Thought | | |
	Neo-liberalism	State Intervention	Community Sovereignty
First level of institutionalization			
Universities, media, research institutions	Strong	Strong	Weak
Grassroots network	Weak	Weak	Strong
Second level of institutionalization			
Multilateral institutions (IMF, World Bank, WTO)	Strong	Weak	Weak
Government institutions	Weak	Strong	Weak
Discourse	Succeeded in consolidating its discourse: Economic growth through liberalization and deregulation	Succeeded in consolidating its discourse. Economic growth through government intervention	Not yet succeeded in consolidating a discourse. Oriented towards local community welfare

The primary enemies of state interventionists are not the defenders of neo-liberalism, who typically sit in government, because their services are needed as technocrats to manage, not control, economic policy. Rather, their main adversaries are the multilateral agencies such as the World Bank, the IMF and the WTO that are pressing the state to implement all-out liberalization, which would effectively dismantle the monopoly held by the bureaucrat-military-conglomerate-politician alliance. Through the ideology of developmentalism they have been successful in getting support from the grassroots by offering short-term programs to lighten the economic burden on the lower social classes, such as the Social Safety Net programs of the late 1990s.

The supporters of community sovereignty face a major array of opponents, from both left and right, market and state, interventionists and liberals. They confront the multilateral agencies by demanding government regulation that guarantees community control over productive resources. They also challenge the bureaucrat-military-conglomerate-politician alliance because it exploits these productive resources, legitimizing their exploits by making reference to Clause 33 of the 1945 Constitution, which states that the earth, water and natural resources of Indonesia belong to the state. These groups have little choice but to seek the first level of institutionalization. Without the full support of the universities, the media, and prominent research institutions, they will not be able to sell their ideas to the general public or develop them into a discourse. And it is critical that thinking become a discourse if it is to exert any influence on the struggle over the management of resources.

There is still the lingering controversy surrounding the creation of the "Berkeley Mafia". Was this a conscious effort, that is, *by design*, aimed at bringing Indonesia into the capitalist orbit or just the unintended consequence of the Ford Foundation's objective to build the capacity of FEUI? Let that question remain unanswered because what is clear is that the development of the community sovereignty school of thought into a discourse must be done *by design*. It cannot be achieved through sporadic and fragmentary capacity-strengthening programs for different communities and supporting organizations. A failure to develop the community sovereignty stream of thinking into a discourse will mean that the negative correlation between economic growth and local community welfare remains intact in Indonesia.

EPILOGUE: NOVEMBER 2004

On 20 October 2004, through a direct presidential election, Susilo Bambang Yudhoyono became the new president of Indonesia. The composition of Yudhoyono's cabinet was actually a *déjà vu* for the proponents of neo-liberalism and state intervention school of economic thought. The success of the neo-liberals to put forward Mari Pangestu as Minister of Trade and Sri Mulyani Indrawati as Minister of National Planning *cum* head of the BAPPENAS was not a ground-breaking accomplishment. In the past, the "Berkeley Mafia" technocrats have occupied key economic positions. Bearing this in mind, it is unlikely that Pangestu and Mulyani, even with the help of multilateral institutions such as the World Bank and IMF, will prevail over proponents of state intervention that enjoyed economic privileges under the Soeharto regime such as Vice President Jusuf Kalla and Coordinating Minister of the Economy Aburizal Bakrie. Rumors that Sri Mulyani might be appointed Coordinating Minister drew heavy criticism from Islamic parties close to President Yudhoyono, who then appointed Bakrie instead. The battle between the two groups over state policies will continue to produce inconclusive results, creating further policy uncertainties in the economy.

The community sovereignty groups actually gain the most from the process and result of the 2004 elections – if they can capitalize on it. Opportunities have opened up for community sovereignty groups to develop the second level of institutionalization by capturing government institutions. People who are critical of the democratic deficit and lack of reforms are starting to discuss the possibility of developing alternative local and national political forces - including parties - for the newly-announced direct elections of heads of local governments, anticipating the 2009 national elections. Platforms are discussed, codes of conduct are drafted, popular political education is designed and parallel meetings have started to merge into a bigger movement. It is now the time for the community sovereignty group to consolidate their first level of institutionalization by establishing a strong network with universities, media and research institutions.

BIBLIOGRAPHY

Aditjondro, George Junus (2003) *Korban-korban pembangunan: tilikan terhadap beberapa kasus perusakan lingkungan di tanah air*, Yogyakarta: Pustaka Pelajar.

Amsden, Alice (1989) *Asia's Next Giant*, Oxford: Oxford University Press.

Antlöv, Hans (2003) "Village Government and Rural Development in Indonesia: The New Democratic Framework", *Bulletin of Indonesian Economic Studies*, 39(2): 193-214.

Anwar, Rosihan (2003) *Against the Current. A Biography of Soedarpo Sastrosatomo*, Jakarta: Pustaka Sinar Harapan.

Arief, Sritua (1982) "Teori ekonomi dan kolonialisme ekonomi", *Prisma*, 11(1): 26-34.

Basri, Faisal (1997) *Perekonomian Indonesia menjelang abad XXII: distorsi, peluang, dan kendala*, Jakarta: Erlangga.

Baswir, Revrisond (2002) "Kita ini jadi taruhan permainan global", *Bisnis Indonesia*, 4 September.

—— (2003) "Indosatgate", 10 February, *Republika*.

Bisnis Indonesia (2003) "CGI dan pemerintahan yang malas", 31 January.

Brooks, Karen Beth (1997) "The Politics of Technocracy in Indonesia", M.A. thesis, Cornell University.

Budiman, Arief (1989) *Sistem perekonomian pancasila dan ideologi ilmu sosial di Indonesia*, Jakarta: PT. Gramedia Pustaka Utama.

Budiman, Arief (1997) "A Socialist Pancasila Economic System", Ian Chalmers and Vedi R. Hadiz (eds), *The Politics of Economic Development in Indonesia: Contending Perspectives*, London: Routledge, pp. 123-127.

Business International Research Division (1978) "Indonesia to 1982: Economic and Political Outlook for Business Planners", Hong Kong: Business International Asia Pacific Ltd.

Chalmers, Ian, and Vedi R. Hadiz (eds) (1997) *The Politics of Economic Development in Indonesia: Contending Perspectives*, London: Routledge.

Dye, Richard W. (1965) "The Jakarta Faculty of Economics", Jakarta: Ford Foundation (mimeographed manuscript).

Forest Watch Indonesia-Global Forest Watch (2001) "Potret keadaan hutan Indonesia", Bogor: Forest Watch Indonesia and Washington DC: Global Forest Watch.

FPPM (2001) "Usulan naskah akademik rancangan undang-undang prakarsa/rancangan undang-undang inisiatif tentang perubahan undang-undang", Jakarta: FPPM.

Glassburner, Bruce (1971) "Mafia Explained", letter to the editor, *Far Eastern Economic Review*, 20 February.

Irwan, Alexander, Giovanni Arrighi, and Satoshi Ikeda (1993) "Kebangkitan ekonomi Asia timur: satu atau banyak keajaiban?" *Prisma* 22(4): 41-64.

Kuntjoro-Jakti, Dorodjatun (1981) "The Political Economy of Development: the Case of Indonesia under the New Order Government, 1966-1978", Ph.D thesis, University of California at Berkeley.

—— (2003) "Strategi pembangunan ekonomi dalam era reformasi dan globalisasi", Speech at ISEI 15th Congress, Malang, 13 July.

Kwik Kian Gie (2003) "Pemberantasan korupsi untuk meraih kemandirian, kemakmuran, kesejahteraan dan keadilan", unpublished manuscript.

Mallarangeng, Rizal (2002) *Mendobrak sentralisme ekonomi: Indonesia 1986-1992*, Jakarta: Kepustakaan Populer Gramedia.

Mubyarto (2002) *Ekonomi pancasila: landasan pikir & misi pendirian pusat studi ekonomi pancasila Universitas Gajah Mada*, Yogyakarta: BPFE.

Munggoro, Dani Wahyu and Andri Novi (2002) "Redistribusi kekayaan alam nusantara", *Jurnal Komuniti Forestri*, 5(6): 7-17.

National Secretariat AMAN (n.d.), "Menyatukan gerak langkah menuju kedaulatan masyarakat adat", Jakarta: AMAN.

Pangestu, Mari (1997) "Only Half-hearted Deregulation", in Ian Chalmers and Vedi R. Hadiz (eds) *The Politics of Economic Development in Indonesia: Contending Perspectives*, London: Routledge, pp. 158-162.

Pangestu, Mari (2003) "That '70s Show: Economist Mari Pangestu Sees Indonesia Returning to the Economic Debate of the Post-Sukarno Era", *Garuda Inflight Magazine*, February.

Panglaykim, Jusuf (1974) *Persoalan masa kini: perusahaan-perusahaan multinasional*, Jakarta: CSIS.

— (1983) (with the assistance of Mari Pangestu), *Japanese Direct Investment in ASEAN: The Indonesian Experience*, Singapore: Maruzen Asia.

Prasetiantono, Tony (2000) *Keluar dari krisis*, Jakarta: PT. Gramedia Pustaka Utama.

Rahardjo, Dawam (1979) "Model pembangunan Cina: ekspresi sosialis di dunia ketiga", *Prisma* 8(5): 16-32.

— (1980) "Pengalaman pembangunan dasawarsa 1970-an: menuju strategi alternatif?", *Prisma* 9(11): 41-55.

Ransom, David (1970) "The Berkeley Mafia and the Indonesian Massacre" *Ramparts* 9(4): 27-29, 40-49.

Robison, Richard (1986) *Indonesia. The Rise of Capital*, North Sydney: Allen and Unwin.

Rostow, W. W. (1971) *The Stages of Economic Growth. A Non-Communist Manifesto*, Cambridge: The Press Syndicate of the University of Cambridge, (2nd edition).

Salim, Emil (1978) "Lingkungan hidup dan pembangunan", *Prisma* 7(8): 3-10.

— (1983) "Tantangan masa depan, pembangunan dengan pemerataan", *Prisma* 7(1): 29-43.

— (1991) "Pembangunan berkelanjutan: strategi alternatif dalam pembangunan dekade sembilan puluhan", *Prisma*, 20(1): 3-13.

— (2002) "Tanpa tedeng aling-aling", in Mohammad Ikhsan, Chris Manning, Hadi Susastro (eds), *80 tahun Mohammad Sadli: ekonomi Indonesia di era politik baru*, Jakarta: PT Kompas Media Nusantara.

Sasono, Adi (1980) "Tesis ketergantungan dan kasus Indonesia", *Prisma* 9(12): 73-85.

— (1983) "Ketergantungan dan hutang dunia ketiga", *Prisma* 12(3) 50-63.

Seda, Frans (1997) "The Impact of the Tapos Summit", in Ian Chalmers and Vedi R. Hadiz (eds) *The Politics of Economic Development in Indonesia: Contending Perspectives*, London: Routledge, pp. 242-246.

Setiawan, Bonnie (2000) *Stop WTO. Dari Seattle sampai Bangkok*, Jakarta: INFID.

— (2001) *Menggugat globalisasi*, Jakarta: INFID and IGJ.

Sjahrir (1997) "The Struggle for Deregulation in Indonesia", in Ian Chalmers and Vedi R. Hadiz (eds), *The Politics of Economic Development in Indonesia: Contending Perspectives*, London: Routledge, pp. 153-157.

Swasono, Sri-Edi (2001) "Mohammad Hatta: Kita merdeka untuk menjadi tuan di negeri sendiri", in Sritua Arief (ed.), *Ekonomi kerakyatan*, Surakarta: Muhammadiyah University Press, pp. 7-22.

WALHI (2003) "Undermining Indonesia: Adverse Social and Environmental Impacts of Rio Tinto's Mining Operations in Indonesia", Jakarta: WALHI and Friends of the Earth Report.

Wallerstein, Immanuel (1997) *Lintas batas ilmu sosial*,Yogyakarta: LKiS.

Weedon, Chris (1987) *Feminist Practice and Poststructuralist Theory*, USA: Basil Blackwell.

Yoshihara, Kunio (1988) *The Rise of Ersatz Capitalism in South-East Asia*, Singapore: Oxford University Press.

-3-

IDEOLOGICAL BAGGAGE AND ORIENTATIONS OF THE SOCIAL SCIENCES IN INDONESIA

Ariel Heryanto

No production of knowledge develops independently or at random. It occurs in a social context, and it helps to create the social dynamics of that context, where various ideologies are pitted against one another. Social sciences have not only studied this, but they are also a part of the phenomena under study. Couched in these general and abstract terms, the observation is too banal to be disputed by social scientists. But, beyond the general statement, there is plenty of room for discussion. For example, how exactly does ideology take an active role in the development of social sciences in a given setting, and how do these processes relate to social relations in the broader sense?

It is rather difficult to determine the beginning of the growth of Indonesian social sciences, because this depends on how we set the boundaries. It is easier to say that Indonesian social sciences, as an academic activity in the field of social studies carried out by Indonesians in a systematic and formal manner within Indonesian society, experienced a sustained and very visible growth that began in the 1960s. Determining such a starting point is not to deny the role, contribution and achievements of those people active in this field in the years before this.

For several decades, there were studies about Indonesia by foreigners and written in foreign languages, circulated mainly outside the territory of the colony of the Dutch Indies or the Republic of Indonesia. Since the beginning of the twentieth century, some residents of the colony of the Dutch Indies, pre-independent Indonesia, and then Indonesia itself received a formal education in the social sciences, usually outside Indonesia, and used a non-Indonesian language for their work. Presented below is a study that concentrates on the social sciences as a part of social change in Indonesia, set in a global context. It is to be expected, therefore, that such a study would have to focus its attention on the rule of the New Order, with references to relevant earlier developments.

Viewed from an extreme vantage point, the social sciences in Indonesia have always openly and almost totally been in the service of whatever government was in power. The change in rulers over the same state, from the formation of the colonial Dutch Indies state to that of the Republic of Indonesia post-1998, has not brought with it any radical change in the character or orientation of the interests of the government, nor in the policies used to promote the development of the social sciences. These interests comprise a rather short list: some projects aimed at creating a stable government administration, the collection of data on "traditional" communities, the modernization of these traditional communities, industrialization and, since 1945, nation building.

There is, therefore, no need for a complex analysis to explain the ideology and partisanship of social sciences and social scientists during this time: they openly served the official interests of the government of the day, and there was no open discussion of the political implications of such a practice.[1] If there is anything to be examined, it is not whether or not there was any ideological interest or baggage in the social sciences in Indonesia or even what the character of the dominant ideology was. Attention needs rather to be focused on the issues of why, how and to what extent these things happened or experienced change. A study of ideology in social sciences would be more challenging in an environment where ideas about neutrality in method, objectivity of data, scientific deduction, the universality of values and meaning, or the autonomy of scientific institutions are respected, either as myth or in practices protected by law and morality. It is only in this environment that we can seek to demolish these myths and expose the ideological interests of different institutions and social science practices.

Examined more closely, and viewed from another extreme vantage point, a range of ideological variations and nuances in the various social science activities in this country can be identified. Although the social sciences may have been in the service of one or two dominant ideologies, the different activities did and do possess

---

[1] Of course, there were exceptions. The prevalence of a formal social science environment so marked by subservience to pragmatic research and in the service of the primary client ordering such research, namely the government, did provoke some independent-minded and critical intellectuals to revolt against this situation. They channeled their energies into activities as intellectual-cum-activists. But they too behaved in the same manner as their opponents: very open in their ideological partisanship.

heterogeneous features. Studies of the differences within a social sciences research institution, among a group of different schools of thought, within a specific period of time, and comparative studies of the works of specific individuals, can be very informative. However, such narrowly based studies need a lot of page space and are outside the scope of this chapter. There are too many variations and the differences between them perhaps do not carry sufficient weight in the main current of the "ecosystem" of the dominant ideology and power in society.

This chapter will try, in more general terms, to study ideological differences in the social sciences in Indonesia through the study of various phenomena: not too narrow or focused on any particular individual, or representing a micro study; nor too broad as to constitute a macro or comprehensive study. Specifically, the chapter will examine the strong bias of New Order "Developmentalism", and also look at some of its critics among social scientists. However, before proceeding, it may be worthwhile to note the approach and biases in this chapter, as well as some of the features of New Order society that have set the context for Indonesian social science.

ON IDEOLOGY IN THE SOCIAL SCIENCES

"Ideology" is used here to refer to a system of knowledge, outlooks, awareness, tastes and values, and general attitude, which coincides with the specific interests of a social group, whether or not those articulating this system are conscious of its partisanship. In the stricter classical Marxist understanding of the term, ideology is restricted to that which reflects the interests of one of two prominent social classes, often in fundamental contradiction to each other. In this chapter, the term is given the broader meaning since such an understanding is more appropriate to the material being analysis, as will be explained below.

Since the 1970s, and perhaps even earlier, it has been difficult to defend the commonly held idea that a specific ideology can monopolize or completely dominate a system of knowledge, which is a scientific discipline, reflecting a total subordination to the general interests of those wielding power, be they the capitalist class, a political party monopolizing state power, or even a dictator and his family and cronies. This outdated notion is not unrelated to the crisis of classical Marxism and some of the social movements inspired by Marxism. This chapter will not, therefore, reproduce the naïve and simplistic perspective that "discipline X" is dominated by "ideology Y", where X and Y are very well defined phenomena.

Another practice of scholars which will not be reproduced here is that of "creating" a "history" of social sciences in Indonesia that develops or proceeds in tandem with political changes at the state level, whether during the Dutch period, the Japanese period, the early independence period, Guided Democracy, the New Order, or *reformasi*. To my understanding, no such history exists, except in the imagination of some writers. Much of the activity in humanities and the social sciences of this society has been dispersed and fragmented.

The following study is based on a number of assumptions that should be presented from the beginning. The first assumption is that every scientific or scholarly activity can adopt or express more than one ideological value, and they are not necessarily mutually supportive. The scholar may or may not be aware of this. Each scholarly discipline is susceptible to the influence of many kinds of mutually incompatible ideologies. This means that within the infrastructures of scholarship in any society, we will find a conglomeration of different ideologies.

The second assumption is that during specific periods in the life of a society, one or two ideological streams might become more dominant. When a social order becomes more stable over an extended period of time, as can be seen in both industrial societies, and pre-industrial and pre-colonial communities in many regions of Asia, there exists one strong and resilient ideology, which is no longer considered to be "ideology" to the members of that social order. At present, many societies are experiencing great changes in many spheres, including ideology. In such a situation, several ideologies compete for dominance. This struggle for dominance may succeed if or when a number of changes or major conflicts are resolved either peacefully or through violence.

Since its formation as a nation at the beginning of the twentieth century, Indonesia has experienced a long history of upheavals and crises in many spheres, including economics, politics, morality, military affairs, and technology. This means that no one ideological form has had the opportunity to assume dominance at any point in time. If there was an extended period of time that was relatively stable, it was the period of the New Order government (1966-1998), although this stability was maintained, initiated and terminated through a series of violent actions and crises. It is therefore possible to identify one ideology that was relatively strong in social life during the New Order. It is also not surprising that we find a development of the scholarly world, including the social sciences, during this New Order period that was marked by stability and by specific ideological features. This ideology can be defined in a number of ways, the most popular being Developmentalism.[2]

There is another point to be noted before we consider the identity or features of an ideology embodied in the social sciences. In relative comparison to Western intellectual

---

[2] As the name of a dominant school of thought or group, the term Developmentalist is spelt with a capital "D", as is also the case with "Development". For a detailed study of the concept of Developmentalism in Indonesia, and its semantic history, see Heryanto (1995).

traditions, the social sciences in this country can not be said to have developed as a well-established institution of influence. The social sciences have developed more slowly and are weaker than in neighboring countries such as Malaysia, Singapore, Thailand or the Philippines (Booth 1999; Nordholt and Visser 1995).

One tell-tale sign of the slow and weak growth of the social sciences in Indonesia is the dearth of comprehensive and serious research into itself. There is still no journal equivalent to the now defunct *Prisma*. Between 1976 and 1990, *Prisma* published six special editions about universities and education. But, there was never an issue devoted to examining the history or growth of the social sciences.[3] The one edition that did examine some such aspects of the social sciences was Volume 12, No. 6, 1983 discussed below. We will also consider one of the few freelance articles discussing this subject, namely that by Benny Subianto (1989). The closure of *Prisma* and the fall of the New Order are perhaps not directly connected. But, the proximity of these two events, particularly at a time that saw a liberalization of the mass media, is evidence that repression by the authoritarian regime was not the sole reason for the weakness of the social sciences in Indonesia.[4]

The book *The Social Sciences in Indonesia*, edited by Koentjaraningrat (1975), is, to my knowledge, the only book published on this topic. It was a collection of articles by many different people, written in English, and was not widely available in Indonesian bookshops or libraries. By comparison, in the neighboring Philippines where English is more widely spoken, a three-volume work entitled *The Philippines Social Sciences in the Life of the Nation* was recently published. This was the product of a 1998 national congress of social scientists.[5] *The Southeast Asian Journal of Social Science* published a special edition (Alatas 2000) on alternative approaches in the social sciences in Southeast Asia. However, not a single article made reference to Indonesia.

This is the reason why the significance and impact of the social sciences in Indonesia on social life, whatever its ideological character, has not been particularly great. This is not to deny that there are other systems of knowledge and sciences. These other systems are usually not recognized as part of the secular, modern system of knowledge and science, a system greatly influenced by formal Western intellectual

---

[3] Perhaps this is not an accident but reflects the dominance of positivism in social science in Indonesia to date. This has wrought criticism from the proponents of post-modernism and cultural studies both of which schools of thought stress self-reflexivity.

[4] See Human Rights Watch (1998) for more information regarding the suppression of academic freedom. For the history of *Prisma*, see Sudibyo (2001).

[5] The writer is grateful to Mara Cynthia Rose Bautista for providing him with the first volume of this work entitled, *The History and Development of Social Science Disciplines in the Philippines* (Miralao 1999).

traditions. The various "indigenous" sciences are referred to as tradition, belief systems, myths or custom. But the truth of the matter is, the development of ideology in a society such as Indonesia does not and has not developed only, or even mainly, through the modern and formal social sciences.

Louis Althusser reminds us that any study of ideology in contemporary society must take educational institutions seriously (1971: 29-31).[6] This has a general validity, but especially in certain societies in Asia, Europe and North America where formal education is well established, where compulsory schooling for 12 years has proven to be fairly effective, and where access to higher education is not a luxury. In such societies, citizens spend a greater part of their time, at least five hours a day over a period of ten years, in school and dealing with the world of ideas, a world filled with ideology. In late twentieth century society, it would be correct to add the mass media, especially television and the internet, to the list of key instruments for the growth and spread of ideologies.

If this chapter were primarily concerned with the question of ideology in Indonesian society, the thing to study would not be the social sciences. Rather, this chapter is about the social sciences and ideology's place within the social sciences. It is not about ideology *per se* or its place in the wider environment. Given that the social sciences in Indonesia are still young and continue to develop slowly, the present chapter does not confine its scope to purely academic works published in peer review journals or ideas embodied in theses. Even *Prisma*, considered the most prestigious journal and the "pioneer of scholarly media" was not a peer reviewed journal. I shall, therefore, also consider articles and opinion columns written by social scientists for the rest of this chapter's discussion. As we know, many social scientists have gained their popularity and authority, not as a result of published academic research, but through appearances at seminars, often without research papers, published opinion pieces or media interviews.

THE NEW ORDER AND THE RISE OF THE INDONESIAN SOCIAL SCIENCES

In a number of liberal countries, the social sciences play a role of social criticism of the status quo. Perhaps more correctly, they are *thought* to have played or should play that role. In many colonial and post-colonial countries, such as Indonesia, the

---

[6] Althusser wrote: "one ideological State apparatus certainly has the dominant role, although hardly anyone lends an ear to its music; it is so silent! This is the School. It takes children from every class at infant-school age, and then for years, the years in which the child is the most 'vulnerable'; ...it drums into them...a certain amount of 'know how' wrapped in the ruling ideology...or simply the ruling ideology in its pure state" (1971: 29).

social sciences have been an instrument to assist state-sponsored projects and to provide the political justification for the rationale or the actual implementation of such projects. Although there are some significant similarities in conditions, spirit, and ideals among the various newly independent nations, their national projects are not uniform, since the conditions and colonial experiences have been sufficiently different (Crouch 1985). The same is true for the development of the social sciences in these countries. The following is an attempt to study, based on the research of many other scholars, the various ideologies that have been strong in the formation of the Indonesian nation-state and which have had an impact on the growth of the social sciences.

From the start, the formation of the Indonesian nation-state constituted a compromise that was necessary but never fully agreed upon by three different social groups or streams of thought. There are different terms used for these groups. In this study we will use the generally used terms of Marxist, Islamist and Developmentalist.[7] These three groups accepted the necessity for compromise because they faced a common enemy, first Dutch colonialists and later Japanese occupation. In addition they shared the common ideal of establishing an independent nation-state and developing an Indonesian identity.

But, there were also major differences between the three groups. The Marxists envisaged a modern, prosperous and independant Indonesian future through the implementation of a fundamental restructuring of the state's economic foundation as part of an international revolution. The Islamists wanted the least possible separation between the teachings of Islam and the task of developing a modern and civilized life, thereby distinguishing itself from the societies of former colonizers or their colonies. The Developmentalists, as described by Cribb (1999: 20), were the supporters of universal, liberal and secular modernity as originally espoused by the modern colonial intellectuals of the Ethical Policy period. During the New Order period, these three elements did not develop into pure or separate forms. Rather, what emerged were combinations of the three, each one exercising some influence over the others.

In reality, there exist in Indonesia many groups, aspirations and ideologies outside of these three. Each of these three groups also has their variant sub-groups. However, it is reasonable to assert that these three groups are the strongest in terms of identity

---

[7]   One recent study of the tensions between these groups is that presented by the Australian historian, Robert Cribb (1999: 20). Cribb uses the term "Muslim" to refer to the second group. In my view, this term is not appropriate for describing the differences between these three groups because there are Muslims in all three groups but not all Muslims propose Islam as the prime orientation or ideal for the nation-state.

orientation and influence. During the Soekarno period, the rivalry between these three groups intensified. Soekarno's efforts in the 1960s to reconcile the three and, at the same time to manage the whole process of government, were given the slogan, Nasakom (*Nasionalis-Agama-Komunis*, or Nationalist-Religious-Communist). It is important to remember that these efforts took place during the Cold War. Developments in Indonesia were not isolated from international tensions. As we all know, the Nasakom slogan and project collapsed in 1965 with the elimination of the communist element from the body of the Indonesian nation-state in one of the biggest mass slaughters in modern history. This event paved the way for the transfer of state power from the Guided Democracy government of Soekarno, who leaned in favor of Beijing, to the New Order under the leadership of Soeharto who was more intimate with Washington.

The New Order government was able to develop cooperation with some, though not all, of the dominant elements in society. But, these alliances were neither static nor between equals. As needs emerged, elements that were promoted or repressed changed. In the early decade of the New Order, the Developmentalists received prominence. Shortly after the New Order consolidated its militaristic power, the New Order suppressed the Islamists until the late 1980s. From that time onwards, a very visible political intimacy developed between the New Order government and sections of the Islamic community.

In the 1970s, the seeds of contradiction and criticism of the dominant ideology were planted. Oriented towards Developmentalism, the project of nation building and modernity was launched in the true spirit of Dutch Indies colonialism, albeit with a strong Javanese flavor. The priorities were economic growth, political stability, increasing formal education opportunities, extending the infrastructure, and cooperation with global international capitalist forces. Because these aspirations were in conflict with Islamist aspirations, the earliest radical criticisms came from this same group. As it turned out, the Islamists became the target of major suppression and destruction by the New Order government once the communists had been destroyed.

Although some changes did occur during the last few years of the New Order[8], the Development ideology was the only ruling ideology for more than thirty years. Because of its dominant position, criticisms of the government almost always implied criticism of the Developmentalist logic. Likewise, criticisms of development projects were also often viewed as an offence against the government. Various aspects of life,

---

[8] Towards the end of his rule, in the 1990s, Soeharto suddenly changed his political strategy. Facing divisions within the political elite and among his former allies, in particular among several retired military officers, the Soeharto government rehabilitated several Islamist leaders who had been in or

including the social sciences, were expected to bow down and serve the national ideology. Public and official activities took place within the framework of a single direction or theme: "In support of Development".

On the other hand, it must also be acknowledged that Developmentalism was the most important sponsor of the quantitative growth in education and research, including the social sciences. This is evidenced by the growth of literacy, the number of children in school, and the increase in research, publishing and library activities.[9] As one observer put it:

> One of the most significant achievements of the New Order regime has been the expansion of education to the point where universal primary education has been almost attained; this also means that illiteracy has almost disappeared among the younger population...For the first time in Indonesian history, then, the secondary educated outnumbered those with no education, Female gains were relatively even greater than male.
>
> Jones 1994: 161

According to another assessment, which was an analysis of the situation in 1941:

> There were only two tertiary education institutions for the social sciences and the humanities,...there were only two Indonesians at professorial level. Now [1983] there are no less than 74 faculties of social sciences and culture...23 faculties of education and teaching under the same system. There are also 32 faculties teaching social sciences and culture.
>
> Abdullah 1983: 24

DEVELOPMENTALISM IN THE NEW ORDER SOCIAL SCIENCES

The Developmentalism that grew in New Order society can be best described as technocratism with a Javanese militaristic accent. Technocratism is neither a specifically Indonesian nor New Order concept. As in many other societies,

---

were in jail, and invited them to share power with him in government (see Hefner 2000). The dominance of Developmentalism during the New Order also did not completely eradicate Marxist and Islamist elements. Islamist thinking developed throughout the 1980s, especially after the formation of the Indonesian Association of Muslim Intellectuals (*Ikatan Cendekiawan Muslim Indonesia* – ICMI) in 1990. To a lesser degree and in secret, the same applied to Marxist thinking after 1965. Marxist books were published (or republished) after the fall of Soeharto in 1998.

[9] For a quantitative picture of developments in formal education in Indonesia during this period, see Juoro (1990), Jones (1994: esp. pp 161-6) and Prijono (1999).

Developmentalism, as a version of technocratism, states that nature is provided as a blessing for humankind; there it exists for humankind to exploit and use for its benefit. The highest form of this exploitation requires the services of experts, science and technology, all working in a secular way, based on universal laws and principles, and neutral in and of themselves. As will be explained below, technocratism in the New Order was adopted selectively and inconsistently, contradicting its other ideological orientations.

In any case, faith in such a notion drove the state to make a strong commitment to the expansion of educational and scientific infrastructure. The state could only, however, accept the legitimacy of education and science that could be considered neutral, that is, which could be and was easily managed by those in power. This is why so many Asian regimes enthusiastically imported science and technology from the liberal West while simultaneously rejecting "liberalism". They hoped that science and technology would become enduring instruments, wielding great power yet remaining subservient, very much like a soldier, machine, worker or thug.

Although technocratism is derived from Western modernity, since the 1980s, post-colonial Singapore has been one of the most fanatical and successful proponents of technocratism. Being more technocratic than the West itself, Singapore has proudly proclaimed its success as a result of a specifically Asian spirit. In Indonesia, in its Javanese militaristic style, Developmentalism was expected to adopt and respect the social and political power structure inspired by Javanese militaristic and *keraton* (royal court) outlooks, giving the New Order the feature of the President as the peak and center of power.[10] In other words, here was a serious contradiction in terms of the New Order's Developmentalism. Universality, neutrality, and objectivity are retained as abstract rhetoric in relation to various managed activities in research and scholarship, but in practice all this was limited and subjugated by the duty to serve the interests and status of the ruling power as the sponsor of scholarship and research.

One good example of how the New Order's technocratism contradicted the feudalism that accompanied it is the program for the cultivation and development of Indonesian languages. Under the New Order, Indonesia was one of just a few countries in the world that carried out large-scale engineering of the national language. This was done on a much bigger scale than anything attempted with the social sciences. On 1 April 1975, this commitment was institutionalized with the establishment of the Center for the Advancement of Development of Language with branches in many provinces. Perhaps Indonesia is the only country in the world

---

[10] Although somewhat out-of-date, Benedict Anderson's (1972) analysis of Javanese power is still useful.

that celebrates a "language month". This is all done in the name of developing "good and correct" usage of the national language according to scholarly criteria and not based on the experience of social intercourse through concrete history, which invariably produces a hybrid, if not a totally mixed character.

In many ways, and perhaps this was not always realized by the experts, the Center for the Development and Advancement of Language assisted the Government's efforts in purifying society's vocabulary and memory of political elements. It was during this period, for example, that the word *buruh* (laborer) was replaced first with *pekerja* (worker) and later *karyawan* (one who strives).[11] Arrest and interrogation by the military became popularly referred to as *diamankan* (to make secure or safe). *Demonstrasi* became *unjuk rasa*, or "to show one's feelings". But, probably the most remarkable achievement was the creation of a reality that had never actually existed: the term *Orde Lama* (Old Order) was invented to enable the projection of the regime as its anti-thesis, the *Orde Baru*, the New Order.[12] A rather unexpected result of this project was that it revealed how the language of government officials themselves was not "good and correct" according to the formal criteria set out by the state! The Language Congress of October 1998 openly criticized the linguistic practices of many officials, for example, the mispronunciation of the suffix "kan" as "ken" in the style of Soeharto. The government chided their critics, arguing that such comments were inappropriate.[13]

This Javanese militaristic accented technocratism never developed into full-blooded technocratism. This is what differentiates Indonesia from Singapore and Malaysia. Technocracy was a useful and temporary instrument to kick-start a method and process that in fact was in contradiction with the basic principles of technocracy. Since 1998, this way of doing things became known as KKN (*korupsi, kolusi dan*

---

[11] TRANSLATOR'S NOTE: *buruh* is the oldest term for "worker" used in political discourse. Meaning "laborer" it has always emphasized the lowly or exploited position of the worker. *Pekerja* is simply the noun made from the verb, to work (bekerja) and has no political connotations one way or the other. *Karyawan* is a more recent invention coming out of the Indonesian army's political interventions in the 1960s and 1970s which created the Golongan Karya or Functional Groups organization. *Berkarya* was politically defined as carrying out one's proper function according to one's occupation (as in the Hindu caste system). A *karyawan* was therefore anybody who carried out the proper function of their occupation. It was meant to negate any sense of workers as an exploited class. Over time in day-to-day usage, *karyawan* came more to mean "white collar worker" or office employee.

[12] These terms were not invented by the Center for Language, but they escaped any criticisms from this Center which was immersed in efforts to Indonesian-ize various technological and technocratic terms. The important thing to note is that the term "Old Order" made its way into the consciousness of those who became critics of the New Order. The habit of referring to the "Old Order" has continued among social scientists, both Indonesian and foreign, even after 1998.

[13] For a more detailed discussion of the relationship between Developmentalism, the language development project and nation building, see Heryanto (1989; 1995).

nepotisme – corruption, collusion, nepotism). However, whatever its limitations, the technocratic commitment of the New Order aided the expansion of the social sciences in this country. For the first time in Indonesian history, several independent bodies were formed that were important for the growth of the social sciences in this country. These included the Institute for Social and Economic Research, Education and Information (*Lembaga Penelitian, Pendidikan dan Penerangan Ekonomi dan Sosial* – LP3ES) in 1971, the Indonesian Association for the Development of Social Sciences (*Himpunan Indonesia untuk Pengembangan Ilmu-Ilmu Sosial* – HIPIIS) in 1975, and the Social Sciences Foundation (*Yayasan Ilmu-ilmu Sosial* – YIIS) in 1976. LP3ES published the most prestigious and enduring social sciences journal in Indonesian history, *Prisma*. Up until that time, most social science research was instituted by government bodies or political parties whose objectives were not to make new discoveries or renew an interest in social knowledge, let alone to espouse any radical criticism of the existing social order.

As explained by Michael Morfit (1981: 68): "Until 1971, almost every ministry established a research and development section to carry out what was referred to as policy oriented research." The same thing was observed by Ruth McVey in the wider context of Southeast Asia: "The main task of scholarship is to fill in the blanks rather than to test the framework." (McVey 1995: 3). This was the reason why "many of the best Southeast Asian scholarly minds have found a purely academic life stultifying and/or repressive, and have turned their energies instead to politics, administration, or other non-research activities" (McVey 1995: 3). The exact nature of the growth of the social sciences in the early decades of the New Order, and the relationship with various social demands and institutions are laid out by Taufik Abdullah (1983).

Social sciences activities were sponsored by New Order government agencies in larger numbers than in any previous period. While there were, no doubt, exceptions from time to time, these activities were carried out as formalities, as part of development projects implemented with government funds or foreign aid. These were not activities aimed at finding "truth and knowledge" to the greatest depth possible. For example, an activity would take the form of a feasibility study prior to the implementation of a development project, or an evaluation after the project had been completed. Almost all were mechanical, focused on the collection of quantitative data, and involved no detailed or critical examination of the validity of the data.

Those collecting the data never received adequate training nor did they have an understanding of the framework being used by the research supervisor, who was usually too busy with other projects in different locations and therefore did not have the time to communicate with the members of his various research teams. As these were almost required purely as a formality, the results of the research would not even receive any attention from the departments that had commissioned the research. They almost never influenced policy decisions, which were based on pragmatic, short-term political considerations.[14] Most of the results of such research were never published and so have never been subject to the critical examination of other social scientists.[15]

Morfit also notes the existence of several semi-autonomous institutions such as the National Social and Economic Institute (*Lembaga Ekonomi dan Kemasyarakatan Nasional* – LEKNAS) and the National Center for Language Development (*Pusat Pembinaan dan Pengembangan Bahasa* – PPPB), both of which come under the umbrella of the Indonesian Institute of Sciences (*Lembaga Ilmu Pengetahuan Indonesia* – LIPI).[16] Again, according to Morfit (1981: 69), there were only a few private institutions worth noting, and only two connected to universities. Apart from LP3ES, there was the Social Science Research Institute at Satya Wacana Christian University (*Lembaga Penelitian Ilmu Sosial* – LPIS), the Research Center at Atma Jaya University, the Development Studies Institute (*Lembaga Studi Pembangunan* – LSP) and the Center for Strategic and International Studies (CSIS). Except for LPIS in Salatiga, they were all based in Jakarta. Although classified as "private", the research conditions and activities were not markedly different in character from the national scene as described by Morfit and McVey. These observations were made in papers presented by LPIS researchers for the first HIPIIS congress held in Bukit Tinggi, 1-6 September 1975 (LPIS 1975).

Of course, not all social sciences produced in Indonesia is as bad as that indicated by the last couple of paragraphs. One of the most important figures to have successfully expressed the spirit of technocracy and modernization in a popular language was the anthropologist Koentjaraningrat. His work, *Kebudayaan, Mentalitet dan Pembangunan* [Culture, Mentality and Development] (1974), comprising a series of articles previously published in the mass media, was reprinted many times because of its popularity. It became an important reference resource for many people. Koentjaraningrat, inspired by the thinking of the American anthropologist, Clyde Kluckhohn, was an Indonesian social scientist who worked tirelessly and with great commitment to explain what was "wrong" with the mentality and spirit of traditional society as it transformed into a modern society. He tried to help society modernize through a change in attitudes and cultural values.

---

[14] TRANSLATOR'S NOTE: This is also the reason why there has been no strong "ideology" behind the practice and structure of the social sciences in Indonesia in the way that such things developed in other former colonies.

[15] This rough outline is based upon the work done by Morfit (1981) and Abdullah (1983).

[16] A more complete list of social science research institutions during this time is provided by Abdullah (1983), but for our modest needs, Morfit's list suffices.

Given, on the one hand, the dearth of other frameworks relevant to the needs of technocratic modernization under the New Order militaristic leadership, and the overflowing need for project based "research" on the other, Koentjaraningrat's model was reproduced, albeit with methodological distortions depending on the practical needs of the different groups making reference to his model. In other words, a specific ideology about the world, truth and social knowledge had gained momentum from the material and immaterial conditions of the time to develop and become dominant in the socio-political context of the New Order. As noted earlier, this had not been a process of one or two elite groups conspiring to fool the people with an instrument called "ideology" in order to extend, defend and justify the interests of the respective groups.

The primary objects of study within this dominant system of thought were non-material things such as mentality, attitudes to life, and cultural values. Yet hundreds, perhaps thousands, of officially sponsored research projects at this time obliged the use of the most "practical and easiest" methodology, namely quantitative surveys.[17] If, in an intangible area such as culture, there was no hesitation in gathering quantitative and empirical data, there was even less hesitation in other fields such as sociology, geography, political science, or history. It is not surprising if those who took the task of critically examining these studies have been disappointed with what they found. It is not just that cultural phenomenon cannot always be measured in quantitative terms, but that basic principles of quantitative research were not properly adhered to by even the most prestigious research teams (see the detailed criticisms provided by Kleden 1987).

Throughout this century, almost every analysis of the social sciences in Indonesia has comprised complaints and statements of grave concern, despite the dramatic increase in the number of graduates, institutions, and research projects. Whilst there are examples of outstanding achievements by individual scholars, there has been no or little development of a support system that facilitates the training of graduates, sustainable research and publications aimed at promoting intellectual works of scholarship. Similarly, many of the outstanding works of individual scholars have not received the public recognition or study they deserve.

These weaknesses are not all related to insufficient funds. Financial assistance from international aid agencies has been more than adequate, at least for the short and medium term needs of individual researchers and research institutions. For

---

[17] This was a very different framework than that of another anthropologist, Clifford Geertz, who had become the inspiration to scholars around the world at that time. This was due the attraction of his use of interpretative anthropology which based itself on ethnography, narration, and subjective and semiotic interpretation (Geertz 1973; 1983).

example, "The YIIS often has more funds than it can use. The difficulty is finding people who can use the funds available in order to implement social sciences research in a systematic way, and be accountable for the results." This was an area of concern, so much so that the founder and leader of the YIIS acknowledged: "We are often being pressured by the international foundations to spend the money that has been allocated to Indonesia." (Soemardjan 1983: 78). Twenty years later, I have personally observed the same phenomenon: the flood of foreign funds for social science research and the difficulty in finding interested and qualified researchers. (Heryanto 1999; 2002).

CRITICISMS OF DEVELOPMENTALISM

Reconciling the stark differences between a technocratism that relentlessly sought rationality, use-value and work efficiency on the one hand, and the parochial and patrimonial New Order social order on the other, was not the only difficulty the government faced. Industrialization under the New Order, partly reflecting its own success, produced in turn other sharp criticisms from several different quarters. The following is a discussion of the three critical perspectives that developed in the social sciences, which can be loosely referred to as the perspectives of the liberals, the populists and the structuralists. As noted earlier, the Islamist, Marxist and Developmentalist elements contributed to the ideological competition, but not in a single, separate and pure form. These various "historical legacies" resulted in the differing natures of these critical groups.

Liberalism, the forerunner of neo-liberalism,[18] was one of the most severe threats to Developmentalism because it had the backing of powerful international forces during and, especially after the Cold War. But liberalism, a force felt so strongly in real life scenarios, was not reflected to its true extent in its rhetorical and public profile (see Irwan, this volume). The public had grown suspicious of liberalism. It was populism that was lauded in public perception and rhetoric. But, facing the powerful tide of global capitalism, populism was often considered a "paper tiger". In the 1980s, Developmentalism, as with liberalism, was the object of serious criticism from the structuralists. For a while, structuralism was a refreshing change for social

---

[18] There are of course important differences between liberalism and neo-liberalism, but these differences are not so significant for the purposes of this chapter. In the context of a discussion of the social sciences in Indonesia, liberalism is a broad category (from the social sciences to the humanities and arts) which emphasizes universal respect for the rights and dignity of the individual – and not a group or the state – as well as a respect for the variety among them, including for minorities. Neo-liberalism is usually considered a more recent generation of liberalism with a narrower orientation to political and economic views, policies and practices.

sciences intellectuals, and it was not long before structuralism transformed into a social movement.

(Neo)Liberalism

Liberalism in colonial and Indonesian social sciences stems from the influence of European liberalism. It has a long history but its influence has always been limited. It is easier to find books and bibliographies that romanticize neo-liberalism in the education system and public discourse than it is to find major works by Indonesians who set out consciously to espouse the spirit of liberalism. If we confine ourselves to looking at the books on university course reading lists or in libraries, we could be led to believe that liberalism, along with neo-classical thought, is indeed influential in fields such as political science and economics. But, this does not reflect the true impact of these ideas on the dynamics of Indonesian social sciences. At this point, it would be appropriate to remind the reader that there was a lack of domestic financial resources available to many social sciences institutions. The large amounts of foreign aid, especially from the United States, came in the form of scholarships, teaching staff, and textbooks that were based on liberal ideas. The foreign resources were accepted and utilized, but not understood in any depth.

Both "capitalism" and "liberalism" are terms that have been generally stigmatized in Indonesian history (Heryanto 1999a). As a result, the entry and growth of liberalism in Indonesia had to put on a "disguise", using other faces and terms. The technocratic aspects of the New Order provided fertile ground, not for the development of liberal thought, but for a normative discussion that romanticized some elements of liberalism, such as the dignity of free, autonomous and rational human beings. This approach would emerge, for example, in attacks on "traditional" society and culture and in the launching of "modernization".

One group usually considered as having played a major role in fostering the growth of one version of liberalism in Indonesia during the New Order is referred to as the Berkeley Mafia. This was a group of graduates from the University of California, Berkeley, who were appointed by the New Order government as "Development Experts" in the cabinet at the end of the 1960s and early 1970s. This version of liberalism was usually very technical and instrumental without the deeper or more comprehensive liberal philosophy or ideology. In any case, their views were quite influential in many, although not all, areas of state policy. They were also influential, to a lesser degree, in the social sciences, especially in nurturing a neo-classical perspective in economics. The private research institution called the Center for Strategic and International Studies (CSIS), founded in 1971 and close, for a time, to the New Order government, also contributed greatly to the spread of the liberal perspective in various social sciences discourses. Overall, however, liberal influences were more strongly reflected in selected government sponsored Development practices than in the formal academic institutions, even though these influences came up against other policies and practices sponsored by the same state.[19]

The chapters by Irwan, as well as Dhakidae and Hadiz in this volume, describe the limited authority and influence of the Berkeley Mafia. Militarism, protectionism, and then corruption and collusion were in partnership with greater forces in the implementation of Development in Indonesia. From time to time, whenever it was felt necessary, government spokespersons would name liberalism as one of the most dangerous threats to the Indonesian nation-state alongside "communism" and "Islamic fundamentalism". These warnings were prolific, for example, when the ideas derived from liberation theology gained currency among non-governmental organizations (NGOs) in Indonesia in the 1980s.

Sympathy for selected elements of liberalism among the Indonesian public grew in the first half of the 1980s encouraged by various parties, among them some government departments. This happened in the aftermath of the economic crisis and the fall in the world price of oil. The key words or "war cry" used to pump up liberalism at that time was *wiraswasta* and *kewiraswastaan*, meaning entrepreneur and entrepreneurship respectively. A major ideological change based on sympathy for liberalism occurred in the late 1980s and early 1990s. Just as a cross-ethnic capitalist class was developing, there was a campaign backing an ideology, which not only justified but also glorified the ideology and dominance of the new capitalist class (Heryanto 1999a). An interesting phenomenon during this period was that the campaign espousing capitalism and liberalism was not just carried out by social scientists, who traditionally wielded little authority, but rather by businessmen and government officials. For the first time in Indonesian history, businessmen appeared at seminars and conferences to present academic style papers. Their companies were often asked to sponsor academic activities and programs in the universities. Some major business figures appeared as new celebrities on the front covers of prestigious magazines, on talk shows, and even appeared on stage to read poetry (ibid.).

The term "globalization" has many widely debated connotations. However, one thing cannot be denied, namely that there has been an expansion of the network of industrial capitalism. Liberalism, in economics, morality and in intellectual affairs, has seeped into Indonesia as part of this process on a scale and depth not before

---

[19] See, for example, Sen and Hill's analysis of the contradictions in the New Order's policies managing the mass media industry (2000).

experienced in Indonesian history. The term "liberal" was consciously chosen by a group of progressive Muslim activists in Jakarta to describe their group, the Liberal Islamic Network, which does not at all mean that they support American style neo-liberal economics. One of the early leaders of this group published his dissertation that openly proclaimed its neo-liberal spirit (Mallarangeng 2002). Sonny Keraf's article (1995) is another example of a perspective that warmly welcomed the liberal outlook during this time.

Despite all of these advances, at the beginning of the 21st century, neither liberalism nor capitalism was considered worthy of more serious thought or deeper understanding by the Indonesian public. Liberalism, like capitalism, is still held in suspicion, even ridiculed. For example, as is described by Wibowo and Wahono (2003)[20], liberalism's influence is more widespread and greater in Indonesia's economic practices than it is a source of inspiration or analytical framework for the social sciences.[21]

Populism

The terms capitalism and liberalism have not been accepted as worthy in Indonesia because of the strength of the history of populist romanticism, as is the case in many agrarian, colonial and post-colonial societies. One of the more resilient manifestations of this populist romanticism is the official history of the struggle for Indonesian independence, and the many sub-plots of that history, which is very much alive in the public fantasy and which has been presented to the public visually through posters, monuments, paintings, banners and decorated village gateways that commemorate independence every 17 August.

Given that New Order Developmentalism defends the interests of the capitalist class, national and city state officials and international capital, it is not surprising that Developmentalism has been seriously challenged by supporters of populism. This is probably because populists gained extra credibility and appeal from the injustices of the New Order. Yet ideologically, populism has motivated them to present sincere and continuing criticisms of New Order Development, which has been based on technocracy, half-hearted liberalism and topped with a Javanese *priyayi*[22] militarism.

---

[20] See reviews of this book by Pramoedya (2003) and Magnis-Suseno (2003).
[21] In an essay regretting the weakness of liberalization in Indonesia, Faisal Basri has written: "I have deliberately put the word liberalization in quotation marks because this term is not popular and by some people is considered *najis* [filthy]: a western idea, giving fanatical support to the Washington consensus, an agent of the IMF, a follower of neoliberalism, a capitalist" (Basri 2003).
[22] TRANSLATOR'S NOTE: *Priyayi* – refers to the layer of state officials and bureaucrats which today still embody the conservative and despotic social, political and cultural outlook of the minor aristocracy of Java which became subservient to the colonial state in the 19th century and which provided much of the colonial state apparatus.

New Order Developmentalism came under attack from two elements that helped the awakening of the Indonesian nation, namely the Marxists and the Islamists, whenever the possibility existed. As mentioned, Marxism, both as a school of thought and a political movement, was physically eliminated as well as formally outlawed at the beginning of 1966. The Islamist forces were subsequently subjugated in the 1970s. This meant that the populist criticisms that did arise during the New Order developed within a system of ideas and vocabulary under the domination of the New Order.

Limited space and my knowledge on the matter do not allow me to give more than one example of sustained populist criticism, namely the school of thought, which calls itself the Pancasila Economic System (*Sistem Ekonomi Pancasila* – SEP). The original source of ideas behind the SEP was the popular socialism of the colonial era, which stressed the importance of cooperatives as a basis of the state economy. This particular form of socialism was popularized by people such as Muhammad Hatta, an intellectual during the colonial period who later became a statesman.

Economist Mubyarto, from Gadjah Mada University, one of the proponents of SEP, defined its five key features. First, "Cooperatives are the basic pillar of the economy"; second, "The wheels of the economy are driven by economic, social and moral incentives"; third, "The strong desire for the whole of society to move in the direction of social egalitarianism"; fourth, "The main priority of economic policy is...to create a resilient national economy"; and fifth, "A clear and firm balance between national planning and decentralization" (*Kompas* 1981; Mubyarto 1987). The merits of the intellectual substance of the SEP aside, it is clear from the wide public response that these ideas developed as a populist criticism of New Order Development. It is not surprising that SEP received broad sympathy from those critical of New Order Development. But, for its own safety, SEP was carefully worded so as to make it acceptable in the political climate of the time. This included using the term "Pancasila", which was at that time also in the process of being sacralized by the New Order as part of the process of justifying the repression of threats from the Islamists.

Cooperatives, the first feature of SEP, represented a populist nostalgia before capitalistic New Order Developmentalism emerged and started to cause problems for "the little people" or common man. By using the relatively old or aged term "cooperatives", which still retained revolutionary populist connotations, these critics were implying that New Order Development had strayed from the consensus and ideals of Indonesian independence. The second feature of SEP, that incentives should be social and moral and not just economic, was a moral criticism of the phenomenon of material greed that developed during the oil boom, and which accompanied the creation and rise of the nouveau riche. Egalitarianism, the third feature of SEP, was a criticism of the gap between rich and poor that had started to cause concern in the 1980s. The fourth, nationalism, and fifth, decentralization, were features that rejected the liberal spirit represented at the time by the technocrats.

SEP can be viewed as an important statement if taken as an expression of populist sentiment and moral criticism. SEP always had, however, serious flaws as an academic concept. From the start, it attracted sharp criticism from those who had been affected by the flourishing of neo-Marxist style structuralist political economy in the 1970s. This brings us to another group of critics of New Order Developmentalism, the structuralists. It must be noted here, however, that despite being subject to very fundamental criticisms since its beginnings, SEP continues to advance.

Structuralist Political-Economy

In the New Order structuralist political economy did not emerge simply as a critical reaction to SEP. Structuralism also launched a general critique of New Order Developmentalism, including a critique of the dominant paradigm within the social sciences. Structuralism thereby opened up a broad new perspective that was very important for the dynamics of the social sciences at that time. This section will not provide an overall analysis of structuralism and its variants that proliferated during the New Order. It will rather concentrate on one version, which became the most popular among the educated public, with a number of reductions and simplifications.[23]

The primary target of structuralist critiques was the so-called, not by its own proponents, "culturalism" or the "cultural approach" to the social sciences and humanities.[24] The criticism of SEP and the social sciences system in general and Development practices in Indonesia was based on the premise that all these had been led astray by culturalism. Because of the importance of these criticisms and the debate that they provoked, this issue is the main object of study for the rest of this chapter. It is regrettable that there was a gross lack of a support system for the social sciences. Consequently, further debate on the impact of culturalism did not take place. Discussed below are (a) a brief sketch of this debate; (b) its contribution to Indonesian social sciences; and (c) its core weaknesses.

---

[23] Several stricter and more thorough uses – to the extent that these characteristics made them less popular in public debate – of the structuralist framework can be studied in a number of seminar papers, thesis and articles in journals such as *Prisma*. Besides the two editors of this book, another Indonesian scholar who was a persistent proponent of the structuralist approach for many different kinds of analysis was the late Farchan Bulkin. The writer thanks the editors, and in particular Vedi Hadiz, for reminding him of the importance of Bulkin's works (1984a; 1984b).

[24] Because these names were attached to this school of thought by critics, references to them should be in quotation marks. To simplify the writing style, the use of quotation marks will not be continued but readers need to bear this note in mind.

The primary criticisms of SEP were that it was nothing more than an idealist and moralist wish list, and therefore not rooted in reality; ahistorical – not rooted in the material reality of economic and political history of Indonesia; and theoretically flawed – not based on theoretical fundamentals from the classical social sciences. One popular proponent of post-1965 structuralism, Arief Budiman, launched a criticism of SEP as part of a larger criticism of the dominant social sciences of the time (Budiman 1981; 1982a; 1989). Although Budiman did provoke some critical responses, none of these are worth mentioning.[25] "Structuralist" criticism became the main reference for those who wished to challenge the social order and the social sciences under the Soeharto regime, which had given birth to this order.

Although he was not alone, and perhaps not the first to put forward structuralism in Indonesia,[26] it can be said that Budiman was one academic who rigorously popularized the concept of structuralism among social scientists. He did this through a series of polemic lectures and opinion columns. Some of his early Indonesian language articles include Budiman 1976; 1977; 1981; 1983; and 1987a and b. Several other writings, including Budiman 1982a and 1982b were compiled into a published book (Budiman 1989). Budiman's views that are relevant to this chapter were expressed in an interview in *Prisma* (Budiman 1983), and will be considered below in some detail.

What Budiman gave to the readers of *Prisma* – the educated Indonesian public not limited to social scientists – was a re-introduction to the basics of classical Marxist thought simple enough to be digested by many people. He had obtained the inspiration for his ideas from his experiences in the United States, where he studied, at a time when structuralism was in vogue. In addition to this, he cited the example of how structuralism was used in dependency theory from as early as the 1960s and 1970s.[27] The primary message of his contributions was historical materialism: that material conditions – the base – determined all other aspects of social life – the superstructure. Unfortunately, there was one important aspect of Marxism, dialectical historicism, which he paid insufficient attention to.

I stated earlier that Budiman's contribution was a re-introduction of Marxism. Classical Marxism and socialism had actually been part of the public discourse in Indonesia throughout the twentieth century until 1965. However, much of this has been forgotten, or its history erased. As a result, it has proven difficult, especially

---

[25] LPIS (1981) published a monograph comprising 28 articles from two major daily newspapers between 1979 and 1981 that were part of a polemic about the Pancasila Economic System.

[26] Sritua Arief and Adi Sasono's (1981) work is considered a pioneering work after 1965 and was also relatively popular.

[27] The results of Arief's study were presented in a doctoral thesis published as Budiman (1987a).

for younger intellectuals who were born and bred during the times of the New Order regime, to revisit their impact on intellectual thought. The irony is that Budiman had, as a student activist, led politically charged actions against leftists before they were wiped out in the mid-1960s. Perhaps Budiman's contribution and role before 1965-6 provided him with the privilege of being able to speak about Marxism and socialism. This privilege was not available to those on the left who survived the mass culling in the mid-1960s because they were stigmatized as communists.[28]

Putting aside the past of the proponent of these ideas, the ideas presented by Budiman to the Indonesian public at the end of the 1970s and early 1980s were a breath of fresh air. He had a huge influence on those who did not have the chance to study overseas and become familiar with ideas forbidden in Indonesia. Over a period of a few short years, Budiman's radical criticisms of the social sciences cast a spell on the students and younger generation who felt dissatisfied with the dominant paradigm that was inspired by the modernization theory. Budiman's popularity as an activist in 1966, especially among students outside Jakarta, added to the credibility of his criticism of the culturalist approach. In a formulation more scholarly than Budiman's more popular presentations, Benny Subianto explained the enemy of structuralism, "the cultural approach":

> ...as an approach in the social sciences that makes culture an independent variable and non-cultural aspects as dependent variables. The cultural approach had the pretension to explain social reality based upon cultural factors through both induction as well as deduction. And in this way to present an empirico-analytical character.
>
> Subianto 1989: 59

In a broader social sciences context, this culturalism is also known by other names such as idealism, humanism, orientalism, or functionalism. The senior scholar who came under the most sustained attack from Budiman was Koentjaraningrat and his book mentioned above, *Kebudayaan, Mentalitet dan Pembangunan* [Culture, Mentality and Development], 1974.

HISTORICAL DIALECTICS, SUBJECT AND STRUCTURE

The above-mentioned article by Subianto is evidence that there was a time when structuralism was "in vogue".[29] Subianto's article is one of the few Indonesian language articles that presents a comprehensive "history" of the social sciences from colonial

---

[28] As of 2003, the Indonesian parliament still rejects Marxism and communism as a legitimate part of political life and open intellectual discussion in this country.

times to the 1990s. The main aim of Subianto's article was to present a lengthy criticism of the cultural approach, which presumably dominated almost the whole history of the social sciences, along with several less fundamental variants, in particular from the colonial and New Order periods.[30] The history presented by Subianto concluded on a happy note, namely the arrival of "the structuralist approach as a criticism of the established groups in the social sciences in Indonesia" (Subianto 1989: 74). This was possible because, according to him, of the availability of study opportunities in the United States for Indonesian scholars in much the same way that "the cultural approach" gained dominance (ibid.).

But, it was not an entirely happy ending. According to Subianto: "The structuralist approach that has developed over the last five years still mainly exists at the margins of the social science community" (1989: 74). This was especially true of the works that were not presented in the same popular manner used by Budiman (see note 23). In practice, structuralism never achieved a position as the most dominant and widespread approach in social sciences research. But, as an ideology, it can be said that structuralism became one of, if not the only, 'politically correct' framework of thought of authority, particularly among independent researchers and public intellectuals, student activists, and non-government organizations, which were flourishing in many regions. Their numbers were not great compared to the number of university graduates, but their status as an "elite", some would even say their celebrity, among the intellectual-activists meant that structuralism became the main rhetoric of criticism and ultimately a new orthodoxy.

As mentioned above, there was no debate in the sense of a genuine dialogue. It appears that the older generation of social scientists, those pursuing culturalism and technocratism had neither the interest nor adequate knowledge in the literature referred to by their critics. On the other hand, the critics were far more familiar with both the material that they were attacking and the new perspective they subscribed to. That is the reason why a balanced or mutually enlightening debate did not ensue. Lacking counter-criticism, or self-criticism from within, the structuralists found it difficult to advance and make more significant contributions to scholarship in the country. In fact in some cases, the reverse happened. As is the case with so many great -isms, after rising to the surface as a radical challenger to the dominant wisdom of the day, becoming popular, if not dominant, Indonesia's

---

[29] The strength of structuralism, at least as a term or slogan, can best be grasped by looking at a number of articles by intellectuals in the mass media at that time. Several examples are Kaiseipo (1982), Budiawan (1987), Massardi (1988), Azhar (1991), Pratikto (1993) and Sutrisno (1994).

[30] In a footnote, Subianto provides a list of examples of "the social scientists who studied in the United States at the end of the 1950s and 1960s...most of the above theses stressed cultural aspects and rarely or indeed never touched on political economy" (Subianto 1989; 69, fn. 35).

structuralism subsequently took on a dogmatic and inflexible character. It experienced the fate of the so-called "cultural approach", an ideology that it had set out to criticize.[31]

An ironic example of the degeneration of the critical and radical character of the structuralist perspective is the development among its supporters of the idea that capitalism and socialism were static, "ready to use" options of development strategy that could be adopted by free and rational human beings already enlightened by structuralism. In other words, the belief was that anyone who swung either towards capitalism or socialism was, in effect, favoring an ideology quite outside the realm of structure and history. The two reified scientific or scholarly approaches, structuralism and the cultural approach, were depicted as two autonomous tools that could be chosen by whomever, whenever. In other words, idealism and humanism, the spirit of the cultural approach that had since become anemic and mechanistic, had staged a comeback under the guise of structuralism or socialism, often involving the very same people who had been the harshest critics of the cultural approach. It was also during this time that an attempt was made to reduce the whole spectrum of social sciences to a simple dichotomy: culturalism versus structuralism.

The following is quoted from a compilation of Budiman's works written in the 1980s, a time when the pro-structuralist debate was waning and the quality of debate declining drastically:

> To simplify things, we can say that there are two approaches that dominate in the social sciences. One is the pole that emphasizes aspects of individual psychology and the system of social values that surround them. We can call this pole as the pole of the cultural/psychological approach. The second pole emphasizes the human being's material environment, that is the social organization and the system of material benefits that it provides....This pole is known as that using the structural approach.
>
> Budiman 1989: 44

This culture-versus-structure dichotomy was reproduced on a massive scale in discussion and consciousness among social scientists, especially among the younger generation. Budiman himself, acknowledged, after presenting this dichotomy: "The division of the social sciences into these two poles is an over-simplification. There are many approaches located somewhere in between these poles" (ibid.).

---

[31] This is the conclusion of Vedi Hadiz (1989) about the political character of the "cultural approach" in Ben Anderson's contributions to Indonesian studies, at least among foreign scholars. However, I am talking here of a more general phenomenon.

Budiman qualifies his statement by saying that he was referring specifically to Indonesian social sciences. However, this important qualification was often passed over or ignored by the public in their excitement to embrace the new ideas being presented. Yet, even this narrowing of focus is not in accord with reality. This is because not only are there many other approaches existent in the social sciences, but these other approaches reside outside, behind, above or on the other end of the spectrum of the dichotomy; they are not located only "between these poles" as Budiman describes. Perhaps it would be more accurate to say that Budiman's statement is more relevant to post-1965 social sciences, particularly in relation to the social scientists who had just returned from study in the United States. The social sciences discussions in Indonesia at this time appeared in many respects to be an extension of lecture-hall discussions in the United States. The topics, figures and schools of thought that they discussed came straight from their reading lists for the courses they were taking in the United States. This is why Indonesian scholars who studied elsewhere other than the United States, scholars such as Y.B. Mangunwijaya, Ignas Kleden and Vedi Hadiz, were not predisposed to popularizing the cultural/structural dichotomy in the 1980s.

Why did structuralism not advance further in Indonesia? To answer this, we must consider the "two-pronged approach" model put forward by the structuralists. However, we need to treat this dialectically, and not as a simple dichotomy. First, we can explain it in a materialist or structuralist manner. Second, we can add to this explanation by looking at the internal weaknesses of the theory as presented in publications in Indonesia in the 1980s.

From a materialist or structuralist point of view, the failure of post-1965 structuralism was due to the fact that this -ism, which appeared radical at first, was, in reality, merely a pretty idea in the minds of a small intellectual elite. It went from essay to essay, from seminar to seminar, and from interview to interview without becoming materially embodied, or manifested in praxis, contrary to what its proponents argued should have happened. In reality, structuralism was raised up as a new superior system of cultural values pushing aside modernity or Development, or Pancasila, but framed once again in terms of idealism, humanism and romanticism. The structuralism that was trumpeted during the New Order period never practiced what it preached.

The irony is that the Pancasila Economic System, as proposed by Mubyarto and his colleagues and which had been criticized as being rooted in the cultural approach, has since continued to develop further in terms of institutional structures. Stepping over the corpse of the structuralist controversy, having never really responded to the rather effective criticisms from the structuralists, Mubyarto founded the Centre for the Study of Pancasila Economy at Gadjah Mada University in September 2002.

At the time of writing, investigations were under way regarding the possibility of setting up five more such centers at tertiary institutions in Semarang and Yogyakarta. The key ideas of Pancasila Economy are still being introduced into high school curricula in 2004 (Wahyuni 2003). And it is ironic that all this is happening at the same time that neo-liberalism has grown stronger in Indonesia, even if it has not yet become the intellectual basis for social science.

Second, theoretically and intellectually, the failure of structuralism in Indonesia after 1965 can be traced back to its failure to explain its own emergence. Its followers did not follow through the logic, or rather the philosophy of structuralism. Therefore, they were unable to explain their own place as products of the structures they were analyzing. In other words, they lost the ability to carry out self-criticism and self-reflection, which actually prepared the ground for the emergence of post-structuralism. To give a clearer picture of what was missing from the Marxist version of structuralism presented by Budiman in the 1980s, I quote below the rather lengthy analytical explanation from Perry Anderson, a prominent figure in western European neo-Marxism:

> To define Marxism as a critical theory simply in terms of a goal of a classless society, or the procedures of a consciously materialist philosophy, is obviously insufficient. The real propriety of the term for Marxism lies elsewhere. What is distinctive about the kind of criticism that historical materialism in principle represents, is that it includes, indivisibly and unremittingly, self-criticism. That is, Marxism is a theory of history that lays claim, at the same stroke, to provide a history of the theory. A Marxism of Marxism was inscribed in its character from the outset, when Marx and Engels defined the conditions of their own intellectual discoveries....
>
> Anderson 1983: 11

How do we explain the rise of a proponent of a Marxist version of structuralism, such as Budiman's, at the end of the 1970s and early 1980s in Indonesia? The spontaneous and typical answer would be that he had the chance to study in the United States at a time when neo-Marxism was briefly on the rise, as explained by Ortner (1984: 138-44). If Budiman had been given a scholarship ten years earlier, it is conceivable that he may have become a proponent of one of the versions of the cultural approach; ten years later and he might have become a proponent of a perspective sympathetic to post-modernism.

Although "historical", such an explanation may not be considered sufficiently "structural" or "Marxist" in terms of the version popularized by Budiman himself, and which was used to criticize SEP. Budiman had attacked the widely held view in Indonesia at the time that education could play an important role in changing an individual, and thus lead to social change.[32] Following classical Marxism in its basic version – neo-Marxist thinkers and cultural studies in western Europe meanwhile were taking things further and carrying out self-criticisms and reformulation – Budiman stressed that changes at the level of thinking could only happen after there was a change in structure: "If we want to change things, then we must change first the basic elements of structure in society. Only then through ideological, educational and other influences, values can change" (1983: 84). According to him: "Everybody, including the social scientist, sees issues from the point of view of their class, namely the social position of the people who received this information" (ibid.: 82). But, how can this theory relate to the experience of Arief Budiman himself? In an interview with *Prisma*, Budiman again embraced all the perspectives he had been attacking so relentlessly, namely, idealism, romanticism, humanism and even fantasized about the emergence of a "superman":

> There are people who can transcend reality, its structure. Most people cannot do this....There are people who can transcend structures of whatever kind. For example, Marx was a bourgeois, but he had a socialist consciousness...I myself do not understand what it is that allows somebody to transcend. Education is perhaps one factor. But it is not the total explanation. So I resolve this dependence between structure and values through the existence of people within the structure who are supernormal. But this is not structural at all....Class interests can be defeated by this....What is clear is that such a person is not tied to the existing social conditions.
>
> Budiman 1983: 84-5

It can be argued that structuralism was denied the chance to develop to a higher level of maturity due to a lack of its being challenged through intense debate. In addition, both structuralism, outside of recent Marxism, and culturalism were poorly understood. The two things had, in fact, shared a history and were profoundly related, were juxtaposed, and eventually caricatured as a dichotomy for the purposes of polemics. In one of his articles on the topic, "The Culture of Power or the Sociology

---

[32] In an interview with *Prisma*, Budiman is reported as saying: "Economists state that the difficulties in Indonesia are a matter of mentality. The social sciences also emphasize mentality. Education is the therapy. The economists also say we have insufficient skills, that we do not have a mastery of technology. The therapy is again education! The conflict between them is very artificial. Their assumptions are liberal assumptions, namely that the problem of development is a problem of individuals and not a problem of improving the social system" (Budiman 1983: 78-9).

of Power?", Budiman (1987b) put forward the question, in an ahistorical manner and based on the dichotomous approach: "Which of the two approaches is the most cogent in explaining power?"

Fortunately, not all the disciples of structuralism and/or Marxism after that period became imprisoned in this caricature of a dichotomy. Several younger scholars made scholarly contributions reflecting a more mature structuralist perspective, in both the Marxist version as well as in other versions. In the culturalism camp, too, there were increasing numbers of cultural studies containing insights into structural issues. It is neither possible, nor necessary to present a long list here. But, there are several names that should be mentioned, including Ignas Kleden, Daniel Dhakidae, Vedi Hadiz, Alexander Irwan, Hilmar Farid, Y.B. Mangunwijaya, and Goenawan Mohamad. In their hands, cultural dynamics is not just a nuisance in an intellectual analysis that should be discarded, or made the object of hostility, but should be taken seriously as part of the dialectics of history, power, political-economic structure, and consciousness.

Although a faithful disciple of Marxism, Vedi Hadiz (1989) appreciates the strengths of the cultural approach as adopted by Benedict Anderson. Perhaps because of his leanings towards Marxism, his analysis, full of praise for this culturalism, concluded with a predictable message, namely, that no matter how far this approach tried to be rebellious, it would soon be tamed by the much bigger conservative current among its followers: "The cultural perspective contributed by him (Anderson), which originally had the quality of an 'intellectual rebellion' against the mainstream in the study of Indonesian politics, will be absorbed into this mainstream, so that it will lose its 'radical' meaning" (ibid.: 30).

Hadiz's assessment was not invalid. But, as has been shown above, the same can be said of many approaches or other -*isms*, including structuralism and Marxism. The pronouncements by Soeharto and so many New Order officials that economic development as the basis of a stable society was a precondition for Indonesia to be able to develop in other areas including law, morality, or culture, does not appear at first glance to be different from the classic propositions of Marxism as popularized by many of its dogmatic proponents.

In his history of the social sciences, Benny Subianto has also tried to be fair by acknowledging that there have been examples of innovative non-structuralist works. He cites the works of Sartono Kartodirdjo on the Banten peasant protests at the end of the 19th century (Subianto 1989: 75). Yet, according to a disciple of the cultural approach, Kartodirdjo's work contains more problems than solutions (Stange 1989: 10). In reality, what is called "culture" usually has a very different meaning for those working in cultural studies from its critics who work from outside these circles. The same applies to many other -*isms*.[33]

CONCLUSIONS

The above discussion shows that the use of certain formal slogans and rhetoric, for example, structuralism, liberalism, or culturalism, in a work of social science does not in itself prove that those involved have represented or have utilized their -*ism* to maximum effect, or even in a systematic and consistent manner. The practice in the social sciences of applying a formal theoretical approach has not in itself been sufficient to demonstrate the character of the "ideology" being proposed and implemented by its proponents. Many -*isms* that at first appear to be radical, break-through forces, become inflexible and frozen as they grow in popularity and dominance. There are good and bad expressions and followers of every -*ism*. In polemics, there is always the temptation to highlight the opposition's worst or weakest examples of theories, ideas and rationale, whilst emphasizing and using only the best among one's own armory.

The most important period of growth in the history of Indonesian social sciences occurred during the period of the New Order militaristic regime. The criticisms put forward by the structuralists and post-1965 Marxists in the late 1970s and early 1980s against the dominant social sciences, the cultural approach, re-energized the social sciences. Almost without exception, the social sciences using the "cultural approach" were subservient to political, material or ideological interests, which were openly formalized by the government.

However, many of these criticisms were delivered in an exaggerated manner, as if the rulers at that time were in great need of the social sciences, or that the social sciences played some major role in sustaining the status quo. In reality, this was not the case. Most of the work of social sciences at that time was technical and formal in character, done for a range of government, social and economic development projects. The government was not really interested in the "substance" of this work but simply whether or not there was "proof" that the research had been done as a formal requirement of the project (Morfit 1981; Abdullah 1983).

It was also unfortunate that the structuralist criticism of the cultural approach was often overdone, extending into unnecessary hostility and dichotomy. The criticisms of the "cultural approach" during the New Order in Indonesia were discussed as if they presented an adequate, if not comprehensive, picture of all academic studies centered on cultural dynamics. It is a pity that some of the outstanding cultural studies from outside Indonesia were not circulated widely in

---

[33] According to Stange: "...every religion defines itself as a hermeneutic circle which has meaning only for those participating within it and never for those just peering in from outside...all systems of thought – at least in this sense – are religions" (1989: 8).

the country until the 1990s. As a result, many social scientists in Indonesia, who generally lack an interest and are not well trained in cultural issues in any case, have a poor understanding of the intellectual dynamics in cultural studies other than those painted by the political economists. Even more ironic is the fact that the structuralism that succeeded in shaming the cultural approach in the social sciences eventually emerged as a new "culture" that was held in awe and glorified with methods and a spirit that differed little from that which propelled culturalism, namely idealism, romanticism, ahistoricism and humanism. In other words, the instrumentalist and liberal ideology that stressed the "autonomy" of the modern subject and which was so compatible with the processes of modern capitalism continued to grow after culturalism had been so relentlessly challenged by structuralism.

From the beginning of the twenty-first century, what was lacking in the growth of contemporary structuralism in Indonesia was self-criticism and self-reflection. This latter feature appeared in the twilight of the last decade of the twentieth century, which was marked by the end of the New Order and of the Cold War that gave birth to the regime. Self-reflection made an appearance in the social sciences arena in Indonesia through the current of post-modernism. Yet, as with other -isms, this new force, which was also deemed radical in its early stages, is not immune from the diseases that afflicted its predecessors.

BIBLIOGRAPHY

Abdullah, Taufik (1983) "Ilmu sosial dan peranannya di Indonesia", *Prisma* 12(6): 22-39.

Alatas (ed.) (2000) "Alternative Discourses in the Social Sciences in Asia", special issue, *Southeast Asian Journal of Social Science*, Singapore: Department of Sociology, NUS.

Althusser, L (1971) "Ideology and ideological state apparatuses" in *Lenin and Philosophy, and Other Essays*, London: New Left Books.

Anderson, Benedict (1972) "The Idea of Power in Javanese Culture", in Claire Holt (ed.) *Culture and Politics in Indonesia*, Ithaca (NY) and London: Cornell University Press, pp. 1-77.

Anderson, Perry (1983) *In the Tracks of Historical Materialism*, London: Verso.

Arief, S. and A. Sasono (1981) *Indonesia, ketergantungan dan keterbelakangan*, Jakarta: Lembaga Studi Pembangunan.

Azhar, Ipong S. (1991) "Problem kultur dan struktur dalam demokrasi kita", *Bernas*, 14 August.

Basri, Faisal (2003) "'Liberalisasi' setengah hati?'", *Tempo* 19-25 May.

Booth, Anne (1999) "Education and Economic Development in Southeast Asia; Myths and Realities", paper delivered at the Second International Malaysian Studies Conference, University of Malaya, Kuala Lumpur, 2-4 August.

Budiawan (1987) "Harmonisasi kultur dan struktur", *Kompas* 20 December.

Budiman, Arief (1976) "Teori dan ahli-ahli ilmu sosial kita", *Kompas* 17 April.

— (1977) "Negara-negara dunia ketiga dan sistem kapitalisme", *Kompas* 23 November.

— (1981) "Sebuah kritik terhadap 'sistem ekonomi pancasila' Mubyarto", *Kompas* 10 June.

— (1982a) "Sistem perekonomian pancasila, kapitalisme dan sosialisme", *Prisma* 11(1): 14-25.

— (1982b) "Bentuk negara dan pemerataan hasil-hasil pembangunan", *Prisma* 11(7): 3-14.

— (1983) "Ilmu-ilmu sosial Indonesia A-historis", *Prisma* 12(6): 74-90.

— (1987a) *Jalan demokrasi ke sosialisme: pengalaman Chili di bawah Allende*, Jakarta: Pustaka Sinar Harapan.

— (1987b) "Kebudayaan kekuasaan atau sosiologi kekuasaan?", *Prisma* 16(3): 61-72.

— (1989) *Sistem perekonomian pancasila dan ideologi ilmu sosial di Indonesia*, Jakarta: Gramedia.

Bulkin, Farchan (1984a) "Kapitalisme, golongan menengah dan negara: penelitia", in *Prisma* 2: 3-22.

— (1984b) "Negara, masyarakat dan ekonomi", in *Prisma* 8: 3-17.

Cribb, Robert (1999) "Nation: Making Indonesia", in Donald K. Emmerson (ed.), *Indonesia Beyond Soeharto*, Armonk (NY): Asia Society, pp. 3-38.

Crouch, Harold (1985) *Economic Change, Social Structure and the Political System in Southeast Asia*, Singapore: SEASP and ISEAS.

Dewanto, Nirwan (1991) "Kebudayaan Indonesia: pandangan 1991", *Prisma* 20(10): 3-21.

Geertz, Clifford (1973) *The Interpretation of Cultures*, New York: Basic Books.

— (1983) *Local Knowledge*, New York: Basic Books.

Hadiz, Vedi (1989) "Politik, budaya, dan perubahan sosial; sebuah rekonstruksi dan kritik terhadap pemikiran Ben Anderson", *Prisma* 18(2): 29-49.

Hefner, Robert W. (2000) *Civil Islam. Muslims and Democratization in Indonesia*, Princeton (MA): Princeton University Press.

Heryanto (1989) "Berjangkitnya bahasa-bangsa di Indonesia", *Prisma* 18(1): 3-16.

— (1995) *Language of Development and Development of Language; The Case of Indonesia*, Canberra: Pacific Linguistics.

— (1999a) "The Years of Living Luxuriously", in Michael Pinches (ed.), *Culture and Privilege in Capitalist Asia*, London: Routledge, pp. 159-87.

— (1999b) "Ilmu sosial Indonesia: krisis berkepanjangan", *Kompas* 18 November.

— (2002) "Can There be Southeast Asians in Southeast Asian Studies?" *Moussons* 5: 3-30.

Human Rights Watch (1998) *Academic Freedom in Indonesia*, New York: Human Rights Watch.

Jones, Gavin W. (1994) "Labour Force and Education", in Hal Hill (ed.) *Indonesia's New Order; the Dynamics of Socio-economic Transformation*, St. Leonards (NSW): Allen & Unwin, pp. 145-78.

Juoro, Umar (1990) "Pendidikan dan pembangunan di Asia", *Prisma* 19(1): 33-48.

Kaisiepo, Manuel (1982) "Ilmu-ilmu sosial dan pendekatan struktural", *Kompas* 16 April.

Keraf, Sonny (1995) "Keadilan, pasar bebas, dan peran pemerintah", *Prisma* 24(9): 3-19.

Kleden, Ignas (1987) *Sikap ilmiah dan kritik kebudayaan*, Jakarta: LP3ES.

Koentjaraningrat (1974) *Kebudayaan, mentalitet dan pembangunan*, Jakarta: Gramedia.

— (ed.) (1975) *The Social Sciences in Indonesia*, Jakarta: LIPI.

LPIS (1975), "Ilmu-ilmu sosial dan pembangunan di Indonesia; penilaian dan prospek", *Cakrawala* 8(1): 61-80.

— (1981) *Ekonomi Pancasila; rangkuman arikel dari suratkabar Sinar Harapan dan Kompas 1979-1982*, Salatiga: LPIS.

Magnis-Suseno, Franz (2003) "Neoliberalisme hitam-putih", *Tempo* 24-30 March.

Mallarangeng, Rizal (2002) *Mendobrak sentralisme ekonomi: Indonesia 1986-1992* Jakarta: Kepustakaan Populer Gramedia.

Massardi, Adhie M. (1988) "Kecengengan struktural", *Kompas* 31 August.

McVey, Ruth (1995) "Change and Continuity in Southeast Asian Studies", *Journal of Southeast Asian Studies* 26(1): 1-9.

Miralao, Virginia A. (ed.) (1999) *The History and Development of Social Science Disclines in the Philippines*, volume 1 of the series *The Philippine Social Sciences in the Life of the Nation*, Quezon City: Philippine Social Science Council.

Morfit, Michael (1981) "Sistem penelitian ilmu sosial", *Prisma* 10(2): 68-74.

Mubyarto (1987) *Ekonomi Pancasila*, Jakarta: PUSTAKA LP3ES

Nordholt, Nico and Leontine Visser (eds) (1995) *Social Sciences in Southeast Asia; from Particularism to Universalism*, Amsterdam: VU Univerity Press.

Ortner, Sherry B. (1984) "Theory in Anthropology since the Sixties", *Comparative Studies in Society and History* 26(1): 126-66.

Pramudya, E Panca (2003) "Kapitalisme paling mutakhir", *Kompas* 24 May.

Pratikto, Fadjar (1993) "Gerakan intelektual atau intelektualisme?", *Bernas* 11 May.

Prijono, Onny S. (1999) "Education: Access, Quality, and Relevance", in R. Baker, M.H. Soesastro, J. Kristiadi, and D.E. Ramage (eds), *Indonesia; The Challenge of Change*, Singapore: Institute of Southeast Asian Studies, pp. 159-78.

Prisma (1983) "Mendobrak jalan buntu ilmu-ilmu sosial", 12 (6): 73-90.

Sen, Krishna and David Hill (2000) *Media, Culture and Politics in Indonesia*, Melbourne: Oxford University Press.

Soemardjan, Selo (1983) "Ilmu itu netral dan ilmuwan harus obyektif", *Prisma* 12(6): 73-80.

Stange, Paul (1989) "'Dekonstruksi': Sebuah orientalisme baru untuk Jawa", *Prisma* 18(2): 3-16.

Subianto, Benny (1989) "Ilmu-ilmu sosial Indonesia: Mencari pendekatan dari masa ke masa", *Prisma* 18(2): 59-76.

Sudibyo, Agus (2001) "Sekali berarti, setelah itu mati", *Pantau* 2(19): 23-9.

Sutrisno, Muji (1994) "Interaksi buduaya: struktural atau kultural", *Jawa Pos* 1 May.

Wahyuni, Sri (2003) "Mubyarto promotes 'Pancasila Economy'", *Jakarta Post* 7 March.

Wibowo I. and Francis Wahono (eds) (2003) *Neoliberalisme*, Yogyakarta: Cindelaras Pustaka Rakyat Cerdas.

-4-

THE NEGATIVE AND POSITIVE USE OF SOCIO-ECONOMIC STATISTICS

Aris Ananta

A knife can be used to cut out a beautiful dress. But, a knife can also be used to kill a living creature. The knife itself can do nothing unless wielded by a human being. Whether harm or benefit comes from a knife depends on the person using it. A knife in itself is a neutral object. A knife can also be forged with a specific purpose in mind. A knife used for slaughtering chickens is different from a vegetable knife. In this instance, the knife is no longer neutral. In addition, even if a knife is made for the purpose of slaughtering chickens, there is no guarantee that it will be used only for this purpose. Everything depends on the human being who is using it. Care and judgment is needed if the knife is to be used properly and for its intended purpose.

The same is true for statistics, including socio-economic statistics. Statistics are merely a source of information. The interpretation and utilization of such information depend very much on who has and uses the information. For example, the availability of statistics on the ethnic composition of the Indonesian population could have both harmful and beneficial effects on Indonesia. It would be harmful if used to divide the Indonesian people. But, the very same data would be beneficial if it were used to improve and encourage harmonious relations among the ethnic groups.

Furthermore, there are many cases where statistics are used to deceive people. In fact, it would not be incorrect to say that they are an outstanding tool with which to mislead people. With statistics, we can present something as if it were the objective truth, even if it were an outright lie. As a result, the recipient of the data can be led to a view that is misguided or even wrong, yet the producers of the data cannot be blamed for this because they have the figures, the statistics, to back up their claim. And so it is with many of the social sciences and other sources of information.

This chapter emphasizes the need for care and judgment when reading statistics, particularly socio-economic statistics. However, it is not such an easy thing to exercize care and judgment when dealing with statistics. The average person is often not trained to use statistics, so it is extremely easy to misunderstand the data. The sadder thing is that there are those who deliberately take advantage of this limitation.

If care and judgment are exercised, statistics can be useful in forging a better understanding of Indonesia. Without the proper care and judgment when interpreting statistics, especially data presented with the intention of distorting the truth, the socio-economic situation in Indonesia is likely to be misunderstood.

There are many examples from many fields with which I can illustrate the need for such care and judgment. In this chapter, I will cite examples from economics and demography, simply because these are the areas in which I have a relatively better understanding. My hope is that readers will also be able to identify examples in their own fields within the social sciences.

Several topics are discussed in this chapter. The first being the substance behind a set of statistics. Statistics can mean different things to different people depending on their approach to a particular issue. Therefore, it is not correct to say, "The figures speak for themselves". This is because it is the person using the figures who does the speaking, not the figures. The substance behind the figures is crucial for any understanding of the figures themselves. This issue of substance behind the statistics is illustrated through the following discussions: (1) How much does the Indonesian economy need to grow every year?; (2) Is unemployment exploding?; and (3) Is poverty spreading?

The second topic relates to the different definitions and concepts used for the same terminology. The definition of national income, for example, is relatively fixed. There is something of a consensus on how to measure national income, although the concept of such a measurement may not be entirely understood by all. On the other hand, the concept of poverty is still confusing. Who are the poor? What does subsistence mean? Skin and bones with nothing to eat, robbed of all energy? Someone who does not enjoy even the minimum standards required to live a healthy life? What is a "healthy life"? Would it include psychological and spiritual life? These issues are discussed in the section, "Is poverty spreading?"

The third topic relates to the process of selection of statistics. If there is more than one source of statistics available, which one do we choose? The decision can be motivated by one's desire to convince listeners or readers and by what one stands to gain from the set of statistics that is ultimately chosen. The discussion on "Infant mortality and life expectancy" illustrates this point.

The fourth topic of discussion relates to how a person's perceptions can influence the way in which they view statistics. As such, statistics can be used as a means to support preconceived perceptions. For example, foreigners who regularly visit Jakarta but who have never witnessed riots, or who have never had their pockets picked, might not believe the city's crime statistics. If they had witnessed a crime or fallen victim to it at some point, they might even go so far as to say that the statistics are not reflective of the severity of the situation. Still others, including scholars and government officials, might even rebuff statistics that do not suit their perceptions or purposes. For example, in early 2004, a certain Indonesian leader attacked population statistics simply because this person had previously visited some remote villages where there happened to be many children. This issue is discussed in the sections, "Is unemployment exploding?" and "What is the percentage of ethnic Chinese in Indonesia?"

The fifth topic discusses statistics as targets; targets in the sense that statistics can be and are often used to set goals and objectives. Used in this way, statistics do not necessarily reflect "reality". They serve the purposes and objectives of those setting the targets. Statistics can also be used as a means to "see into the future", projections, if you will, of what might occur under different circumstances. Setting targets and making projections are two distinct scenarios, and it is important that we make this distinction from the outset. This distinction between the two is discussed further in the section, "How to estimate population figures for the future."

All the data used in this chapter is taken from the Central Bureau of Statistics (*Badan Pusat Stastik* – BPS) publications or data collated based on information provided in BPS publications. The decision to refer to BPS data was made for purely practical reasons; BPS data is readily available and is already used by the government and others as reference material.

HOW MUCH DOES THE INDONESIAN ECONOMY NEED TO GROW?

Statistics show that the Indonesian economy grew by 4.1 percent in 2003. What does this figure mean? Is the Indonesian economy in good or bad shape? If we are interested in attacking the Indonesian government, this data could be a powerful weapon, since the growth figure is way below what it was before the Asian economic crisis, namely 6 percent per annum. The logical conclusion is that, over the last five to six years, the government has not succeeded in reviving the country's flagging economy. Experts in this field, be they government officials, economists or foreign consultants, imply that economic growth is the best indicator of a healthy economy. As far as the health of Indonesia's economy is concerned, there is an eagerness for it to return to pre-crisis conditions. This eagerness is fuelled by the belief that high economic growth rates are necessary to tackle the massive unemployment in the country. The issue of unemployment is discussed further in the next section.

Conversely, a 4.1 percent figure could be used to say that the government has managed to drag the economy out of the economic crisis doldrums; after all, the economy was at its worst in 1998 with minus 13.13 percent growth; 1999 was only marginally better at 0.79 percent growth, and 2002 figures stood at a slightly healthier 3.66 percent.

So, is the Indonesian economy improving or not? The answer depends on which set of figures one relies on. The question that remains, however, is when Indonesia will achieve pre-crisis growth figures.

Care must be exercised when attempting to answer this question since it assumes that the higher the growth of national income, the better the economy. But, what is economic growth a measure of? And what of the distribution of income or the issue of poverty itself? How does the environment feature in the equation? These and other similar questions are not answered by economic growth statistics.

If we hold the view that the sustainable progress of an economy is not only measured by its growth rate, but also by other seemingly "non-economic" factors, then we would not be asking when pre-crisis growth conditions will be achieved. This is because, according to this view, it is possible that a growth rate of less than 5 percent, accompanied by other elements of a growing economy such as favorable income distribution, a significant reduction in poverty, and improvement in environmental concerns, could actually be preferable to an 8 percent growth rate marred by environment degradation, disparate income distribution, and little progress in poverty reduction.

What factors determine the national income? There are many different answers depending on who is answering the question and what school or schools of thought have influenced them. However, all these schools accept that aggregate demand is one key factor in determining national income. If there is no aggregate demand, the economy will not grow. In popular terms, if aggregate demand declines, the economy is said to be weak. Everyday observation also shows that a marketplace is considered busy and doing well if it is bustling with shoppers and consumers. Textbooks on macroeconomics always include a considerably lengthy discussion on this issue.

In this context, large savings are not good for the economy. If everybody, including producers, wants to save their money, and that desire is strong, then the aggregate demand will decline. A decline in aggregate demand will lead to a decline in production. A decline in production will result in a decline in income, and a decline in income will lead to a further decline in production, and so on. It becomes a vicious cycle. Saving is considered "bad behavior" in a recession, when the economy is slow. Spending, even excessive spending, can be good medicine for a weak economy. Such high expenditure will lead to a rise in aggregate demand. In other words, spending big, which is contrary to savings, will be excellent for the economy.

Theoretically, funds used to quell political disturbances in a region, let us call it X, could be a "blessing" for the economy outside X because it would increase the aggregate demand outside X. Production outside X rises, income rises, and so demand outside X will rise further. In other words, disturbances can help increase economic growth outside X, and the economy in general. Was not the World War II an important reason for the awakening of the United States economy after the Great Depression of the 1930s?

Corruption, controversially, could also be a blessing for the economy if it is measured in terms of economic growth. For example, if the Social Security Net (*Jaringan Pengaman Sosial* - JPS) funds actually reached the poor, then, the impact on the economy, in theory, would be small. The poor only spend their income on inexpensive goods and services whose stimulatory impact on the economy is weak. The impact on macroeconomic growth would also be weak. On the other hand, if JPS funds are embezzled by those in high positions, the money could be spent on luxury goods and services, thereby increasing economic activity, and generating employment. Aggregate income could increase quickly and this could, in turn, be reflected in high growth statistics.

Theoretically, environmental damage can also have a positive impact on economic growth, when measured simply in terms of national income. The air and water are heavily polluted. The government deals with this by creating projects to clean up air and water supplies. They are large-scale projects. There is a lot of money involved. This creates more aggregate demand and creates employment. Production increases, especially if part of the money is siphoned into the pockets and private bank accounts of officials, because they could spend the money on expensive goods and services, as described above.

These are just some examples of how I believe that "bad" things could actually boost the economy and reduce poverty. They also show that economic growth figures can hide many things. In addition, the above examples illustrate how economic growth statistics are interpreted is dependent on a pre-existing understanding of economic development.

IS UNEMPLOYMENT EXPLODING?

By definition, according to the International Labor Organization (ILO), a person is unemployed if he does not do any work at all but is looking for work. This is also the definition applied by the BPS to Indonesia. Specifically, the definition provides that a person is said to work if he works at least one hour continuously during the week preceding the survey. If this definition is applied strictly to the unemployment situation in Indonesia, unemployment rates have always been very low, hovering in the single-digit zone. These rates, however, have been steadily increasing since the 1970s, a period of high economic growth in Indonesia, whilst managing to remain below the 10 percent mark.

On the other hand, as explained in established macroeconomic textbooks, unemployment rates will explode if the economy deteriorates. During a recession, unemployment will increase dramatically. This is especially so during a regional economic crisis. Applying this theory to Indonesia, many, including government officials, and local and international scholars, are skeptical of statistics reflecting low unemployment rates. Common sense and logic suggest that unemployment rates must have been high, particularly in 1997 and 1998, simply because they have first-hand knowledge of the difficulties people had when trying to earn a living, themselves included.

Having said that, it should be noted that such macroeconomic figures are typically produced in industrialized countries that provide unemployment benefits. One could argue, therefore, that the "unemployed" referred to in the textbooks are those with no work at all, who are looking for work, *and* who are subsidized by the state, even if only with the minimum. However, this is not the system in Indonesia. If someone has no work at all, how is the person to live? Those with the capacity or "ability" to be unemployed are those with savings, who are supported by friends and family, or who receive good severance packages. Without savings or other means of financial support, an unemployed person in Indonesia accepts any job there is to be had in order to survive; in which case, he is no longer, technically speaking, unemployed.

In other words, the international definition of "unemployed" or "unemployment" does not reflect the realities or financial hardships of the people in Indonesia. Here are some anecdotes to illustrate this point:

I once met a resident of a luxurious housing estate in Jakarta. Both his home and car were very nice. His two children were studying in America. He had been a manager of a large corporation. When the crisis hit, he was dismissed with a "golden handshake". Nine months after his dismissal, he still had not found a job, but not for want of offers. He had been offered a managerial position with another company, but he turned it down. In the meantime, his lifestyle had not changed. He still had his nice home and car. His two children were still studying in America. But, by the definition, he was an unemployed person.

On the other end of the spectrum, there was a construction site laborer. He was a day laborer. There was no work for him when the crisis hit. He was dismissed and received no severance payment at all. Unfortunately for him, with no substantial savings, and with a family to feed, he could not afford not to work. As soon as a position for an unskilled laborer opened up, he took it despite the fact that it paid much less than his previous job. He had to. By a cruel twist of fate, this laborer, by the definition again, was not an unemployed person.

It is not surprising, therefore, that some efforts were made to "upgrade" the statistics on unemployment after the 1997 economic crisis to suit the textbook definition of "unemployment" and/or the differing individual perceptions of unemployment.

These efforts included a revision of the definition of "unemployment". It was argued that the unemployment rates were low because the concept of "unemployment" only covered a situation of so-called "open unemployment", thus not covering people who were forced to take whatever was available for their survival. Even the ILO itself argued that the operational definition of "open unemployment" should be widened. As a result, the definition now includes those who are not working but are preparing themselves for work; those who are not working but had a job previously; and those who did not have a job and had no hope of finding a job again. As a result, in part, of this new definition, unemployment rose in 2001. In 2002, the open unemployment rate in Indonesia was 9.06 percent.

Efforts were also made to include the "disguised unemployed" or "under-employed", namely those who work less than 35 hours per week, as part of the definition of unemployment. As a result of these efforts, the unemployment rate, open and under employment collectively, soared to 37.71 percent. In other words, almost four of every 10 members of the workforce were unemployed.

As with the concept of open unemployment, this measurement of under-employment gives rise to many questions. For example, who can afford to work less than 35 hours a week? BPS (2003) posed the question, arguing that some of those who work less than 35 hours a week do so voluntarily, in which case, they cannot be considered to be experiencing financial hardship. Still others are forced to work less than 35 hours a week, there not being enough work to go around. But, is this really the case? What does it mean to be "forced" to work less than 35 hours a week?

Perhaps there are jobs to be had, but not necessarily suitable ones. Further, how do they support themselves working less than 35 hours a week? If they have other means of financial support, be it from friends or relatives, they should not be considered when trying to reflect financial hardship. Even on this basis, the unemployment rate in 2002 was only 20.97 percent.

On the other hand, what about someone who works more than 50 hours per week on a minimum wage, or perhaps even less? Is such a person unemployed or not? As illustrated earlier, those who work less than 35 hours a week, and are considered to be under-employed, might actually be better off financially that those who work 50 or 80 hours a week.

In view of these contradictions, and of the inconsistencies in measurement procedures, do we still need statistics on unemployment?

The debate goes on. Whether or not the employment situation is, in reality, improving is beyond the scope of this chapter. If statistics are to suit theories and perceptions, we do not need them. If the statistics are wrong, it is quite likely that the theory or perception behind them is also wrong.

IS POVERTY SPREADING?

Who are the poor? It is not easy to define who the poor are. Are they the needy, the destitute, the hunger-stricken people? What is the benchmark?

One common quantitative measurement of poverty is premised on the definition of the minimum that a person needs to sustain a proper life. Yet, it is debatable what "proper life" is or should mean. Different scholars may have different definitions of what is regarded as "proper". Each approach has its own weaknesses and strengths, but it is beyond the scope of this paper to evaluate different measurements of poverty. This section discusses poverty only to illustrate how different measurements can be applied to a single concept.

BPS applies an economic definition of poverty. BPS classifies a poor person as someone who cannot meet his basic needs, that is, both food and non-food needs. Therefore, this poverty line comprises a food and non-food poverty line. The food poverty line refers to the amount of rupiah needed by a person to consume 2100 calories of energy per day for a month. On average, an adult needs 2100 calories a day to live a healthy life. The non-food poverty line is determined by basic needs such as housing, clothing, healthcare, education, and transportation.

Therefore, the poor as defined by BPS are not necessarily the hunger-stricken people, the destitute, or the needy, who have nothing and must seek the help of others. The BPS definition of poverty is relatively more "humane" and reasonable. With this broad definition of poverty, the number of poor people in Indonesia dropped from 47,974,600 (23.43 percent) in 2000 to 38,743,700 (19.14 percent) in 2001; 38,867,000 (18.41 percent) in 2002; and declined only slightly to 38,394,000 (18.20 percent) in 2003.

It is interesting to see how BPS has changed the measurement of poverty, to adjust to the dynamics of the society and to attempt to improve the coverage of the poor. These changes are all made to make the statistics on poverty more relevant. Yet, those reading such statistics might not be aware of these changes and might be inclined to make wrong conclusions.

For example, the figures for poverty in 1996 showed 22.5 million or 11.34 percent of the population as being poor. In 1998, the data showed a dramatic increase to 49.5 million or 24.23 percent. The increase of 27 million was "good news" for those that believed the impact on poverty of the crisis that began in 1997 was great. The data supported this belief.

Yet, we must be careful when studying these statistics. In a certain BPS publication, it was stated that the calculation of the non-food poverty line had been changed in December 1998 to bring it in line with developments in society with regard to non-food needs. The definition of "needs" was expanded because BPS realized that the needs of society had expanded. Hence, BPS raised the poverty line. With these changes, it is no surprise that poverty figures also increased. Of the increase of 27 million, some of this represented a genuine increase and the rest was simply a result of an adjustment of method of calculation.

BPS also carried out a comparison using the adjusted method. The 1996 poverty data was recalculated using the 1998 poverty line measurement. With these figures, the 1996 poverty figures became 34.5 million and not 22.5 million. This means that there was "only" a 15 million increase in poverty from 1996 to1999. In other words, the poverty situation would have been more severe had we not been aware of the changes in the measurements of poverty.

These statistics have been useful in providing information on poverty in Indonesia. However, these figures do not give a true picture of the extent of the poverty, or how low poor peoples' incomes have dropped. Do the poor live just under the poverty line or far below it? In the absence of more in-depth studies, the total number of poor might remain constant, but the number of people living far below the poverty line might actually increase.

To respond to this question, BPS has also measured the depth of poverty using the *poverty gap index*. The higher this figure, the greater the depth of poverty, and the greater the distance between the lower incomes and the poverty line. Using the

1998 poverty line, this index rises from 2.5 in 1996 to 4.4 in 1998 for the urban areas, and 3.5 to 5.0 in the rural areas. These statistics show that not only does the number of the poor increase, but the gap between the poorest and those near the poverty line also increased.

There is also the question of how income is distributed among the poor. Even if poverty numbers decrease, income distribution could remain disparate. Again, the BPS has responded to this issue, by calculating the *poverty severity index*, using the 1998 poverty line: The higher the index, the more uneven the distribution.

These three sets of figures show that poverty worsened at the beginning of the Asian economic crisis. What, then, happened in 1999? Based on the 1998 poverty line, the number of poor dropped by 12 million to 37.5 million or 18.17 percent of the population. This is very close to the 1996 figure of 17.65 percent. The *poverty gap index* and the *poverty severity index* also declined although they both remained higher than in 1996. In other words, there had been some improvement in the poverty situation in Indonesia.

We may ask further questions about the concept of measurement of poverty. For instance, there are countries where clean water is readily available, and can be consumed without boiling. In Indonesia, all water must first be boiled, unless it is bottled water. Further, in many parts of Indonesia where water is hard to come by, it must be bought on a daily basis. In such a situation, do we need to include the price of water in the calculation of basic needs?

And what about air pollution? Do we need to include the cost of obtaining "clean air" through purification methods when calculating the cost of basic needs? In a city like Jakarta, for example, "clean air" is relatively difficult to obtain and we often have to pay a high price to obtain such clean air.

We could also include the cost of security in the cost of minimum needs. If our money can be easily stolen, then we need to spend money on our security. People who live in area where there are many thugs must spend more to obtain security. How much does security cost? Should this be included in calculations of the cost of minimum needs?

Nevertheless, this is not a discussion on poverty per se. There are many more statistics on this, from different sources, collected using different methods. This is simply to show that the BPS has tried hard to improve the measurement of poverty. Yet, people should not perceive that these statistics are necessarily the ideal ones. I believe the BPS itself continues to improve their methods of measurement. The most important point of this discussion on poverty is that users of statistics should be aware of the concept behind the statistics and the possibility of changes in definition and measurement, even if the terminology remains the same.

INFANT MORTALITY RATES AND LIFE EXPECTANCY

In this section, mortality and life expectancy are used to illustrate how statistics can be used to suit certain objectives or purposes. There might not be anything wrong with the statistics per se, but it is the choice of statistics that determines the impact of those statistics on those being presented with them.

In demography, we have infant mortality and life expectancy figures at the time of birth. These are two different concepts. Infant mortality rates show the situation regarding deaths of children under one year of age. Life expectancy, on the other hand, summarizes mortality rates for people of all ages. Infant mortality rates are a necessary element in the assessment of life expectancy, but they are only one element of many. These two figures together can provide a better picture of a society's general state of health.

In Indonesia's case, the problem is that we only have statistics for infant deaths, and deaths of children below the age of five years. While there have been several attempts to calculate adult death rates based on empirical data, there is still no consensus on any figures. The absence of such critical data has forced demographers to use a "model" popular with countries that do not have the necessary empirical data with which to compile death statistics. There are many available models, but most demographers, in and out of Indonesia, would use the so-called Coale model, which is based on a formula that links infant mortality with life expectancy.

With this Coale model, life expectancy figures are calculated based on infant mortality rates. In countries where there is accurate or adequate death rate data, infant mortality rates can give a different picture than that portrayed by life expectancy. But in Indonesia, where there is no reliable information on death for the adult population, the infant mortality rate and the life expectancy figures give similar information. As such, it would not be correct to present the two sets of data together.

I have a friend who once did exactly that. I at first thought that this friend did not understand the limitations of these statistics. Therefore, I explained the issue. But, I was startled to learn that my friend indeed knew of the Coale model. He explained to seminar attendees that the continuous drop in infant mortality rates showed that the health/healthcare situation was improving. Presenting life expectancy figures, he added that they were additional evidence of the improving situation: "See, life expectancy is also going up."

"*Pak*, should we not use just one of these, not both together?" I asked him after the seminar.

"Yes..." he said. He continued: "What I have done is not academically correct, but we need to convince these people that health conditions in Indonesia are improving. So, we need to present both sets, so they will be more convinced."

This is not the only example of statistics not being properly utilized. In the 1980s, the physical quality of life index (PQLI) was very popular in many countries, including Indonesia. This index was based on two variables, health and education. It seemed to be the ideal index. Unfortunately, health was measured based on life expectancy and infant mortality. In Indonesia, these two figures were based on the same information, and this is precisely why only one of these figures should be used at any one time. We mislead the reader if we use both giving the impression that we are presenting two independently obtained figures, when in fact they are both based on the same statistical data. This index was used for a long time in Indonesia, but fortunately, not any longer.

There is another measure, developed by the United Nations Development Program (UNDP), and also used by Indonesia, namely the Human Development Index (HDI), which combines education, health and economic statistics. To measure health, the index uses life expectancy without combining it with infant mortality. The HDI calculations are free of the error characteristic of the PQLI method.

Here is another anecdote. Another friend of mine did not want to mislead his audience. He did not want to use both statistics together, because it was not ethical. So, he chose just one. He chose life expectancy.

I asked him: "Why did you choose life expectancy and not infant mortality, given that they are both based on the same information?"

"Academically they are identical, but listen....", he explained.

I do not recall the exact figures he quoted. But, I think they were as follows: Infant mortality declined from 44.54 per 1,000 to 31.63 per 1,000. Life expectancy rose from 67.86 to 70.92 years.

"Declined from 44 per 1,000 to 31 per 1,000? It sounds like a very small decline," he explained. He then continued: "But, increasing from 67 years to 70 is much better sounding. Also, the word 'decline' does not sound as good as 'increase' in the life expectancy statistics."

I was interested in this explanation. The two statistics were the same, but my friend was able to make them different. I later thought: "Well, if health conditions were deteriorating, then he would use the infant mortality rate so the situation would not appear as dire."

HOW MANY ETHNIC CHINESE ARE THERE IN INDONESIA?

What percentage of the Indonesia population is ethnic Chinese? Is it 1 percent, 3 percent, 5 percent, or 10 percent? Are there three million, five million, 10 million, or 20 million ethnic Chinese in the country? There have been many estimates of the number and percentage of ethnic Chinese in Indonesia. The interesting thing is that, for a long time, the only data available were results from a 1930 census. It was only 70 years later that statistical data on the ethnic Chinese were collected in the Indonesian Population Census in 2000. Before this, it was taboo to collect data on ethnicity. The act of collecting data on ethnicity was thought to risk social unrest or even the disintegration of the Indonesian people or nation.

Without this data, researchers, planners, and politicians were busy guessing the number and percentage of ethnic Chinese in Indonesia. Perceptions have played a big role in determining the "correct" figures. These perceptions include both the perceptions of academics as well as the "desires" of the politicians.

The 1930 census produced a figure of 1.2 million ethnic Chinese or 2.05 percent of the population in Indonesia. Since then, there have been only estimations of their numbers and no accurate research data to rely on. Further, because these figures frequently appear in the media and public documents, they tend to influence society's perceptions on this issue. These perceptions are also influenced by what appears to be the case in working and living environments.

A friend of mine took issue with the data published in the book, *Indonesia's Population: Ethnicity and Religion in a Changing Political Landscape,* that I co-wrote with Leo Suryadinata and Evi Nurvidya Arifin. This book stated that in 2000, there were 3 million ethnic Chinese in Indonesia, or 1.5 percent of the population. In my friend's opinion, the figure was too small.

He said: "I often see Chinese around me. These statistics are a lie."

"These figures are for the whole of Indonesia and not just for the area where you live and work," I answered.

He parried: "I know, but the figure is too small."

"Where do you live?"

"In Jakarta."

"Oh, in that case...the percentage for Jakarta is 5.5 percent or 7 percent if you include those who don't call themselves Chinese. So, perhaps your perception is right," I answered.

"Oh, I see, yes..." he said. "I think even 5 or 7 percent is too low. There are Chinese everywhere..."

"Yes, of course. But we are talking about all of Jakarta not just your part of Jakarta, where you live or work."

"Yes, of course, but the figure is still too low, I am sure there are more Chinese than that," he answered confidently.

"Where do you live in Jakarta?"

"North Jakarta."

"Well then, of course. The percentage there is 11 percent or perhaps 14 percent."

"Ah. That is also too low," he answered sharply. "Those statistics are lying. I meet and see Chinese all the time. The statistics are lying."

"Where do you live in North Jakarta?"

"Kelapa Gading Permai!"

I smiled. Of course he would meet and see many ethnic Chinese in that area; it is a housing estate popular with them. And it was clear to me why he had taken issue with the statistics; he compared them to what he saw every day in the Kelapa Gading Permai housing estate in North Jakarta!

The 1.5 percent figure, as was given in our book, was derived from the 2000 population census. Incidentally, this was the first census or survey that included ethnicity in the count. All prior estimates were based on the 1930 data combined with speculation and guesswork. The example above of my Kelapa Gading Permai friend illustrates this point: When statistics, even if collated from the results of a general survey, do not coincide with what is perceived to be, their correctness is disbelieved or doubted.

HOW IS THE FUTURE POPULATION OF INDONESIA TO BE CALCULATED?

In this section, we discuss how statistics are used to set targets in the planning process. There is nothing wrong per se with using statistics in this way, but it is necessary to distinguish *targets* from *projections*.

In the early 1990s, the Demographic Institute of the Faculty of Economics at the University of Indonesia attempted to project the Indonesian population in 2020. We prepared several scenarios. One scenario we used, which we thought was very plausible, was that Indonesia would achieve *replacement level fertility* between 2000 and 2005.[1] In this scenario, Indonesia would achieve "advanced country" status demographically in the period 2000-05. When we presented these results to the National Family Planning Coordination Board (*Badan Koordinasi Keluarga Berencana Nasional* – BKKBN), we were criticized for being too pessimistic about their family planning efforts. They were of the view that replacement level fertility would be achieved as early as between 1995 and 2000.

Still others felt that we were being too optimistic. They were of the view that replacement level fertility would only be achieved in 2005-10. The interesting twist is that, after several months of discussions, the BKKBN eventually opted for the 2005-10 scenario.

---

[1] Replacement level fertility is the point at which a country or region completes the transition from "developing" country conditions to "advanced" country conditions as regards births and deaths. Indonesia will enter a *below replacement level* stage after it has achieved *replacement level*.

Its decision was rationalized as follows: If the BKKBN had adopted the 2000-05 scenario, and replacement level fertility was actually achieved, it would have been an expected result, one that would not warrant any special congratulations for the BKKBN. The converse is also true. If, based on the 2000-05 scenario, replacement level fertility was achieved only in 2005-10, the BKKBN's efforts would be deemed to have failed, and it would be in for harsh criticisms. By adopting the 2005-10 scenario, the BKKBN would be on a safer middle ground.

As it turned out, data from the 2000 census seemed to indicate that the replacement level would be achieved around the year 2000, more in line with what our friends at the BKKBN had argued initially. The 2000 Population Census showed a total fertility rate in 1996-2000 of 2.3. Based on this data, replacement level fertility should be achieved *before* 2005-10, which has become the government target. So, the BKKBN can expect hearty praise and congratulations for reaching their targets.

It is important to note, however, that there is another source of information with which fertility levels in or around 2000 can be measured. The data from the Indonesian Health and Demography Survey (*Survai Demografi dan Kesehatan Indonesia* – SDKI) for 2002-03 provided a total fertility rate of 2.6 for 1999-2002. This is a much higher figure than the 2.3 for the 1996-99 period, produced by the 2000 Population Census. If the SDKI data is adopted, the government will achieve its replacement level fertility target in 2005-10. The target would be achieved on time, and not too early.

But, how are we to know which source of information is correct; the 2000 population census or the 2002-03 SDKI data? Demographers still debate this issue. One view is that the economic crisis and the reduced role of the BKKBN should have slowed the decline in birth rates in Indonesia. The crisis, which also resulted in the government's difficulties in providing adequate healthcare, could also contribute to a slowdown in declining death rates. According to this view, the SDKI data would be more reliable. Another group was of the view that the crisis would have no impact on births and deaths. The impact of the crisis was not as bad as expected in 1998. In fact, said this group, people would be under more pressure to reduce births during a crisis. This second group, therefore, would prefer the 2000 Population Census results.

CONCLUSION

Statistics have many limitations. Statistics can be used to deceive, to mislead the listener or reader, but they can also be used to benefit many people. This chapter has presented various examples of the kind of care and judgment that needs to be exercised when dealing with information of any sort, including statistics. With keen judgment, statistics can indeed help us to understand economic and social conditions better.

Government officials may tend to choose statistics that help to improve their image. They might also hide behind statistics. As a result, people might not trust the statistics supplied by government officials. Similarly, critics of the government are usually suspicious of statistics that highlight how well the government has performed.

My opinion is that we need more statisticians who are aware of the limitation of statistics, and who can help in making better use of available data. They will be able to contribute a great deal to a better analysis of social, economic and political affairs as part of achieving a more accurate understanding of Indonesia's situation. The dissemination of statistics and other accompanying information must also be improved. One practical problem that stands in the way of achieving these goals is the fact that statisticians are not well paid. Prospects, too, are not entirely promising. Yet, national planning, research and development are highly dependent on good quality statistics and even better interpretation of those statistics.

BIBLIOGRAPHY

Badan Pusat Statistik (2002a) *Laporan perekonomian Indonesia 2002,* Jakarta: Badan Pusat Statistik.

Badan Pusat Statistik (2002b) *Data dan informasi kemiskinan tahun 2002, Volume 1: Propinsi,* Jakarta: Badan Pusat Statistik.

Badan Pusat Statistik (2003) *Pengembangan metode perhitungan pengangguran: pengangguran terbuka dan setengah pengangguran di Indonesia 2000-2002*, Jakarta: Badan Pusat Statistik.

Badan Pusat Statistik (n.d.a) *Penyempurnaan metodologi penghitungan penduduk miskin dan profil kemiskinan,* Jakarta: Badan Pusat Statistik.

Badan Pusat Statistik (n.d.b) *Perkembangan tingkat kemiskinan dan beberapa dimensi sosial-ekonominya 1996-1999: sebuah kajian sederhana,* Seri Publikasi Susenas Mini 1999, Volume 2, Jakarta: Badan Pusat Statistik.

BPS, Bappenas, UNDP (2001) *Menuju konsensus baru. Demokrasi dan pembangunan manusia di Indonesia,* Jakarta: BPS, Bappenas, UNDP.

-5-

BETWEEN APOLOGIA AND CRITICAL DISCOURSE: AGRARIAN TRANSITIONS AND SCHOLARLY ENGAGEMENT IN INDONESIA[1]

Ben White

This chapter traces the development of scholarly work in Indonesian agrarian studies from the late colonial period to the present. By "agrarian studies" we mean broadly: social sciences research and teaching on agrarian structures, agrarian history, agrarian and rural poverty, agrarian reform and rural development. The main focus is on *"Indonesian* agrarian studies", that is, the role of Indonesian academics in agrarian studies rather than a general overview of "agrarian studies in/on Indonesia", in which case the role of foreign academics might have been given more prominence. It also focuses particularly on the work of those Indonesian academics who have expressed critical voices on agricultural and rural development trends and policies, and explores the tensions, sometimes destructive, sometimes creative, between state policies and scholarly engagement on agrarian matters in four main periods: the late colonial period (1920s-1940s), the Soekarno era of the 1950s-1960s, the Soeharto period (late 1960s to late 1990s) and finally the current era known, perhaps optimistically, as the *era reformasi*.

---

[1] This chapter draws and expands on two earlier studies on the history of agrarian research and debate in and on Indonesia since the late colonial period (White 2002; 2004). I am grateful to Jan Breman, Gunawan Wiradi, Mubyarto, Sediono Tjondronegoro and Vedi Hadiz for helpful comments on earlier drafts. A fellowship at the Netherlands Institute of Advanced Studies during 2000-2001 made possible much of the groundwork for this study. Thanks also to the staff of the Rockefeller Archive Centre for their help during a short visit in 2003.

We begin with a few general propositions:

1. Despite the dominant progressive rhetoric used by succeeding regimes to characterize each of these four periods, Indonesia has essentially experienced a series of secular transitions from one inherently conservative regime to the next, the present regime not excluded, each of them without a strong social base and without serious commitment to fundamental social change in rural areas. In each period, therefore, critical or progressive social scientists committed to fundamental social change have encountered difficulties with conservative structures of power and control in teaching and research.

2. Agrarian developments have been a key arena in which tensions between state power holders and the intellectual community have been played out. This is not surprising in view of the importance of the agrarian sector as both a key and, until the mid 1970s, major source of state revenues and corporate profits, as well as of the livelihood for the majority (until the early 1990s) of the Indonesian population. It was also a key arena of resource contestation both within communities and between local populations and the state. On the one hand, successive regimes have needed the expertise of graduates and staff of agricultural faculties to serve in government departments and agribusiness enterprise, and to make agricultural and rural development policies more effective. On the other, the agrarian social scientists, with their first-hand knowledge of agrarian conditions and comparative knowledge of other societies, made them potentially harsh critics of dominant agrarian policies and their ramifications.

3. Throughout the period under discussion, there has been tension between two opposing visions of Indonesian rural society. One, dominant among policy makers, academics and urban elite, promotes the image of rural society, especially in Java, as being made up of egalitarian and homogeneous communities of "peasants" or "small farmers", practicing "subsistence farming" and to a large degree isolated from the cash economy. The other underlines the dependence of most rural Indonesians on a cash economy, at least from the early 20th century, and the importance of processes of social differentiation, pointing to the emergence of agrarian classes, including a substantial landless class in many regions, based primarily on differential access to land.

4. The influence of (mainly US-based) foreign donors on the agricultural faculties, whether through scholarships, library support, research grants or other means, was already strong in the Soekarno period. Although some authors view the period of the 1950s and 1960s as a relatively barren period in (indigenous) Indonesian agrarian studies, several important field studies were undertaken during this time, including some innovative experiments in "participatory action research".

5. The 1965-66 political purges in Indonesia's chief centers of agrarian social science and the constrained political atmosphere on campus in the succeeding decades have had a far-reaching impact over both the subject matter and analytical approaches used in teaching and research, right up to the present.

6. The large amounts of funds devoted to human resource development have strengthened this trend. The great majority of agrarian social scientists and economists awarded fellowships for study abroad in the 1960s and 1970s, mainly to the land-grant universities of the USA, returned with some mainstream versions of neo-classical agricultural economics or a rural "modernization theory" which then became the basic frameworks of teaching, whether explicitly or implicitly.

7. While Indonesian university-based researchers have on the whole avoided controversial or politically sensitive topics, there are important exceptions, including those who have exercised considerable influence on thought and consciousness. Since the mid-1980s, there has been an increasing tendency for critical voices to be heard outside the campus, in the framework of research- and action-oriented non-governmental organizations or NGOs. While on the one hand a positive tendency, it also signals a problem that continues into the *reformasi* period: if critical voices flee the campus, how are university students going to learn critical thinking?

8. The fall of the Soeharto regime unleashed a flood of pent-up peasant and environmental activism and a burgeoning of NGOs and NGO-based discourse. Besides the ongoing, complex and difficult discussions on agrarian reform, current NGO discourse includes idealistic notions and anti-globalization slogans. Like other keywords of agrarian discourse which have come before and which will come in future, the current "fashionable" discourse also needs to be continually and critically questioned. Given the current state of the universities, it is doubtful that students are being prepared for such a challenge.

THE LATE COLONIAL PERIOD AND ITS LEGACY

The last two decades of the Dutch colonial period, that is, the 1920s and 1930s, produced a large body of research and debate on agrarian conditions in Indonesia, in which the main participants were the graduates and faculty of the *Landbouwhogeschool Wageningen*[2], the *Economische Hogeschool Rotterdam*[3] and

---

[2] Now the Wageningen University and Research Centre
[3] Now the Erasmus University Rotterdam

the University of Leiden (among them Boeke 1910; 1953; Kolff 1953; Ploegsma 1936; Scheltema 1931; Vink 1941; Vries 1931; Wertheim 1959; Wertheim and van der Kolff 1966). This collection of literature points to two main traditions among the colonial agrarian scientists. First, a strong tradition of empirical study; detailed, field-based analyses of agriculture and village economy. Second, a tradition of lively, more theoretically informed debates on the fundamental nature of Indonesian agrarian economy and society. Critical comments on agrarian policies, and on agrarian poverty in both Java and other islands were not uncommon; we should remember that Dutch intellectuals and officials occupied a range of positions in the Dutch political spectrum, including the left. The influence of Dutch intellectuals continued in Indonesian rural studies, particularly in Bogor, until the expulsion of the Dutch in the late 1950s.

M.A. Jaspan noted the co-existence of an apologetic majority and a smaller critical minority in late-colonial scholarship.[4] Colonial social sciences, he notes, was characterized by "colonial apologia...[which] has diminished the accuracy and reliability of much that was written". However:

> Although the majority of Dutch scholars were closely identified with the colonial ethos and were prepared to justify it...there were a few outstanding workers who challenged the prevailing assumptions and retained an independent scientific outlook. Foremost among the latter is Wertheim. [...] His refusal to identify himself with colonialism during the colonial period, combined with his penetrating insight into the nature and prospects of the independence movement enabled him, alone among his former colleagues, to withstand the impact of the long and bitter conflict between the newly established republic and the Netherlands government during the period 1945-50.
>
> Jaspan 1961: 8

Among Wertheim's influential works that focus on a broad range of social changes in Indonesia yet give due attention to agrarian changes is his *Indonesian Society in Transition* (Wertheim 1959)[5]. According to him, Indonesian progressive intellectuals, including the young nationalists, were on the whole "composed almost exclusively of elitists" (Paget 1975: lvi) who were not very interested in agrarian conditions or issues of rural poverty.[6] To my knowledge, there were only two important exceptions.

---

[4] An anthropologist of British origin who was affiliated to Gadjah Mada University in the late 1950s and early 1960s

[5] Re-published in an Indonesian-language version in 2002.

[6] This contrasts with the strong interest in agrarian issues of the nationalist movements in British India and French Indochina (Breman, et al. 1997: 28-9).

The first is Iwa Kusuma Sumantri's remarkable booklet, *The Peasants' Movement in Indonesia*, written in Moscow in 1927 (Dingley 1927). The author, who had grown up in small-town West Java and graduated in Law from Leiden University,[7] studied at Moscow's Eastern University in 1925 and undertook research on commission from the Farmers' and Peasants' International *Krestintern* in order to supplement his meager income.[8] Using available statistics from the *Statistical Abstracts of the Netherlands Indies* and some other standard sources,[9] this study provides a basic account of social and economic conditions of the Indonesian peasantry and plantation workers. The chapter, "Social and economic conditions of the peasantry", based on available secondary sources, devotes much attention to the struggles over land between large European agro-enterprises and peasants, and to the heavy burdens on the peasantry imposed by tax and service obligations to government, large landowners and native princes, a situation made worse by the "monstrous activities of the numerous usurers [who] usually consist of Chinese merchants and native hadjis" (ibid.: 25). The study also underlines the very low educational level of peasants and their almost complete lack of political rights, and concludes with a strong argument for the need for Indonesia's young progressives to pay greater attention to peasant problems and to promote the emergence of peasant organizations catering to their material interests such as producers' and consumers' cooperatives (ibid. 59). He does not enter into discussions on class differentiation within the peasantry or the class nature of the peasantry, although these were matters of debate in the Russian context at the time.

The second exception, and one which continues to influence perceptions of Indonesian rural social structure up to the present day, is Soekarno's various writings and speeches on the subject of "Marhaen" and "Marhaenisme". It was apparently in 1924 that Soekarno, walking in the countryside south of Cigelereng near Bandung, met Marhaen, the Sundanese "chicken-flea peasant" [*petani sieur*] whose situation as owner-operator of a small farm – destitute, but not a member of the proletariat – seemed to have been a genuine source of political revelation. Marhaen (and his notional Javanese counterpart 'Kromo') became the standard referents in Soekarno's (and Soekarnoist) discourse for a specific, non-Marxist-textbook kind of poverty and agrarian structure that is frequently alluded to in some of Soekarno's most important works of the 1930s, including his electrifying defence plea, *Indonesia*

---

[7]   He later became Minister of Education and Rector of Bandung's Pajajaran University.
[8]   This study was originally written in French and published in translation in English and Russian. The curious choice of nom-de-plume 'S. Dingley' is explained by the fact that during the writing of the book his young Ukrainian wife Anna Ivanova gave birth to his first child, Sumira Dingli (Iwa Kusuma Sumantri 1966: 43)
[9]   Few citations or references are given, but among them is (Huender 1921).

Accuses! that was published in the pamphlet, *Towards Indonesian Independence*. The pamphlet chronicled the political trials of 1930 and 1933.

Soekarno was largely a self-taught man, who reached adulthood with a high degree of political consciousness but with minimum indebtedness to Dutch or European ideas. He was, however, widely read,[10] and made extensive references to the works of European writers and political activists in developing his discourse on imperialism and his "attempt to reach an intelligible explanation for himself and for the Indonesian people of how they had arrived at the present" (Paget 1975: lvi). He drew particularly on Kautsky's insights into the respective roles of the masses, political parties and individual leaders in political struggle. The meeting with Marhaen reflects a classic confrontation between textbook Marxist ideas of class structure and Indonesian realities. Further, it is probably mainly to Kautsky (the textbook) and "Marhaen", the "field" reality, that we owe his insistence that political dialogue must be first and foremost with the masses, rather than among elites, and that the PNI must, by necessity, become a "mass party":

> The structure of Indonesian society is at present *kromoistic, marhaenistic*, that is, a society for the most part consisting of *little farmers, little laborers, little traders,* and *little seamen....*A powerful national bourgeoisie, such as in India, whose strength must be used in the struggle against imperialism...cannot be said to exist here....The Indonesian movement can only be a movement which draws its strength almost exclusively from the circles of *brothers Kromo* and *Marhaen....*
>
> Soekarno 1975 (orig. 1930): 96-7 (*emphasis in the original*)

Soekarno's exclusive populist focus on the impoverished petty commodity producer and his apparent ignorance, or perhaps, neglect for political purposes, of internal differentiation in Indonesian society has been mirrored in subsequent elite and academic discourse on Indonesian society, including that of Clifford Geertz. As Onghokham perceptively notes:

> Soekarno ignored such groups as village heads and officials, larger land-owning 'Marhaens', wholesale traders and wealthy batik traders; he also did not raise the issue of the millions who did not own any land but worked as share tenants or wage labourers, because to raise these issues would have been divisive....For

---

[10] It is interesting to speculate how such a figure, who never studied outside Indonesia, could have gained access to reading matter. Like many critical Indonesians today who do not find much in a largely collapsed academic library system, the most important sources of his reading were probably the private libraries of sympathetic foreigners (Paget 1975: xxxxiii).

Soekarno, the main reason for launching the concept of Marhaen was to convince the educated Indonesian elite to abandon their preconceptions about the common people. Elite perceptions, as reflected in terms like *'rakyat bodoh'*, *'kampungan'*, *'orang dusun'*[11] and so on were battered down and replaced with the term 'Marhaen', since the term 'proletarian' besides being inaccurate would be more shocking to the elite."

Onghokham 1978: 32

THE 1950S AND 1960S: YEARS OF LIVING DANGEROUSLY

One of the distinguishing features of colonial agrarian studies as noted above, the tradition of detailed empirical work, be they rural surveys or "descriptive sociology", became firmly embedded in the new universities of independent Indonesia; the other tradition of broader theoretical debate and critical thinking on the nature of Indonesian agrarian structures and transitions did not. Some scholars have commented on the lack of communication between Indonesian social scientists favoring structural-functional and Marxist approaches in this period (Tjondronegoro 1995). Given the similar lack of communication in the early Cold War period between bourgeois and Marxist traditions in the American universities, which made cooperation agreements with Indonesia's main universities (see below), it is not surprising that the period was marked by a relative absence of theoretical debate. Yet at the same time, agrarian scholars involved themselves in the pressing issues of the day, especially of course on problems of mass rural poverty and the need for agrarian reform. It is perhaps also relevant that many of Indonesia's first indigenous lecturers and professors in (rural) sociology originally came from other, more technical departments, which perhaps made them relatively less at home with social-science theorizing.[12] To be fair, we should also note that Western and particularly North American "rural sociology", departments in which many Indonesians studied, is not known as an arena of vibrant theoretical debate.

Readers should remember the relative weakness of *all* social sciences in Indonesia post-independence, including the rural social sciences. This reflects the appalling record of Dutch colonialism in providing education at any level, and specifically their failure to establish a single university in this nation of 60 million people until the 1940s, when two faculties were established in Jakarta and Bogor

---

[11] All pejorative or dismissive terms for ignorant rural people
[12] For example Sajogyo and Anwas Adiwilaga, pioneers of indigenous rural sociology at IPB and Unpad, were both originally students in agronomy.

(Koentjaraningrat and Harsja Bachtiar 1975).[13] Among independent Indonesia's first national universities, the University of Indonesia (UI) began with a large contingent of European teaching staff, the language of instruction in the 1940s being Dutch. Meanwhile, Gadjah Mada University (UGM) was staffed largely by Indonesians using the Indonesian language. Very few Indonesian social scientists had the opportunity to study abroad until the late 1950s when funding became available from foundations such as Ford and Rockefeller as well as from the Eastern bloc countries,[14] and when various North American universities established affiliation programs with Indonesian faculties (for example, Berkeley with the Economics Faculty of UI; Wisconsin with the Economics Faculty of Gadjah Mada; Kentucky with the Bandung Institute of Technology (ITB) and the Agriculture Faculty of UI at Bogor).

When the new agricultural faculties were established within the new universities, their library resources were minimal. Library support in agrarian sciences was one important contribution of the Council on Economic and Cultural Affairs (CECA)[15] established by John D. Rockefeller III in 1953 with John Lossing Buck[16] as its first Director. The CECA's primary objective was the "development and training in agricultural economics" in Asia, with an intention in later years to support related disciplines such as rural sociology, agricultural extension and community development.[17] In 1955-56, Buck approved book grants to various universities and faculties in Jakarta, Bogor and Yogyakarta. It is interesting to note that both Buck and, after 1957, his successor, Arthur T. Mosher, exercised considerable censorship in response to these requests in the early years. This was before ADC developed the "standard ADC list" of book titles that found their way into many Agricultural Faculty libraries in and outside Java.[18] In 1956, Soedarsono Hadisapoetro, the then Assistant Professor in the Faculty of Agriculture and Forestry at Gadjah Mada University, requested 123 book titles in social sciences and farm management, including some

---

[13] These were the Faculty of Letters and Philosophy in Jakarta (1940) and the Faculty of Agriculture in Bogor (1941) which together with six other faculties were to become the University of Indonesia (1947).

[14] During this period young Indonesian academics went in two main directions to study: (a) the Eastern bloc countries (especially the USSR and E. Germany) and (b) to the USA (including Harvard, MIT, Berkeley and Cornell) funded mainly by the Ford and Rockefeller Foundations; this is the group made (in)famous by the controversial 'Ramparts' article (Ransom 1970). Post-1965, the first group either could not come home, or were marginalized on Indonesian campuses; the second group had large influence on the direction of all social sciences and certainly agrarian social science.

[15] Later to change its name to The Agricultural Development Council (ADC).

[16] Buck had been since 1921 Professor of Agricultural Economics at the University of Nanking and is best known as the author of a detailed field study entitled *Chinese Farm Economy* (1930).

[17] See documents in Rockefeller Archive Centre (RAC), RBF Series 3 Box 37 Folder 286.

[18] And which, from the mid 1960s onwards, always included two copies of Geertz' *Agricultural Involution*.

general works on anthropology, including Malinowski and Benedict, and on agrarian change such as Jacoby's *Agrarian Unrest in Southeast Asia*. Buck informed Soedarsono: "I shall go through this list of books carefully and may wish to make some substitutions of books which are considered superior to those you have mentioned." Eventually, UGM received only 51 titles, nearly all of them technical works on aspects of farm management in the USA. In 1960, to "acquire a library to help in sociological research", the Department of Social Economic Sciences in the Faculty of Agriculture at Bogor sent a request for a list of books seven pages long, totalling 118 books worth some US$500. Mosher scrapped many titles from the list. Among those not approved were Cooley's *Social Organization,* Weber's *Methodology of the Social Sciences*, Merton, Brown & Cottrell's *Sociology Today,* Hogbin's *Social Change,* Gerth & Wright Mills' *Character and Social Structure,* and Wertheim's *Indonesian Society in Transition*. Among those approved were Hoselitz' *Sociological Aspects of Economic Growth*, Parsons' *Structure of Social Action*, and *Structure and Process in Modern Societies*, Lazarsfeld & Rosenberg's *Language of Social Research*, and Geertz' *Religion of Java*.[19]

Despite the weak human and infrastructural resource base in the universities, research on indigenous agrarian issues at this time was not as weak, absent or inconsequential as was sometimes claimed. See for example, statements made in the 1950s by Held or later by Geertz (Geertz 1974; 1995). The 1950s was a time in which the need for a concrete understanding of agrarian conditions and problems grew more acute, in the context of the heated discussions and conflicts surrounding the long process of drafting of Indonesia's new Agrarian Law. During this time, while a series of committees established in 1948, 1951, 1956, 1958 and 1959 wrestled with the task of formulating the new laws (Wiradi 1999), Indonesian researchers carried out a number of important field studies.

Space constraints here prevent a detailed account of those field studies, but some key individuals and groups of the 1950s can be mentioned briefly. In Bandung, the agronomist Anwas Adiwilaga, who was to later become Professor in Agricultural Sociology at Bandung's Pajajaran University, carried out detailed research on land tenure and relations between poor and wealthy peasants in West Java (Adiwilaga 1954a; 1954b). Together with ten Dam's well-known study of Cibodas, these reports provide a good picture of the problems of land concentration, absentee ownership, the poor and often declining state of landlord-tenant relations, competition and the absence of mutual assistance as the basis of rural social structure, and the chronic indebtedness of small peasants, tenants and landless workers.

---

[19] See correspondence in RAC, ADC IV 3B1.13 Box 1 Folder 63, Box 2 Folder 44.

Another cluster of village studies emerged from Gadjah Mada University. A social science research group had been established in 1951, primarily to manage the planned collaboration with the Massachusetts Institute of Technology (MIT) "Indonesia Field Team", comprising six young Harvard Ph.D candidates, including Clifford and Hildred Geertz, Alice Dewey and Robert Jay. Although the planned collaboration with the MIT Team failed,[20] the group was not dissolved, and instead proceeded with its own research. Some years later, under the leadership of the anthropologist, M.A. Jaspan, the committee was transformed into a research institute, namely the *Lembaga Sosiografi dan Hukum Adat*, which published its own journal *Sosiografi Indonesia* (Koentjaraningrat 1975: 224). Among the 30 or so published outputs, several fieldwork-based studies of rural Javanese villages again point to rural social stratification and land-based inequalities rather than poverty-sharing as the basis of social structure (Gadjah Mada University 1956; Guritno 1958; Sosrodihardjo 1955; 1958). We should also mention the more economics-oriented studies carried out in 23 villages in Central and East Java by the University of Indonesia's Institute for Economic and Social Research (*Lembaga Penyelidikan Ekonomi dan Masyarakat* – LPEM) in cooperation with the Ministry of Home Affairs in 1954-55 (Ismael 1960; Salim 1959; Nitisastro 1956; Nitisastro and Ismael 1959), and Selo Soemardjan's Cornell-based dissertation on *Social Changes in Yogyakarta,* based more on the author's personal experience rather than on systematic fieldwork, which throws light on rural social structure and the impact on different social groups of both the 1930s recession and the turbulent times of the Japanese occupation and subsequent nationalist struggle (Soemardjan 1962). Within the Agricultural Faculty of UI in Bogor (later renamed IPB), important Ph.D theses were written by Bachtiar Rifai on land tenure and share tenancy in Javanese villages (Rifai 1958) and by Kampto Utomo (later to be known as Sajogyo) on Javanese "spontaneous" transmigrants in Lampung (Kampto Utomo 1957).

Also influential in both university and political circles were the path-breaking attempts at rural "participatory action research" sponsored by the Indonesian Communist Party (*Partai Komunis Indonesia* – PKI) and/or its peasant affiliate, the Indonesian Peasant Front (*Barisan Tani Indonesia* – BTI), in 1959, 1964 and 1965. These studies, which also received government support, were based on an explicit recognition of the weaknesses of the positivistic, questionnaire-based studies (*angket*) that were characteristic of previous research on agrarian problems.[21] The new

---

[20] Koentjaraningrat (1975:225) and Geertz (1995: 105) give quite different accounts of the background to this breakdown, the first in a long series of troubled relations between foreign Ph.D researchers and their Indonesian host institutes. Wherever 'truth' lies (perhaps somewhere in between the two) it is the Geertzian version, now adapted and further exaggerated by Geertz' intellectual biographer (Inglis 2000:13-14), which will stick in international circles.

[21] The reasons for abandoning conventional research methods are explained in Aidit 1964: Ch.1.

participatory studies produced a series of accounts of rural class differentiation, landlessness, indebtedness and so on (Aidit 1964; Slamet 1988). These accounts are a stark contrast to Geertz' work in the same period with its picture of "involution" and homogeneous, poverty-sharing peasants (Geertz 1963a). While these studies were not themselves carried out by professional social scientists, academics were involved in training and advising the PKI/BTI cadres who went to the field, practicing the "three togethers" (3 sama), the "four don'ts" (4 jangan) and the "four musts" (4 harus). These methods of field practice can be described as the forerunners to the "bottom-up", "participatory action research" strategies now popular with the NGO community and, more recently, with mainstream organizations such as the World Bank.[22]

Comparing the two traditions of sample survey research on the one hand, and "participation and direct observation" on the other, Kampto Utomo noted with interest the strategic decision of Aidit and his colleagues to adopt the latter approach:

> On the one hand, the participatory method is really objective...because [the researchers] seek information directly from the subjects, the primary agents in the matters under study, not through village heads or the leaders of their own constituencies in the village. On the other hand this classic anthropological 'approach' lasted only one week per village, though possibly we may find compensation in the scale of the survey: 3,300 cadres in 124 subdistricts in Java, with every participant researcher in the field for an average of twelve weeks. However...possibly the large scope of the survey was largely influenced by a policy of 'therapie' for the cadres: so that through this research they would better integrate with the people.
>
> Kampto Utomo 1965: 259

The first results of these studies, which covered 15 villages in Java and documented considerable inequalities in land control, were widely publicized at the 1959 National Farmers' Conference and in the press. These studies resulted, for example, in the PKI's identification of the *tujuh setan desa*, the "seven village devils who suck the

---

[22] The 'three togethers' are: work together, eat together and sleep together with the poor peasants and landless workers ['sama bekerja, sama makan dan sama tidur dengan buruhtani atau tani miskin']. The 'four don'ts' are: don't sleep in houses of village elites; don't lecture the peasants; don't be the causes of material losses to your host families or the peasants, and don't take notes in front of the peasants [jangan tidur dirumah kaum penghisap didesa; jangan menggurui kaum tani; jangan merugikan tuanrumah dan kaum tani, jangan mencatat dihadapan kaum tani], while the 'four musts' are: practice the 'three togethers'; be modest, polite and ready to learn from the peasants; know and respect the local language and customs, and help to solve the problems of the host family, the peasants and the local Party (Aidit 1964:18).

blood of the peasants": landlords, usurers, advance purchasers of crops, middlemen, bureaucratic capitalists (those who use state funds to pressure peasants to sell their products to state enterprises at low prices), village bandits (local strongmen who commit crimes to defend the interests of exploiting classes) and evil village officials *[tuan-tanah jahat, lintahdarat, tukang-ijon, kapitalis birokrat, tengkulak jahat, bandit desa dan penguasa jahat]* (Aidit 1964: Ch.2). This is indeed a robust list, and in retrospect, not an inaccurate one. Contrast this with the contemporaneous characterizations of social-economic relations and processes in rural Java by Geertz, who claimed inexplicably that Javanese peasant vernacular recognized no "haves" and "have-nots", but only *"tjukupans"* and *"kekurangans"*, or "just-enoughs" and "not-quite-enoughs" (Geertz 1963a: 97). Further, Geertz describes a situation where land-holdings and wealth reflect a process of "near-equal fractionalization" (Geertz 1956: 141), and where poverty is shared.[23]

While readers might reasonably expect some bias in the PKI/BTI studies, they do little more than confirm, in more colorful prose, the picture that already emerged from the university-based studies just mentioned, as noted by the anti-communist observer, van der Kroef:

> Compared to what is known from other, non-Communist sources, of the concentration of landownership, mortgaging of crops, pawning of land, peasant indebtedness, and rural underemployment in Indonesia (especially in Java), the general conclusions of the PKI researchers are not without some foundation.
>
> van der Kroef 1960: 12

The results of the earlier studies found their way into one of the few textbooks on rural development issues to be produced in the Soekarno period: Universitas Indonesia lecturer, Ina Slamet's *Pokok-Pokok Pembangunan Masyarakat Desa* [Fundamentals of Rural Development] (Slamet 1965).[24] These studies were, therefore, widely known.

---

[23] The impact of the work of the 'Modjokuto' team (who completed their fieldwork in 1953) was not widely felt in Indonesia until many years later. Of the major books produced by team members, only Geertz' *The Religion of Java* was published by 1960 (Geertz 1960). This was followed by Hildred Geertz' *the Javanese Family* (Geertz 1961), Alice Dewey's *Javanese Traders* (Dewey 1962), Clifford Geertz' *Agricultural Involution* and *Peddlers and Princes* (Geertz 1963a; Geertz 1963b) and his *Social History of an Indonesian Town* (Geertz 1965) while the only 'real' rural-fieldwork based product, Robert Jay's *Javanese Villagers* was not published until 1969 (Jay 1969).

[24] The first version of this book was distributed as lecture notes in 1960, the first edition of the book was published in 1962 and the second edition in 1964. This was one of the few Indonesian-language textbooks on rural development widely available in libraries and bookshops in the first decade of the Soeharto period.

Ina Slamet wrote an important retrospective summary and discussion of the third and last study carried out in early 1965 in villages of West, Central and East Java, Bali and Lampung by Peasants' Front and PKI cadres, under the sponsorship of the Aliarcham Academy of Social Sciences and the Ministry of Science and Research. This study, the official aim of which was to study the conditions of food production, involved somewhat longer periods of "participatory" fieldwork, and the results, while initially in a series of stenciled village monographs, were never summarized or published. It is interesting to note that in these studies the importance of women's participation in research was stressed; several of the researchers were women, reflecting also the mixed membership of the BTI (Slamet 1988: 40). Slamet recalls that stress was placed on objective reporting, albeit for the specific purpose of providing the BTI and PKI with more comprehensive knowledge of rural conditions (ibid.: 1). This is indirectly confirmed by the enormous variety of conditions reported from the various villages in West, Central and East Java, suggesting that the cadres were hardly pressured into following a standard line. While the PKI and BTI based their initial thinking on a basic, "classical" agrarian class categorization (landlords, rich peasants, middle peasants, poor peasants, agricultural laborers), they made important modifications to this framework based on the realities observed in the field, combining land and income-based indicators to arrive at a classification of social-economic groups in rural society, which "though it did not resolve all ambiguities, was nevertheless fairly realistic" (ibid.: 30).

Subsequent claims by expatriate scholars that the PKI failed to understand the agrarian structure, basing itself on a too-rigid application of the Maoist model of rural class divisions (Lyon 1970; Mortimer 1972; Törnquist 1984) need to be reconsidered in the light of these studies. Both the published and unpublished studies of 1964 and 1965 clearly show that the PKI were willing to adapt theories and concepts to Indonesian realities as revealed in field research. The "seven village devils" discourse was precisely an attempt to underline that Indonesia's rural poor were exploited in complex ways and that "concentration of surplus" was based not only on land rent and extraction of surplus value from wage labor, but also on a much richer combination of economic, political and ideological mechanisms (Slamet 1988: 31).

Meanwhile, on campus and perhaps influenced by the PKI's innovations in rural research, another experimental version of "participatory action research" emerged in the early 1960s through what Franke has called an indigenous Indonesian theory of a "Green Revolution". This theory was based not only on the introduction of new technology but also, unlike its corporate and corporatist successors in the Soeharto period, on a transformation of village institutions and mass mobilization, thereby breaking the barriers between the professional elite and peasants. The idea originated in Bogor in 1963. Students went to live with farmers in villages, sometimes for an entire cropping season, to teach and learn from them, offering suggestions for improved cultivation techniques, interceding with local officials on the farmers' behalf and bringing their experiences back to the next group of students. In 1964 and 1965, the Ministry of Agriculture adopted the program, sending 440 students to the field in 1964 and 1,200 in 1965 (Franke 1972; Rieffel 1969; Roekasah and Penny 1967). Two independent sources estimated that yields had reached more than 50 percent above the national average on the 175,000 hectares covered by this early version of the Bimas program (Mears and Saleh Affif 1968; Rieffel 1969).

Recalling earlier remarks about the lack of dialogue between different intellectual traditions at this time, Geertz, whose "agricultural involution" is perhaps the only lasting theoretical contribution made by a foreign scholar in this period, seems to have stayed firmly within his own camp (Geertz 1963a). Whether or not he was aware of the many village-level studies carried out by Indonesian researchers during the 1950s is unclear, but not one of those we have cited here is mentioned in *Agricultural Involution* (ibid.). This reluctance to see anything of worth in the fieldwork-based research of his Indonesian contemporaries is reflected again in Geertz's sweeping dismissal, a few years later, of the "usual [Indonesian] view" of research: "A brief 'study trip' in search of written records, a generalized summary of the accessible "literature" on a subject, or a fish-net type of fact-gathering survey" (Geertz 1974). This was a grossly inaccurate characterization, which does no justice to the actual research practice and commitment of many Indonesian rural social scientists during this period.

AGRARIAN CHANGE, APOLOGETICS AND SCHOLARLY ENGAGEMENT IN THE SOEHARTO PERIOD

Both pre-colonial states and colonial regimes at various times instituted changes, some of them radical ones, to structures and systems of access to agricultural land over large parts of Indonesia. It is therefore not surprising that post-colonial peasants, activists and policy-makers – and, until the mid-1960s, some of their expatriate advisors – felt it imperative to introduce agrarian reforms to correct some of the distortions introduced by earlier feudal and colonial regimes. Indonesia's experience of agrarian reform during the height of the Cold War period is a particularly tragic and ironic one. After the enactment in 1959 and 1960 of land and tenancy reform laws based on political compromise, which basically reproduced the typical "anti-communist" model[25] (as applied successfully with US backing in Japan, S. Korea and Taiwan and unsuccessfully in South Vietnam), organizations and groups which pressed at local level for the implementation of these (anti-communist) reforms, themselves fell victim to the anti-communist purges of 1965-66.

Similar purges occurred in the universities, both before and after Minister of Education, Brigadier-General Syarif Thayeb, instructed university rectors to suspend all administrative and academic staff linked to the PKI or any of its affiliate organizations on 29 October 1965. The influence of the campus purges on agrarian studies should not be underestimated. These purges produced victims, survivors and winners. Large numbers of academic staff in IPB, UI, Unpad and UGM, including some of Indonesia's most promising young scholars on agrarian matters, were expelled from their campuses. Some never returned, others returned under severe constraints, including regular interrogation by the resident Opsus staff and travel restrictions. Their experiences colored the subsequent academic work of those who did not find themselves in any kind of political trouble.

This period was characterized by enormous investment in agricultural infrastructure and research, as well as investment in university infrastructure and human capital. This enabled state officials to exercise some degree of thought control over the universities through the allocation of rewards, whether in the form of projects, facilities, secondments to (quasi)-government bodies, overseas study and so on. Further control was exercised by the presence of military interrogation centers on or near campuses. This environment certainly affected what was taught, what research projects were funded, what was written, and what subjects students selected for thesis research.[26] It was an environment that imposed the corporatist understanding of introducing rural modernization (*pembangunan masyarakat desa*) in backward "traditional" peasant society, backed by Soeharto's personal interests and commitment, from Repelita I onwards, in promoting a self-sufficiency in food, and agricultural modernization generally.

The post-1965 policy shift from "agrarian reform, mass mobilization and intensification" to "green revolution from the top down, without land reform" in

---

[25] Based on the strengthening of small-scale private ownership, conversion of tenancy into ownership rights, maximum and minimum holdings limits, and compensation for appropriated land.

[26] I should note that Sajogyo (referring to an earlier draft of this chapter) expressed some disagreement on this point: "this was certainly not what I or my colleagues and students in social sciences experienced in the Agriculture Faculty of IPB. As supervisors, our tradition was to offer students a free choice of topics and issues for their field research! The staff also tried to set an example: behave like 'innocents'" (Sajogyo 2003: 9). It may have indeed have been not so much pressure from supervisors as the more general political atmosphere on campus which encouraged a choice of relatively "safe" research topics.

fact had been foreshadowed prior to 1965 by the shift among external agencies (USAID, the World Bank, the Ford Foundation, the Rockefeller-funded Agricultural Development Council – ADC) from interest in and even support for (non-communist or anti-communist) agrarian reform to technocracy-inspired "green revolution" approaches to food production and agricultural development.[27] The main external agencies sponsoring training and other investments in the agrarian social sciences also tended, with some notable exceptions, to promote a rather flat, de-politicised approach to agricultural economics and rural sociology with scholarships mainly to the agricultural economics and rural sociology departments of US universities. In the 1950s and early 1960s, despite the urgent need for postgraduate training, key sponsors like CECA had found it difficult to identify candidates who were both qualified and available for study abroad (Wharton 1959). From 1961 to 1973, however, CECA-ADC sponsored 20 fellows for Master's or Ph.D studies overseas, almost all to US universities, and almost all in the field of Agricultural Economics.[28] The list, although short, reads like a "who's who" of teaching, research and policy-making on agriculture in New Order Indonesia: Saleh Afiff, Alhambra Rahman, Affendi Anwar, Syarifuddin Baharsyah, Achmad Birowo, Faisal Kasryno, Margono Slamet, Roekasah Adiratma, Rudolf Sinaga, I. Gusti Bagus Teken. They all held prominent leadership or advisory positions, in addition to their university jobs, in Bappenas, the Department of Agriculture and/or the Agro-Economic Survey of Indonesia in the 1970s.

The paternalistic stance of at least some major donor agencies can be seen in the ADC's vision of the "ideal pattern of ADC-aided career development". Having identified promising undergraduate students, ADC aimed to provide them with "constant exposure to ADC publications and training materials" and "constant contact and correspondence with ADC (field) Associates" for the individual's entire subsequent career through ADC-sponsored Master's and Ph.D studies abroad, research grants, short courses and conferences during the years of teaching or research in between study programs, and finally "career continuation" support in the form of ADC sponsorship of research, sabbaticals, travel grants and consultancies

---

[27] This shift is perhaps most clearly seen in the series of consultancy visits made by the US-based anti-communist land reform adviser Wolf Ladejinsky in 1961, 1962 and 1963. Reports from the first two of these visits resulted in memos on how Indonesia's land reform laws were too conservative, 'an example of how not to give land to the landless'; in contrast, the final policy memorandum addressed to Minister Sadjarwo basically suggested abandoning land reform efforts and focusing energies instead on small-farm intensification efforts to raise peasant productivity (Ladejinsky 1961; 1964)

[28] ADC (1973). The exceptions were three scholarships to University of the Philippines and one to Australian National University; the non-economist was M. Amin Aziz of Sosek-IPB who was sponsored for an MA in Rural Sociology at University of the Philippines.

in other Asian countries (ADC 1968). One important additional element was the provision of teaching materials in the rural social sciences through a program that was initiated in 1963 with a Ford Foundation grant to CECA. The program involved the "collection and distribution of materials relating to agricultural development" by both reprinting existing publications and commissioning new ones. The three staff members assigned to this Asia-focused project were all North American, as was its Advisory Board of six representatives of US universities and foundations. The most influential product of this program was the first commissioned book written by the CECA-ADC Director himself, A.T. Mosher, entitled *Getting Agriculture Moving: Essentials for Development and Modernization* (Mosher 1965). This small book, with an initial print-run of 5,000 (and subsequently 25,000) copies, was translated into numerous languages including Indonesian (Mosher 1967). It completely reflects the dominant modernization theory in rural development discourse, and the new focus on the "green revolution" package of productivity-enhancing measures and the shift, both by governments and donors, away from politically difficult measures like land reform. No "village devils", or the means to deal with them, are to be found in the book, only the "five essentials" and "five accelerators" of agricultural modernization. A first batch of 200 copies was distributed to agricultural faculties throughout Indonesia, and free copies were sent to all ADC Fellowship recipients and others departing for study abroad, with the suggestion that they read it before departing for their studies.[29]

The early 1970s also saw the establishment of key campus-based research institutes or centers. In agrarian studies, the more influential of these were the Institute of Rural Sociology Research, from 1972, headed by Professor Sajogyo at IPB, and the Center for Rural and Regional Studies, from 1973, headed by Professor Sartono at UGM. In New Order Indonesia, the development of critical discourse on key issues of agrarian transformation was hindered by the long periods during which public and academic discussion of agrarian reform or even agrarian poverty was either impossible, or severely constrained by the hostile political climate.[30] For a period of about 10 years, from 1966 to1976, public discussion of land reform issues was virtually impossible.

In the repressive climate surrounding academic activity during this period, it was not surprising that Indonesian researchers in these institutes and other centers, on the whole, avoided controversial topics or at least couched their concerns about the direction of rural development policies in careful terms, at least when publishing

---

[29] RAC, ADC IV 3B1.4 Box 6 folders 46 and 48.
[30] The late Buddy Prasadja told me in 1973 how as a final-year student at UI he had been harshly criticized by the examiners of his *skripsi* for the frank discussion of rural poverty in his Cirebon field study (Prasadja 1972).

for domestic readers. For an indication of the kinds of research and discussions prevailing at the time, readers could scan, for example, the titles and abstracts of the monthly seminars at UGM's Center for Rural and Regional Studies between 1983 and 1991 (Mubyarto and Ari Basuki 1989; 1992), or those of the Master's and Ph.D theses in Rural Sociology at IPB between 1975 and 1994 (Sajogyo et al. 1995). Two general patterns are clear. First, the relatively scant attention given to issues of land tenure and agrarian relations, and broader theoretical issues in both centers[31] , and second, the predominant tendency towards topics that validated the prevailing New Order rural development models and strategies.

The most important exception here is Sajogyo whose critical overview of studies of the impact of New Order agricultural intensification programs, as described in *Modernization without Development in Rural Java* (1973), was widely circulated inside and outside Indonesia, but never published in the Indonesian language. Both Sajogyo in Bogor, and Masri Singarimbun in Yogyakarta, squarely addressed the issue of mass rural poverty through empirical research (Sajogyo 1974; 1977; Singarimbun and Penny 1976), and in 1976 Sajogyo publicly re-introduced for the first time the issue of land reform (Sajogyo 1976).[32] Loekman Soetrisno and Mubyarto at UGM also frequently wrote on issues of rural poverty in the 1980s. These interventions paved the way for subsequent, albeit cautious, legitimization of these topics in academic and policy discussions, as seen in the Indonesian Social Science Association's selection of the sensitive theme of "Structural Poverty" [*Kemiskinan Struktural*] for its 1978 Congress in Malang (Alfian et.al. 1980),[33] and the Agro-Economic Survey's organization of an International Workshop on "Agrarian Reform in Comparative Perspective" in Sukabumi in 1980.[34]

---

[31] About one in ten of the IPB theses, and virtually none of the P3PK seminars focused on land tenure and/or agrarian relations.

[32] When asked at the time why he had decided to re-introduce the issue of land reform in such a low-profile way – as foreword to another author's book, but with a characteristic Sajogyian exclamation mark (Sajogyo 1976: 17) – Profesor Sajogyo told the author that it was intended as a *"proefbalon"* (weather balloon), i.e. a testing of the political wind.

[33] In this volume, two papers by university-based academics provide field-based analysis of agrarian structures and plead for structural solutions (Hotman Siahaan 1980; Sinaga and White 1980), in contrast to the apologetic contributions of power holders (Adam Malik 1980; Emil Salim 1980; Kartidjo 1980) and the ambivalent, euphemistic meanderings of those who straddled the worlds of power and academia (Selo Soemardjan 1980; Soedjatmoko 1980)

[34] Both these gatherings were heavily attended by members of the security apparatus. In the 1980 "Agrarian Reform" workshop, the security personnel hovering outside on occasions outnumbered the 30 participants. All media reporting on the workshop was prohibited. The workshop's recommendation (White and Wiradi 1984: 7) to establish an autonomous "land tenure research, training and information centre" in Indonesia, with support from the Institute of Social Studies (The Hague) and the Land Tenure Center (Madison) – never subsequently implemented – is perhaps one of the great missed opportunities of the 1980s.

While agricultural economics has had its own disciplinary journal *Agro-Ekonomika* since 1969,[35] the rural sociologists have not. The interdisciplinary journal, *Prisma*[36], however, offers an excellent representative view of the general tone and content of public academic discourse on agrarian issues in New Order Indonesia, and also the limits to which this discourse could stretch. From the early 1970s onwards, *Prisma* became the most widely read source of Indonesian-language research articles and essays among agrarian scholars. Besides some important individual articles on the early impact of the green revolution,[37] eleven issues or sections of *Prisma* were devoted to issues of land tenure, rural development, food policy, plantations, and other related topics between 1978 and 1995, with contributions from both established and younger-generation researchers.[38]

In the years of the New Order government and green revolution, the Agro-Economic Survey's (AES) long-term research programs, funded mainly by the Ford Foundation through grants to the ADC, involved repeated visits to samples of villages in Java from 1969 onwards (in the "Rice Intensification Study") and 1976 onwards (in the "Rural Dynamics Study"). These studies were to become important elements in both policy discussions and academic debate concerning agricultural intensification and rural change in Java. Their influence was felt not only through the various survey results published by AES researchers themselves, but also from the frequent involvement of policy-makers in policy workshops from the AES' early years (de Vries 1969; Penny 1971; Strout 1985), and through the fact that many of the better-known green revolution dissertations and other studies by foreigners were based on research carried out in AES sample villages (among them Breman 1995; Collier et al. 1974a; Franke 1972; Hart 1986; Hayami and Kikuchi 1981; Pincus 1996; White and Wiradi 1989).[39] The AES villages, in this way, provided raw material for many prominent foreign critics as well as apologists for Indonesia's green revolution.

Green revolution studies from the early 1970s onwards have shown their own

---

[35] *Agro-Ekonomika* began life robustly in 1969 with a first issue completely devoted to critiques of the ill-fated Bimas Gotong Royong programme, but in later years has not been known for critical work on dominant development models.

[36] First published in 1971, and sadly defunct since October 1998.

[37] Astika 1978; Collier, et al. 1974b; Mubyarto 1976; Mubyarto 1978; Sairin 1976; Soejono and Birowo 1976

[38] These include *Desa* 7(3) 1978 *Pengembangan masyarakat* 8(3) 1979, *Tanah* 8(9) 1979, *Desa* again 17(1) 1988, *Politik agraria* 18(4) 1989, *Pertanian* 19(2) 1990, *Industri Perkebunan: Kemakmuran Siapa?* 20(4) 1991, *Kemiskinan* 22(3) 1993, *Pangan* 22(5) 1993, *25 tahun revolusi hijau* 23(3) 1994 and *Pola pembangunan ekonomi desa* 24(8) 1995.

[39] Collier was assigned by the Agricultural Development Council as full-time consultant with the Agro-Economic Survey from 1967-1975, and White from 1975-1980.

progression, which is complex enough to require its own chapter and can only be briefly summarized here.[40] First, the studies of the early to mid-1970s, particularly those by Sajogyo, Collier and his other Indonesian colleagues in the various reports of the AES, and the young Social Science Research Institute at Satya Wacana Christian University, served a purely empirical purpose, namely to draw attention to some of the social-economic concomitants of the green revolution in lowland irrigated rice cultivation. The early 1970s in fact played witness to a rare moment when a number of young scholars from research institutes in Bogor, Yogyakarta, Jakarta and Salatiga all turned their attention to an issue of common concern: the negative impacts of green revolution technologies, and practices on employment and income opportunities for the marginal-peasant and landless groups who formed the majority of most rural communities. These studies produced some excellent empirical work (Budhisantoso 1975; Collier et al. 1973; Collier et al. 1974a; LPIS 1976; Sairin 1976; Sinaga and Collier 1975; Stoler 1975; Utami and Ihalauw 1973) which succeeded in drawing the attention of policy makers and foreign donors to issues of the distributional consequences of agricultural modernization in the "unreformed" agrarian structures of Java and other islands, and played some role in the official shift to discourses of *pemerataan* (equality), which emerged in the late 1970s. However, these authors entered rarely, if at all, into dialogue with general theory or comparative literature. They also were generally out of touch with earlier work on agrarian labor relations in Javanese rice agriculture, written mainly by Dutch authors.

Some of the authors of the 1970s and early 1980s, particularly foreigners, were of course concerned with looking critically at the "involution" thesis, as this had by that time become the "label" attached in the minds of outsiders, and some insiders, to agrarian Java. Authors who have questioned the involution thesis can be divided roughly into three kinds. First, those who accepted the validity of "involution" as characterization of colonial and early post-independence Javanese society until the 1960s – or in some cases, did not presume to judge on this matter – but argued that in Soeharto's New Order Indonesia, with the green revolution intensifying and the commercialization of rural economy, "involutional" mechanisms and concepts of shared poverty were breaking down. Second, those who questioned the validity and usefulness of "involution" as a characterization of Javanese rural society both during the colonial period and more recently; and third, somewhere in between, those who accepted that "involutionary" processes might at times have been at work, but only as short-lived processes generally associated with secular contractions of colonial export-crop production.

---

[40] Various aspects of these studies are discussed further in (White 1989; 2000).

In contrast and partly in reaction to these studies, the later 1970s and 1980s saw many researchers, particularly foreigners, engaging in a more *reflective* kind of green revolution study, relating field observations on changing agrarian relations to classic ideas of agrarian differentiation and diversification, often with an explicitly comparative purpose and sometimes with a broader historical perspective (Hart 1986; Hayami and Kikuchi 1981; Husken 1989; Maurer 1986; Pincus 1996; White and Wiradi 1989). These authors on the whole, like the authors of various Dutch agrarian dissertations of the 1920s and 1930s, had read the classic European works on agrarian differentiation processes and were, among other things, somewhat concerned with exploring the relevance of a mainstream or "global" model for the understanding of the dynamics of agrarian change in Java. Although some of them devoted space to critiques of "involution", they certainly did not see this as their main objective.

Several prominent Indonesian historians such as Sartono and Onghokham have achieved international reputations with their work on the history of Javanese peasant society and protest in the colonial period.[41] Their work, and that of others who followed such as Kuntowijoyo and Soehartono, is important not only for its content, but for its demonstration of the value of holistic, political-economy inspired analyses of agrarian structures and relations and their dynamics, rather than for the sterile frameworks of Parsonian sociology and neo-classical (agricultural) economics which characterized so much of the sponsored research during the green revolution.

Indonesian agricultural economics has remained a largely conservative discipline, rooted in neo-classical frameworks and neo-liberal policy prescriptions although sometimes with a neo-populist tone, and largely uninterested in issues of agrarian inequality and agrarian reform. This is the case in Bogor, although economics and sociology are still linked together in the Departments of Social Economy in the Faculties of Agriculture and Animal Husbandry (see below), and in many provincial and private university departments that have recruited IPB graduates. An important exception here is UGM's Professor Mubyarto.[42] Although trained in the mainstream tradition, namely in Wisconsin, USA, his widely-used 1973 textbook, *Pengantar Ekonomi Pertanian*, keeps the neo-classical framework in the background and makes widespread use of sociological and other works to try to provide a view of agricultural economy adapted to actual Indonesian conditions (Mubyarto 1973). In his many

---

[41] Between Indonesia's two main Departments of History it is Gadjah Mada which has developed a strong tradition of agrarian history under the influence of Professor Sartono Kartodirdjo. UI historians, despite the colourful presence of Onghokham have focused more on political and military history.

[42] Mention should also be made of Mubyarto's colleague Ace Partadiredja, author of some pioneering studies on *ijon* debt relations in Java (Partadiredja 1973a and b; 1974).

writings on *Ekonomi Pancasila* and other works on agricultural and rural development policy (Mubyarto 1983), he has consistently argued for another form of economics, one in which issues of social justice have a stronger place.

In Bogor, it is Professor Sajogyo who has done the most to promote interdisciplinary work between sociologists and economists.[43] Sajogyo has reminded us of the beginnings of agrarian social sciences in Bogor. W.J. Timmer, a former *landbouwconsulent* and the first Professor (1948-51) in the new Department of Social and Economic Agricultural Sciences (*Ilmu-ilmu Sosial Ekonomi Pertanian*) wrote a book on *Totale Landbouw-wetenschappen* or "Total Agricultural Sciences", auguring well for interdisciplinary work. Even today, undergraduates at IPB do not study rural sociology as such but *sosial-ekonomi pertanian*,[44] in which the specialization in rural sociology occupies only the last four semesters. Sajogyo also argues that Rural Sociology in Bogor:

> "...is not a mirror of the curriculum of those US agricultural faculties originating in the Landgrant Colleges....Among the core staff of the S2 program in Bogor, graduates from the US are not at all dominant. In fact in Bogor, we have developed a 'hybrid' Rural Sociology, a combination of sociology (the legacy of industrial nations), anthropology (a Western legacy, product of the study of indigenous tribes before they were marginalized) and social psychology (for rural extension based on adult education principles)."

> Sajogyo et al. 1995: xii-xiii

It is unfortunate, however, that neither Sajogyo nor Tjondronegoro, or other key figures at IPB, produced a textbook outlining the basic principles of rural sociology à la IPB.[45]

Gender studies in the agrarian social sciences, also pioneered in Bogor, began sometime in the late 1970s and developed rapidly thereafter. Social-science attention to women and gender in Indonesia emerged in the early and mid 1970s largely for instrumental reasons in connection with the policy focus on family planning and population control.[46] Many of the early green revolution studies already mentioned

---

[43] Mubyarto has called Sajogyo an "economic sociologist, or the father of Indonesian sociological economics" *["Sosiolog yang ekonom, atau Bapak ekonomi-sosiologi Indonesia"]* (Mubyarto 1996).

[44] Normally translated awkwardly as "socio-economics of agriculture".

[45] The core rural sociology handbook used in the 1980s and 1990s is the two-volume reader edited by the two Sajogyos, and reprinted 13 times between 1982 and 2002. The 13th edition still includes classic works by the Dutch authors ten Dam on agrarian structure in Cibodas and Wertheim on the changing status system (Sajogyo and Pudjwati Sajogyo 2002).

[46] A representative collection at this time is *Prisma*'s theme issue *Wanita dan Cakrawala Baru*, 4(5) 1975).

had underlined the impact of technical and institutional change on (near-) landless women, but systematic studies of women and gender relations in agricultural communities did not emerge until the late 1970s.[47] Of 100 S-2 and S-3 theses on Rural Sociology completed in Bogor between 1975 and 1994, the largest group was those focusing on *Peranan Wanita* or "Women's Roles" (Sajogyo et al. 1995: xxi-xxii). Gender studies in this field, as in others, began as critical/alternative discourse, followed rapidly by attempts to "tame" and incorporate this discourse through institutionalization, including the PSWs in every state university and many private ones. Like all such attempts, incorporation has been only partly successful, but it is largely true to say that the Centers of Women's Studies in Bogor and other universities have become sites of (non-radical) "women's studies", while more critical, feminist perspectives on "gender studies" are based largely off-campus in a number of NGOs, such as Kalyanamitra, Solidaritas Perempuan, the Jurnal Perempuan group, Komnas Perempuan, and LBH Apik. Sadly, however, the exponents of more critical gender studies have published very little on agrarian matters.[48]

Finally, we should note the emergence of a strong focus on environmental issues in agrarian studies, including critical social sciences work on forestry, and shifting cultivation from the early 1980s, often supported by programs of the Ford and Rockefeller Foundations.[49] This was also linked to some important and often courageous critical work on marginalization of indigenous peoples, forced displacement as a result of large infrastructure or resettlement projects amongst others. Space constraints here do not allow for a discussion on work in this field. Readers are referred to *Environmental Politics and Power in Indonesia,* to be published in 2005 for Ford Foundation's *Celebrating Indonesia* series.

---

[47] The first systematic study of women's rural economic activity and decision-making by Indonesians was an FAO-funded study in West Java, carried out in 1977-79 by Pudjiwati Sajogyo and a combined AES-IPB team (Sajogyo 1980; 1983; Sajogyo et al. 1995; White and Hastuti 1980). A Ford Foundation grant for IPB's Women's Studies Project (1981-1986), including a substantial number of S-2 fellowships, helped to establish this field of study as one of the flagships of rural sociology in Bogor.

[48] An important exception is Indira Simbolon's pioneering work on gender and land in North Sumatra (Simbolon 1998). An influential Indonesian-language introductory textbook on gender studies from a feminist standpoint is Ratna Saptari and Brigitte Holzner's *Perempuan, Kerja dan Perubahan Sosial* (Saptari and Holzner 1997).

[49] If we use the appearance of a theme issue of *Prisma* to indicate the emergence of a critical mass of scholarship in this field, the first issue on the environment was in 1978: 7(8).

REFORMASI AND THE NEW GENERATION OF SCHOLAR-ACTIVISTS

The fall of Soeharto and the ensuing turbulent period of *reformasi* unleashed a flood of pent-up peasant and environmental activism and a burgeoning of NGOs and NGO-based discourse. Recent years have seen a rich profusion of new publications on agrarian issues, many by younger scholars with the majority of them based off-campus in NGO centers of research and activism. The NGO phenomenon in intellectual life actually had already made itself felt in the later years of the Soeharto government (mid-1980s–late 1990s). Theirs was the critical voice that grew progressively louder and the tendency was for critical research to be increasingly undertaken outside the campus, in the framework of a new generation of NGOs undertaking research explicitly in the service of activism. Those with a strong interest in agrarian issues include Akatiga, KPA *(Konsorsium Pembaruan Agraria)*, INSIST, PERCIK, YAPIKA, LAPPERA, amongst many others.

These researchers publish their work in established or in NGO presses and in NGO-based journals, some of them short-lived,[50] rather than in the mainstream journals such as *Masyarakat Indonesia* and *Agro-Ekonomika*. Their research publications vary in quality; much of the new material is unreferenced and poorly edited, often confronting the reader with wild, enthusiastic generalizations amid a jungle of misprints.

The NGO phenomenon is a key development that needs discussion. Paradoxically, it contributed to the trend that gave birth to it, that is, the augmenting sterility of academic life on campus and the divergence of more-critical "NGO" and less-critical "formal academic" discourses in many areas. This may be seen for example in discussions on poverty, including those on women and poverty, and of course on agrarian reform, for example World Bank models in the universities and more radical versions outside. The two worlds, however, are not completely isolated from each other; some prominent university academics use the NGOs to escape the constraints of academia, and some key NGO activists spend part of their time teaching.

In the new, NGO-driven agrarian studies issues of land tenure, land conflict and land reform have fused to become one key issue (Adhie and Menggala 2002; Al Araf and Awan Puryadi 2002; Anu Lounela and Zakaria 2002; Endang Suhendar et al. 2002; Endang Suhendar and Winarni 1998; Noer 1997; 1999; Pujo Suharso 2002; Wiradi 2000). Other popular issues include village democratization and peasant rights (Jati Wijaya et al. 2000; Juliantara 2000; Wahono 2002), and the impact of

---

[50] Two NGO-based journals which have achieved relative stability are Akatiga's *Journal Analysis Sosial* and PERCIK's *Renai*. It is a great pity that LP3ES's *Prisma* ceased publication in 1998, just missing the chance to derive new strength from the outpouring of new critical social science in the heyday of the early *reformasi* period.

agri-business, commercial forestry and infrastructure projects on local people (Sangaji 2000; Bachriadi 1995; Wiradi 1999). There have also appeared a number of interesting village- or local-level studies, often revisions of S1 or S2 theses indicating that critical research still survives in some corners of academia, studies of particular social groups such as rural child workers, and critiques of current agricultural policy (Afandi 2001; Sangaji 2000; Tjandraningsih and Anarita 2002; Maula 2001; Pratikto 2000; Setyobudi 2001). These works are generally written with spirit and, with some notable exceptions (Noer 1999; Wiradi 2000), with little explicit reference to theory or with little or no historical depth.

While NGO discussions and publications on the whole are more interesting than those emerging from the universities,[51] they are often inspired by rhetoric and a rather uncritical adoption of radical theories. It should also be noted that critical NGOs are a minority and will remain so, reflecting the tendency for critical NGOs to attract mainstream sponsorship, thereby eventually becoming "corporatized", requiring a constant cyclical emergence of new critical NGOs.

In criticizing the mainstream discourse of rural modernization that characterized the Soeharto period, current NGO discourse often relies, rather uncritically, on idealistic notions of community, as in "community-based forestry", *adat* or "customary law", as in *masyarakat adat* meaning "customary society", and anti-globalization notions such as *kedaulatan pangan* or "food sovereignty".[52] Such concepts, like other keywords of agrarian discourse which have come before and which will come in future, need to be continually and critically interrogated. Will it be the (still-to-be-"reformed") campuses of state and private universities, or the more fragile and ephemeral world of extra-campus NGO centers that will promote and nourish such critical discourse?

At the height of the Soeharto period, Gunawan Wiradi and I wrote:

Although public discussion of [agrarian reform] issues is now quite acceptable, one result of this hiatus [in public discussion of land reform issues] is the serious lack of local and comparative research materials both on land tenure problems and on the theory and practice of land reform and agrarian reform. Furthermore, formal training in the theory and practice of land reform and agrarian reform is now virtually absent from the curricula of most departments concerned with agricultural and rural development problems in Indonesian universities.

White and Wiradi 1984: v-vi

---

[51] A common saying among activists is 'when I enter the university I leave my brains behind'
[52] Gender issues, inexplicably, have largely disappeared from this discourse as the main feminist NGOs and scholars have turned their attention to other issues during *reformasi*.

How much progress in this area has been made in the last two decades, and especially in the recent years of *reformasi*? How many Indonesian universities and departments now include teaching modules on Theory and Practice of Agrarian Reform at undergraduate (S1) or post-graduate (S2) level? And, where can researchers, activists, interested journalists, political party campaigners and others who might be interested find a good library or database on questions of agrarian structure, agrarian poverty and agrarian reform? After all the decades of external support for university library development, what library still subscribes to the key international journals in the field or even purchases the latest Indonesian-language books in agrarian studies, let alone preserves the various Indonesian publications that I have cited (with the excellent help of Dutch libraries) on the period of the 1950-80s? How, then, can young Indonesian scholars develop their comparative and theoretical capacities, or even study the history of their own indigenous Indonesian agrarian studies, without going abroad?

And who will write the much-needed new Indonesian-language textbook on rural sociology? Will the teaching of rural sociology on-campus respond to the new demands of rural reform and encourage students to return to the idealism that characterized the 1950s and 1960s? The latest post-Soeharto rural sociology textbook that I picked up on a recent visit to Gramedia, written in 2002 by Jabal Ibrahim, is still based on ideas from US sociology and modernization theory of the 1960. For example it cites Arthur Mosher and Everett Rogers with no mention of social class differentiation, agrarian conflicts or agrarian reforms or structural issues in general. Further, the chapter on "social change" appears towards the end of the book, almost as an afterthought. These ideas, imparted in lectures and textbooks and reproduced in the theoretical frameworks of student theses, stand in the way of attempts to bring critical discourse back to where it belongs, in university-based teaching and research.

These questions become increasingly urgent as new decentralization measures open up new potentials, but also new problems and hazards, for creative agrarian development and reform measures at the regional level. The critical mass of awareness and expertise is now needed, more than ever before, at the regional level. When will every region have its own campus-based Centers of Agrarian Studies (*Pusat Kajian Agraria*), its own (branch of) the KPA, or similar bases for the support of research, documentation, advocacy and informed policy debate on agrarian reform?

It is this crucial interplay between "passion" and "reason" that is required to make progress on issues of agrarian poverty and social justice. Further, it is primarily the universities that have historically played a crucial mediating role, as centers of both teaching and research. This role was played by universities, however imperfectly, in the Soekarno period and was largely taken away from them during the decades of the New Order, for reasons described in earlier sections. While critical and creative thinking may currently flourish off-campus, its existence there is inherently unstable and vulnerable. For example, if, as is quite possible, the conservative tendencies of the current "reform" regime are consolidated into a harsher version after the 2004 elections, and the freedom of expression of the first few post-Soeharto years yields to a more repressive environment, critical scholarship might increasingly feel the need for the protection and legitimization that the university can potentially offer. However, given the current state of the universities – which seem in many ways to have remained largely unchanged in the *reformasi* years, even as their students became active in movements for political change off-campus – it is doubtful whether they are busy preparing their staff and students for such a challenge.

BIBLIOGRAPHY

ADC (1968) *Program and Method of Operation*, New York: The Agricultural Development Council.

ADC (1973) *Directory of Fellows*, New York: The Agricultural Development Council.

Adhie, B., and Hasan B. N. Menggala (eds) (2002) *Reformasi pertanahan: Pemberdayaan hak-hak atas tanah ditinjau dari aspek hukum, sosial, politik, ekonomi, hankam, teknis, agama dan budaya*, Bandung: Penerbit Mandar Maju.

Adiwilaga, A. (1954a) *Daerah aliran sungai Tjikapundung-Hulu*, Bandung: Kantor Perantjang Tata-Bumi Djawa Barat.

—— (1954b) *Land Tenure in the Village of Tjipalago (Bandung Regency)*, Bandung: Kantor Perantjang Tata-Bumi Djawa Barat.

Afandi, Andik (2001) *Tragedi petani: 'Musibah' panen raya padi 2000*, Yogyakarta: Lembaga Analisis Informasi.

Aidit, D.N. (1964) *Kaum tani mengganjang setan-setan desa: laporan singkat tentang hasil riset mengenai keadaan kaum tani dan gerakan tani Djawa Barat*, Jakarta: Yayasan Pembaruan.

Al Araf and Awan Puryadi (2002) *Perebutan kuasa tanah*, Yogyakarta: Lappera Pustaka Utama.

Alfian, Mely G. Tan and Selo Soemardjan (eds) (1980) *Kemiskinan Struktural: Suatu bunga rampai*, Jakarta: Pulsar/Yayasan Ilmu-Ilmu Sosial/HIPIIS.

Astika, Ketut Sudhana (1978) "Pengaruh sosial ekonomi program intensifikasi padi di Desa Abiansemal", *Prisma* 7(1): 77-90.

Bachriadi, Dianto (1995) *Ketergantungan petani dan penetrasi kapital*, Bandung: Akatiga Foundation.

Boeke, J. H. (1910) *Tropisch-koloniale staathuiskunde: het probleem*, Ph.D thesis, University of Leiden.

—— (1953) *Economics and Economic Policy of Dual Societies as Exemplified by Indonesia*, Haarlem: Tjeenk Willink.

Breman, Jan C. (1995) "Work and life of the rural proletariat in Java's coastal plain," *Modern Asian Studies* 29(1):1-44.

Breman, Jan, Peter Kloos and A. Saith (eds) (1997) *The Village in Asia Revisited*, Delhi: Oxford University Press.

Budhisantoso, S. (1975) *Rice Harvesting in the Krawang Region (West Java) in Relation to High-yielding Varieties*, Melbourne: Centre for Southeast Asian Studies, Monash University.

Buck, John Lossing (1930) *Chinese Farm Economy: A Study of 2866 Farms in Seventeen Localities and Seven Povinces in China*, Nangking: University of Nanking.

Collier, William L., Gunawan Wiradi, and Soentoro (1973) "Recent changes in rice harvesting methods," *Bulletin of Indonesian Economic Studies* 9(2):36-45.

Collier, William L., et al. (1974a) "Agricultural technology and institutional change in Java," *Food Research Institute Studies* 13(2):169-194.

—— (1974b) "Sistim tebasan, bibit unggul dan pembaharuan desa di Jawa," *Prisma* 3(6): 13-30.

de Vries, E. (1969) "The Agro-economic Survey of Indonesia," *Bulletin of Indonesian Economic Studies* 5(1):73-77.

Dewey, Alice (1962) *Peasant Marketing in Rural Java*, Glencoe: Free Press.

Dingley, S. (1927) *The Peasants' Movement in Indonesia*, Berlin: R.L. Prager.

Franke, Richard W. (1972) *The Green Revolution in a Javanese Village*, Ph.D thesis, Harvard University.

Gadjah Mada University (1956) *Laporan penyelidikan ilmu djiwa sosial di Palidjan*, Yogyakarta: Gadjah Mada University, Faculty of Education.

Geertz, Clifford (1956) *The Development of the Javanese Economy: a Sociocultural Approach*, Cambridge: MIT Center for International Studies.

—— (1960) *The Religion of Java*. New York: Free Press.

—— (1963a) *Agricultural Involution: the Processes of Ecological Change in Indonesia*, Berkeley: University of California Press.

—— (1963b) *Peddlers and Princes: Social Development and Economic Change in Two Indonesian Towns*, Chicago: University of Chicago Press.

—— (1965) *The Social History of an Indonesian Town*, Cambridge (MA): MIT Press.

—— (1974) "Social science policy in a new state: a programme for the stimulation of the social sciences in Indonesia", *Minerva* 12(3): 365-381.

—— (1995) *After the Fact: Two Countries, Four Decades, One Anthropologist*, Cambridge (MA): Harvard University Press.

Geertz, Hildred (1961) *The Javanese Family: A Study of Kinship and Socialization*, Glencoe: Free Press.

Gunawan, Rimbo, Juni Thamrin and Endang Suhendar (1998) *Industrialisasi kehutanan dan dampaknya terhadap masyarakat adat: kasus Kalimantan Timur*, Bandung: Akatiga.

Guritno, Pandam (1958) *Masyarakat marangan: sebuah laporan sosiografi ketjamatan Prambanan daerah istimewa Jogjakarta*, Yogyakarta: Gadjah Mada University, Panitya Social Research.

Hart, Gillian (1986) *Power, Labour and Livelihood: Processes of Change in Rural Java*, Berkeley: University of California Press.

Hayami, Y. and M. Kikuchi (1981) *Asian Village Economy at the Crossroads: An Economic Approach to Institutional Change*, Tokyo: University Press.

Huender, W. (1921) *Overzicht van den economischen toestand der inheemsche bevolking van Java en Madoera* (Survey of the economic condition of the indigenous population of Java and Madura), The Hague.

Hüsken, Frans (1989) "Cycles of commercialization and accumulation in a Javanese village", in *Agrarian Transformations: Local Processes and the State in Southeast Asia*, Gillian Hart, Andrew Turton and Ben White (eds), Berkeley: University of California Press, pp. 303-331.

Ibrahim, Jabal Tarik (2002) *Sosiologi pedesaan*, Malang: Penerbitan Universitas Muhammadiyah.

Inglis, Brian (2000) *Clifford Geertz: Culture, Custom and Ethics*, Cambridge (MA): Polity Press.

Ismael, J.E. (1960) *Keadaan penduduk di 23 desa di Djawa*, Jakarta: Lembaga Penyelidikan Ekonomi dan Masyarakat, University of Indonesia.

Iwa Kusuma Sumantri (1966) *Riwajat hidup seorang perintis kemerdekaan*, Bandung: unpublished manuscript.

Jadul Maula, M. (ed.) (2001) *Ngesuhi deso sak kukuban: lokalitas, pluralisme, modal sosial demokrasi*, Yogyakarta: LKiS.

Jaspan, M.A. (1961) *Social Stratification and Social Mobility in Indonesia: A Trend Report and Annotated Bibliography*, Jakarta: Gunung Agung.

Jati Wijaya, Angger et al. (eds) (2000) *Reformasi tata pemerintahan desa menuju demokrasi*, Yogyakarta: Pustaka Pelajar/Yapika/Forum LSM DIY.

Jay, Robert (1969) *Javanese Villagers: Social Relations in Rural Modjokuto*, Cambridge (MA): MIT Press.

Juliantara, Dadang (ed.) (2000) *Arus bawah demokrasi: otonomi dan pemberdayaan desa*, Yogyakarta: Lapera Pustaka Utama.

Kampto Utomo (1957) *Masyarakat transmigran spontan di daerah w. Sekampung*, Bogor: Penerbitan Universitas Indonesia.

— (1965) "Research sosiologi pedesaan di Indonesia" in Sadikin Soemintawikarta (ed.) *Research di Indonesia 1945-1965*, Jakarta: PN Balai Pustaka/Departemen Urusan Research Nasional, pp. 251-265.

Kartodirdjo, Sartono (1980) "Struktur masyarakat Indonesia dan masalah kemiskinan", in Alfian, Mely G. Tan and Selo Soemardjan (eds) *Kemiskinan struktural*, Jakarta: Pulsar/YIIS/HIPIIS, pp. 20-30.

Koentjaraningrat (1975) *Anthropology in Indonesia*, The Hague: Martinus Nijhoff.

Koentjaraningrat and Harsja Bachtiar (1975) "Higher education in the social sciences in Indonesia", in Koentjaraningrat (ed.), in *The Social Sciences in Indonesia*, Jakarta: Indonesian Institute of Sciences, pp. 1-42.

Kolff, G. H. van der (1953) "An economic case study: sugar and welfare in Java", in *Approaches to Community Development*, P. Ruopp, (ed.), The Hague and Bandung: van Hoeve, pp. 188-206.

Ladejinsky, Wolf (1961) "Land reform in Indonesia (memorandum, 24 January 1961)", in *Land Reform as Unfinished Business: the Selected Papers of Wolf Ladejinsky*, L. Walinsky, (ed.), Oxford: Oxford University Press for the World Bank, pp. 297-299.

—— (1964) "Land reform in Indonesia" (memorandum, 27 February 1964), in *Land Reform as Unfinished Business: the Selected Papers of Wolf Ladejinsky*. L. Walinsky, (ed.), Oxford: Oxford University Press for the World Bank, pp. 340-352.

Lounela, Anu and R. Yando Zakaria (eds) (2002) *Berebut tanah: beberapa perspektif kampus dan kampung*, Yogyakarta: Insist Press/Jurnal Antropologi Indonesia/ Karsa.

LPIS (1976) *Tebasan dan beberapa perubahan sosial ekonomi lain di pedesaan Jawa Tengah*. Salatiga: Lembaga Penelitian Ilum-ilmu Sosial, Universitas Kristen Satya Wacana.

Lyon, Margo (1970) *Bases of Conflict in Rural Java*, Berkeley: University of California, Centre for South and Southeast Asian Studies, Research Monograph no. 3.

Malik, Adam (1980) "Kemiskinan struktural di Indonesia dan perubahan struktur masyarakat", in *Kemiskinan struktural*, Alfian, Mely G. Tan, and Selo Soemardjan (eds), Jakarta: Pulsar/YIIS/HIPIIS, pp. 14-19.

Maurer, Jean-Luc (1986) *Modernisation agricole, developpement economique et changement social: le riz, la terre et l'homme a Java*, Geneva: Presses Universitaires de France.

Mears, Leon, and Saleh Affif (1968) "A new look at the Bimas programme and rice production", *Bulletin of Indonesian Economic Studies* 10:29-47.

Mortimer, Rex (1972) *The Indonesian Communist Party and Land Reform, 1959-1965*. Clayton: Monash University Centre of Southeast Asian Studies, Papers on Southeast Asia No. 1.

Mosher, Art T. (1965) *Getting Agriculture Moving: Essentials for Development and Modernization*, New York: Praeger Publishers for the Agricultural Development Council.

—— (1969) *Creating a Progressive Rural Structure*, New York: Praeger Publishers for the Agricultural Development Council.

—— (1974a) *Menciptakan struktur pedesaan progresif untuk melayani pertanian*, Jakarta: CV Yasaguna for the Agricultural Development Council.

—— (1974b) *Menggerakkan dan membangun pertanian*, Jakarta: CV Yasaguna for the Agricultural Development Council.

Mubyarto (1973) *Pengantar ekonomi pertanian*, Jakarta: LP3ES.

—— (1976) "Response penduduk terhadap penciutan kesempatan kerja di pedesaan", *Prisma* 5(9):50-58.

—— (1978) "Involusi pertanian dan pemberantasan kemiskinan: kritik terhadap Clifford Geertz", *Prisma* 7(2):55-64.

—— (1983) *Politik pertanian dan pembangunan pedesaan*, Jakarta: Sinar Harapan.

—— (1996) "Prof. Sajogyo: sosiolog yang ekonom, atau Bapak ekonomi-sosiologi Indonesia", in *Sajogyo: Bapak, guru dan sahabat*, Mubyarto, B. Ismawan, O.S. Pamuji, and Yati Widayati (eds), Jakarta: Yayasan Agro-Ekonomika.

Mubyarto and Ari Basuki (eds) (1989) "Rural Development Seminars: Collected Abstracts From Monthly Seminars 1983-1988", Yogyakarta: Centre for Rural and Regional Studies, Gadjah Mada University.

—— (1992) "Seminar pedesaan: abstrak makalah-makalah Seminar Bulanan P3PK UGM. Yogyakarta: Pusat Penelitian Pedesaan dan Kawasan, Universitas Gadjah Mada.

Nitisastro, Widjojo (1956) "Some data on the population of Djabres, a village in central Java", *Ekonomi dan Keuangan Indonesia* 9:731-784.

Nitisastro, Widjojo and J.E. Ismael (1959) *The Government, Economy and Taxes of a Central Javanese Village*, Ithaca (NY): Cornell University.

Noer, Fauzi (ed.) (1997) *Tanah dan pembangunan: risalah dari konferensi INFID ke-10*, Jakarta: Pustaka Sinar Harapan.

—— (1999) *Petani dan penguasa: dinamika perjalanan politik agraria Indonesia*. Yogyakarta: Insist/KPA/Pustaka Pelajar.

Onghokham (1978) "Soekarno: Mitos dan Realitas", in *Manusia dalam kemelut sejarah*, T. Abdullah, A. Mahasin, and D. Dhakidae (eds), Jakarta: LP3ES, pp. 20-46.

Paget, R. (1975) "Introduction" in R. Paget (ed.) *Indonesia Accuses! Soekarno's Defence Oration in the Political Trial of 1930*, Oxford: Oxford University Press.

Partadiredja, Ace (1974) "Rural credit: the ijon system", *Bulletin of Indonesian Economic Studies* 10(3): 54-71.

Partadiredja, Ace et al. (1973a) "Ijon di Jawa Barat: Laporan penelitian ke-2", Yogyakarta: Lembaga Penelitian Ekonomi Universitas Gadjah Mada.

—— (1973b) "Ijon di Jawa Tengah, dareah instimewa Yogyakarta dan Jawa Timur", Yogyakarta: Lembaga Penelitian Ekonomi Universitas Gadjah Mada.

Penny, David (1971) "The Agro-economic Survey of Indonesia: an Appreciation". *Indonesia* 11.

Pincus, Jonathan (1996) *Class, Power and Agrarian Change*, London: Macmillan.

Ploegsma, N.D. (1936) "Oorspronkelijkheid en economisch aspect van het dorp op Java en Madoera" Ph.D. thesis, Leiden University.

Prasadja, Buddy A. (1972) *Pembangunan desa dan masalah kepemimpinannya*, Jakarta: Fakultas Ilmu-ilmu Sosial Universitas Indonesia.

Pratikto, Fadjar (2000) *Gerakan rayat kelaparan: gagalnya politik radikalisasi petani*, Yogyakarta: Media Pressindo.

Ransom, David (1970) "The Berkeley Mafia and the Indonesian Massacre", *Ramparts* 9(4): 27-29, 40-49.

Rieffel, Alexis (1969) "The Bimas programme for self-sufficiency in rice production", *Indonesia* 8: 103-133.

Rifai, Bachtiar (1958) *Bentuk milik tanah dan tingkat kemakmuran: penyelidikan pedesaan didaerah Pati, Jawa Tengah*, Ph.D thesis, University of Indonesia (Bogor).

Roekasah, E, and David Penny (1967) "Bimas: a new approach to agricultural extension", *Bulletin of Indonesian Economic Studies*, 7:60-69.

Sairin, Sjafri (1976) "Beberapa masalah derep: studi kasus Yogyakarta", *Prisma* 5(9): 59-67.

Sajogyo (1973) "Modernization without development in rural Java", a paper contributed to the study on Changes in Agrarian Structures organized by the FAO of the UN, 1972-73. Bogor, unpublished mimeo.

— (1974) *Usaha perbaikan gizi keluarga*, Bogor: LPSP, Bogor Agricultural University.

— (1976) "Pengantar", in Masri Singarimbun & David H. Penny, *Penduduk dan kemiskinan: kasus Sriharjo di pedesaan Jawa*, Jakarta: Bhratara Karya Aksara, pp. 7-21.

— (1977) *Garis kemiskinan dan kebutuhan minimum pangan*, Bogor: Agricultural University (unpublished).

— (2003) "Dari praktek ke teori dan ke praktek yang berteori", paper presented at the Refleksi Sajogyo seminar, Jakarta, December.

Sajogyo and Pudjwati Sajogyo (eds) (2002) *Sosiologi pedesaan: kumpulan bacaan,* 13th edition, Yogyakarta: UGM Press.

Sajogyo, et al. (eds) (1995) *Panen 20 tahun: ringkasan tesis dan disertasi 1975-1994 studi sosiologi pedesaan program pasca sarjana Institut Pertanian Bogor*, Bogor: DOKIS/ISI/PERHEPI/YAE/PUSPA SWARA.

Sajogyo, Pudjiwati (1980) *The Role of Women in Different Perspectives*, Bogor: Agro Economic Survey and Centre for Rural Sociological Studies, Bogor Agricultural University.

— (1983) *Peranan wanita dalam perkembangan masyarakat desa*, Jakarta: Rajawali.

Sajogyo, Pudjiwati et al. (1979) "Studying rural women in West Java", *Studies in Family Planning* 10(11-12): 364-9.Salim, Emil (1980) "Kebijaksanaan pemerataan mengatasi kemiskinan," in Alfian, Mely G. Tan, and Selo Soemardjan (eds) *Kemiskinan struktural*, Jakarta: Pulsar/YIIS/HIPIIS, pp. 31-45.

Salim, Emil et al. (1959) *Kehidupan desa di Indonesia: suatu case study daripada 23 desa di Djawa*, Jakarta: Lembaga Penyelidikan dan Ekonomi Masyarakat, University of Indonesia.

Sangaji, Arianto (2000) *PLTA Lore Lindu: orang Lindu menolak pindah*, Yogyakarta: Yayasan Tanah Merdeka, ED Walhi Sulawesi Tengah, Pustaka Pelajar.

Saptari, Ratna, and Brigitte Holzner (1997) *Perempuan, kerja dan perubahan sosial*, Jakarta: Grafiti/Kalyanamitra.

Scheltema, A.M.P.A. (1931) *Deelbouw in Nederlandsch-indie*, Ph.D thesis, Wageningen Agricultural University.

Setyobudi, Imam (2001) *Menari di antara sawah dan kota: ambiguitas diri, petani-petani terakhir di Yogyakarta*, Magelang: Indonesiatera.

Siahaan, Hotman (1980) "Struktur sosial dan kemiskinan petani", in Alfian, Mely G. Tan, and Selo Soemardjan (eds) *Kemiskinan struktural*, Jakarta: Pulsar/YIIS/HIPIIS pp. 111-121.

Simbolon, Indira J. (1998) *Peasant Women and Access to Land. Customary Law, State Law and Gender-based Ideology: the Case of the Toba-Batak (North Sumatra)*, Ph.D thesis, Wageningen Agricultural University.

Sinaga, Rudolf and William L. Collier (1975) "Social and regional implications of agricultural development policy", *Prisma* (English version) 1(2):24-35.

Sinaga, Rudolf, and Ben White (1980) "Beberapa aspek kelembagaan di pedesaan Jawa dalam hubungannya dengan kemiskinan struktural", in Alfian, Mely G. Tan, and Selo Soemardjan, (eds), *Kemiskinan struktural*, Jakarta: Pulsar/YIIS/HIPIIS, pp. 138-158.

Singarimbun, Masri and David H. Penny (1976) *Penduduk dan kemiskinan: kasus Sriharjo di pedesaan Jawa*, Jakarta: Bhratara Karya Aksara.

Slamet, Ina (1965) *Pokok-pokok pembangunan masyarakat desa*, Jakarta: Bhratara.

—— (1988) *Views and Strategies of the Indonesian Peasant Movement on the Eve of its Annihilation in 1965-66*, The Hague: Institute of Social Studies.

Soedjatmoko (1980) "Dimensi-dimensi struktural kemiskinan", in Alfian, Mely G. Tan, and Selo Soemardjan (eds) *Kemiskinan struktural*, Jakarta: Pulsar/YIIS/HIPIIS, pp. 46-64.

Soejono, Irlan and Achmad T. Birowo (1976) "Distribusi pendapatan di pedesaan padi sawah di Jawa Tengah", *Prisma* 5(1):26-32.

Soekarno (1961) (orig. 1933) *Indonesia menggugat! Pidato pembelaan Bung Karno dimuka hakim kolonial*, Jakarta: Departement Penerangan / Percetakan Daja Upaja.

—— (1975) (orig. 1930) "Indonesia Accuses!" in R. Paget (ed.) *Indonesia Accuses! Soekarno's Defence Oration in the Political trial of 1930*, Kuala Lumpur: Cornell University Press.

Soemardjan, Selo (1962) *Social Changes in Jogjakarta*, Ithaca (NY): Cornell University Press.

—— (1980) "Kemiskinan struktural dan pembangunan", in Alfian, Mely G. Tan and Selo Soemardjan (eds) *Kemiskinan struktural*, Jakarta: Pulsar/YIIS/HIPIIS.

Sosrodihardjo, Soedjito (1955) "Preliminary report of social research in the Daerah Istimewa Jogjakarta", Yogyakarta: Gadjah Mada University.

— (1958) *Kedudukan pemimpin didalam masyarakat desa. Volume I*, Yogyakarta: Gadjah Mada University, Panitya Social Research.

Stoler, Ann (1975) "Some socio-economic aspects of rice harvesting in a Javanese village", *Masyarakat Indonesia* 2(1):51-88.

Strout, A. (1985) "Managing the agricultural transformation on Java: a review of the Survey Agro-Ekonomi", *Bulletin of Indonesian Economic Studies* 21(1):62-80.

Suharso, Pujo (2002) *Tanah, petani, politik pedesaan*, Solo: Pondok Edukasi.

Suhendar, Endang and Y. B. Winarni (1998) *Petani dan konflik agraria*, Bandung: Akatiga.

Suhendar, Endang et al. (eds) (2002) *Menuju keadilan agraria*, Bandung: Akatiga.

Tjandraningsih, Indrasari and Popon Anarita (2002) *Pekerja anak di perkebunan tembakau*, Bandung: Akatiga.

Tjondronegoro, Sediono M.P. (1995) "Indonesia's social science agenda: a personal view", in Leontine Visser and Nico Schulte Nordholt (eds) *Social sciences in Southeast Asia: from Particularism to Universalism*, CASA Comparative Asian Studies 17, Amsterdam: Free University Press, pp. 59-78.

Törnquist, Olle (1984) *Dilemmas of Third World Communism: Strategic Problems in Soekarno's Indonesia*, London: Zed Books.

Utami, W., and John Ihalauw (1973) "Some consequences of small farm size", *Bulletin of Indonesian Economic Studies* 9(2):46-56.

van der Kroef, Julius (1960) "Agrarian reform and the Indonesian communist party", *Far Eastern Survey*, January, 5-13.

Vink, G.J. (1941) *De grondslagen van het Indonesische landbouwbedrijf*, Ph.D thesis, Wageningen Agricultural University.

Vries, E. de (1931) *Landbouw en welvaart in de regentschap Pasoeroean. 2 vols.* Wageningen: H. Veenman & Zonen.

Wahono, Francis (ed.) (2002) *Hak-Hak asasi petani dan proses perumusannya*, Yogyakarta: Cinderleras Pustaka Rakyat Cerdas.

Wertheim, W.F. (1959) *Indonesian Society in Transition: a Study of Social Change*, The Hague & Bandung: W. van Hoeve.

Wertheim, W.F., and G.H. van der Kolff (eds) (1966) *Indonesian Economics: the Concept of Dualism in Theory and Policy, Volume VI*, The Hague: van Hoeve.

Wharton, C.R. (1959) *The US Graduate Training of Asian Agricultural Economists*, New York: The Council for Economic and Cultural Affairs.

White, Ben (1989) "Java's green revolution in long-term perspective", *Prisma* 48:66-81.

— (2000) "Rice Harvesting and Social Change in Java: An Unfinished Debate", *The Asia Pacific Journal of Anthropology* 1(1):79-102.

— (2002) "Agrarian debates and agrarian research in Java, past and present," in Gunawan Wiradi, E. Suhendar, S. Sunito, M.F. Sitorus, A. Satria, I. Agusta, and A.H. Dharmawan (eds) *Menuju keadilan Agraria: 70 tahun*, Bandung: AKATIGA, pp. 41-82,

—— (2004) "Java and social theory: agrarian debates, past and present" in Hans Antlöv and Jörgen Hellman (eds) *The Java that Never Was*, Berlin: LIT Verlag.

White, Ben and E. Hastuti (1980) "Different and unequal: male and female influence in household and community affairs in two West Javanese villages", Bogor: Agro Economic Survey, Rural Dynamics Study, Working Paper no. 6.

White, B., and Gunawan Wiradi (1984) *Agrarian Reform in Comparative Perspective*, The Hague: Institute of Social Studies.

—— (1989) "Agrarian and nonagrarian bases of inequality in nine Javanese villages" in Gillian Hart, Andrew Turton and Ben White (eds) *Agrarian Transformations: Local Processes and the State in Southeast Asia*, Berkeley: University of California Press, pp. 266-302.

Wiradi, Gunawan (1999) "Tinjauan ulang istiqarah/wacana agraria" in *Laporan penyeleggaraan dialog merumuskan arah dan strategi reformasi agraria*, Bogor: Institute Pertanian Bogor.

—— (2000) *Reforma agraria: Perjalanan yang belum berakhir*, Yogyakarta: Insist, KPA, Pustaka Pelajar.

-6-

THE POLITICAL ECONOMY OF HIGHER EDUCATION: THE UNIVERSITY AS AN ARENA FOR THE STRUGGLE FOR POWER

Heru Nugroho

Higher education, both during the period of the New Order as well as in the *reformasi* era, has several unresolved issues. These issues include the grip that the government bureaucracy had on higher education, its increasing costs, the marginalization of the poor, the low quality of education, research and publications, as well as an underdeveloped academic culture. In 2000, *Asiaweek* reported that even the most prestigious universities in Indonesia ranked below most other universities in Asia. The University of Malaya and the Putra University in Malaysia were ranked 47 and 52 respectively while the University of Indonesia and Gadjah Mada University ranked 61 and 68 respectively.

Perhaps the words *universitas magistrorum et scholarium* can be used to define the normative function of higher education. A university is not defined just by impressive buildings set on acres of land, but by the organization of human beings engaged in academic activity. The university is where scholars come together to seek academic truth and to advance their individual capacities through each of their academic disciplines. The university is also an institution where scholars have the responsibility to teach students, to exchange ideas through discussion, debate, publications and polemics, based on the results of their research. The concept of the university does not just refer to its existence as an object, but rather to its existence as a process. The university is a place for the meeting of minds of the members of the *civitas academica* and is not only defined by the dimensions of time, space or place.

Ironically, even now, academic activities such as serious education, sustained research, the continuous development of critical perspectives, or sustained scholarly debates are not apparent. Lecturers who have graduated with higher degrees are not busy with academic activity but only with teaching and research that can produce instant rupiah, that is, activities that hold the promise of economic benefit. Research and teaching are no longer carried out as the duty of an academic, but take the form now of "projects" aimed at bringing in money, whether in small or large amounts. These projects either supplement one's income or constitute one's primary source of income.

Project activity is evident in the mushrooming of seemingly unconventional or non-mainstream education. These would be in addition to the usual degree courses available at most universities such as diploma programs, B.A. extension courses, M.A. programs such as special classes, long distance classes, or through the opening of regional branches. Such activities can be very profitable for the lecturers involved in them. The new policy on higher education autonomy for the University of Indonesia (UI), Gadjah Mada University, Bandung Institute of Technology (ITB) and the Bogor Institute of Agriculture (IPB), which will make them State Owned Legal Bodies (*Badan Hukum Milik Negara* – BHMN), have implications of financial independence. These policies have turned education into a moneymaking business activity. The time and energy of a majority of lecturers are now taken up with these teaching activities because it is the way they can save themselves from the confines of the small salaries they receive as civil servants. Serious research is only carried out by a small number of lecturers who are motivated, or who have contacts with external sources of funding. Even then, most of this research is research that will instantly make money and not research that will produce serious academic results. So it is not surprising if there is infertility of thought and intellectual involution.

Academic culture, that should be the mainstay of activity in higher education, seems to be have disappeared, overshadowed by the fervor with which the *civitas academica* strive to enrich themselves economically. There is little incentive to become a lecturer producing serious work and distancing oneself from material things, termed "asceticism" by Weber. Academics are more interested in teaching and research activities that generate profit, or in securing bureaucratic positions on-campus, such as those of university vice-chancellor or president, dean, heads of centers or assistants to the heads. If the academic has strong "social-political" networks, he can seek positions within the government apparatus, for example as expert adviser to ministers, the main aim being to increase one's access to power in order to increase one's income. The situation of higher education in Indonesia is like that of a "toothless tiger". On the one hand, the universities are admired because of the idealism associated with them; on the other, academic authority and status have greatly declined.

The scholastic ideals of higher education have been reduced to economic and political functions. It is true that higher education practices everywhere are multi-dimensional, a mix of social, cultural, political, economic, amongst others. But one has to remember the *Tri Dharma*, or Three Functions, of universities, namely the provision of educational, research and social benefits. Higher education today is no longer a platform for implementing the *Tri Dharma*, but one that involves the struggle for political and economic resources. The major stakeholders are the state, market and the *civitas academica*. The erosion of the spirit and ideals of higher education is a cultural tragedy that threatens the very existence of Indonesian society in the global context.

Before seeking a solution that will awaken higher education in Indonesia and help it to attain a level of international competence, it is necessary to describe the factors that have contributed to this erosion.

STATE, MARKET AND HIGHER EDUCATION

The experience of the developed capitalist countries provides us with the information that higher education has become an arena for the struggle between the state and the market. The form of government of a country determines the extent to which higher education is controlled by the state or is integrated into the market. According to Charles Lindblom:

> ...the greatest distinction between one government and another is in the degree to which market replaces government or government replaces market. One is social organization through the authority of government. One is social organization through exchange and market.
>
> Lindblom 1977: 4

If a country adopts a centralistic economic system, then higher education will tend to be under the subordination and made one of the instruments of state power. The state intervenes in higher education policy on the understanding that the state covers all costs. The price of education is kept low to ensure that all citizens have access to it. In a liberal economic system, higher education is significantly influenced by market mechanisms. There is a tendency for the cost of education to be high with the result that poorer sections of the community would need some form of subsidy if they are to have access to it.

These two "state versus market" models are the extreme variants. In reality, there is more overlap between the two forms. This overlap creates the mixed economy, that is, a mixed economic system that accommodates both socialist and capitalist perspectives. It can create the privatization of education on the one hand, and protection for poorer citizens on the other. According to Gosper Esping-Anderson, the mixed economy has a number of variants classified as regimes of welfare capitalism (Esping-Andersen 1999). There are three forms of this regime, namely, conservative, social democratic and liberal, which base their policies on market mechanisms whilst, at the same time, providing assistance to citizens who do not directly benefit from these market mechanisms. These policies are called de-commodification, and include things such as welfare payments and affordable public services.

In several Western European countries, the policy of de-commodification has made higher education affordable for all its citizens; while in the USA, higher education remains expensive, but scholarships are available to the poor giving them the opportunity to attend private universities. These countries are now also experiencing a wave of privatization imbued with the spirit of neo-liberalism. Variations in the de-commodification policies have not had an influence on the quality of education, the quality of research or its applications in these countries. Even neo-liberal policies maintain the de-commodification of higher education, keeping these countries at the forefront of research and higher education.

Indonesia has adopted a duel system of education. There is a state system of higher education that is fully funded by the state and a private system that receives only partial subsidization. Because the New Order system was authoritarian, the state intervened in both these systems. After *reformasi*, political democratization and economic liberalization came into play. In the education sector, the *reformasi* governments implemented the policy of autonomy for institutions of higher education by changing the status of state tertiary institutions to BHMN or state-owned legal bodies. This status means that they can now raise additional funds directly from the general public. Indeed, several experts have emphasized that quality education is expensive. This helped to legitimize the BHMN policy, although it has meant an increase in university fees, and incited public protests because the policy marginalizes the poor, effectively closing off their access to higher education.

The facts show that tertiary institutions in Indonesia are more an arena for political games between the state, the market and the *civitas academica* than a gathering place for academic activity. The change to campus autonomy has not really done anything more than institute a change from state tyranny to market domination. The reality is that the *civitas academica* has not been able to critique the social marginalization that has resulted from this policy. During the New Order, the tyranny of the state brought benefits to those academics that were loyal to the state. Now in the era of campus autonomy, academics are benefiting from the education and research business, so that again they are failing to take a critical position towards this policy. The problem of the poor quality of higher education, a legacy of the New Order, has still not been solved. The weakening of academic culture, which has had a negative impact on the quality of higher education, is a cumulative result of state intervention, the pull of the market and the political games of the academics alongside the weak work ethic of society-at-large. The policy of changing the status of universities to that of BHMN appears to be a negative development characterized by moral hazards, such as the commodification of higher education.

HIGHER EDUCATION IN THE NEW ORDER AND REFORMASI PERIODS

In practice, institutions of higher education do not exist in a vacuum, but are influenced by the social conditions that surround them. The experience of the industrial countries shows that higher education, which is independent of the state and therefore free to determine its own academic activity, has the ability to innovate and take critical attitudes. Such institutions do not become instruments of the state, but in fact become instruments of criticism and are a source of ideas that are beneficial to the broader social and state interests. For example, many major universities in the USA have established centers for Southeast Asian studies with state funding but without state intervention in their activities.[1] Research results produced by such centers are typically used by the US government to formulate policies relating to Southeast Asia. This situation changes once there is a centralistic and authoritarian government. An authoritarian system of government tends to make higher education subservient to state power, which in turn results in bureaucratization, the domestication of scholarly activity and the curtailing of academic freedom.

The state of higher education during the New Order is an example of a high degree of state intervention in national interests. During that time, higher education was subordinate to the state and its task was to support state policies. The fact that higher education was primarily government-funded meant that all research, education and civil service programs had to comply with state development policies. As a result, educational institutions, which ought to have been criticizing the phenomenon of developmentalism, failed to do so. This is because the majority of

---

[1]   This information is from an interview with Dr Bambang Cipto, a lecturer at the Muhammidiyah University in Yogyakarta. He stated that: "In America there are Centers for Southeast Asian Studies. They receive very large funding from Congress, and there are many of these centers. So there must be support from the legislature to ensure that higher education can act as an optimal agent for change."

lecturers preferred to serve the government in return for economic and political gains: economic gain in the form of additional income, and political gain in the form of positions in the government bureaucracy.

The Pancasila ideology was used to enforce hegemony in all aspects of life. In the case of higher education, academics who openly challenged Pancasila or refused to accept it as the sole ideology faced the prospect of being stigmatized as communists. Working within this single ideology was the preferred option. Many were involved in P4 Training (*Pedoman Penghayatan dan Pengamalan Pancasila* – Upgrading Course on the Directives for the Realization and Implementation of Pancasila), which provided substantial additional income as well as extended the networks necessary for achieving upward mobility into the government bureaucracy. Lecturers who held certificates as P4 trainers would find it easier to secure positions in government departments. This was because they would be considered loyal to the rulers. The phenomenon of Pancasila as a sole ideology turned the P4 Training programs in the universities (both state and private) into economic and political activities.

For appointment as a lecturer, both in state and private institutions, the requirement was either a P4 certificate or proven participation in programs including classes on the Pancasila doctrine as the sole ideology. Most of these pre-appointment programs were about the doctrines of how to be a good civil servant, about loyalty to the state, and discipline and obedience to the central government.[2] Candidates were given three chances to pass pre-appointment tests. A pre-appointment certificate was essential for a Candidate Civil Servant (*calon pegawai negeri sipil* – CPNS) to be appointed a full civil servant (*pegawai negeri sipil* – PNS). Candidate lecturers in private universities were caught in the same trap in that such a certificate was also a pre-requisite for appointment as a PNS *Kopertis* lecturer on secondment to a private university. There were two categories of lecturers in the private universities, those with PNS status and those without. Those with PNS status were seconded to private universities by the government as part of the *Kopertis* program to advance private universities. Non-PNS lecturers were employees of the foundation responsible for setting up the private universities. Lecturers employed by such foundations also had to have received P4 Training in order to be appointed lecturers. In this way, the New Order's domination was not only over PNS lecturers, but also lecturers who were, in effect, private employees.

---

[2]   The use of a dominant state ideology as an instrument of hegemony and domination is not confined to New Order Indonesia and former communist countries but also occurred in ancient China. Weber (1920) stressed that Confucianism was an ethical doctrine that all government employees must know and practice (see also Schroeder 2002).

There were some academics, albeit a minority, who criticized the government's policy of turning Pancasila into a business project. These academics were, invariably, economically and politically marginalized by the government. However, in most cases, they had socio-political networks that extended beyond the government. These networks gave them alternative, non-government economic and political resources that they could utilize. Such critical academics were often not interested in the research projects ordered by government departments and preferred projects commissioned by non-governmental organizations (NGOs) and international networks. This community of "rogue" academics, which was critical of the government, sought their funding from independent sources such as Ford Foundation, Asia Foundation and Toyota Foundation, through international academic cooperation and so on. These academics were usually more productive in terms of research and contributing to academic publications.

There were also the ambivalent academics. They were, at times, critical of the government, and at others not. This type of academic was often stigmatized as an opportunist scholar. They wanted respect from their "leftist" colleagues, and they wanted to assure the government that they loyally supported its programs. The reasons for this ambiguity can, in the end, be traced to their concern for continued access to economic resources. They wanted to be considered for projects or bureaucratic recruitment on the one hand, and retain legitimacy as critics on the other. This is how these ambiguous academics survived in the Soeharto era, although in the *reformasi* era, many became "free riders" and emerged as *reformasi* figures on renowned campuses.

To consolidate state domination over higher education institutions, the New Order implemented a "de-politicization" of the campuses, the so-called Normalization of Campus Life (*Normalisasi Kehidupan Kampus* – NKK), a doctrine of social order in higher education institutions. Students were forbidden from carrying out political activities. They were forbidden from taking to the streets because it would disturb the political stability of the government. What was stressed was that they should study, graduate as quickly as possible and obtain suitable work. The NKK policy changed the role of members of the *civitas academica* in politics. It was marked by the disbanding of student councils and their replacement with student representative bodies. Marxist and neo-Marxist thinking, which struggled for justice and defended the interests of the poor, were prohibited from being taught. The government stressed that institutions of higher learning were part of the government bureaucracy. Therefore, bureaucratic positions on the campuses such as university presidents (and their assistants) and deans (and their assistants) were political rather than academic appointments. Such political appointments had to be approved by the central government, in this case, the Minister for Education and Culture. Although there were institutions that elected their own university presidents and deans, the government had veto rights. The centralized system of state power was replicated in the universities with ultimate power being in the hands of the university president.

Although political change towards democracy has now taken place, the education bureaucracy has not changed significantly. University organization remains substantially the same as under the New Order, where the president is the ultimate power, with decision-making and veto rights. Further, the university president is essentially an extension of the power of the Minister for National Education, that is, the government. The procedure for appointing a university president or dean remains the same: elected candidates must be approved the Minister. As between BHMN and non-BHMN institutions, there have been some minor changes in procedure. In non-BHMN institutions, potential candidates are nominated by the University Senate, which then sends the nominations and its recommendations to the Minister for National Education. In BHMN institutions, candidates are also nominated by the Senate, but candidates with the three highest numbers of votes then stand before the University Senate (*Majelis Wali Amanat* – MWA) for election. The Minister sits on the MWA and wields 35 percent of the voting rights. As such, the election of a university president in a BHMN institution is still greatly influenced by socio-political networks.

The policy of campus autonomy whereby a university is independent of state power remains, sadly, merely an ideal. *Reformasi* has started the process of democratization, but the changes have yet to filter into higher education institutions. The process is hampered largely by academics who have goals other than the advancement of higher education.

CURRICULUM, STATE INTERVENTION AND CONFUSION IN A TIME OF TRANSITION

It can be said that higher education had more autonomy under the Soekarno government than that of the Soeharto era. In Soeharto's opinion, this autonomy was the cause of Indonesia's political instability. History has shown that, in addition to the military, the student movement, manipulated and managed by the Armed Forces, played an important part in the toppling of the Soekarno government. The New Order regime was fully aware of the political usefulness of the student movement, and therefore instituted very tight controls over higher education through the de-politicization of university campuses. For example, curricula were designed in accordance with government guidelines. The aim was to mould the consciousness of the students, ensuring that they chose to work for rather than against the government. The result was that students adopted a pragmatic approach to education: pass the examinations, graduate and get a job quickly.

The Soeharto government's intervention in the curriculum began in 1968 when the then Ministry for Education and Culture moved to standardize all curricula across the country. In 1970, the Directorate of Higher Education initiated the formation of consortia for each of the different subject areas. These consortia were to formulate national curriculum standards. With the availability of major funds, these efforts produced concrete results. In 1979, a significant change was made in the education system; course lengths or durations, previously calculated according to years, were changed to a system of credit points. The new system shortened the study time for students. One of the reasons for the change was that it was thought the old system wasted a lot of time and created "perpetual students".

Although these consortia produced many benefits for curriculum development in higher education, they grew less energetic over time. In the 1980s, their activities were hampered by a decrease in government funding. The reason for this decrease was that the government had already achieved its aims, namely of dominating and intervening in higher education. As a result, the consortia were no longer of any use to it. The interesting thing to note here is that these curricula became the mainstay for universities throughout the country. Even now in the *reformasi* era, these curricula, which some feel are no longer appropriate, are still used by most tertiary institutions.

The general definition of a curriculum is: a collection of subjects formulated into an educational program aimed at achieving a specific outcome. The normative outcome of an ideal curriculum comprises the ability to think for oneself, to master the relevant skills or expertise, and to have a critical outlook. But a curriculum is more than just a collection of subjects; it also includes content, method, orientation, composition and a system of assessment. The various consortia had succeeded in formulating national curricula that had become the references in the various fields of study. The subjects that had been formulated in the National Curricula were divided into different categories: General Basic Subjects (*Mata Kuliah Dasar Umum* – MKDU), Specialist Basic Subjects (*Mata Kuliah dasar Keahlian* – MKDK), Specialist Subjects (*Mata Kuliah Keahlian* – MKK) and Supporting Subjects (*Mata Kulian Penunjang* – MKP).

For both the social and natural sciences, 7 percent of the curriculum, had to include MKDU. MKDU comprised subjects such as Religion, Pancasila, Civics and Basic Culture (for those in the natural sciences disciplines) and Basic Sciences (for those in disciplines outside of the natural sciences). Religious education was provided in every discipline so that students would develop a high moral character, honesty and conformity. It was hoped that if the students were taught to behave in a certain ordered manner, political instability could be avoided. The irony was that this religious education worked against the teachings, appreciation and practice of pluralism. As the teachings in this subject tended to be normative, students were placed in socially exclusive religious groups. As these normative teachings taught "good" and "evil" according to each belief, the net result was that this system of teaching tended to work against the possibility of religious harmony. Perhaps this was the outcome that the government desired. If a pluralist and critical spirited religion was taught, it could have stimulated a critically spirited religious social movement. As such, religion could not have been used as a political instrument of the government. Such a development represented a threat to the power of the authoritarian regime.

The subject Pancasila was aimed at educating students in each of the five *sila* or principles. A normative Pancasila human being was a religious person, who respected the meaning of humanity, was aware of the unity of Indonesia, and who was democratic and socially just. The unfortunate thing was that the institutions of higher education that should have held freedom of thought and the test of logic in high esteem were faced with a doctrinaire system of teaching Pancasila. As the state ideology, Pancasila could not be criticized and was taught as if it was an irrefutable truth. Anyone who disagreed with the compulsory teaching of Pancasila in the institutions of higher education was considered to have strayed. Even worse, that person would be labeled a communist; a label that often brought with it dire consequences. Reference material on Pancasila was even borrowed from the discipline of philosophy to prove that Pancasila was an indigenous product. There were no critical philosophical studies to refute this claim. As a result, this state ideology became something of a "civil religion".

MKDK and MKK accounted for 93 percent of the curriculum and were compulsory for all disciplines. The relevant consortia determined the core subjects for each discipline. For example, the following subjects were decided upon for sociology: Introduction to Political Science; The Indonesian Social System; Classic Sociology Theory; Modern Sociology Theory; Sociology Research Methods I and II; Development Sociology; and The Sociology of Industry. There were two subjects that the state considered important and strategic in its efforts to achieve domination. These were The Indonesian Social System and Development Sociology. Similar subjects to these were not only prescribed for the discipline of sociology but other

---

[3] Subjects with the aroma of development became very important accompanying the hegemonic developmentalism of the government. However in an interview with Drs Solatun, Msi, he emphasized that for Ph.D students at Padjajaran University, while development subjects were important in a normative sense, this was not true in the case of all students. For those choosing inter-disciplinary

disciplines as well. For example, the Indonesian Communication System[3] and Sociology of Communication were also subjects in Communications. The economics consortium had also devised the subjects Indonesian Economic System and Development Economics. The Indonesian Social System subject was intended to convince students that there was a need for national integration so that, in the future, there would not be a danger of disintegration. However, this subject was artificial because empirically, there is no Indonesian social system. This was a subject that had been devised "by order" from the state, through a consensus in the consortium. It took on more of an ideological character. This was the same for the Sociology of Development, which should ideally have also included a discussion of the Sociology of Underdevelopment. But, because discussion of topics such as dependency and underdevelopment originated from leftwing thinking, the regime did not want them taught in the universities. The government was seeking academic justification for its policies and as a result every social sciences discipline had to discuss development. By "discuss", I mean lectures had to provide an academic defense for development, not a platform to criticize it.

With the onset of *reformasi*, the *civitas academica* realized that the old curricula had become out-of-date and needed revision. Unfortunately, academe was not equipped to make the revisions due to a lack of resources at the local level. Further, there was the argument that a national curriculum was necessary to ensure uniformity between departments and faculties in the various universities. The current national curriculum, called the core curriculum, has been revised to constitute only 40 percent of core credit points. However, there still lacks a consensus on the core subjects that form the core curriculum. Having said that, the decision should and must lie with the academics, and not the government. A core curriculum must be developed by experts in their respective disciplines, working in cooperation with one another, and putting aside competitive egotism.[4]

FROM ACADEMIC TO ADMINISTRATIVE AUTHORITY

One significantly negative impact of the New Order's implementation of de-politicization was the transformation of the academia into an administrative component of the ruling regime. During Soekarno's rule, universities had political autonomy as well as freedom in terms of administration and academic life. The primary result of making the campus a part of the political administration of the government was that it was no longer an autonomous academic arena but an extension of the government bureaucracy. The militaristic leadership structure of the New Order meant that the campus came under government command. The command structure in the education bureaucracy was clear in the hierarchy of authority: President, Minister for Education and Culture, Director General of Higher Education, University President, Dean or Head of Studies Centre, Head of Department or Head of Studies Program or Head of Laboratory, lecturers, and students.

This was an administration pyramid. Universities were only authorized to make decisions relating to the administration of their departments and faculties. Other decisions like major promotions, for instance, had to be made at the highest level in the Ministry of Education and Culture. For example, a lecturer who was prime for promotion had to fulfill conditions set down by the Minister. To be promoted from Level III/a (the entry level for a young lecturer) to III/d, the candidate's qualifications had to be examined and approved by a team in the university. But for a promotion to Level IV/a, that is, to the position of a full-fledged lecturer, up to Level IV/e, or that of Professor, authority rested in the hands of the Minister. Indeed, the letter of appointment of a professor had to be signed by the president. There have been several instances where fully qualified academics, with openly opposing views to the government's, have been by-passed for professorships. There have been other less compelling reasons for non-appointment; for example, refusal to don the official civil servants organization uniform, or non-attendance at 17 August commemoration celebrations. Further, whether or not one qualified for promotion was not a question of academic merit alone. It was not unheard of for a candidate's private life to be dragged into the discussion of promotion. In short, it was an arbitrary system of evaluation, one highly dependent on with whom one found favor.

This is a form of militarization of the organization of higher education.[5] Umar Kayam once described higher education in Indonesia as a "government bureau". This government bureau, in the guise of a university, was headed by a university president who, more likely than not, took no interest in the scholarly pursuits of the institution. But he received the highest salary, up to five times that of a professor.

Today, professors in many of the world's renowned research centers and

---

[5]   The organization of universities in Indonesia is identical to military organization with the university president as commander and the professors and heads of laboratory as corporals. If an academic organization was implemented, then the opposite would be the case with the president as the corporal implementing orders issued under the academic authority of those running the laboratories (Pedju 2002).

universities do not take up administrative positions. They prefer to remain as scholars and, in any case, such positions are more prestigious than administrative positions. Here in Indonesia, however, it is the administrative positions over which people fight. This is a result of the feudal culture and also flows from all the allowances and perks that are attached to these positions. The motivation to become a campus bureaucrat has more to do with increasing one's income than with academic achievement. This, in turn, has contributed to a situation where academic authority is subordinate to administrative authority, a situation that influences the way in which policy is decided. Campus officials often confuse the academic and administrative authority that they possess, with the result that academic policy is often made by campus bureaucrats exercising their administrative authority.

RESEARCH: THE STRUGGLE FOR POWER

One way in which the state exercises control over higher education is through the provision of research funds and research *pembinaan* (cultivation or guidance). *Pembinaan* is carried out through the government bureaucracy, namely the Directorate General of Research and Community Service. Its task is to provide guidance/help in developing research areas and to distribute funds to the Research Institute (*Lembaga Penelitian* – LEMLIT) in each university. In each LEMLIT there is a research commission that must assess all proposals that it receives. Supervision of the approved research proposals is also carried out by the LEMLIT. The LEMLIT commission can suggest improvements and/or amendments to the proposals, but its role is really that of a conduit, passing proposals on to the Director General for final approval – especially so if the Director General provides funding for the research. If the university funds the project, then it is the LEMLIT that decides which proposals are accepted and which are not.

In the case of a university funding its own research, it is "community funds" that are used. These are essentially fees paid by the students. The LEMLIT is, in this case, responsible for both the administration and supervision of the approved research projects.

Funds are also set aside for research at the faculty level. The amount varies according to the number of students enrolled. The funds are not allocated in a competitive manner, but allocated to all staff on a basis agreed within the departments. The funds are intended to help promote academic activity, such as to enable staff to increase their credit points for research that is required for promotion. But it is often the case that the only real motivation is the money itself and not the advancement of quality of research.

Research funds that do not originate from the central government or from student fees are offered through LEMLIT or the various university study centers. [6] This means that the bureaucratic hierarchy is not so relevant to funds coming from international donors or ministries proposing research cooperation.

There are other ways in which research activities can and do become the site of struggle over economic and political resources. Those with greater access to research have a greater economic capacity. They will also have the ability to form "cliques", a system of patronage that can also be used politically. Those who control research projects become "godfathers"[7] of sorts and can carry out a "social mobilization" of the academics involved. At the right moment, strategic persons can use this support for political purposes, such as swinging votes at when electing university presidents or deans.

A LEMLIT has no research staff. This body comprises only a chairperson, secretary and administrative staff. But this body has research commissions whose members come from the different faculties. Members of the commission receive a stipend if they attend meetings or are required to examine proposals as part of the selection process. This institution is not important in terms of the struggle over resources as the amount of money involved is not great and not very strategic. Although a LEMLIT is supposed to coordinate research in the study centers, in reality and in this era of BHMN, these centers are not subordinate to the LEMLIT. They have their own strategic leaders who have their own access to national and international funding.[8] Such "private" networks that can bring in money are also a political resource. The position of chairperson and secretary of LEMLIT are not economically lucrative, but are somewhat prestigious because they are a doorway to the university president, assistant rector, postgraduate program director and so on.

---

[6] Sources of funding for research through LEMLIT includes:
  1. Funds from the Director General of Higher Education such as competitive grants, grants for cooperation between institutions of higher education, postgraduate team grants, and funds from the Director General of Research and Community Service (competitive)
  2. Cooperation with government departments (competitive)
  3. Research funds from the university, such as that from the community through student fees and the routine university budget (not competitive)
  4. Research funds from overseas foundations such as Toyota, Sumitomo and so on (competitive)
[7] As expressed in an interview with Drs Purwanto, the head of the Sociology Department in the Faculty of Social and Political Sciences, Gadjah Mada University. He emphasized that a lecturer with a wide network and many research projects would become a "godfather". A system based on returning a favor develops as people are invited into research projects and receive monies that sometimes can be greater than their actual wages. Dr. Fathur Rochman, a senior researcher in the Center for Population and Policy Studies at Gadjah Mada University, has said that those that feel they have debt to repay because they have been invited to join in *proyek* (projects) can be used as political supporters and supporters of ideas and thus as a crony supporter.
[8] As stated by Haryanto, a civil servant working as an administrator at the UGM Research Institute.

The study centers are multi-disciplinary. Ideally these centers should realize the goal of breaking down barriers between disciplines. But this rarely happens in practice. Everything depends on who heads the center. Typically, researchers and specialists are recruited on the basis of friendship networks and not expertise. As a result, these study centers are run by people or groups of people who, if given the opportunity, are ready to move up the ranks into the campus bureaucracy. This can and does dilute the multi-disciplinary character and ideals of a study center. [9]

The study centers also obtain research funds from government departments, whether through cooperation projects, tenders or open competition. These funds are usually tied to departmental programs. Departments often want research done that will justify their programs. One example was a project funded by the Ministry of State for the Advancement of Women to research their operational efficiency and which intended to confirm the effectiveness of their programs as being in accord with the Broad Outlines of State Policy (*Garis-garis Besar Haluan Negara* – GBHN). When the research showed otherwise, the officials of the Ministry were angry. They were of the view that it defied logic that the research should target for criticism the very source of funding for the research (Nugroho 2001: 157-61).

Lecturers working in study centers are financially better off than those who teach in the faculties and who are not involved in S2 and S3 teaching programs. One need only look at the cars, houses and other material possessions of study center lecturers to appreciate the disparity. Whether or not a study center has a large range of research projects can be seen from the types and number of cars parked outside. The parking areas outside economic faculties with good research links outside the university are like luxury car showrooms. Every make of luxury car, including the latest models, are to be found there!

Not all lecturers become researchers in research centers based within the university.[10] There are many more lecturers who only teach. These are more dependent on the resources in the faculties. As a result, the competition for access to the economic and power resources at the faculty level is intense. Those who have contacts with research donors are few but they dominate the political game. The

---

[9] Sources of research funds available to studies centers comprise:
    1. Information from LEMLIT
    2. Research funds from within Indonesia, such as from government departments, companies and so on.
    3. International funds such as those from the Ford Foundation, Plan International, Pact Indonesia, USAID, UNESCO, and so on.
    4. Large centers will institute independent research projects for its staff.
[10] Dr. Fathur Rochman expressed this in Javanese: "wong sing ngekeki dhuwit aku, kok nuthuki aku" ("I have the money, yet they hit me").

way they build patronage and loyalty is by recruiting their juniors and colleagues for research projects, at the same time making them a part of their political constituency.

The political economy of the struggles around research produces four typologies of academics:

1. Lecturers who have networks with research donors who dominate the political economy of the faculty;

2. Lecturers who have networks but not very good ones, with the result that these lecturers are at times beholden to research project "lords", and at others independent;

3. Lecturers with insufficient or inadequate networks with research donors and who end up as subordinates to those with stronger networks. They usually take on positions such as assistant researcher; and

4. Lecturers who have no networks at all and have little interest in academic activity, seeking work outside of academe, for example, dabbling in sideline businesses such as the buying and selling of cars, land, and so on.

AUTONOMY AND THE COMMODIFICATION OF HIGHER EDUCATION

The relatively adequate funding provided to the universities during the New Order was not provided simply as an expression of the state's responsibility to the education sector, but was intended to placate it so as to prevent any opposition to its policies.

There are two types of institutions of higher education: state and privately run universities, both of which receive state funding, although to different proportions. State institutions receive more benefits both in terms of financial and non-financial facilities. Since private institutions do raise their own funds, the assistance they receive from the state tends to be more non-financial in nature. Several high profile state institutions such as University of Indonesia, Bandung Institute of Technology, Bogor Institute of Agriculture and Gadjah Mada University have become supervisors of the education activities in smaller universities, including new state universities or private universities. These supervising universities provide assistance in the betterment of the quality of education. In the case of private universities, supervising universities help in raising the status of a private university from the lowest category, that of a registered university, to that of a state university. This supervision and assistance can include seconding expert lecturers and other staff, providing training for researchers and so on.

In the 1980s, these four main universities established the Inter-University Center (*Pusat Antar Universitas* – PAU), whose aim was to assist marginalized state and private universities in obtaining more adequate academic resources. Besides arranging M.A. and Ph.D overseas education for staff, PAU also instituted upgrading training. PAU at times also provides research funds for specific projects. During the New Order, PAU obtained assistance from the World Bank through the Ministry of Education and Culture. For lecturers with doctorates in these four universities, PAU is another good source of additional income as well as a test-bed for new academic activities. The activities designed by PAU differ little from the government projects that bring with them a lot of money. Unfortunately, the presence of a PAU office at a university becomes the target of strategic struggles over political and economic resources.

Most of PAU's funds come from the World Bank. Postgraduates returning home with their doctorates and who ought to be carrying out serious research get drawn into PAU activities. Although they do not or might not produce anything very worthwhile, they are handsomely rewarded for their trouble. By channeling abundant funds to PAU, the government has succeeded in domesticating the youngest and brightest minds by drawing them into the *proyek* practice. Sadly for PAU, the post New Order period saw its importance fade. PAU is still in existence but it has ceased to play a strategic role in the ever-tenuous relationship between the state and higher education.

Although funds for education declined in the final days of the Soeharto government, it was still better than the situation as it is now in the *reformasi* era.[11] The cutback in funds and the new government's interest in the free market have resulted in a stagnant education sector. The government liberalized many aspects and sectors of life, including higher education. But, funds to develop education ran dry and the education sector was left to fend for itself. When the Minister for National Education made the announcement that some of Indonesia's universities were to be given BHMN status, similar to being a state owned corporation, the government was already officially in the process of reducing funding for higher education. The four universities whose statuses were changed were UI, ITB, IPB and UGM. Meanwhile, the University of North Sumatra (Medan), Padjadjaran University (Bandung), Diponegoro University (Semarang) and Airlangga University (Surabaya) are in process of attaining BHMN status. In this regard, it is entirely possible that the government will stop funding altogether.

---

[11] Sources of research funds at faculty levels in the advanced (BHMN) campuses comprise:
1. Funds drawn from student fees (SPP) (not competitive and tend to be distributed as set share)
2. Research co-operation with government departments and companies (not producing publications, only the reports for the bodies concerned)
3. International funds (Ford Foundation, Rockefeller Foundation, Plan International, USAID, UNICEF and so on)
4. Strategic persons who have networks that can access national or international funds.

If that happens, these universities will have to raise their funds directly from "the market", that is, they will have to "sell their wares". The most immediate result is that student fees will be severely hiked and this will further marginalize those who are already marginalized, that is, the poor and underprivileged.[12] Another potential problem is that the institutions that have recently obtained BHMN status, generally do not have any experience as private bodies having to seek their own funding. The speediest way to make money is to sell new educational programs, at all levels from extension to Ph.D programs. For example, an institution might start extension and higher diploma programs off campus.. There are now also part-time M.A. programs for those who work full-time, with courses organized as all-day courses on Saturdays and Sundays. In addition, diploma and degree undergraduates pay additional fees, apart from the basic student fees, including Contributions to the Advance for Education (*Sumbangan Pembinaan Pendidikan* – SPP); Operation and Maintenance Fees (*Biaya Operasional dan Pemiliharaan* – BOP); and an Academic Development Contribution (*Sumbangan Pembinaan Akademik* – SPA).

Because the BHMN universities are instituting new programs at every level, this has increased the competition in private universities. The BHMN universities have become "general stores"[13] selling every kind of merchandise, from sewing needles, to motorcycles to cars. To use another term, the process is one of the "McDonaldization of Higher Education"[14], with university branch offices and off-site campuses mushrooming everywhere, delivering instant education that can be purchased wherever and whenever. This McDonaldization of higher education follows four principles: quantification, efficiency, predictability, and "technologization". Quantification upholds the principle of the more graduates, the better. Efficiency refers to a belt-tightening process motivated by purely economic factors. Programs that make a lot of money, such as economics, technical courses, and so on, are developed and aggressively marketed, while courses in the humanities, with typically fewer sub-topics, are done away with. Predictability relates to connecting courses with the labor market in a kind of "link and match" process. Technologization refers to the implementation of hi-tech methods of teaching and course development.

It has to be acknowledged that the commodification of education has improved the material wealth of lecturers and other higher education employees. Just as

---

[12] As stated by Dr Bambang Cipto in an interview in Yogyakarta, March 2003.

[13] A term invented by Ki Supriyoko to describe the greed of the BHMN institutions (*Kompas*, 12 December 2002).

[14] The term McDonaldization has been taken from Ritzer (1996) to describe the process of irrational rationalisation in modern society.

McDonalds runs a delivery service that brings "burgers to its customers", so, too, do the universities with their "go to the client" divisions where lecturers travel across the country to conduct classes.

The commodification is not restricted to the education arena or, as some cynics call it, the "the degree market". It also extends to research, which is another funding resource. It also cannot be denied that with so many research contracts currently ongoing, researchers and their administrative staff are benefited materially. But with an abundance of research activity comes a corresponding drop in quality of the research and education being carried out.[15] Lecturers are kept busy with long teaching and research hours, motivated primarily by money. There is little or no time for self-reflection or contemplation. They have become factory workers who happen to have teaching skills. The researchers also become very mechanical researchers, with no self-initiated research oriented towards the advancement of knowledge.

The commodification of education is the cause of its own downfall. It has produced growth and the need to secure the greatest output possible. The BHMN policy had a rational starting point: autonomy to the universities for increased creative and critical freedom. However, it has instead produced irrationality, the further marginalization of the poor, dehumanization and a decline in the quality of higher education. This is the tragedy of higher education in the *reformasi* era.

THE STAGNANT ACADEMIC CULTURE

An academic culture can be defined as the system of values that is the basic reference for the behavior of the *civitas academica* in carrying out education, research and the practical applications of that research. An academic work ethic is also a necessary element of an academic culture. Academic activity comprises: (1) the transfer knowledge, sharpness of analysis and enlightenment; (2) untiring research to uncover truth and to push the boundaries of innovation; (3) the opening up of a sustained critical discourse that enables ongoing debate within the academic community, free of any enmity; (4) publication of research results;(5) the critical application of the results of research and thought to solving social and economic problems. Without a true academic culture, a university is a collection of impressive buildings set on acres of land.

---

[15] The decline in the quality of lecturers is a result of people being too busy with teaching, supervision, research and other activities driven only by the search for additional income. To achieve good results however what is needed is seriousness, concentration and enough time. This kind of opinion was put forward by Dr Dedy Mulyana, a post-graduate teacher at Padjadjaran University.

Ignas Kleden, wrote some ten years ago that the social sciences today have taken on the character or the life of a traditional market or bazaar (*Kompas*, 17-18 July 1995). Social scientists are the peddlers hawking their wares; they work alone, with no coordination and cooperation among colleagues, with the result that much of their work is duplicated by others. Further, they do not take the time to critically evaluate their work, resulting in collections of barren, unexcited and dispassionate studies. Kleden called this "bazaar intellectualism". If we observe the evidence closely, we will see that this was not a phenomenon of the New Order only. It continues today, even under a very different regime.

This bazaar intellectualism is manifested in the universities in all the hubbub of their activity, such as building new physical infrastructure, increasing the number of *civitas academica* from year to year, establishing research centers, and increasing the number of people with higher degrees and professorships. Scholars do not know what their colleagues are doing, except that they are involved in teaching, research and social service.

Compartmentalization is another backlash of commodification. The different disciplines have become increasingly exclusive and specialized, almost self-protectionist. This is because one's expertise or skill in a particular area of study or discipline has become one's primary source of income, the proverbial "rice bowl". For example, an economics professor might be offended if an anthropologist makes reference to markets without prior consultation with the economist.

Anticipating this trend towards compartmentalization, research centers were established, each focusing on a specific topic, including Environmental Studies, Women's Studies, Population Studies, Rural Studies, Cultural Studies, Tourism Studies, Southeast Asian Studies and so on. There are a number of normative goals set out for these centers. First, these centers are not set in a purely scholarly framework, but they are intended to have an engagement with reality, with the added ability to test and thereby improve their theories. Second, these centers are meant to break down the walls between the disciplines and forge an inter-disciplinary approach. Third, they are to prepare higher education institutions to work towards becoming research universities.

However, in reality, these mechanisms and institutions have not functioned in the ideal way for the university. There has been a tendency to avoid inter-disciplinary movement between campuses with the emergence of new walls alienating the different centers from one another, often with overlapping themes because they do not communicate with one another. Further, each self-funding center sees itself as the leader in its specific area of study. For example, women's studies should be carried out in an inter-disciplinary manner in Women's Studies Centers, wherever there is one, and not in other centers because this can result in a blurring of lines between the different areas of concentration between centers.

Another disturbing trend is that research centers have become overrun by dominant cliques with particular political inclinations. As such, an academic who has been active in one center will not be able to be active in others that do not share his political inclinations. This creates another barrier within the university that is not at all helpful to developing a scholarly community.

The low level of academic culture in the country now is a product of the mismanagement of the higher education system. During the New Order, the state was too dominant in intervening in our higher education system, while in the *reformasi* era the market is driving academic activity based on financial incentives. As a result, the *civitas academica* does not possess the academic work ethos and initiative that is befitting of scholars.

CONCLUSION

The development of higher education in the country cannot be separated from its cultural, economic and political context. Higher education has been an arena of competing demands between the state, the market and the *civitas academica*. This has been the situation that has contributed to determining the quality of academic endeavor. The most visible result of this is that higher education has betrayed its credo: namely the system's universities should be a place for academic endeavor, but its economic and political characteristics overshadow the academic. The result is that intellectual involution, characterized by infertile academic work, now prevails throughout our country.

During the New Order, higher education was an instrument of state power, which made it a part of the government administration and bureaucracy. The reproduction of the system of state power was reflected in the position of university president as the commandant of the university with supreme power outstripping the academic authority of the professors in charge of departments or laboratories. The subordination of higher education to the state resulted in academic authority being smothered by administrative authority. An academic's success was evaluated according to whether he had succeeded in winning administrative posts, and not his academic work. The curricula were also an area of intervention with the state forming consortia to formulate curricula that would support development and which were standardized into an official National Curriculum. Research also became a battlefield between the state, the market and academics as each sought to win control of the resources made available to the universities. The state provided funding in order to domesticate the universities and preempt any criticism. Meanwhile, the members of the *civitas academica* battled over access to research projects through patronage. Those with access to government or international donor funds were able to obtain social and political support from the client academics that they had invited to *proyeks*.

Higher education has experienced no significant change in the *reformasi* era. The government has responded to the global changes implementing privatization, namely with the policy of changing the status of the universities from state institutions to BHMN. Four universities (UI, ITB, IPB, UGM) considered to have the capacity to attract funds directly from society have been transformed to BHMN. This policy will be implemented gradually in relation to other universities with the goal of steadily decreasing government funding for higher education. The commercialization that began during the last years of the New Order has grown to fantastic proportions since the BHMN policy was implemented. The policy was implemented to contain the exploding cost of education in order to achieve a higher quality of education. Ironically, the result has been the commodification of all levels of higher education, from diploma programs through to higher degrees. Another by-product of the BHMN policy is the increased marginalization of the poor and a constricting of their access to higher education. Although the *civitas academica* has benefited financially from the policy implementation, there has been no corresponding improvement in the quality of higher education. As the atmosphere in institutions of higher education has not provided any stimulation to the *civitas academica* to strive for academic achievement, it has been as if such desires have been contained in their private realm. This is the prevailing state of higher education at the moment.

The reality shows that the pressure of the market on higher education has produced negative results. If a de-commodification of higher education accompanied by an administrative tightening is not embarked upon, higher education in our country will continue to drag its feet and will ultimately lose its ability to produce quality academic work.

BIBLIOGRAPHY

Esping-Andersen, Gøsta (1999) *Social Foundations of Postindustrial Economies*, Oxford: Oxford University Press.

Lindblom, Charles E. (1977) *Politics and Markets: The World's Political Economic Systems*, New York: HarperCollins.

Nugroho, Heru (2001) *Menggugat kekuasaan negara*, Surakarta: UMS Press.

Pedju, Ary Mochtar (2002) "Universitas, Organisasi Militer atau Akademik?" *Kompas*, 12 December.

Ritzer, George (1996) *The McDonaldization of Society*, Thousand Oaks (CA): Pine Forge Press (revised edition).

Schroeder, R. (2002) *Max Weber tentang Hegemoni Sistem Kepercayaan*, Yogyakarta: Kanisius

Weber, Max (1920) *Gesammelte Aufsätze zur Religionssoziologie*, Tübingen: J.C.B. Mohr.

-7-

THE CLASS QUESTION IN INDONESIAN SOCIAL SCIENCES

Hilmar Farid

A nybody who set out to write about the class issue in New Order Indonesia would have soon realized how sparse the available literature was on the subject. The dearth of reference material was so obvious that even a young undergraduate student, just starting on his studies on Indonesia, was able to make the observation (Levine 1969). Levine argued that the scholars of the 1960s were only interested in studying the daily politics of parliament, the political parties and government bureaucracy. Labor, peasants, unemployment, the urban middle class, traders and small landowners only ever appear in their writings as "the masses". Although Levine was referring to literature published in Australia and America, this criticism applies to Indonesian social sciences as well. Several years after Levine made this comment, Benedict Anderson, a prominent Indonesian studies scholar, said in passing that that there had been several works to "show that Levine's call (to pay more attention to class) had not gone unheeded" (Anderson 1982: 89). It is not clear what works he was referring to, but a simple search of the electronic databases or library catalogues will show that not one of the people to whom Anderson was referring might have been an Indonesian scholar.

Those who observe modern Indonesian history will quickly relate the disappearance of the concept of, and discourse about, class from the Indonesian social sciences to the rise of the New Order. While the destruction of class cleared the way for development (Farid 2000), repression in academe cleansed thought, accompanied by what one writer calls "dis-education" (Ward 1973: 75). The New

Order made sure that the concept of class disappeared by getting rid of the intellectuals who had used the term "dis-education". Further, it replaced all the terms that these intellectuals had used previously with new terms that the regime considered more appropriate. The result of this repression cut very deep, perhaps deeper than the regime itself expected. Writers and scholars began to compromise their stands, even as they thought about issues, avoiding sensitive terms and topics, and often, in the end, losing the ability to explain what they really meant.

The first part of this chapter examines the changes and discursive practices that began after the events of 1965-66 and that have contributed to the nature of the social sciences today. Anti-communism, the doctrine of development through growth and stability, the policy of "floating mass", the role of the United States and the idea of modernization that was born during the Cold War are all important in understanding the discursive formation of the Indonesian social sciences during the New Order. These issues have all had an important role in influencing what have emerged as concerns for scholars of the social sciences, such as low quality of research, the project mentality, the dearth of critical theory and the disappearance of important concepts such as class and gender.[1] Since the 1970s, a number of intellectuals have put forward criticisms of the dominant liberal perspective and have offered a "historical social science" as the alternative, which has, among other things, re-introduced the concept of class. This endeavor was relatively successful in challenging the dominant paradigm by exposing its political and ideological bias, but was unsuccessful in achieving a radical turn-around of what they criticized.

From an examination of studies and articles written in the "historical social science" mode and by comparing them with orthodox Marxist class analysis, I attempt in this chapter to formulate a class analysis framework that will be useful to get to "more than what just appears on the surface" (Levine 1969: 5). Contrary to the view that class is no longer relevant in this "post-everything" world, I want to show that an analysis of capitalism and class still has an important role, not only in understanding reality, but also in changing it.

THE NEW ORDER AND THE DISAPPEARANCE OF CLASS

The anti-communist mobilizations organized by the New Order rulers culminated in the dissolution of the Indonesian Communist Party (*Partai Komunis Indonesia* – PKI)

---

[1] The slander campaign about the castration of the generals at Lubang Buaya by Gerwani on 1 October 1965 was a culminating point in the New Order's instituting of control over sexuality and sexual politics in the coming period (Wieringa 2003). In the social sciences, the campaign resulted in the rejection, belittling and even humiliation of gender and sexuality studies which can be felt even today.

and the banning of Marxism by the highest state institution. To ensure that all radical political jargon was driven out of public discourse and of the academic world, the regime created new terms and then enforced their usage. The word *buruh* was banned and replaced with *karyawan* or *pekerja*, while *tionghoa* was replaced with *cina*.[2] In the social sciences, we also saw the emergence of generic concepts such as "the poor" or "low income groups" as replacements for workers or the proletariat. If these terms operated as euphemisms in public discourse, they had a deeper impact in the social sciences. These generic concepts had no analytical power, were politically empty and so strengthened the apolitical character of the social sciences during the New Order. This change also echoes the myth of the "breaking down of class delineation" that was very strong in the American social sciences at the beginning of the 1950s (Westergaard 1972). However, in the United States and Europe, this myth grew in the course of a long debate on class analysis that originated with Marxism. In Indonesia, the intelligentsia embraced the myth under circumstances where a political vacuum had been created by repression.

It is still not clear today how many social sciences scholars, teachers, researchers and students were killed, arrested, or exiled and unable to return to Indonesia since October 1965. But, given the extent of the repression and the tight control over the academic world, we can be sure that almost all intellectuals who upheld a radical egalitarian perspective were removed from the scene. As a result of this suppression, some campuses even suffered a deficiency in teaching staff (Danandjaja 1989: 390). Those that later returned from exile were usually not allowed to teach or continue their activities in the scholarly arena. Others who, for one reason or another, were unable to return played no role in the formation of social sciences perspectives in Indonesia.

These developments meant that academic life in Indonesia since 1965 has been dominated by intellectuals who supported the New Order, either because of ideology and politics or because of reasons of personal safety. Most of these people came from aristocratic backgrounds, were the children of small businessmen or civil servants, who had graduated from Dutch schools and who had continued higher education studies after independence (MacDougall 1975). As part of a rising elite after independence and because of their ties to the aristocracy, they had no interest in a radical change to the social order, especially not one that might threaten their

---

[2] TRANSLATOR'S NOTE: The replacement of the word *buruh* with *karyawan* was connected to the struggle for power between the left workers movement under leadership of the All-Indonesia Central Workers' Organization (*Sentral Organisasi Buruh Seluruh Indonesia* – SOBSI) and the military who had formed the All-Indonesia Central Employees' Organization (*Sentral Organisasi Karyawan Seluruh Indonesia* – SOKSI) as a rival organization (Leclerc 1972). The New Order paid special attention to the politics of language since the beginning of its rule and in the course of its rule several *keywords* emerged as important in strengthening its legitimacy (Van Langenberg 1986). "Cina" (Chinese) emerged as a pejorative term for Chinese during the New Order displacing the older, more neutral term, Tionghoa.

own position (McVey 1969: 10). Sharp division since independence over the direction of Indonesian development, made more intense as a result of the Cold War, pushed this group into the anti-communist camp that struggled resolutely to find a way to ensure that Indonesia did not fall into the hands of communists. Some of these people developed strong links with the military in the early 1960s, which later emerged as the military-civilian axis that overthrew Soekarno and established the New Order.[3] These people's presence not only presented a civilian face to the military regime, but also helped them work out concrete plans to seize power. A development plan based on the market economy and concepts of modernization provided the "scientific basis" for the anti-communist stance of then New Order rulers (Salim 1997; Sumawinata 1992).

This process proceeded slowly within the social sciences in the universities in the 1960s. In the first years after the repression, social sciences academics were primarily kept busy with technical issues, such as the shortage of teachers, the opening of faculties and social sciences programs in the different universities. There were only a few scholars with enough knowledge and confidence to be able to simultaneously pump anti-communist and anti-politics sentiments into their fields of study. The modernization theory thus emerged, not as one of several theories available to understand society, but as the one and only theory. In fact, it became the social sciences itself. The dream of a modern, rational and advanced Indonesia achieved through a market economy, combined with "bad" memories, implanted by New Order rulers, of a chaotic past rife with the danger of political radicalism, slowly nurtured a real belief in this "theory".

The concept of class clearly stood outside this belief because "there was a social and political cultural prejudice that our society was already very egalitarian" (Tjondronegoro 1997: 83). Society was pictured as an integral unit, where the division between the elite or leadership and the masses was not as a result of inequalities in the social structure. Rather, it was deemed to be the ascribed status steeped in history.[4] The absence of sharp conflict in the villages, after the mass killings petered out in the 1960s, strengthened the view that in any "normal" given situation,

---

[3] The role of these intellectuals was even more important because of the support they received from the United States. The United States had provided scholarships for economics and social science graduates to study in American universities. American government documents explicitly described this program as part of a "controlled experiment of modernization" to create "agents of modernization" that could transform Indonesian society into a modern and rational one (*Foreign Relations* 2001: 549-50). It stated, "moving Indonesians to an outside vantage point is undoubtedly the best way to show them the deficiencies in their own social structure and stimulate a desire for this change."

[4] These ideas were consistent with the organic state discourse developed by the New Order military and which became the point of contact between the social sciences and [state] power. The principle of

Indonesian society was harmonious despite the differences in income, work ethic and life situation. In these circumstances, the social sciences not only became a source of scholarly confirmation for government policy, but an integral part of it.

Uncertainty arose when the growth-oriented development began to harden social divisions. The New Order regime and the intellectuals who supported it were faced with a dilemma. On the one hand, their organic state discourse did not acknowledge class differences. On the other, in order to devise policies that ensured they maintained control, they had to acknowledge the existence of such differences and divisions. In industry, for example, the doctrine of partnership between worker and employer came into conflict with the regime's endeavors to implement labor laws that aimed for the protection of the latter's interests as against the former. When worker unrest emerged in the 1980s, the regime stuck to its concept of partnership claiming that the workers were being manipulated by radical groups that wanted to overthrow the government. Any disturbances in the organic state are always blamed on foreign groups, usually described as being alien to Indonesian history and culture. Differences within society itself would never lead to conflict because "it was not in accord with the basis of the state, namely Pancasila" (Moertopo 1980: 33-34). This view leads to a disastrous logical fallacy. A social reality exists or does not exist depending on state ideology, on whether the rulers and its supporting intellectuals want it to exist.[5] In this context, the replacement of the term "class" by "group", which flows from the argument that Indonesian society is egalitarian and does not have classes as in the West, is more than just the adoption of a euphemism; it is an *argumentum ad baculum,* which persists in public as well as in social sciences discourse.

An understanding of the thinking that flows from the architecture of the discursive formation must be informed as much by a study of what scholars say as what they do not say. Studies by New Order intellectuals of industry, for example, concentrate on issues of market, employment, investment and growth as well as the issue of whether

---

floating mass which was derived from the organic state discourse became the "scientific foundation" of the social engineering that was born from the modernisation theory. No figure better represents the alliance between intellectual scholarship and power than Ali Moertopo, an intelligence officer who played an important role in consolidating military power after October 1965 and also held a respected position as a New Order political thinker. His writings on accelerated modernisation became one of the primary narrations of the organic state discourse and development during the New Order period (Moertopo 1974).

[5] This *ad baculum* logic can be found in the pronouncements of public officials or in scholarly writings even today. Concern about gender inequality or discrimination is dismissed by the government and intellectuals, for example, because such inequality is "is not known in Eastern culture". Military killings in Aceh or East Timor never happened because it would be "contrary to the principles upheld by the military which hold human rights in high esteem."

society is ready and mentally prepared to enter the industrial era. Such studies are usually prepared as part of policy advice to decision-makers of government policies and development projects.[6] The seizure of land, enforced labor, the discrimination of women, violence and repression are not mentioned in discussions of the industrialization process. In fact, they are avoided. The New Order rulers aggressively indicated their objections to such studies and the intellectuals defended this attitude by describing these phenomena as "incidents" outside of the scholarly realm.

CRISIS AND CRITICAL SOCIAL SCIENCES

Discontent and dissatisfaction with the New Order had begun to grow since the early 1970s. Elements in the elite, intellectual and student strata, that originally supported the New Order, grew progressively uncertain of it because the modernization project did not appear to be proceeding as smoothly as originally anticipated. The strategy of technological diffusion, investment and strong leadership was not giving rise to modernity and democracy. Instead, the opening up of the economy to international trade and capital was helping to create a corrupt and authoritarian military oligarchy. There were two different responses from within the social sciences orthodoxy. The majority made a conservative turn and further stressed the need for political order alongside economic growth as the path to modernization.[7] In their view, pre-modern societies were not ready to receive a true distribution of power. They argued their case by showing the weaknesses of social leadership in village and traditional institutions, while also emphasizing the role of the military in accelerating modernization in Indonesia (Moertopo 1972). Others made the "criticism" that the modernization that was being implemented was based solely on Western values, when, according to them, there were many positive traditional values that could have been used to encourage modernization (Amman 1971; Mattulada 1979).

---

[6] The proximity of the social sciences and policy making was born from and then served to strengthen the alliance between intellectual endeavor or scholarship and state power that has been described earlier. The management of this alliance was completely in the hands of the government bureaucracy who decided on the priorities, time span and funding for this research as well as which researchers would be involved. Research institutions based in the universities were formally independent but were very dependent on government projects and had almost no space to develop independent, basic research (Abdullah 1983). Participating in research contracted by the government was considered far more important (though less prestigious) than producing internationally recognized academic work.

[7] This was development in the social sciences everywhere in response to the emergence of authoritarian regimes in the Third World. In order to give legitimacy and a scientific basis for US policy supporting Goulart in Brazil, Mobutu in Zaire, Pinochet in Chile and Soeharto in Indonesia, the bureaucrat-scholars wrote about the need for political order as the key to the success of modernization (Huntington 1968).

Sharper criticism emerged from outside the orthodoxy, in particular from the intellectuals and students who had been protesting against many of the government's development projects and policies (Budiman 1978; Akhmadi 1981).[8] They criticized the orthodoxy for blaming poverty and other social ills and problems on laziness and cultural backwardness (Soedjatmoko 1980; Siahaan 1983; Alfian et al. 1980). Inequality and poverty, including the social divisions of society, were a legacy of colonialism, which had not experienced any change after independence, but had led Indonesia to become a backward country dependent on international capital (Sasono and Arief 1981). As a criticism of the orthodoxy, some social scientists argued the need for a "historical social science" or a "critical social science" (Budiman 1983; Bulkin 1984).

The framework for this thinking was, however, united only as a criticism of the orthodoxy, in particular the idea of modernization, rather than a comprehensive agenda for research or a coherent theoretical framework. The analysis of the social basis of New Order authoritarianism brought the intellectuals in contact with the dependency theory and neo-Marxism. Debates over the state, such as that between Poulantzas and Miliband, and debates on the mode of production in the Third World colored discussions among students in many towns (see Heryanto's chapter in this volume). The concept of class entered these discussions making reference to a wide range of literature, beginning with Barrington Moore, Anthony Giddens, Louis Althusser and Mao Zedong. There were some initiatives, such as the formation of the Forum for Transformative Social Sciences (*Forum Ilmu Sosial Transformatif* – FIST), aimed at consolidating these discussions. However, they were short-lived and represented more an attempt to establish an intellectual opposition rather than a systematic and coherent intellectual project. The writers involved addressed various themes, which were deemed relevant, in a sporadic manner, but almost never attempted to synthesize their theoretical arguments or empirical research results. As such, these discourses never developed into a significant body of literature.

One of the most important "projects" to emerge from within this approach was the study of the middle class and its role in democratization. The critical intellectuals

---

[8] Within the establishment there were also discussions of poverty and inequality. However these phenomena were seen as "social problems" that (a) occurred naturally as a result of modernization and industrialization and (b) had not yet been addressed by appropriate government policies. There was a belief that a correct policy approach by the government would be the solution for every social problem and that the aim of social research was to identify those things that could be managed through policy. No development of any kind of critical thought or theory could develop because of the apolitical mentality that had been planted within the establishment since the beginning of the New Order. It became an "unstated belief" that objectivity resided in a neutral stance that chose to neither support nor reject any specific theories (Kleden 1984: 141).

saw the student movement, non-governmental organization (NGO) activities, and the social criticisms in the mass media and the arts as signs of the awakening of the middle class. As a result, they wanted to equip themselves with the theoretical tools to be able to understand and encourage this middle class movement to proceed further. Most of these studies attempted to understand the middle class through an examination of their incomes, lifestyle, language and social behavior. There were only a few studies that actually attempted to locate the middle class in the Indonesian capitalist system (Bulkin 1983; 1984; Kuntowidjojo 1985; Muhaimin 1985; Mahasin 1990; Heryanto 1990). Even among these more systematic studies, it was clear that there was strong motivation to discuss the middle class as an agent of change. There was little consciousness that the concept and term "middle class" was itself problematic, and there were few who were moved to examine this issue in greater depth.

In the meantime, the search for an agent of change received new impetus with the emergence of the concept of "civil society" (Budiman 1983). The discussion of the middle class subsided because, to paraphrase the words of Hegel: "All the cows were allowed to be grey". Differences between the classes and the tensions created by those differences were hardly ever mentioned again.[9] The concept of civil society became a powerful tool to expose the inequality in the relationship between state and society, whilst providing a scientific basis for anti-authoritarianism. But, this belief did not hold out for long. The collapse of a centralized state authority opened the way for many new and unpredicted trends: the emergence of militant ethnic and religious groups; the dominance of groups of armed thugs in politics; the emergence of communal violence and riots. Faced with this reality, many intellectuals turned back to some of the old axioms related to modernization theory and started to talk about "civilized society", as opposed to "civil society", pluralism, modern political ethics and good governance. These ideas were championed by a strange alliance of public intellectuals, civil society organizations, international financial organizations and business groups.

The NGO movement, student activists and some public intellectuals pushed the valorization of civil society in a different direction. They are, in general, very critical of neo-liberal globalization, foreign debt, international financial institutions and militarism. In their view, the civil society movement, is a viable alternative to

---

[9] There is a view that the middle class – especially the educated layer such as students and public intellectuals – are the 'advance elements' of civil society who can overcome major differences in the course of fighting authoritarianism. This view manifests in particular a serious gender bias because most of the educated layer since colonial times has been male. This view is saying that educated middle class males, because their education and knowledge can represent the interests of men and women form other classes. Such issues as this shows that in many ways "critical social science" has not moved far from the dominant paradigm that it wishes to criticize.

"building a new world" based on participation, respect for the autonomy of communities and a welfare-oriented economics. The inspiration for these ideas has been the new social movements, which stretch across classes, are not dogmatic and have a pro-people perspective. The dominant political form of action in this movement was advocacy and campaigns to raise the awareness of those being defended, and a section of the elite that shared similar concerns.

Although these two civil society movements have a very different theoretical basis and political orientation, neither gives an important place to class in social analysis or political discourse. For those holding a liberal or (neo-liberal) outlook, any discussion on class or class tensions is anathema. Those with a more critical outlook look upon political practice based on class as out-of-date and irrelevant in the face of an increasingly complex social reality. Both of these approaches, with their different emphases, are based on the premise that it is important to establish a new social contract with the rulers to decrease, not eliminate, injustices, support clean and authoritative electoral politics, and struggle to reform the political institutions. From the point of view of these perspectives, the alternative perspectives that emphasize class differences are out-of-date and only serve as obstacles to achieving the unity that is considered absolutely necessary to resist authoritarianism.

I hold the opposite view. In this increasingly "complex" situation, class analysis is relevant and can help to find a way out of the theoretical and political quagmire faced by the democratic movement. The first step necessary in developing a class analysis and discourse is to unpack the myths and doctrines that surround such analysis. The current of historical social sciences was relatively successful in unpacking the ideological baggage of the modernization theory and liberal thinking, but it did not advance at all in terms of starting a dialogue with Marxist tradition.

THE COLD WAR, CLASS AND MARXISM

The term "class" was part of the vocabulary of the nationalist movement since the beginning of the 20th century when its leaders came into contact with socialist activists from the Netherlands. The sharp inequalities between the native residents and Europeans, the presence of plantations and the colonial state meant that the class discourse over-lapped with a throng of concepts that were born out of the resistance to the foreign powers, such as *bangsa* ("a people" or sometimes "nation") and *rakyat* (the [oppressed] people).[10] It was the PKI and trade unions that began a systematic

---

[10] In 1870 the per capita income of native residents was 47.2 guilder as compared to 2,163 guilder per capita for Europeans, a ration of 1 to 46. In 1913 when socialist ideas started to penetrate the nationalist movement the ratio was 1:65 (Maddison 1989: 665). There were also differences in wages between

use of class analysis as they began to absorb Marxism, or more accurately the Comintern line, into the movement's discourse (McVey 1965; Shiraishi 1990). The closeness to the Comintern's class analysis and the tendency to proletariatize the nationalist movement became a serious issue and provoked a series of debates which sometimes led to splits (Farid 1994). The violent suppression by the colonial powers of the 1926-27 rebellion ended this process and transformed the nationalist movement.

The class discourse in Indonesia was always very influenced by the Marxist orthodoxy propagated by the Soviet Union under Stalin.[11] This orthodoxy changed Marx's thinking from a theoretical analysis of the antagonistic conflict between capitalist exploitation and workers struggle for emancipation into a theoretical justification for socialist accumulation and centralization of power. At the heart of this analysis was a teleological idea of a linear development of society. It was conceived that all societies in the world would develop from primitive communism, to slavery to feudalism and, eventually, to capitalism. The unending pressure from the forces of production meant that relations between parties and production life cycles or processes would undergo continual transformation. In capitalist society, this means smashing the worker-capitalist relationship that holds back the productive forces from moving society to a more advanced form, namely socialism.

Although there was contact with this orthodoxy in the 1920s, its influence on class discourse only strengthened in the 1950s. The first attempt at using this orthodox thinking to analyze the class situation in Indonesia in a comprehensive manner is contained in the book, *Indonesian Society and the Indonesian Revolution*, by the PKI leader, D.N. Aidit (1957).[12] Following the orthodox historiography regarding stages in the development of society, Aidit traced Indonesia's journey through primitive communism, slavery and feudalism. Colonialism prevented development to the next stage, that is capitalism, thereby creating a "semi-colonial and semi-feudal" country.[13] This course of development meant that Indonesia, like other former colonies, had a different class structure from the capitalist countries of

---

European and native workers which hindered the development of a movement that could bring the two together.

[11] This doctrine was known as Marxism-Leninism and was developed in the 1920s as the theoretical reference for many communist parties throughout the world (*Fundamentals of Marxism-Leninism* 1952). During the Cold War, this doctrine received a high dosage injection of *scientism* which elevated its status to that of a holistic science and the primary source of all knowledge.

[12] This work was originally intended as an educational resource for PKI members. Almost all party literature, including the writings of other party leaders, used this as a reference (*Partai Komunis Indonesia* 1962; 1964). Other theoretical works of PKI leaders, which were not great in number, show the closeness of their thinking to the orthodoxy (Aidit 1962a and b, 1964; Njoto 1962).

[13] This argument is the same as that put forward by Mao Zedong for Chinese society (Mao 1954). Almost all his understanding of pre-capitalist society and the division of society into classes was taken from

Europe. Aidit divided society into six main classes which were determined by their economic as well as social positions: feudal landlords, comprador capitalists, national bourgeoisie, urban petty bourgeoisie, peasants and proletariat. The rest of the analysis is mostly concerned with the potential, or lack thereof, of these classes to act as revolutionary forces. The dynamics of class conflict are virtually absent from this analysis because, as reflected in the PKI's politics, it cannot be a priority during national democratic struggle.

If we examine it closely, it is clear the PKI's class discourse was more tied to the political situation than to an analysis of capitalism. The "comprador bourgeoisie", for example, was used almost exclusively to refer to the anti-communist political forces, the Masyumi and the Indonesian Socialist Party (PSI). After these two parties were banned for their participation in the rebellion to establish the Revolutionary Government of the Republic of Indonesia (PRRI), this category disappeared from the PKI's discourse and was replaced by "capitalist bureaucrats", which was primarily aimed at state officials who were hostile to the party. The same approach can be seen in the party's analysis of class divisions in the village (Aidit 1964). This report, a result of research conducted in villages in West Java, based class categories not just on economic and social criteria, but also on political stands, so much so that it produced categories such as "good landlord" and "bad landlord"[14] (see also White, this volume). The PKI analysis appeared more as a political analysis using class jargon rather than as a class analysis of the political situation.

The Cold War situation, which divided the world into two camps, also strengthened state-ism, a concept that blurred class divisions in society. This, in turn, influenced the class discourse developed by the PKI and other radical organizations. As part of a front fighting imperialism, the leaders of the PKI more often espoused a radical nationalism rather than class struggle, where the revolutionary people were a part of the unit fighting imperialism and the remnants of feudalism. Indonesian society was divided into those who, alongside the government, opposed these two "forces of evil", and who therefore were a part of

---

this work. Some sections quote Mao word for word. Following Mao, Aidit drew the conclusion that the party could not struggle directly for socialism but would have to pass through a national democratic stage of struggle to liberate the country from imperialism and to eliminate the hold of the remnants of feudalism. Yet, differing from Mao Zedong who advocated armed struggle during the national democratic stage, the PKI believed that the struggle could be carried out as a peaceful, parliamentary struggle. This approach provided the scientific basis for the national front politics line it pursued until its destruction in October, 1965.

[14] This research was the only massive attempt by the PKI to understand social dynamics based on empirical observation. For the PKI leadership, especially Aidit, this research was an important step in strengthening the understanding of cadres of the village situation as well as a way of challenging the methods and findings of "bourgeois studies" (Mortimer 1975: 304).

the "people" no matter what their class origins or interests, and those who supported them. This shift in interpretation produced tensions inside the party, especially when Aidit announced that the class struggle must subordinate itself to national interests (Mortimer 1975: 160-3). This tension only emerged in the form of a critique after October 1965, when a surviving section of the party leadership wrote a self-criticism and exposed the "bourgeois" character of the party leadership and other mistakes made by the PKI in trying to understand the dynamics of class struggles.

As far as I am aware, no Indonesian social scientist has written a comprehensive study of the PKI's class analysis. Yet, almost all writers, whether because of academic integrity or security reasons, have wished to stress the differences they have with "Marxist orthodoxy" (Bulkin 1983, 1984).[15] A closer examination shows that their differences were more to do with terminology rather than substance. The historical social sciences stream, which attempts to reject all these orthodoxies, Soviet, Chinese or PKI, actually shares a fundamentally similar approach with these orthodoxies. They both make classifications that divide society into boxes or compartments they call "class". They start with an abstraction from reality by isolating the subject in order to analyze its form and content. This abstraction is then formulated as a "class" according to various criteria. The differences between the approaches lie more with the method and criteria used and the class schema that emerges from the attempts at classification. Marxism-Leninism states that class conflict is inherent in any schema and represents the primary contradiction that moves history, while liberal analysis and historical social science views conflict as resulting not only from class, but also from ethnic, national, religious and racial issues.

The similarities between the PKI class analysis and the historical social sciences stream can be seen through a comparison of how they each deal with the issue of the "middle class". For Bulkin, the middle class was a "social grouping in society comprising the intellectuals, students, newspaper editors, indigenous businessmen and merchants, lawyers and other professionals" (Bulkin 1984: 6). Mahasin sets the criteria for being

---

[15] In the Marxist tradition the tendency to produce a more complex class map comes from dissatisfaction with the bi-polar class analysis or three primary classes presented by Marx. This framework is adequate, they say, in understanding social divisions in a more complex society. There then sometimes develop the desire to go beyond classical Marxism with an analysis that is more 'scientific', sometimes using mathematical calculations on exploitation and class location. Ellen Meiksins has said that the motivation behind scientism comes from the wish to respond to attacks from neo-classical economics on class analysis as unscientific. There is a desire to give a "more scientific basis" to class analysis and Marxist theory. The proponents of scientism, such as Jon Elster and Erik Olin Wright who are quite well known in Indonesia, have tried to 'correct' Marx's ideas and Marxist theory, which had become misinterpreted during the Cold War as had happened in the New Order. They wanted Marxism to have equal status with other "respected" social sciences (Wood 1989: 75). However, while the intention was to produce a new sharper framework of thought, these efforts only brought Marxism closer to the liberal thought which was in fact its antecedent in the history of modern thought.

middle class as social origins in *priyayi* (aristocratic) families, rich peasants and small businesspeople, and especially differing culture and life styles (Mahasin 1990: 91). These ideas are not very different from those of Aidit who also used such criteria as political influence and social authority in his analysis of class in the villages (Aidit 1964). The categorization of intellectuals as part of the urban middle class because of their open outlook is not very different from the "progressive intellectuals", described by Aidit as a part of the urban petty bourgeoisie. This kind of classification often ends up making a fetish of categories that are not only weak in theory, but also politically problematic.

This kind of class categorization is usually used to stick a label on some or a group of people who share similar characteristics. The problem with this approach becomes apparent when it involves itself with a dynamic social reality. When Indonesia was hit by the economic crisis, thousands of "professional workers", who would ordinarily have been described as middle class, lost their jobs. If we follow this logic, these jobless middle class folk would then have become, even if only for a while, "classless" people because they had no work. Those who eventually did find low-paying jobs as taxi drivers, for example, would become members of the working class. If they opened a shop after receiving a capital injection from their capitalist parents, they would return to the "urban petty bourgeoisie". The same applies to the hundreds of thousands of workers who were dismissed and – if we follow Aidit's categorization – became the "petty bourgeois" because they no longer worked in a factory but maintained themselves by becoming some kind of operator in the informal sector of the large cities. Attempts to define classes this way come into difficulty when dealing with concrete reality. This is because the categorization approach is in a constant state of flux. Criteria of categorizations change so often that the categories themselves lose their meaning. Apart from not furthering an understanding of social dynamics, this approach is very much open to attack from mainstream views that it sets out to criticize.

The capitalist class schema provided by Richard Robison (1986) is not problem-free (Glassburner 1987). This schema is quite powerful compared to most class schemas produced by the historical social sciences stream in Indonesia and is useful in identifying the "who's who" in the New Order elite. However, his analysis faces the same difficulties as described earlier. For example, if it had to deal with the film and TV series industry, which is dominated by "Indian capitalists", a category which is not to be found in his class schema. In studies of other regions, there are many writers who have developed more coherent, complex and credible schemas compared to those available for Indonesia and Southeast Asia (Portes 1985, 2003; de Little 1992; Wright 1997). In the end, however, they all operate within the same framework and come up against the same theoretical problems. In other words, the issue is not the brilliance of a particular system of classification of classes, but rather the very attempt at classification itself.

Giving definite and certain categorizations to class differences based on various criteria can have serious consequences. In the Soviet Union, for example, Stalin used this approach as the basis for oppressing the "*kulak* class" or rich peasants that held back the revolution. In China, Mao Zedong's ideas about class became the basis for defining "enemies of the people" who later were to be punished in accordance with their anti-revolutionary class character during the Cultural Revolution.[16] In this context, a social class defined by a certain social aggregation is dangerous and can kill. As an analysis that can support a movement for change, a class categorization such as this can also be very misleading. For example, the labor movement in Indonesia has just been hit by a wave of mass dismissals that has left hundreds of thousands of people, including a large number of trade union militants, unemployed. If a tight class categorization is used, these newly unemployed persons are no longer a part of the working class. In which case, trade unions cannot (and should not) take up their struggle. Labor organizations today will face many difficulties in determining an organizing strategy in a time of "labor market flexibility" if they stick to using very rigid class concepts. Activists and trade union leaders, who struggle for certainty in employment and do not speak out against contract labor could end up a conservative force and, ironically, an obstacle to the development of the labor movement.

TOWARDS A CLASS ANALYSIS OF INDONESIA

The deadlock in the class analysis that has developed in Indonesia is rooted in two problems. First, there has been a failure to locate the discourse in an analysis of the capitalist system. Whilst claiming to emphasize the importance of history, the historical social sciences school exhibits many ahistorical traits. The teleological view that they adopt means that their primary reference is the degree to which a capitalist society has reached an ideal, fully developed or mature form and the failures it has experienced and obstacles it has faced in that regard. They are less concerned

---

[16] The film *To Live* directed by Zhang Zimou (1994) provides a comical depiction of the confusion that arose as a result of the categorization of classes during the Cultural Revolution. In one scene, the poor husband and wife protagonists of the film discuss the arrest of a neighbor, a local communist party leader, who has been accused of being capitalist for no clear reason, except that he was accumulating some valuable goods in his house. Worried that they too might be visited by a party official, they discuss which 'class category' is appropriate for themselves. Finally they completely convince themselves (because of the frightening prospect of arrest) that they are a part of the proletariat.

with how the capitalist system has actually grown and developed in reality. [17] The second problem has been the failure to understand the capitalist system itself. In this regard both the PKI and the historical social sciences school are not far removed from neo-classical political economy, such as is represented in the works of Walt Rostow, which are the mirror image of the Soviet Marxist analysis of the stages of development of society.

In his elucidation of the capitalist production process, Marx (1867) highlighted the mistake made by classical economics in confusing form with substance, and in viewing complex relations between humans as *things*. His whole explanation is an effort to pull apart this reification by analysis of the capitalist system element by element, beginning with the commodity as the most elementary form of prosperity in capitalist society. In his analysis, a commodity was not simply an object that was bought and sold, but a manifestation of the conflict between capital and labor, and so it was better appreciated as a social relationship. For Marx, the next most important question was how to understand how this form (and the relations underpinning it) grew and spread in society. He showed that this system was only possible through the imposition of work, where people are coerced to work and sell their labor power as a commodity. This coercion is inherent in capital, and throughout history, a struggle has existed between labor and capital to determine (a) whether this work can be imposed; (b) the intensity of the work being imposed; and (c) the price to be paid for this imposed work. The feature that differentiates the production of commodities under capitalism from pre-capitalist commodity production is that it is continuous and boundless. It is only through this imposition of work through the commodity form that capital is sustained and class divisions maintained.

Capital is not just a thing, but the totality of process as set out by Marx in the formula M-C-M, or in other words, a social relation in motion. This is an elementary point, but is often ignored both by orthodox Marxists as well as the critical social sciences stream in Indonesia. In their view, following the vulgar, classical economics that was actually criticized by Marx, capital is money, goods, machines and tools that are used in commodity production. Classes develop around the ownership of the means of production and they enter into conflict with one another when "who gets what" is decided unjustly or unfairly. For Marx, capital is a social relationship within which is embedded a contradiction, and which can only sustain itself by arranging all human activity into work that creates commodities. While political economy is satisfied with using economic growth figures or capital flows to measure

---

[17] This tendency can be seen, for example, in Yoshihara's (1988) writings on "ersatz capitalism" which have been very popular in Indonesian social science circles.

the growth of capital, Marx emphasized the importance of studying production and the appropriation of surplus in reality. "Capital", understood as money, goods, machines or tools, would not become capital without labor that would create value.[18]

This concept of class is used to understand the antagonistic relations in capital as a social relation. The division of society into classes is a pre-requisite for capitalist production, which is achieved through coercion, primarily the separation of people from the means of production and social reproduction, with the consequence that they must sell their labor power in order to live. This process took a long time in many places. Marx himself used the example of Britain where capitalism had achieved a more solid condition. Class, in Britain's case, is not something that appears like "the sun over the eastern horizon", as is often imagined in the classification method described earlier. Class is also not an abstract category that operates outside or across history, but a key concept in understanding capitalism. Marx's ideas and those of many writers outside the Soviet and Chinese orthodoxy who reject fetishizing categories and call for a return to class as an analysis of the capitalist system are a good starting point for the development of a class analysis of Indonesia. This is not the place to attempt a comprehensive explanation of the method that is required. I wish rather to focus attention on one crucial aspect of class analysis, namely class formation, which is rarely discussed in the critical social science literature in Indonesia. The discussion below will make use of several studies that either because of the inadequacy or adequacy can help in developing this starting point.

Robison's *The Rise of Capital* (1986) is often cited as the first effort to develop a class analysis of contemporary Indonesian politics. This book provides detailed information on the capitalist class, divided into four categories based on their differing relationships with state power. Critiques of this work often concern the empirical data used for the argument, or doubtful formulations regarding the various class factions or the extent to which the class analysis is useful in explaining economic policy changes (Glassburner 1987; Basri 1992).[19] However, the real problem with this work relates to class and capitalism. Robison focuses his attention on the

---

[18] This labor theory of value is an element in the thinking of Marx that has always attracted much controversy. One point of controversy has been the "problem of transformation" where Marx is considered to have failed – and to have been inconsistent – in explaining the transformation of surplus value created by labor into price and profit (Morishima 1973; Steedman 1977). Another more powerful criticism has been that which says that contemporary capitalism has created "new" forms of work and a heterogeneity of work that makes Marx's idea of the centrality of work in producing surplus and thereby the labor theory of value out-of-date (Offe 1985).

[19] Glassburner and Basri's critiques are based on neoclassical economic concepts, which were not discussed much in Robison's work. Interestingly to date there has been no response by Robison to these kinds of criticisms, which could in fact be easily demolished even from within their own perspectives on class and capitalism.

"capitalist revolution" brought on by the New Order that, according to him, created new classes, including a domestic capitalist class. The capitalist class' differing interests, political orientations and relationships with the bureaucracy meant that it experienced weakness and disunity from within long before the state did. Robison traces the origins of the weakness of this class back to colonial times. The colonialists had failed to provide the foundations necessary for the development of a strong capitalist class. Using a selection of historical data that backs his argument, he is able to present a description of the growth of the capitalist class in Indonesia and explain why this class was unable to play the major role traditionally played by the bourgeoisie in a capitalist society. But, this framework, in effect, works to his disadvantage in that he is unable to see the process and dynamics of the expansion of the capitalist system in Indonesia.

By focusing solely on the differences among the factions of the capitalist class meant that there was no discussion of the issue of the tension and conflict between the capitalist and working classes. The literal interpretation of his approach is that capital accumulation equals to the piling up of wealth, primarily money, which has been planted in a particular sector of the economy. With this approach, the key issues become the resources, relations and political patronage of the different factions of capital and their respective access to sources of finance. The way in which "capital" is realized as capital does not appear to him as problematic. His discussion of growth figures, international capital flows, the growth of exports and the manufacturing industry shows that Robison, as well as other writers of Indonesian social sciences, sees capital as an asset or thing caught up in *Verdinglichung* (Marx 1867: 76-89). To him, class formation is constituted by the consolidation of groups of people into various "categories" in accordance with criteria that have no connection with the antagonistic contradictions inherent in capital. His analysis of the "capitalist revolution" is totally centered on the process of policy change under the New Order, which was aimed at facilitating the return of foreign capital and encouraging growth, while the social order which forced people to become "a ready work force" before "capital" flowed back into the country and realized as capital, which further strengthened the order, was not touched upon.

Class analysis based on an understanding of capital as a social relation sees things differently. Capital accumulation does involve the gathering of money and assets on the hands of capitalists, but it also involves the accumulation of labor power, and more important, a strengthening of the social order that rests on the commodity form. What Robison called a "revolution" was also a revolution in the way of life of a great many people who were forced to work under the commodity form. "The missing chapter" in Robison's writings was then filled in by several other studies on the Indonesian working class under the New Order (Bourchier 1994; Hadiz 1997). Robison described the rise of capital, while the writings about industrial workers described the other side of the rise of capital, ignoring the latent tension and conflict between the two issues. Just as Robison explained the rise of the capitalist class as a result of the flow of foreign aid and capital into Indonesia, Hadiz states: "[The] new industrial working class is largely the product of Indonesia's increasingly important manufacturing sector." (Hadiz 1997: 111). But neither of them explains that "capital" can only be realized through forcing people to work under the logic of capitalism. Several indications that do arise in Hadiz's work are not discussed further and so the question of class formation is left undeveloped. The presence of a "cheap and docile labor force" (Deyo 1989; Hadiz 1997) is accepted as a reality in newly industrialized countries without any discussion on the process that results in people being "willing" to work under appalling conditions and for low wages. The separation of people from the means of production, commodification and accumulation of labor power in capitalist production is absent from their explanations, with the result that their analyses tend towards a mechanistic view of the working class as a by-product of industrialization.

Marx's discussions on *ursprungliche Akkumulation* (primitive accumulation), and on the expansion of capital as a social relation are very important for overcoming these theoretical weaknesses, and for a better understanding of their implications. Marx's concepts explain the historical basis for capitalist production in the separation of the producers from the means of production, thereby transforming the means of subsistence and production into capital while the producers are transformed into wage-workers (Marx 1867: 753). This process shows us that capitalist production, which now appears to be a natural phenomenon, actually achieved dominance through coercion, sometimes using very brutal methods. This *ursprungliche Akkumulation* is not something that happens just once in history. In Marx's words: "Once this separation is given, the production process can only produce it anew, reproduce it, and reproduce it on an expanded scale" (Marx 1858: 462). Resistance to this process and *disruption* to the capitalist production process always pushes capital to secure its continued existence by strengthening and renewing methods of domination.

The history of the rubber, tobacco and sugar industries in Java and Sumatra clearly illustrate the *ursprungliche Akkumulation* process (Stoler 1985; Elson 1986; Knight 1989, 1992; Breman 1989). The forced cultivation system in Java, the enforcement of the *koelie ordonnantie* and the *poenale sanctie* in Sumatra, which stipulated harsh penalties for workers who broke contracts, and the penetration of the money economy, were the colonial rulers' strategies for ensuring there was a

THE CLASS QUESTION IN INDONESIAN SOCIAL SCIENCES   185

ready workforce that could turn "capital" into capital. The most important thing here was not the value that was created. In fact, there are many studies to show that the money made during this period was not important in "capital" formation in the Netherlands (Maddison 1989; van der Eng 1998). The more important issue was the separation of the producer from the means of subsistence and means of production, in other words, the destruction of the pre-capitalist mode of production through forcing people to work in the commodity system in order to live. Repeated separation over an extended period becomes the basis for the continued development of capital.

The wave of violence that wreaked Indonesia in 1965-66, apart from being a crime against humanity, is an example of the *ursprungliche Akkumulation* in action (Farid 2000). It illustrates the other aspect of the "capitalist revolution" that Robison talked about. The mass killings were often accompanied by theft of land and property, and a condemning of the families that survived to a position of being "free labor".[20] The "PKI stigma" forced these victims and their families to accept any work there was no matter how bad the conditions. In exchange for work, their status as "ex-prisoner" or "PKI family" was kept secret. They formed a "cheap and docile labor force" in Indonesia. The New Order rulers used the "communist issue" as a tool to tighten their control over industrial relations and to overcome the resistance to the expansion of capital into the villages. During this time, the New Order re-introduced forced labor and physical repression of workers in places that previously played an important role in economic growth and the expansion of capital.

Ironically, as was the case with the *ursprungliche Akkumulation* in colonial times, the 1965-66 violence did not play an important role in the gathering of wealth and the formation of "capital" in the reign of the New Order. As Robison shows, "capital" was brought into Indonesia through aid and loans from overseas (1986; 1990). Be that as it may, following Marx's ideas on the capital as a social relation, these violent events played an important role in separating labor from the means of subsistence and means of production as a pre-condition for the realization of "capital" into capital. The system of industrial relations that was then enforced, with violence, made it possible for the expansion of intensification of capital. This does not mean that the New Order used slavery to achieve an accumulation of capital, although there was,

---

[20] The number of people killed in this sequence of violence was between 500,000 to one million people. Approximately the same number of people was arrested or accused of being communists and so became social and political pariahs (Budiardjo 1998). The number of people affected by these killings, indirectly as well as directly, including the families of victims or those accused of being communists, was between six and seven million.

in actual fact, some element of slavery involved.[21] Class formation in the New Order did not happen overnight but was a long drawn-out process that was very complex and can only be understood through close historical observation.

This analysis, taken further, will lead us to an understanding of the working class, which has so far been considered identical to laborers, or more specifically with industrial labor, who work for a low wage. An analysis of capital as a social relation shows that the most important factor in the formation of class is not the official status of a person, but the imposition of work that divides society into two categories: those who work under the commodity form and, those who oversee the process and reap the profits. Of course, in reality this is a very complex process. For example, in the plantations at harvest time, most of the workers who are recruited are peasants contracted for a fixed period of time. But, as Stoler has shown in her study of plantations in East Sumatra, the presence of the plantations had an impact on "the core of community relations and domestic organization" (Stoler 1985: 189). The capitalist system is a process that carries out a continuous division through the imposition of work, and which influences the whole of society by dragging all aspects of life into commodity production. The working class comprises not only those who sell their labor for a wage, but also those who create value and play a role in producing surplus even though they may not receive a wage.[22]

This analysis also has implications on thought and consciousness in Indonesia. Robison appears inconsistent on this question in a number of his writings (1982; 1985; 1986). In certain sections, he stresses the existence of a capitalist class. Yet, in others, he casts doubts on his own conclusions (Winters 1996). This uncertainty occurs primarily because Robison, as with many critical social scientists, locates his analysis within the framework of the nation-state, or Indonesia, when capital is, in fact, global in character. The attempt to find a "domestic capitalist class" tends to lead to absurd conclusions because it confuses the operational basis of capital with national identity. The category of "national bourgeoisie" used by Robison needs to

---

[21] In *Das Kapital* (1867) Marx repeatedly showed the importance of unpaid labor and all kinds of forced labor in the capital accumulation process. The idea that the capitalist system is fully based on "free wage labor" actually originates with the Stalinist interpretation of the stages in the development of society, which sees capitalism as a system that is completely different from the preceding systems. For example, the oil industry in Indonesia, one of the pillars of capitalist accumulation in Indonesia, always used state repression to secure industrial stability.

[22] Feminist theoreticians have taken up the issue of *unpaid labor* in the capitalist production system (Mies 1986; Federeci 1999). Several researchers have started on such studies in Indonesia although they have not yet provided detailed explanations of the contribution of *unpaid labor* in the process of capital accumulation. One major issue is that statistics – which are often a primary reference in studies of labor – have never recognized unpaid labor, such as that carried out by women and children, as work (Holzner 1992).

be redefined because many of the key figures he identifies in this category no longer exist in Indonesia. The differentiation between foreign and national capital is useful perhaps only insofar as understanding the different interests in relation to economic policy is concerned. However, it is of little use in terms of understanding the dynamics of capital.[23] Within the framework of the nation-state, the New Order formed a ruling class that played an important role in managing labor and capitalist production. But, in an international context, the function of the ruling class was that of watchdog and an extension of foreign capital. In neo-liberal globalization terms, nation-state borders are of little consequence to capital dynamics, notwithstanding that state institutions play an important role in securing the continuity of this system in the regions they dominate.

CLASS, THEORY AND POLITICS

The most fundamental theoretical implication of the class analysis framework discussed above is the need to rethink the disciplinary division, a concept strongly held in the orthodox social sciences in Indonesia.[24] The discussion above also shows the need for contributions to the study of class from all branches of the social sciences – from economics, sociology and political science – and law and criminology. A project such as this cannot be tackled in the realm of the orthodox social sciences because of their definite and fixed "boundaries". In other words, it is not only the strong anti-communist sentiment in intellectual circles in Indonesia that holds back class analysis, but also the division of the social sciences into different disciplines. Any serious study of class and capitalism in Indonesia must cut across these artificial boundaries. Given the strength of these divisions in the social sciences, perhaps what is needed is not only a rethinking but an unthinking to find a new basic paradigm (Wallerstein 1996).

Another issue is the embedded state-ism in the social sciences that is reflected in the nation state as a unit of analysis. This orientation is problematic since it directs discussions to national policy issues rather than to the concrete social reality where administrative borders are not always relevant. Analysis of class and capitalism in Indonesia has so far only busied itself with Java and Sumatra and has paid little attention to other areas, which are usually left to anthropology, so that even the

---

[23] Politically this kind of discussion is of more help to policy makers than the social forces seeking an alternative to the capitalist system. This perhaps explains why writing on contemporary Indonesian political economy has generally attracted the interest of bureaucrats, business people and middle class intellectuals rather than labor movement activists.

[24] The separation of social sciences into various disciplines was inherited from early 20th century trends in the United States and Europe (Wallerstein 1996).

claim of the analysis being "national" is dubious.[25] It is difficult at the moment to place Indonesia at a certain stage of development of society, whether merchant capitalist, agrarian capitalist or semi-industrial capitalist. This is not because Indonesia is a unique country, as is often absurdly put forward by social scientists trying to hide their inability to explain things, but because the tendency to categorize is, in itself, a mistake.

If we follow Marx's analysis about the different "phases" in the expansion of capitalism, Indonesia, as are many other countries, is experiencing different phases but all at the same time. Industrial manufacturing representing mature capitalism with clear and legally regulated labor relations, free wage labor and set wage standards, stands beside, and is connected with, *ursprungliche Akkumulation* that involves the theft of land and the introduction of other means of subsistence, as well as forms of enforced labor akin to human bondage and unpaid labor. Any analysis of Indonesia using the nation state as a unit of analysis must take into account the inter-relationships between the different phases in order to reach a satisfactory conclusion about class and capitalism in Indonesia.

This class analysis, based on the idea of capital as a social relationship, also has implications on the political agenda of any class-based political movement. In orthodox Marxism, the primary force used to confront capitalism is the working class and in particular, industrial workers who are considered to be the most able to organize themselves by virtue of the nature of their work. The most important task of this working class is to expropriate the means of production and establish a new social order without exploitation. The experience of the Soviet Union and China, as the two major proponents of the orthodoxy in the world, shows that these tasks have never been successfully carried out. The socialist order that was established certainly removed the bourgeoisie from political life as well as production, but it did not actually remove the heart of capitalist production: the endless imposition of work. Marx's analysis of class and capitalism clearly showed that the biggest issue with capitalism was not only how work was organized, but also how all aspects of social life was organized throughout the community. Class divisions do not end merely with the declaration of the formation of a workers state because what follows

---

[25] Studies of capital and state that stress the importance of "relative autonomy" of the state usually have policy making at the national level as the object of their study. At this level, the argument that the state bureaucracy is autonomous from the influence of factions of capital perhaps has some truth (although can be questioned if related to the capitalist class as a whole), but is of course incorrect as a generalization. In Papua and Kalimantan, for example, the giant mining and plantation companies not only influence government policy but also control and finance the instruments of state repression such as the police and army, which can be mobilized at a moments notice to confront any resistance to these corporations.

is the same organization of work only carried out by a new and different power.

The most important thing in class politics, therefore, is not the strengthening of the bargaining power of workers in the face of capital, but the elimination of relations that force people to work under the commodity form. This struggle, as shown by Marx, not only occurs under conditions of "mature capitalism", as imagined by orthodox Marxists and Indonesian critical social sciences, but in every phase of the expansion of capitalism. The peasants' struggle to defend their land from the take-over of capital is just as important as the struggle of workers seeking wage improvements or attempting to form cooperatives aimed at taking them out of the commodity system in order to fulfill their needs. The understanding of class based on the concept of capital as a social relation merely assists in identifying where these different forms of resistance overlap in their resistance to capital.[26] In present-day Indonesia, the struggle against the rule of capital is broken up into sectors, reflecting the inflexible approach to classification using strictly defined categories. A historical analysis, which can capture the dynamics of class conflict and can supercede this kind of categorization effort, is greatly needed if the current deadlock faced by many social and political movements is to be overcome.

CONCLUSION

The to-ing and fro-ing of the class discourse in Indonesia exemplifies the close connection between the social sciences and power. The arrival of the New Order, which opposed and suppressed class-based movements was accompanied by a cleansing of academic discourse on class concepts and by making public discourse on the subject taboo. However, it would be a mistake to think that suppression was the only obstacle holding back class analysis in the Indonesian social sciences. As in many former colonies, class concepts came up against other concepts arising out of struggles in society, especially the concepts of nation and the people. The PKI, as the main representative of a class-based movement in Indonesia, began to shift from orthodox Marxist ideas on class in the 1960s to a discourse based on "the struggle of the people against imperialism". It was the New Order that later accused the PKI of pretending to "advocate the class struggle", something that the PKI had, in fact,

---

[26] In an analysis of the French peasants at the beginning of the 19th century, Marx stressed the importance of the *dynamic collective self-activity* and strong community bonds in the class formation process (Marx 1851: 187). Contemporary Marxist theory develops this idea further when it talks about the *ruling class* as a class that is not always united by its socio-economic interests but by its political orientation to defending the disparity created by the capitalist system. The Indonesian military, for example, while having a hierarchy of rank that reflects "class" differences (from the point of view of income and influence) is a part of the ruling class in the domestic political context.

long abandoned. The New Order also demanded that people reject class analysis on the basis that it had been advocated by the PKI.

Facing the deadlock of the modernization paradigm, some social scientists developed the historical school of social sciences, or historical social sciences, which appeared to be a viable alternative more because of its criticisms of the dominant paradigm than the fact that it might have developed a research agenda of its own. This historical social sciences school was a part of the overall criticism by student activists and intellectuals of New Order authoritarianism and its development agenda. The discussion about class began with the search for an "agent of change" or other force that could face up to or take on the New Order. The belief in the importance of social structure in any political analysis pushed study and discussion to seek the social basis of democratization, and in particular, a more in-depth look at the middle class, which began to grow and wield its influence in the 1980s. The discourse on the middle class heralded a significant drop in discussions on the struggle against authoritarianism. It was during this time also that the concept of "civil society" was on the rise, further blurring class boundaries.

This analysis has shown that the social sciences are a fundamental part of social struggles and are not exempt from issues of political bias and interests. On the subject of political bias and interests, far too much emphasis and attention were given to the Cold War framework of capitalism versus socialism. As a result, the theoretical debate was stifled and the continuing political struggle hints at an apocalyptic tendency. In current liberal thinking or thought, the doctrine has emerged that "there is no alternative"; that there is nothing better to be achieved than that which has already been achieved by the capitalist system. At the other end of the spectrum, in orthodox Marxist doctrine, there is the slogan: Socialism or Barbarism. A class discourse based on historical analysis, including a study of both leftist and rightist orthodoxies, shows that there are, in reality, many alternative "fates" of the people.

BIBLIOGRAPHY

Abdullah, Taufik (1983) "Ilmu sosial dan peranannya di Indonesia", *Prisma* 12(6) 22-39.

Aidit, Dipa Nusantara (1957) *Masyarakat Indonesia dan revolusi Indonesia*, Djakarta: Jajasan Pembaruan.

—— (1962a) *Marxisme dan pembinaan nasion Indonesia*, Djakarta: Jajasan Pembaruan.

—— (1962b) *Sosialisme Indonesia dan sjarat-sjarat pelaksanaannja*, Djakarta: Jajasan Pembaruan.

—— (1964) *Kaum tani mengganjang setan-setan desa*, Djakarta: Jajasan Pembaruan.

Akhmadi. Heri (1981) *Breaking the Chains of Oppression of the Indonesian People*, Ithaca: Cornell Modern Indonesian Project, Translation Series.

Alfian, Mely G. Tan and Selo Soemardjan (eds) (1980) *Kemiskinan struktural: suatu bunga rampai*, Jakarta: Pulsar.

Alisjahbana, Iskandar, et al. (1985) *Komunikasi dan pembangunan*, Jakarta: Sinar Harapan

Amaluddin, Mohammad (1987) *Kemiskinan dan polarisasi sosial: studi kasus di desa Bulugede, Kabupaten Kendal, Jawa Tengah*, Jakarta: Penerbit Universitas Indonesia.

Amman, Paul (1971) "Tradisi sebagai dasar modernisasi", *Basis* 20(7):194-202.

Anderson, Ben (1982), "Perspective and method in American research on Indonesia," in Ben Anderson and Audrey Kahin (eds) *Interpreting Indonesian politics: thirteen contributions to the debate*, Ithaca: Cornell Modern Indonesian Project, Cornell University, pp. 69-83.

Basri, Muhammad Chatib (1992) "Catatan dari pergulatan ekonomi di Indonesia: sebuah upaya merambah pemikiran Richard Robison", *Ekonomi dan Keuangan*, 42(3): 235-262.

Bourchier, David (ed.) (1994) *Indonesia's Emerging Proletariat: Workers and Their Struggles*, Indonesia Annual Lecture Series, Clayton: Center of Southeast Asian Studies.

Breman, Jan (1989) *Taming the Coolie Beast: Plantation Society and the Colonial Order in Southeast Asia*, Delhi: Oxford University Press.

Budiardjo, Carmel (1996) *Surviving Indonesia's Gulag: A Western Woman tells her Story*, London: Cassell.

Budiman, Arief (1978) "The student movement in Indonesia: a study of the relationship between culture and structure," *Asian Survey* 18(6):609-625.

— (1983) "Ilmu-ilmu sosial a-historis", *Prisma* 12(6):74-90.

Bulkin, Farchan (1983) "State and Society: Indonesian Politics Under the New Order, 1966-1978," Ph.D thesis, University of Washington.

— (1984) "Kapitalisme, golongan menengah dan negara: sebuah catatan penelitian," *Prisma*, 13(2):3-22.

Caffentzis, George (2002) "On the notion of a crisis of social reproduction: a theoretical review," *The Commoner*, 5:1-22.

Cleaver, Harry (1979) *Reading Capital Politically*, Austin: University of Texas Press.

— (1986) "Karl Marx: Economist or Revolutionary?" in Suzanne W. Helburn and David F. Bramhall (eds) *Marx, Schumpter & Keynes*, Armonk (NY): M.E. Sharpe, pp.121-146

— (1989) "Work, value and domination: on the continuing relevance of the Marxian labour theory of value in the crisis of the Keynesian planner state," Austin (TX).

Colleta, Nat J. and Umar Kayam (eds) (1987) *Kebudayaan dan pembangunan: sebuah pendekatan terhadap antropologi terapan di Indonesia*, Jakarta: Yayasan Obor Indonesia.

Collier, David (ed.) (1979) *The New Authoritarianism in Latin America*, Princeton (NJ): Princeton University Press.

Danandjaja, James (1989) "Antropologi", in Manasse Malo (ed.) *Pengembangan ilmu-*

ilmu sosial di Indonesia sampai dekade '80-an, Jakarta: Pusat Antar Universitas Ilmu-ilmu Sosial UI and Rajawali Press, pp.277-401.

de Angelis, Massimo (1995) "Beyond the technological and the social paradigm: a political reading of abstract labour as substance of value", *Capital and Class*, 57:107-134.

de Little, Daniel (1992) "Interest, class and identity: microfoundations for Asian studies", paper presented to the Association for Asian Studies, April 3.

Deyo, Frederic (1989) *Beneath the Miracle: Labour Subordination in the New Asian Industrialism*, Berkeley: University of California Press.

Elson, Robert E. (1986) "Sugar factory workers and the emergence of 'free labour' in nineteenth century Java", *Modern Asian Studies*, 20(1):139-174.

Farid, Hilmar (1994) "Mencipta Bahasa, Menemukan Bangsa: Politik, Bahasa dan Nasionalisme," *Kalam* 3:24-36.

— (2000) "Clearing the ground for *pembangunan*: the mass extermination in Indonesia, 1965-66," paper presented at the conference 'The Politics of Identity in Contemporary Indonesia', University of Tasmania, 8-9 December.

Federici, Silvia (1999) "Reproduction and feminist struggle in the new international division of labour", in M. Dalla Costa and F. Dalla Costa (eds) *Women, Development and Labor of Reproduction: Struggles and Movements*, Trenton (NJ): Africa World Press.

Fine, Ben (2001) "The continuing imperative of value theory", *Capital & Class*, 75: 41-52

Glassburner, Bruce (1987) "Book review: *Indonesia, the Rise of Capital*", *Bulletin of Indonesian Economic Studies*, 23(3):109-112.

Hadiz, Vedi R. (1997) *Workers and the State in Indonesia*, London: Routledge.

Heryanto, Ariel (1990) "Kelas menengah Indonesia: tinjauan kepustakaan", *Prisma* 19(4):53-67.

Hindley, Donald (1964) *The communist party of Indonesia 1951-1963*, Berkeley: University of California Press.

Holzner, Brigitte (1992) "Gender dan kerja rumahan", *Prisma* 21(3):35-60.

Huntington, Samuel (1968) *Political Order in Changing Societies*, New Haven (MA): Yale University Press.

Kleden, Ignas (1984) "Kritik teori sebagai masalah ilmu sosial," in *Krisis ilmu-ilmu sosial dalam pembangunan di dunia ketiga*, Yogyakarta: Pusat Latihan, Penelitian dan Pengembangan Masyarakat, pp.139-154.

Knight, G.R. (1989) "Sugar, peasants and proletarians: colonial Southeastern Asia 1830-1940," *Critique of Anthropology* 9(2):39-63.

— (1992) "The Java sugar industry as a capitalist plantation," *Journal of Peasant Studies*, 19 (3-4):68-86.

Koentjaraningrat (1974) *Kebudayaan, mentalitet dan pembangunan*, Jakarta: Gramedia.

— (ed.) (1975, 1979) *The Social Sciences in Indonesia*, 2 vols, Jakarta: Lembaga Ilmu Pengetahuan Indonesia.

Kuntowidjojo (1985) "Muslim kelas menengah Indonesia dalam mencari identitas, 1910-1950", *Prisma* 11:35-51.

Leclerc, Jacques (1972) "An ideological problem of Indonesian trade unionism in the sixties: 'karyawan' versus 'buruh'", *Review of Indonesian and Malaysian Affairs* 6(1):76-91.

Levine, David (1969) "History and social structure in the study of contemporary Indonesia", *Indonesia* 9:5-19.

Lukman, M.H. (1960) *Tentang front persatuan nasional*, Djakarta: Jajasan Pembaruan.

MacDougall, John James (1975) "Technocrats as modernizers: the economists of Indonesia's New Order," Ph.D thesis, University of Michigan.

Maddison, Angus (1989) "Dutch income in and from Indonesia 1700-1938," *Modern Asian Studies*, 23(4):645-670.

Mahasin, Aswab (1990) "The santri middle-class," *Prisma* 49:91-96.

Mao Tse-tung (1954) "The Chinese Revolution and the Chinese Communist Party," *Selected Works of Mao Tse-tung*, London: Lawrence and Wishart.

Marx, Karl (1851) "The Eighteenth Brumaire of Louis Bonaparte," in *Marx and Engels Collected Works*, Vol. 11, New York: International Publishers, 1969.

—— (1867) *Das Kapital: Kritik der Politicshen Oekonomie*, Volume I, Berlin: Dietz Verlag, 1957.

—— (1858) *Grundrisse der Kritik der Politische Oekonomie*, Berlin: Dietz Verlag, 1953.

Mattulada (1979) "Pengaruh tradisi dan modernisasi dalam pembangunan masyarakat desa di Indonesia", *Wawasan* 1(2):19-24.

McVey, Ruth T. (1965) *The Rise of Indonesian communism*, Ithaca: Cornell University Press.

—— (1969) "Introduction," in Soekarno (1926) *Nationalism, Islam and Marxism*, Ithaca: Cornell Modern Indonesia Project.

Mies, Maria (1986) *Patriarchy and Accumulation on a World Scale*, London: Zed Books.

Morishima, Michio (1973) *Marx's Economics*, Cambridge: Cambridge University Press.

Mortimer, Rex (1975) *Indonesian Communism under Soekarno: Ideology and Politics, 1959-1965*, Ithaca: Cornell University Press.

Muhaimin, Yahya (1984) "Politik, pengusaha nasional dan kelas menengah Indonesia," *Prisma* 13(3):63-72.

Moertopo, Ali (1972) *Dasar-dasar pemahaman tentang akselerasi modernisasi pembangunan 25 tahun*, Jakarta: Center for Strategic and International Studies.

—— (1980) "Hubungan perburuhan Pancasila sebagai manifestasi falsafah Pancasila di bidang perburuhan," in Suntjono (ed.) *Hubungan pemerintah, pengusaha dan buruh dalam era pembangunan*, Jakarta: Yayasan Marga Jaya.

Njoto (1962) *Marxisme: ilmu dan amalnja*, Djakarta: Jajasan Pembaruan.

Notosusanto, Nugroho (1974) "The historical development of the dual function of the Indonesian armed forces," *Indonesian Quarterly* 3(1):64-73.

Offe, Claus (ed.) (1985) *Disorganized Capitalism*, Cambridge (MA): MIT Press.

Partai Komunis Indonesia (1962) *ABC Revolusi Indonesia*. Djakarta: Jajasan Pembaruan.

—— (1964) *Bagaimana masjarakat berkembang*, Djakarta: Jajasan Pembaruan.

Portes, Alejandro (1985) "Latin American class structures: the composition and change during the last decades", *Latin American Research Review* 20(3):7-39.

—— (2003) "Latin American class structures: their composition and change during the neoliberal era", *Latin American Research Review* 38(1):41-82.

Robison, Richard (1978) "Toward a class analysis of the Indonesian military bureaucratic state," *Indonesia* 25:17-39.

—— (1986) *Indonesia: The Rise of Capital*, Sydney: Allen and Unwin.

—— (1990) *Power and Economy in Soeharto's Indonesia*, Manila: Journal of Contemporary Asia Publishers.

Rosen, George (1985) *Western Economists and Eastern Societies: Agents of Social Change in South Asia, 1950-1970*, Baltimore: John Hopkins University Press.

Saad-Filho, Alfredo (2002) "Production, exploitation and control: value relations in capitalist society," Working Paper, Department of Development Studies, University of London.

Sadli, Mohamad (1993) "Recollections of my career", *Bulletin of Indonesian Economic Studies* 29(1):35-51.

Salim, Emil (1997) "Recollections of my career", *Bulletin of Indonesian Economic Studies* 33(1):45-74.

Sanit, Arbi (1981) *Sistem politik Indonesia: kestabilan, kekuatan politik dan pembangunan*, Jakarta: Rajawali Press.

Sapiie, Soedjana (1974) "Transfer of technology, a proposed solution for Indonesia", *Indonesian Quarterly* 3(1):37-59.

Sasono, Adi and Arief Sritua (1981) *Indonesia: ketergantungan dan keterbelakangan*, Jakarta: Lembaga Studi Pembangunan.

Shiraishi, Takashi (1990) *An Age in Motion: Popular Radicalism in Java, 1912-1926*, Ithaca: Cornell University Press.

Siahaan, Hotman M. (1983) "Tekanan struktural dan mobilisasi petani di pedesaan", *Prisma* 12(11-12):50-63.

Soedjatmoko (1980) "Dimensi-dimensi struktural kemiskinan", *Prisma* 9(2): 66-75.

Steedman, Ian (1977) *Marx after Sraffa*, London: New Left Books.

Stoler, Ann Laura (1985) *Capitalism and Confrontation in Sumatra's Plantation Belt, 1870-1979*, New Haven: Yale University Press.

Sumawinata, Sarbini (1992) "Recollections of my career," *Bulletin of Indonesian Economic Studies* 28(2):43-53.

Sutrisno, Lukman (1980) "The sugar industry and rural development: the impact of cane cultivation for export on rural Java, 1830-1934", Ph.D thesis, Cornell University.

Tan, Mely G. (1973) "The role of sociologists in social development: the Indonesian case", *Masyarakat Indonesia* 1(1): 39-43.

Thompson, Edward P. (1968) *The Making of the English Working Class*, London: Penguin Books.

Tjondronegoro, Sediono M.P. (1997) "Agenda ilmu sosial Indonesia: tinjauan pribadi," in Visser, Leontine and Nico Schulte-Nordholt (eds) *Ilmu sosial di Asia Tenggara: dari partikularisme ke universalisme,* Jakarta: LP3ES.

van der Eng, Pierre (1998) "Economic benefits from colonial assets: the case of the Netherlands and Indonesia 1870-1958," Research Memorandum (GD-39), June.

van Langenberg, Michael (1986) "Analysing Indonesia's New Order state: a keywords approach", *Review of Indonesian and Malaysian Affairs* 20(2): 1-47.

Visser, Leontine and Nico Schulte-Nordholt (eds) (1997) *Ilmu sosial di Asia Tenggara: dari partikularisme ke universalisme,* Jakarta: LP3ES.

Wallerstein, Immanuel et al. (1996) *Open the Social Sciences: Report of the Gulbenkian Commission on the Restructuring of the Social Sciences,* Stanford: Stanford University Press.

Ward, Ken (1973) "Indonesia's modernisation: ideology and practice," in Rex Mortimer (ed.) *Showcase State: the Illusion of Indonesia's Accelerated Modernisation,* Sydney: Angus and Robertson, pp. 67-82.

Wennerlind, Carl (2002) "The labour theory of value and the strategic role of alienation," *Capital and Class* 77:1-21.

Westergaard, J. H. (1972) "Sociology: the myth of classlessness," in Robin Blackburn (ed.) *Ideology in Social Science,* London: Fontana, 119-163

Wieringa, Saskia (2003) "The birth of the New Order state in Indonesia: sexual politics and nationalism," *Journal of Women's History* 15(1):70-91.

Winters, Jeffrey (1996) *Power in Motion: Capital Mobility and the Indonesian State,* Ithaca: Cornell University Press.

Wood, Ellen Meiksins (1989) "Rational choice Marxism: is the game worth the candle?" *New Left Review* 177:41-88.

—— (1998) *The Retreat from Class: a New 'True' Socialism,* London: Verso.

Wright, Erik Olin (1997) *Class Counts: Comparative Studies in Class Analysis,* Cambridge: Cambridge University Press.

Yoshihara, Kunio (1988) *The Rise of Ersatz Capitalism in South-East Asia,* Singapore: Oxford University Press.

-8-

INCLUSION AND EXCLUSION: NGOS AND CRITICAL SOCIAL KNOWLEDGE

Meuthia Ganie-Rochman and Rochman Achwan

In the 1970s, during Soeharto's rule, critical social knowledge emerged as a reaction to two developments: the domination of empiricist analysis in the social sciences and very strong state powers. Where empirical analytical social science stressed effectiveness in mastery of the technical structures of causal relations in the study of society, critical social knowledge centered its studies on the effort to liberate human beings from dominant power structures (Giddens 1982).

These two forms of social knowledge, in all their variants, existed and developed in and outside the universities forming the panorama of social thought in Indonesia. Indonesian universities have been hotbeds for social empiricist analysis-based sciences. In addition, critical social thought developed in these same universities with the aim of exposing the assumptions and theories of modernization that dominated thinking about development in the Soeharto era. At the same time, outside the universities, there developed a number of non-governmental organizations or NGOs (LSM – *Lembaga Swadaya Masyarakat*, the literal translation being "Self-Reliant Community Institutions") that were active in the development sphere and that used the empiricist-analytical social science approach. These developments enriched socially critical knowledge both as it was developed by NGOs that had an orientation to academic research about development and by those oriented to social research and training in support of advocacy. This chapter focuses its analysis on the latter type of NGO, which, for practical reasons, we will call "critical NGOs".

Given its major contributions to developmental politics, empiricist-analysis social science is positioned as the "mainstream" and was protected and kept in dominance by the state in order to define scientific truth. Critical social knowledge found itself in a "peripheral" position, with the counter-hegemonic aim of overturning dominant power structures. This critical knowledge has been defended and developed by the critical NGOs. It is interesting to study the development of critical knowledge and its struggle with the state and the mainstream in the liberation of social groups from an unjust dominant power structure during the Soeharto era.

This paper presents the following arguments. First, the system of state power played an important role in pushing the supporters of critical NGOs to the margins. Second, the weak development of critical ideas is closely connected with the weak position of its supporters in the configuration of power, domination and hegemony. This is why the aspirations of social knowledge that were being fought for were adopted by mainstream social sciences and the state as a means of maintaining their position and legitimizing the politics of development. The adoption of these aspirations was reflected in the changes in direction and approach of development during the Soeharto era. Third, and this is connected with the second argument, the thinkers of the critical NGOs failed in developing an alternative paradigm. In short, both inclusion (the adoption of aspirations) and, at the same time, exclusion (the marginalization of critical NGOs) were principles of management in the Soeharto era with respect to critical knowledge. In the post-Soeharto era, in an open political playing field, the critical NGOs have tended to become a part of the political system, thereby often losing their critical edge.

As briefly discussed above, the state's management of mainstream social sciences was a part of building legitimacy for development policy. Attention will be paid now to the tactics of inclusion and exclusion developed by the state and the responses of the activists and thinkers of the critical NGOs to the social issues that then emerged. Second, it will focus on the institutions and perspectives of some critical NGOs and the areas of study that concerned them. Third, it will look at the media and participatory methods they used. Fourth, it will explain the inclusion-exclusion-inclusion process of critical knowledge and the role played by critical NGOs in the Soeharto and post-Soeharto era. This chapter will conclude with a discussion of the condition and future prospects of critical knowledge and mainstream social sciences in the post-Soeharto era.

THE STATE AND THE MANIPULATION OF MAINSTREAM SOCIAL SCIENCES

The Soeharto government has been both criticized and praised during its more than thirty years of rule. The United Nations designated Indonesia as a middle-income country during this period. Several programs, such as family planning, self-sufficiency, particularly in the production of rice, and community health, received international recognition. Yet at the same time, criticisms of many different kinds also developed over time. This began with criticism on the issue of equity in distribution in the 1970s, economic justice in the 1980s and human rights in the 1990s.

In this kind of situation, inclusion and exclusion are not easy to define. There are frequent debates over how to explain inclusion and exclusion. In the liberal tradition, the issue of inclusion and exclusion is influenced by the view that people end up marginalized as a result of an emphasis on individual competency. In this view, through economic expansion and diversification, the Soeharto government appeared to provide adequate opportunities for people to improve their economic situation.[1] But its critics based their definition of the problem of inclusion and exclusion on whether the state was able to manage the economy in a way that upheld principles of justice. They considered that exclusion took place although there might have been a general increase in income. Critical NGOs see the problem of inclusion and exclusion as something inherent at the level of social interaction.

The Soeharto government, as with many other governments, always instituted both dimensions of inclusion and exclusion. Objective criteria are often difficult to reach because these depend on the theories and concepts being used. Furthermore, when a government utilizes theories and concepts, these are often adjusted to suit certain political goals – although this is not always the case – making it even harder to measure levels of objectivity. Development policy in the Soeharto era based itself on the contrived use of theories used by mainstream social sciences, which then became the focus of the critics who brought forward competing ideas.

This manipulation of mainstream social sciences involved three aspects, namely the legitimacy of policy, the positioning of strategy groups and the boundaries of state authority. First, the aspect of legitimacy was supported by modernization theories, comprising the growth theory and the socio-political modernization theory. Both these theories assumed a strong role for the state in encouraging economic development. The primary theses of these theories are that modernization is a process of social change carried out in accordance with predetermined plans (Pieterse 2001). The concept of "trickle down effects" as a part of the growth theory was used to justify policy for the development of capital-intensive industry as a means of creating prosperity. But what occurred was state-induced growth because taxation never

---

[1] This statement is not meant to deny that in some sectors the Soeharto government established monopolies and provided selective protection to certain groups. During the oil boom, it was possible to provide both expanded economic opportunities and privileges.

became an important instrument in achieving equity of distribution. Further, the development of the industrial sector was not well planned. As a result, it was unable to act as the locomotive for the development of a people's economy.

The economists who supported this approach argued that an increase in prosperity had occurred as a result of the allocation of resources to basic needs. The state facilitated agricultural inputs, health centers, family planning, basic education, and so on. The critics argued that this capital-intensive development policy created regional inequities, one of the big issues of the Soeharto period. It was shown that state resources were concentrated in Jakarta and in other large cities on the island of Java (Thee 1981).

In the 1980s, a new perspective arose, namely neo-liberalism, that aimed to limit the role of the state in economic life. If, in the past, the state was viewed as a problem solver, it was now viewed as the source of the problem. As a result, deregulation and privatization arose as new jargon in the development policy discourse in Indonesia. This was supported by the demands of the market for a policy of rationalization, and pressure from the International Monetary Fund (IMF) for the abolition of state subsidies. At this time, the economists supporting neo-liberalism were given a bigger say in government economic policy. But the neo-liberal concept still had, and has, to operate within the framework of the Indonesian political system.

The second aspect of the manipulation of mainstream social sciences relates to the positioning of strategic groups. This aspect was partly supported by the modernization theory that identified individual ability as the driving force for lifting standards of living. It was also partly supported by the concept of quasi-corporatism, which identifies the state as the representative of various groups, especially economically weaker groups (Ganie-Rochman 2002). Quasi-corporatism stresses control, unlike the concept of corporatism that stresses the state's role in balancing different interests. Thus, the government felt it necessary to form various umbrella organizations for different strategic groups, such as journalists, lawyers, workers, students and businessmen. For the poor, the representation of the state went beyond defining the scale and scope of popular welfare; the state also provided substantial budgets for basic needs. The state made itself the "protector" of the interests of the poor, giving society the chance to question whether the model being presented was a just one.

Democracy was also used by the government to maintain a hold over its people. This concept, which stresses the rights of citizens and a mutual respect for differences, was described by Soeharto as a process, and one that should not be seen through "Western eyes". While saying that democracy was necessary, the Soeharto government maintained its tight control, through co-option and pressure, over all strategic groups.

A third aspect relates to the limits of the state's authority. The Soeharto government had an interest in blurring these limits so as to eliminate the possibility of a legitimacy crisis and the buildup of any opposition force. This was done by its adopting a communitarian perspective to define "nation" as a collective life where conflict and differences in interests were not emphasized. The government translated this into a more paternalistic version of the state ideology of Pancasila. Collectivity was the theme used to justify state hegemony. Through this mechanism, the government administered politics, economic allocation, and the legitimization of social activity through secretly formulated definitions. An integrated system was established, although this was not social integration. Because of its centralistic character, this type of integration resulted in the various social organizations losing their ability to develop themselves and cooperate. Collective ties became artificial and social solidarity was empty due to lack of a basis in praxis.

The totality of government policy produced what was called the politics of the development state (Leftwich 1994).[2] These policies became popular at the international level. Its emergence was encouraged by economic growth in Asia, including Indonesia, which was seen as a success by the international institutions such as the World Bank and the IMF. Mainstream social sciences in Indonesia were a replication of the social sciences that dominated development thinking in the West. These concepts and theories entered Indonesia at different times.[3] Several domestic and international factors worked to influence, sustain and develop these theories and concepts. Social scientists, in particular economists, political scientists, sociologists and anthropologists, play important roles in making use of these social sciences. The economists must be mentioned first because the Soeharto government sought its legitimacy from improving the economy. After rehabilitation of the economy, a new phase was planned to transform the economic structure from agrarian to industrial. Using money from oil, the state developed an import-substitution industrial structure that became the driving force of industrialization.

In the 1970s, the social scientists working in the universities and the government bureaucracy were all trying to answer the same question: How can the skills, attitude and mentality of the nation be transformed so as to support a modern economy? A

---

[2]   These political characteristics are: (a) there is an elite group with a development orientation; (b) it has relative autonomy; (c) a strong and competent bureaucracy; (d) a weak and subordinated civil society; (e) effective management of forces outside the state; (f) legitimacy based on the appearance of economic achievement.

[3]   The modernization theory was popular in the 1950s but its influence in Indonesia continued until the 1980s. The human development perspective was popular in the 1980s and its influence continued in Indonesia in the 1990s. Neo-liberalism entered Indonesia at the same time it became popular at the international level and remains influential in Indonesia today.

functional structural approach was adopted because it was the basis of social and political analysis of social issues. In other words, social scientists sought to evaluate how far institutions supported modern public and social life.

In the 1980s, there was an economic downturn caused by a drop in oil prices, as well as the strengthening perceptions of inequalities and a trend towards authoritarianism. As a result, some social scientists began to ask critical questions about the workings of the Soeharto government. The themes of modernization and the state as the motor for change no longer seemed convincing. They began to examine the impact of development on life in general; the seizing of agricultural land for industry, the weakening of traditional and social bonds, and the marginalization of people's industries by the big industries in the cities. The development of critical knowledge at the international level also brought in ideas from the structural approach and theories of dependency. A number of younger academics returning home from overseas won considerable popularity using these theories.

In the following years, right up until the end of the Soeharto era, the social scientists in the universities and government had to deal with the criticisms launched by NGO activists and critical social scientists who wanted political democracy and a renewal in the administration of the state. NGO activists were calling for a reorientation of development that gave society a larger role. A participative approach, in the sense of giving opportunities to the people in politics, was also advocated. The mainstream social sciences began to adopt the themes, calls and approaches advocated by the NGOs. This is how human development, sustainable development, capacity building, and a role for NGOs became an integral part of the mainstream social sciences.

In the 1990s, the concept of good governance emerged. This concept was defined as the use of authority through participation, transparency and accountability so as to encourage the efficient and more equal management of resources. The World Bank, and other international development cooperation agencies subsequently, have popularized this concept (Kaufmann et al. 1999). Parallel to this idea, and parallel to the waves of democratization in Latin America, Asia and Eastern Europe, the concept of "civil society" became popular; a concept based on the assumption of the existence of a public arena as a structured platform for communication and cooperation among citizens in voluntary and independent civil associations. The formation of such citizens' associations is a condition of the development of democracy.

In the post-Soeharto era, civil society and good governance have become the main frameworks for social and state administration used by institutions involved in reform of public institutions and social empowerment in Indonesia. Pro-democracy groups, especially the NGOs, have been very encouraged by this new situation. However, this situation, as will be discussed in the final section of this paper, has eroded the critical edge of Indonesia's NGOs.

INSTITUTIONS AND PERSPECTIVES

In January 1980, *Prisma*, a magazine published by the Institute for Social Economic Education, Development and Research (*Lembaga Penelitian, Pengembangan, dan Pendidikan Ekonomi Sosial* – LP3ES), one of the more established NGOs, published an issue about social inequalities resulting from government economic policy. The issue of social inequality has remained an issue in research in Indonesia ever since. This issue is closely connected to the problem of relations between social classes, and the imbalances between villages and towns. This issue had already started to develop with the student protests of 1974 and 1978. But the *Prisma* edition took the issue into more prestigious circles, namely those of academics and educated people.

This magazine was first published in 1971 as a vehicle for the critical ideas of former student leaders who had sensed the trend towards political centralization at the beginning of the Soeharto era. The founders of *Prisma* wanted the magazine to be a forum for contemplating the future of Indonesia. Motivated in the search for alternative ideas, *Prisma* was able to capture constructive and critical ideas. With very intellectually capable people behind *Prisma*, this magazine was able to attract the country's foremost intellectuals to contribute articles, thereby establishing itself as a respected vehicle among Indonesian intellectuals. Even so, as set out by Dhakidae (2003), the magazine provided an important bridge between the New Order bureaucracy, the technocrats and society. This bridge was built upon the belief that modernization and technocracy can be combined with a populist consciousness.

Most NGO activists, such as those enrolled in the Secretariat for Indonesian Forest Preservation (*Sekretariat Pelestarian Hutan Indonesia* – SKEPHI) and the Institution of Social Transformation Research (*Lembaga Penelitian Ilmu Sosial Transformatif* – LPIST), received university education, and developed their own approaches to this issue of inequality. To date, many activist research groups emerged, also studying the issue of inequalities. They formed their own associations of researchers that rival those supported by the government. These inequalities, they said, must be studied objectively in the context of development in Indonesia today.

Several economic experts expressed a different opinion to the NGO activists, saying that income inequalities in Indonesia were moderate compared to other countries. They argue that industrial development in the cities was very prominent in the 1980s and much agricultural land was taken for these purposes. This change of function in the use of land meant a loss of income for many farmers. Yet, on the other hand, employment was created outside agriculture. Separate from the issue of dependency and job security, the reality was that there has been an increase in income in the village areas. However, the NGO researchers have not accepted this argument. Using the dependency theory, they argue that this social inequality was and is caused by an exploitative social structure.

Apart from LP3ES, there was another NGO that developed critical ideas about Indonesian development, namely LPIST.[4] Differing from LP3ES, LPIST was formed by people trying to understand the issues as experienced and understood by marginalized groups. As with other NGOs, LPIST was initially interested in how inequality produced marginalized groups such as peasants, the urban poor, women and the ethnic minorities such as the *pesantren*. LPIST initially carried out research to uncover the mechanisms that produced poverty. The dependency and structural approaches colored much of the analysis of this research. This sustained research, accompanied by high levels of lively discussion, has enriched the tools for analysis and understanding of the dimensions of poverty.

In the early 1990s, LPIST developed a more advanced approach than other NGOs. It argued that development in Indonesia had damaged local social institutions making them vulnerable to pressures from outside. LPIST argued that "re-institutionalization" was necessary to solve many problems. It is interesting to note that LPIST analysis saw the dimension of "social trust" as being an important part of social solidarity.[5] Developments flowing from these research activities led LPIST to search for a methodology to understand how to achieve social transformation.[6]

This approach has the reverse approach to that of mainstream social sciences because it questions the values of development actors. LPIST developed the idea that the development of knowledge should be embedded in the community participation process. The development of knowledge for change must be located in specific social networks that comprise academics, activists and the people. LPIST instituted training in transformative social science methodology and theory for scores of NGO activists throughout Indonesia.[7] These activities brought new ideas into the NGO community. However, it did not create any important or new

---

[4]   This groups was active from the second half of the 1980s until the mid-1990s.

[5]   See LPIST (1990), *Asas*, May-June.

[6]   This methodology was defined as a way of understanding theory and research methodology that was oriented towards emancipatory change. LPIST (1990).

[7]   It is stated that the aim of the training, was "apart from theoretical understanding, also aimed to reflect collective experience and conditions, and help formulate values in influencing choices in action; deepen studies and concern for the themes of poverty and social marginality; sharpen and extend dimensions of respective activities and to pioneer networks which can make possible ongoing exchanges of experience." See LPIST (1990).

intellectual dimension in the NGO movement in Indonesia.

The dependency theory led NGO activists to view the "middle class" with skepticism.[8] This was reinforced by the fact that the urban middle class was born out of government economic policy and that many of them were tied to government projects (Ganie-Rochman 1986). This view also meant that NGO activists did not even try to see any potential in the "middle class" as a group that could be encouraged to join in the process of change.

Their view of the state changed from seeing it as the "agent of capitalism", the state being a passive institution in the face of outside interests, to seeing it as a more active institution, namely a "bureaucratic patrimonial" institution. These critics also made reference to "the government" when talking about the ruling power, a term less abstract than "state". Soeharto was seen as the center of all government policies, in addition to political forces such as the military, bureaucrats, and business groups. In addition, these critics zeroed in on policies relating to, in particular, transmigration, labor, or the take-over of land for development projects. The issue of women in development policies also began to emerge at this time.

The basic criticism put forward regarding state policy towards women was that it was freezing traditional gender roles in the interests of the government's political and economic policies. Women activists shared the view of other activists that the state had a militaristic and authoritarian character.[9] They added that the state also had a patriarchal character, one that was reflected in its policies and in the legal system. The result, they argued, was that women had limited recourse or opportunities to protect their interests in public life. The first policy that was discussed was that in relation to population where women were compartmentalized into a domestic role and were expected to take responsibility for procreation.[10] In the economic sphere, women did not qualify as the main breadwinners, and this justified a system of lower wages for women workers; a system that was developed in accordance with the government's cheap labor policies. The government was also accused of using women for the purposes of stabilizing political support, particularly through Dharma Wanita, an institution set up especially for the wives of civil servants.[11]

---

[8] As reflected in the research and writings published by SKEHPI, LPIST and LSP.
[9] Two of the first women's NGOs established were Kalyanamitra and Solidaritas Perempuan. Kalyanamitra issued a bulletin, namely *Dongbret*. This was a pioneering publication in campaigning for women's issues. Later, many other organizations emerged in several larger cities.
[10] Women were the primary objects of family planning programs. The critics stated that these programs were often not sensitive to the differences among women's bodies, let alone to women's own perspectives regarding these programs.
[11] The leadership structure of this organization mirrored the hierarchy of the husbands of the women members and instituted programs to absorb the energies and thoughts of the wives.

The criticisms of these policies led women activists to develop a women's perspective. They argued that development planners and researchers in general did not take into account the feelings, ideals and desires of women as an objective reality. They only understood, the argument continued, general standards and categories behind which specific economic and political interests hid. To back up their claim, activists highlighted the example of government programs, the success of which were measured by economic growth and the physical tasks involved.

The struggle of pro-women's issues activists ("women activists") was difficult. For years, they faced the ridicule of both policy makers and society. They even faced difficulties in getting their agendas accepted in the NGO community. Many NGO activists were of the view that the first priority was to struggle for a change in the political system under which the NGOs themselves were being pressured. Adding women's issues into the fray would only create more difficulties for the struggle. In the same breath, women activists argued that a democratic system would have a gender perspective. The weakness of this analysis was perhaps related to the thinking of pro-democracy activists in general. Their ideas about democratic systems were very simple. More important, they clearly reflected close political interaction with the government (Ganie-Rochman 2002).

Women activists, however, maintained their view that political change must necessarily include a gender perspective if that change was to settle issues for women.

After the fall of the Soeharto government, women activists faced a new government that was not effective in either formulating or implementing public policy. It appeared difficult for women's issues to attract attention from policy makers or the international institutions involved in the reformation process.[12] At the same time, regional autonomy brought new concerns for women activists. For instance, regional governments, whether with religious or traditional backgrounds or otherwise, were and are reputed to have implemented regulations that are damaging to the interests of women. Although not opposed to religion per se, the activists believe that religion is a powerful tool that is often used to further the interests of a patriarchal power system.

To the NGOs, "participation" was a key element of change in the Soeharto era. They attributed all the social ills and issues that plagued Indonesia to the lack of opportunity for participation by the people in policy and development. Participation was defined as the right to a voice in decision-making. When talking about participation, the NGO activists were referring both to society in general and the local communities in particular. The issue of participation was often connected with government. Political participation meant the opportunity to build large

---

[12] The exception was the issue of public violence against women which emerged as an issue as a result of riots in various areas, including Jakarta.

political organizations or parties. When talking about local communities, participation was seen as the people having a say regarding government development projects. Their views on participation were very simple and essentially reflexive.

Towards the end of the Soeharto regime, many NGO activists no longer saw participation as a concept of their struggle. NGO publications, such as those published by the International NGO Forum for Indonesian Development (INFID) and the Foundation of the Indonesian Legal Aid Institute (*Yayasan Lembaga Bantuan Hukum Indonesia* – YLBHI), two of the more prominent NGOs in the 1990s, began to speak of democratization. This was because participation was slowly losing its ground as a political demand. Their focus had shifted to empowering marginalized groups. To achieve this, the NGOs had to rally the support of these marginalized groups through democratization.

THE MEDIA AND THE PARTICIPATORY METHOD

The break away from the prevailing or dominant sources of information started with the publication of bulletins by student activists and NGOs, an activity that was popular in the mid-1980s. These were low-budget bulletins aimed at providing accessible information about the critical perspectives on marginalized socio-economic groups. Most of them depicted the unjust actions of the military and bureaucratic apparatus.

Aditjondro labeled this form of media "non-mainstream" and divided it into three categories: religious media, anti-capitalist media, and the student press (Aditjondro 1993). Aditjondro also provided a circulation breakdown of the three: religious media constituted 200,000 copies or 2.6 percent of print media, that is, newspapers and magazines; anti-capitalist publications or bulletins, usually published by NGOs, had an average print run of between 500 and 1000 copies; and the student press had smaller print runs.

Funded for the most part by donor institutions, NGO bulletins, targeted at the marginalized groups including farmers, workers and street traders, carried reports of violations by the military, bureaucracy and/or capitalists. Their key messages were clear: anti-inequality, anti-capitalist, anti-military, and anti-bureaucracy. In addition, some bulletins provided more constructive information relating to the various projects and programs being implemented by the NGOs.

As the NGOs grew in prominence and presence, so, too, did the funding by foreign donors. The additional funding enabled them to publish books based on library research or research reports, thereby enabling them to reach a much wider audience. By the mid-1990s, some 300 books and publications were reported to have been published by the NGO community (Akatiga n.d.), but the acutal number was far greater. Almost all of their books, as with the bulletins, carry a direct message, and often have provocative titles.[13] Issues were reported through the direct presentation of evidence, such as statistics on deforestation, wages, rape, and human rights violations.

In the second half of the 1980s, structural poverty was a popular topic of discussion in NGO publications and research. What is interesting is that there were claims that this research was carried out using the participatory method. This points to a transition from the popularity of the structural approach to that of participatory research. Kleden (1995) notes that NGO researchers used Participatory Action Research with little reference to academic sources. There were three main reasons for this: first, their attitude towards universities; second, their orientation to problem solving; and third, the emphasis on the role of the NGOs.

This period in the 1980s exposed a weakness in the connection between structural analysis in studying social economic conditions and the reality as depicted by members of the marginalized groups. NGO researchers had a strong desire to refute modernization theories. They wanted to show that these theoretical icons would end up damaging the interests of the weaker sections of society. The participatory methods used in research were still simple and were not discussed in great depth. In fact, it is more accurate to describe this period as a time of trying to bring the voices of the poor into research results. It should be noted that there was an absence of identification in their research of any agents, processes or institutions that could have provided a connection between the macro background and experiences of the individual.

The participatory approach then developed more as a part of the NGOs' actual program of action. There are very few books published by the NGOs depicting this participatory method. Almost all of the NGOs' participatory research was a part of specific projects or programs. This of course had specific implications for the results of the process. The participatory research carried out was often captured by the aims and processes that were part of that project or program. There has long been criticism among the NGOs of their participatory method. This criticism was not of the method itself but rather of the nature of the commitment of the marginalized groups with whom they were working. They were criticized for bringing middle class attitudes and thinking and of not adequately fusing with the interests of the

---

[13] Such as: *Developing Small Enterprises: A Half-hearted Partisanship* (Akatiga); *In the Name of Development: Human Rights and the World Bank in Indonesia* (Elsam); *Land, the People and Democracy* (Yogyakarta NGOs Forum); *Prisoners of Progress* (INFID); *Women and Handicrafts: Between Myth and Reality* (Kalyanamitra); *Industry Deregulation and a Sustainable Development Perspective* (Konphalindo), *New Economic Imperialism* (Konphalindo); *Communication for Human Dignity* (Yakoma); *The Life of Women Workers* (Yasanti); *Demanding Rights* (YLKI).

weaker sectors of the people. The criticism was that the participatory method was of limited use because there was little real opportunity for using this method outside of a specific project or program.

With regard to gender issues, however, there are arguments supporting the implementation of the participatory concept by NGOs. The programs that were supported by foreign donors were aimed specifically at raising awareness of women's issues and raising the status of women in Indonesia. Because women's issues were approached from the point of view of increasing individual capacity, it was possible to implement a more consistent and systematic participatory approach. For example, one pioneering women's NGO, Kalyanamitra, developed a schema of activity that, for years, has comprised three spheres: gender orientation, training in gender analysis, and in-depth analysis of gender analysis.

The women's movement in Indonesia was responding to the same basic issue as the critical movement in general, namely, an authoritarian and militaristic government. It was this background that determined the way in which the participatory approach adopted by women's NGOs developed. For example, books aimed at raising awareness or gender analysis would always contain sections analyzing government policy. Gender training provided more opportunity compared to other types of NGO training for conceptual bridges between the macro level and the influence on individuals. In gender training, the concept of "access" to social institutions and organizations was one key concept. There was a systematic explanation of the influence of social institutions and organizations on women. This was carried out in the midst of also explaining the cultural role of gender. Putting aside for a moment any of its weaknesses, it can be stated that the gender analysis developed by the Indonesian women's NGOs took a "middle ground" perspective, stressing the process of interconnection between actors, agents, and institutions or organizations.

Another proposition of gender analysis was that society is heterogeneous. This heterogeneity was not treated merely as a category. Instead, it was the starting point for various social groups when looking at and solving problems. This proposition was implemented in the study of the consequences of development policy through to family relations. Opposing mainstream social sciences, which had been adopted widely in government policy, gender analysis explained the issues hidden behind the figures showing the successes of government programs. This argument was closely connected with the metaphor that they promoted, namely the private is political. This metaphor reflected the reality that public appearances did not convey the true situation as far as women were concerned. Women activists also used this proposition to oppose the Soeharto government's perspective on the domestic role of women. The activists argued that legitimizing this domestic role concealed the various domestic problems experienced by women including physical abuse and so on.

The women activists honed their research skills by learning from their international colleagues who had already developed and refined the participatory method. They were also assisted by a number of NGO figures who paid particular attention to popular education. Popular education was targeted at raising critical awareness as well as socio-economic capacity of marginalized groups. Proponents of popular education were particularly interested in ensuring that participation was motivated by a real desire on the part of the marginalized groups to contribute to change.

In the early 1990s, several women NGO activists were involved in efforts that questioned the activities and orientation of NGOs as organizations working for and in the interest of marginalized groups. A reflection or evaluation exercise was embarked upon in several parts of Indonesia and involved various strata of groups. This exercise concluded that many NGOs had a conformist, rather than reformist, outlook on change. Very few NGOs saw change as transformative, that is, change that would alter the structural and cultural basis of society. In fact, there were inconsistencies and contradictions in the "paradigms", vision, methodology, approach and management of the various NGOs that wanted transformative change (Fakih 1996).

An "education committee" was therefore established to change the orientation and actions of the NGOs. The committee was tasked with developing plans for a system of education, including curriculum, training methodology, process, readings, selecting participants, facilitators and teachers. This committee had an important influence on the NGO community because of its involvement in a variety of processes for training activists. The aim, as set out in its manual, was to develop a critical awareness about social structure. The method used was dialogical, one that raised consciousness and was focused on analyzing the socio-economic structure. Some of the members of this committee later established an NGO based in Yogyakarta called the Institute for Social Transformation or INSIST. INSIST went on to become one of the main centers of the NGO movement in Indonesia.

In the post-Soeharto era, INSIST has involved itself with political education, focusing on regional autonomy. Its view is that despite the political changes that have taken place, the marginalized communities have not yet been liberated from their shackles. Adopting Freirean thinking, it always seeks to understand the social relations that hold back critical thinking. INSIST is of the view that the militarist nature of Indonesia's style of governance – defined as a tendency to force one's will on others – still prevails, whether within the government itself, political parties or other segments of society. As a result, the training courses that it has developed concentrate not only on the liberation of consciousness, but also on political structures, especially those in the region. This is so that the participants can understand the room for change, including for changing government regulations. INSIST is trying to unify two areas, namely social organization and the formal arena of policy change.

INSIST apparently subscribes to the Gramscian concept of "organic intellectuals", that is, intellectuals who help the process of liberation. Yet, its interpretation of the concept appears to be that even organic intellectuals are not able to determine either the problems or the solutions for "oppressed groups", the term they use to describe the marginalized groups (Fakih 2002; Fakih et al. 1999). The organic intellectuals and the "oppressed groups" move together in a continuous action-reflection manner. This method is intended not only to understand the truth, but also to explain the role of knowledge and how it can be used to achieve social change. Based on these ideas, this group has developed a program for social empowerment with the aim of achieving change together with marginalized groups.

One program that was considered a success was the empowerment of farmer organizations where peasant representatives, facilitated by NGO activists, formulated and carried out action plans demanding changes in agrarian policy.

For the most part, however, INSIST carries out study programs about democracy based on popular awareness of social, economic and political rights. They have initiated research programs for the purposes of reflection, published books and magazines, organized capacity building programs in communities and other activities geared towards cultural liberation (INSIST 2002).

In the post-Soeharto era, with aid from international donor organizations, many other NGOs are now concentrating on strengthening civil society organizations and reforming laws in the framework of good governance. These programs usually take the form of capacity building for the NGOs themselves and for local level social organization. These programs for strengthening civil society organization are aimed at building transparent and accountable public organizations. For example, many NGOs work towards setting up citizen's forums as part of a program for strengthening civil society. These forums are places where different social groups can meet to discuss the allocation of resources in their area. Focus group discussion methods are often used to identify the aspirations of the different groups.

However, barely two years into these civil society organization activities, these NGOs have attracted criticism from "the organic intellectuals", or groups such as INSIST. Critics argue that these NGOs have accepted the ideas for change as promoted by donor institutions whose interests lie in maintaining capitalism and the free market economy. Even under the guise of the good governance framework, they have been accused of having forgotten the plight of the marginalized groups. Critics further argue that the good governance framework has neither the perspective nor methods to awaken the critical thinking or social capacity of the "oppressed groups".

INCLUSION – EXCLUSION – INCLUSION

Indonesia's critical NGOs were instrumental during the Soeharto era in introducing and using critical knowledge to understand and solve social problems. The discussion above shows how extensive their range of critical terminology and concepts was; terminology and concepts that were introduced to the public arena of development politics in this country. Their concepts included inequality, poverty, anti-capitalism, dependency, participation, participatory action research (PAR) and empowerment. The NGOs tried to play two very difficult roles: actor of theory and actor of action. They carried out these two roles with the aim of overturning an unjust power structure of domination.

Their concepts were always the antithesis of those developed by the state and the mainstream. If the state and the mainstream talked about growth, they talked about inequality. Against modernization, there was anti-capitalism; against top-down was bottom-up; for state-led development, there was society-led development; and for the survey method of research, there was the PAR method. While all these ideas and aspirations were very important, this critical knowledge tended to be reactive as opposed to proactive, responding only to the concepts of mainstream social science.

As will be explained below, due to the 1. breadth of topics that were open to study, 2. anti-science tendencies, 3. limited international support and 4. undemocratic state power, critical knowledge came to occupy a peripheral position during the New Order. The critical NGOs with their concepts of critical knowledge only had limited success in achieving their mission of changing the unjust social structure of domination. However, the mainstream social sciences and the state made use of their aspirations, so much so that critical knowledge as well as the critical NGOs have been brought into the fold of state power and the social sciences. The course of development of critical knowledge and the role of NGOs can be described as a process of inclusion-exclusion-inclusion.

The emergence and development of critical knowledge and critical NGOs cannot be separated from the nation's disappointment in development. Soeharto's development policy promised an industrial society supported by a strong state. The Modernization theory, very popular internationally at the time, played an important role in providing justification for this policy. At the beginning of the Soeharto era, the state adopted a growth strategy. In the next decade, it adopted the strategy of bringing equity to development. This change in strategy was a result of the work of the critical NGOs who raised the issue of increasing social inequality at that time. The state and mainstream social sciences were also able to adopt the bottom-up orientation through a development approach oriented to basic needs. All this time, however, the critical NGOs leaders remained on the margins of the Indonesian political arena.

We need to ask why there was such limited success in overturning the unjust social structure of domination. The simple answer is that the system of state power did not provide the space needed for critical knowledge to develop. However, the internal factors - mentioned earlier in this section - played an important role in holding back the development of critical social knowledge. Having said that, the weaknesses of this knowledge are not wholly attributable to its supporters in Indonesia. It could be argued that the inability of its international thinkers to make it a "paradigm" was also to blame (Pieterse 2001: 74-83).[14]

The social sciences have two key characteristics: explanatory and prescriptive (Katouzian 1980). The first one explains accurately two or more social events and analyzes the relationship between these events. The second formulates policy that is useful for the sustainability of social development. In addition, social science requires institutional backing to support its development.

At the international level, the critical knowledge thinkers covered a wide range of topics including the spread of poverty, environmental destruction, labor exploitation, the role of NGOs, grass-roots movements, human rights, predatory states, and opposition to global capitalism. The problem was that each of these wide-ranging topics was studied independently of the others, without connection or continuity. Furthermore, debates over the validity of a particular concept in each area rarely occurred. As a result of the lack of any real co-ordination among the thinkers, a variety of terms emerged in the critical knowledge arena: appropriate development, participatory development, human development, consciousness raising and liberation. A clash of concepts, the lifeblood of scientific innovation, therefore never materialized among these thinkers. This school of thought failed to develop a paradigm. Perhaps this failure can be attributed to the stronger orientation

---

[14] In this context, the international thinkers are those who have been concerned with alternative models of development. These models include those concentrating on a people-centered approach, development as social transformation, development as endogenously self-reliant. All these models flowed from disappointment with mainstream social science, which defined development as growth. Their endeavors to break from mainstream social science have instead strengthened the latter. The dialectics between these two forms of knowledge have grown rapidly.

to and greater concern for practical affairs rather than focusing only on theoretical matters (see also Irwan, this volume).

Critical knowledge in Indonesia is a replica of the complexity experienced by the international critical knowledge thinkers. The scope of study for the Indonesian thinkers was also very wide: the domestication of women, impoverishment, labor exploitation, and global capitalism. They also used a wide variety of concepts without any effort at critical questioning: empowerment, social transformation, civil society, grass roots and so on. As with their international colleagues, most of the critical NGOs thinkers were not very interested in codifying or systematizing the data they gathered in their field studies. Their reluctance to systematize their data and their weakness in questioning the validity of concepts gave rise to the view that they were and are anti-science and anti-scholarship.

By comparison, it is a very different with mainstream social science. While the mainstream is considered to be "neutral" because it disguises the form of legitimization of the structure of domination (Giddens 1982), it is still equipped with a powerful methodology for analyzing the causal relations between social events. This would explain why the ideas and concepts brought to the fore by the critical NGOs were so easily adopted without any real damage to the mainstream social science machinery. In fact, the lack of academic tradition and institutional basis of the majority of NGOs in the Soeharto era resulted in the terminology they used being taken over by the state. The terminology of participation, for example, appeared in official government documents as a new metaphor in the development discourse in the 1980s.

Ironically, the critical concept of *participation*, which the NGOs advocated for the overthrow of unjust structures, did not appear to have an impact within the NGOs themselves. In one study, Hannam (1988) reported that decision-making in the NGOs was a process undertaken by leaders without reference to staff. The NGOs' social programs were formulated without dialogue with the target groups. This stemmed from the fact that most NGOs in Indonesia were created by foundations where the founding committee or board of patrons had the final say on all matters such as funding, focus and direction, and research. This position went against the grain of the anti-organization stand.[15] At the moment, the internal management of NGOs is weak. They have confused order as necessary to produce predictability and accountability with order for order's sake. Dependency on leaders has made the NGOs very open to personal impediments such as ill feelings and conflict.

Pressure for NGOs to become participatory organizations arose at the beginning

---

[15] Anti-organization means being against the renewal of work mechanisms that could produce effective organizations.

of the 1990s. People raised problems again with the foundation form of organization. The argument that the foundation form provided protection against infiltration by the government no longer held water. In fact, the argument was put forward that the foundation form was on of the factors that explained why NGOs did not develop into broader movements. An external factor, namely politically motivated interaction with the government, had affected ideas about how to organize an NGO. Alternative ideas on form then started to emerge, such as unions and associations. These alternative forms were popular as they were seen to provide opportunity for greater involvement by the people, both by staff as well the various groups that were stakeholders. Another factor was that the NGOs had not been able to develop substantive relations with the marginalized groups. NGO activities with marginalized groups had been constrained by the project cycle. Not many NGOs had the capacity to sustain ongoing programs of mobilizing or engaging the people.

In the post-Soeharto era, both politics and social sciences have opened up greatly. New roles and new ideas have and continue to develop, so much so that there is scope for NGOs to exist within the system rather than on the periphery. Their critical aspirations and ideas have also received academic justification. These critical aspirations have become important components in the new paradigms of good governance and civil society. If development was the "religion" of the Soeharto era, these new paradigms are the "new religion" in the post-Soeharto era. In this new era, and for the first time in Indonesian political history, NGOs occupy a relatively good position, having built cordial working relations with the state and business.

It is important to point out, however, that with this recognition and renewed status come greater responsibility and more complex problems to tackle. Today they are involved in education programs relating to citizenship and democracy. These programs are necessary but insufficient to liberate many communities from the grip of unjust structures. The experience of Porto Alegre, Brazil (Aber 2000), shows the importance of combining civics education with the provision of resources. Through the participatory budget process the governor of Porto Alegre provides funds and resources for social programs planned by the various civic groups. But, note that these funds must be earned or won competitively. This is where Indonesian NGOs falter.

Indonesian NGOs, having introduced a "new religion" to the country, have found for themselves a comfortable place in the realm of good governance and civil society. As presented by Törnquist (2002), these "religions" stress the importance of the role of the elite in instituting the rule of law, human rights and a suitable constitutional system for the country. This paradigm, as described by Törnquist begs the following questions: Does Indonesia have a ruling elite that is capable of doing the things described by Törnquist; and does this paradigm give sufficient attention to the social context involving patterns of power relations, the role of "actors" and the political culture in Indonesia today?

To answer the first question: Indonesian political history is marked by the constant failure of the political elite in establishing good institutions. Second, the Indonesian social context tends not to support the working of this paradigm. The mushrooming of political parties and the dominance of parliamentary politics has tended to produce discontinuity. Party politicians and leaders have transformed themselves into political bosses. The media in Indonesia frequently reports on collusion between politicians, bureaucrats and businessmen.

The Thai experience might provide valuable lessons for Indonesian NGO activists and thinkers. Thailand carried out political reformation in the beginning of the 1980s and found its momentum in the beginning of the 1990s after the fall of the military government. The new "religion" of good governance also appeared and developed in Thailand. But, unlike in Indonesia, Thai NGOs had and have thinkers who are able to expose the weaknesses of the good governance paradigm. Thirayuth Boonmee, an NGO thinker and former student leader in the 1970s, reformulated a definition of good governance that did not need make reference to the formal state institutions:

> National good governance lies in the power of the movement of local organizations, peoples' communities to understand problems, be self reliant, help themselves, reform themselves; and at the same time, be forceful in monitoring whatever is bad and ugly in society.
>
> Phongpaichit 1999: 11

These ideas have inspired Thai NGOs to carry out an empowerment of the social movements at the local level. As explained by Phongpaichit (ibid.), working towards empowerment defines NGOs as the catalyst and facilitator for the development of social movements at the local or community level. The strength of the NGOs must come from these social movements and not from the funds or human resources of the NGOs. Based on these ideas, the NGOs can develop umbrella organizations such as the Council of the Poor, Farmers Council and so on.

When plans to change the Thai Constitution were announced, Thai NGOs argued for a right to contribute to that change. One change they proposed was the elimination of extra-legal power relations by strengthening the legal monitoring of politicians and bureaucrats, particularly by the public. This movement, because of its wide support, was able to make a valuable contribution to the new constitution.

In Indonesia, some NGOs tried to do the same thing. A network of critical NGOs prepared a draft of a new Constitution that provided for the political rights of the citizens. However, the Peoples Consultative Assembly did not adopt this draft, leaving much of the rules of the political game in Indonesia intact.

CONCLUSION

Even though critical knowledge faced enormous obstacles, it provided important inspiration for many different critical NGOs in the Soeharto era. In addition, the work done by the NGOs made a difference to the lives of the farmers of Kedung Ombo, the poor of Jakarta, and the workers in the labor-intensive industries. However, the NGOs thinkers have been reluctant to pull apart, question and re-formulate the critical concepts and theories as well as the mainstream ideas that have developed in Indonesia or internationally.

The same weakness applies to mainstream social science. Indonesian universities have failed to adapt mainstream thought to Indonesian conditions. In their introduction to this book, Hadiz and Dhakidae state that Indonesian scholars have contributed much less to the international academic literature on their own country than scholars of the neighboring countries of Malaysia, Thailand, Singapore and the Philippines. Nugroho even states a general concern about the state of universities in Indonesia. He argues that these institutions are an arena for the struggle over economic and political resources. We should be concerned about the weakening of the academic tradition in the Indonesian social sciences.

In the post-Soeharto era, the international financial bodies are playing a very important role not only in the economy but also in the development of the social sciences. At this juncture, it is worth quoting the economist John Maynard Keynes from 67 years ago:

> Practical men [sic], who believe themselves to be quite exempt from any intellectual influences, are usually the slaves of some defunct economist. Mad men [sic] in authority, who hear voices in the air, are distilling their frenzy from some academic scribbler of a few years back."
>
> Keynes, quoted in Block 1996: 3

Now is the time for both the critical NGO's thinkers and those from the mainstream social sciences to awaken from their slumber and work together to throw light on the dark corners of the Indonesian social sciences. In this way, they will be able to pull apart, question and then reformulate all these foreign ideas in accordance with the conditions of our society.

BIBLIOGRAPHY

Aber, Rebecca (2000) *From Clientilism to Co-operation: Local Government, Participatory Policy and Civic Organizing in Porto Alegre, Brazil.* World Development.

Aditjondro, George Y. (1993) "The Media as Development Textbook: A Case Study on Information Distortion in the Debate about the Social Impact of an Indonesian Dam", Ph.D thesis, Cornell University.

Akatiga (n.d.) *Buku dan publikasi alternatif ornop Indonesia: menguak potensi publikasi organisasi non-pemerintah,* Bandung: Akatiga and Oxfam Australia.

Block, Fred L. (1996) *The Vampire State,* New York: The New Press.

Dhakidae, Daniel (2003) *Cendekiawan dan kekuasaan dalam negara Orde Baru,* Jakarta: Gramedia.

Fakih, Mansoer (1996) *Masyarakat sipil untuk transformasi: Pergolakan ideologi NGOs Indonesia,* Yogyakarta: Insist Press.

— (2002) *Jalan lain: manifesto intelektual organik,* Yogyakarta: Insist Press.

Fakih, Mansoer, et al. (1999) *Panduan pendidikan politik untuk rakyat,* Yogyakarta: Insist Press.

Ganie-Rochman, Meuthia (1986). *Golongan menengah atas di jakarta: suatu pendekatan struktural.* M.A. Thesis, Faculty of Social and Political Sciences, University of Indonesia.

— (2002) *An Uphill Struggle: Advocacy NGOs Under Soeharto's New Order,* Jakarta: LabSosio.

Giddens, Anthony (1982) *New Rules of Sociological Method,* London: Hutchinson

Hannam, Peter (1988) *Pengembangan bentuk pembangunan alternatif: pengalaman NGOs Indonesia, Prisma* 17(4).

Insist (2002) *Gerakan sosial intelektual organik,* Yogyakarta: Insist Press.

Katouzian, Homa (1980) *Ideology and Method in Economics,* London: Macmillan

Kaufmann, Daniel, Aart Kraay and Pablo Zoido-Lobaton (1999) *Governance Matters,* Washington (DC): The World Bank Development Research Group on Macroeconomics and Growth and World Bank Institute Governance, Regulation, and Finance.

Kleden, Ignas (1995) "Social science in Indonesia: action and reflection in the Southeast Asian perspective" in Visser, Leontine and Nico Schulte-Nordholt (eds) *Social Science in Southeast Asia: From Particularism to Universalism.* Amsterdam: VU Univerisity Press.

LPIST (1990) *Asas* Bulletin (May-June).

Leftwich, A (1994) "Governance, the state, and the politics of development" *Development and Change* 25:363-383.

Pieterse, Jan Nederveen (2001) *Development Theory: Deconstructions/Reconstructions,* London: Sage.

Phongpaichit, Pasuk (1999) *Civilising the State: State, Civil Society and Politics in Thailand,* Amsterdam: The Center for Asian Studies Wertheim Lecture Series.

Törnquist, Olle (2002) *Popular Development and Democracy: Case Studies with Rural Dimensions in the Philippines, Indonesia, and Kerala*, Oslo: Centre for Development and the Environment, University of Oslo.

Thee Kian Wie (1981) "Pembangunan ekonomi dan pemerataan: beberapa pendekatan Alternatif" in Thee Kian Wie (ed.) *Pembanguan ekonomi dan pemerataan: beberapa pendekatan alternatif,* Jakarta: LP3ES.

-9-

SOCIAL SCIENCE ASSOCIATIONS

P.M. Laksono

In his reflections on the New Order, primarily based on a study of written documentation, Daniel Dhakidae (2003: 291-330) describes the social sciences as a form of power. At the same time, their professional association – in this case, the Indonesian Association for the Development of Social Sciences (*Himpunan Indonesia untuk Pengembangan Ilmu-Ilmu Sosial* – HIPIIS) – has played, in a rather ambiguous manner, a prophetic role. It raised objections to and warned of the impending failure or dangers of policy making. This, of course, was a political strategy intended to make it possible for these professionals to present their policy recommendations and ideas, refined and articulated in a form invented by the New Order itself: the *himbauan* (petition). In Dhakidae's terminology (ibid.: 328), this new form then became a kind of *madah* (a form of praise or supplication). Producing these *madah*, critical intellectual sense was ignored, so much so that the position and standing of social science professionals were secondary to that of key government officials, serving *ex officio* only to the president.

Dhakidae's argument stems from the New Order's "weapon", namely "the state secret". The secret in question was in connection with the 1965 coup d'état. The facts relating to that event became *sesengkeran*; hidden behind a wall, and kept away from others, never to be discussed or touched.[1] As a result of this "state secret", power was born.

---

[1] In Bali and Lombok many people build their homes within a *panyengker* or wall that encircles their home hiding the complex of houses belonging to the members of the *dadia* or extended patrilineal family. Inside this *panyengkar*, in the north eastern corner, can be found a family temple and some households whose activities can not be seen from outside. Each *panyengker* hides a complexity of mysterious life activities.

In a footnote, Dhakidae (2003: 291) quite aptly quotes Carl Schmitt when he says that secrecy is created to justify a raison d'être that allows its creator to stand above the conflict between "what was truth and what was not truth". So, the creator becomes an anti-intellectual, refusing the test of truth, thereby forcing the intellectuals into hiding. Efforts to expose injustices and wrongdoing are therefore conducted under the veil of secrecy. But, these efforts are critical in increasing awareness among the oppressed and exploited, which leads them to struggle and fight for their liberation (Freire 1999: 207).

Under the New Order, all academic activity in search of truth was permitted only with a research permit from a special directorate. In other words, the concept and theoretical notion of research were permitted, but not if research that crossed the line into the realm of the *sesengkeran*. At that time, however, almost all areas were considered behind the walls of *sesengkeran* and were taboo subjects for open and critical discussion. Everything, including poverty, family planning, sexuality and religion were taboo. This is how the term "intellectual prostitution" arose. The term referred to how academia was used only to satisfy and strengthen the *sesengkeran*, that is, the ruling power. According to Paulo Freire (1999: 194), this was a process called "mystification" where people were not actually forbidden to think, but where illusions and/or myths, created by the ruling power, were the order of the day. Such illusions and myths were created to ensure that the dominated society would find it difficult to use its powers of reason. So, it makes sense that Dhakidae, adapting his framework from Pierre Bordieu's[2], analyses the intellectual associations and institutions as the manifestation of a relationship between spheres of power, where the intellectual sphere is in the subordinated, subjugated position.

More than just that, Dhakidae (2003: 302-303) shows that the academics and intellectuals, after finding themselves unable to take a divergent stand against the tide of Guided Democracy before 1965, were also unable to put up any form of resistance to the post-1966 wave of intellectual neutering. The academics and intellectuals once again found themselves subdued when 800 academicians, lecturers, writers and journalists were exiled to Buru Island. Dhakidae described this process of exile by quoting from a letter written by Pramoedya Ananta Toer to his daughter

---

[2] The intellectual arena is depicted by Bourdieu (1994: 140-145) as a space for competing power relationships in a symbolic struggle. The intellectual arena is an arena of struggle which has its won stakes, namely who is to be considered a "genuine" intellectual. The intellectual arena is also wrought with structures of power. The intellectuals are a faction of the dominant class insofar as they possess power and privilege which derives from cultural capital, but they are dominated by those who have political and economic power.

on the eve of his own departure to Buru on 17 August 1969. Pramoedya began with a quote from a Lieutenant Marzuki at the Salemba jail:

> You have no rights except to breathe. And some of us have even had that right stolen...We sailed [*sic*] in a space behind a door of iron bars, locked in, prisoners, in three large areas below deck. We had no right even to see the sky, let alone to own it or share in owning it.

Dhakidae depicts how, from that time on, a new alliance was formed between the intelligentsia and the New Order; an alliance based on new equations of civic responsibility. This alliance became more explicit when the party system in Indonesia was disbanded in 1973. The institutions that had been used to represent the will of the people, but which were considered rowdy, emotional and prone to conflict, were eliminated. The citizen's participation in the republic was confined then to an ordered common sense. Society as a whole underwent what Dhakidae aptly called "scientification". All sectors of society were thus ordered and science became the basis for the justification of all policies, which were seen as free from any binding values. In order to carry out this process of "scientification", the National Development Planning Board (*Badan Perencanaan Nasional* – BAPPENAS) was established. This was followed by the setting up of a Regional Development Planning Board (*Badan Perencanaan Daerah* – BAPPEDA) in every province and district throughout the archipelago. These bodies, apart from providing permits for research, mobilized information and knowledge for the purposes of development planning. Each ministry and most local governments also established a Research and Development Agency (*Badan DikLat*). Similarly, the universities as well as the private sector set up research institutions and/or specialist departments. The orchestration of science and learning by the state power, backed of course by capital, therefore became a reality. The realization of learning in the intellectual sphere was no longer free but had become subordinated to state power. Even campus life was controlled through the Normalization of Campus Life, or the NKK program (see Nugroho, this volume).

The professional associations gradually took on the role of institutional mediators and facilitators between the interests of the intellectuals or specialists, who operated within the academic/scholarly rhetoric, and the politicians who deposited their political messages within that academic rhetoric. The implication was that academic rhetoric then transformed into something transcendent separated from the interaction with (political) interests, which became latent, hidden and deferred. The intellectuals also created a *sesengkeran* to hide the "shameful truth" of their subordination.

For the purposes of this chapter, these professional intellectual/political associations are studied primarily from a phenomenological and reflective perspective, and from a structural functional perspective. The functional and structural aspects of these associations are included in this study as "significations bearing the traces" (Sarup 1993: 4) [3] of where academic and political interests intersect or meet. Further, this chapter delves into the struggle to strike a balance between the advancement of knowledge and learning on the one hand, and the need or desire for social advancement on the other.

These associations are not only unique, but also complex in nature because they have become enmeshed in the power struggle. As a result, their existence cannot be separated from the developing historical context. Time, place, and funding are important factors in understanding the roles or functions of these associations. Based on their determined roles and functions, one can then move on to study the mission and vision of each association. It is through such a study that one is exposed to the infighting and tensions among members of the various associations.

Finally, this chapter studies the efficacy of these associations by measuring the extent to which the associations' implementation of missions and visions has managed to retain the active participation of members.

THE GENESIS OF THE ASSOCIATIONS

Many professional social sciences associations have been established since the 1970s. Several association members were interviewed for this chapter.[4] It is interesting to note that not one of the interviewees alluded to any connection between the formation of their associations with the dissolution of Indonesia's political parties in 1973. Coincidence? Perhaps. Yet the fact that these associations were more than mere affiliates of political parties, and that partisan scholars became a thing of the past, were indeed indications that these new associations were different from the partisan scholars of the Old Order period. The one striking similarity, however, was that both Old and New Order era associations existed at the heart of the political arena.

---

[3] I am using the meaning of "traces" as used by Jacques Derrida in post-structural discourse. He says that each signifier contains traces of other interconnected signifiers which never have direct contact with the always absent substance.

[4] These included members from Indonesian Association of Economists (ISEI), Indonesian Association for the Development of Social Sciences (HIPIIS), Association of Indonesian Pre-historians (API), Association of Indonesian Sociologists (ISI), Association of Indonesian Literary Scholars (HISKI), Association of Indonesian Anthropologists (AAI), Association of Indonesian Archeologists (IAAI), Association of Indonesian Epigraphists (AAEI), Indonesian Linguistics Community (MLI) and Indonesian Historians Community (MSI).

TABLE 1: SCHOLARLY PROFESSIONAL ASSOCIATIONS IN INDONESIA, CA. 1990			
Profession	Total	Jakarta	Outside Jakarta
Social humanities	18	17	1
Health	25	22	3
Natural Sciences	21	16	5
Technical	12	8	4
Agricultural	8	5	3
Inter-disciplinary	15	9	6
Others	7	3	4
Total	106	80	26
Percentage	100	75	25

In the list issued by the Indonesian Scholarly Professional Associations (*Organisasi Profesi Ilmiah Indonesia* – OPII) there were at least 106 Scholarly Professional Associations, including some in the social sciences. This is not a comprehensive list, as associations such as the Association of Indonesian Sociologists (*Ikatan Sosiologi Indonesia* – ISI) or the Association of Indonesian Pre-historians (*Assosiasi Prehistori Indonesia* – API) are not included in this list. The data provided is also very limited, confined to just the name and address of each association. The associations cover a wide range of scholarly disciplines such as anthropology, archaeology, criminology, psychology, linguistics, and demography. They also include those that focus on issues such as public health, women's issues and the environment. The political stand of the associations is also stated in the preamble on ethics. The preamble claims that every scholar is a citizen. This claim is also made by the pre-historians: "The Indonesian Association of Pre-Historians is based on the Pancasila and the 1945 Constitution, and as a professional association is founded on scholarship."[5] It was in this way that these associations' professional activities were ethically and politically subordinated to citizenship, and were neither mediated by political parties nor controlled by the state.

We can examine the claim to be different for the partisan associations of the 1950s. As for scholarship-based associations, there is the example of the Indonesian Association of Economists (*Ikatan Sarjana Ekonomi Indonesia* – ISEI). According to Dibyo Prabowo, ISEI, which was established in the 1950s, experienced something of a revival in the early 1970s. Its vision was to advance the science, that is, to study why and to resolve the decline of economic science during the time of Soekarno[6], and to

---

[5] Quoted from an information sheet about API signed by its chairperson, Prof. Dr R.P. Soejono.
[6] They said that economics, as envisaged by the liberals, stagnated as a result of the influence of communist, socialist and anti-American ideas.

avoid partisanship. ISEI's objective was to advance or develop economics in accordance with economic conditions of the time, that is, when individuals were free to exploit and enjoy a free market economy. ISEI itself stated that it wanted to develop a pure science of economics. Budi Santoso, from the Association of Indonesian Anthropologists (*Asosiasi Antropologi Indonesia* – AAI), also presented the same reason for establishing the AAI, namely, a desire to avoid political segregation.[7]

The reality, however, was rather different. If we look at the structure of these associations, which were mostly headquartered in Jakarta and with branches in the regions[8], we can see that they were focused on membership. On 29 June 2002, for example, the Surabaya branch of ISEI held the Management and Economic Research Symposium I (SINREM I). There were 60 members in the organizing committee, most of whom had Masters degrees in management. SINREM I was a one-day affair and the program included a half hour speech by each of the ISEI branch chairpersons, the General Chairperson and the President of the host university. There were also two half hour speeches by ministers. Four hours were allocated for the presentation of research papers and another half-hour set aside for the presentation of a prize to the best paper. This example shows how science and scholarship were no more than covers for a mass movement of a vested interest, something we call politics, and the entire seminar was, in effect, dominated and run by the government. First, there was obviously no point in putting together such a large organizing committee other than to ensure that a large-enough audience attended to hear the ministers' speeches. Second, four hours was hardly sufficient for a dialectical discussion coupled with the added insult of wrapping up the proceedings with an awards presentation for the best paper, as if it was a school writing competition.

The ISEI experience is not unique. And given the organizational model of ISEI, it would not be incorrect to say that ISEI was merely a holding ground for large numbers of social sciences professionals in Indonesia.

HIPIIS started out somewhat differently, although it eventually went the way of ISEI. The only difference between the two is that HIPIIS has not yet set up a foundation for fundraising purposes.

---

[7] Budi Santoso: "We initiated AAI building from the Anthropology Fellowship Union (*Ikatan Kekerabatan Antropologi* – IKA) which had operated at the level of students. We had formed that organization because there was nothing to get involved in after lectures. AAI was formed around 1965 because it was a heated up period and we did not want the anthropologists to be drawn into conflict caused by the political parties. Actually, I formed IKA in the 1960s for the same reason. At that time the political parties were competing to win students as their main constituency. There was GMNI, GMKI, PMKRI and so many others. I was the first chair and remained as chair until 1993. Because in those days, only UI taught anthropology most of the members were from UI."

[8] Of the 106 professional organizations, 87 had the head office in Jakarta; 9 in Bogor; 7 in Bandung and one each in Yogyakarta, Malang and Jatinangor Sumedang.

ISEI was brought into being by Professor Sumitro and former Vice-President Hatta (Dhakidae 2003: 307) and was headed during the New Order period by a professor at the University of Indonesia who was also head of BAPPENAS. HIPIIS's story is somewhat different. HIPIIS was established by Jakarta-based professors and specialists with mainly peripheral positions in government. The highest bureaucratic positions held by the founders of HIPIIS were Secretary to the Vice President of Indonesia (e.g. Selo Soemardjan), and Director of LEKNAS LIPI (e.g. Taufik Abdullah). This is the story of the establishment of HIPIIS as remembered and told by its first chairman, Taufik Abdullah, to Ons Untoro on 7 August 2003 in his office at LIPI, Jakarta:

One day, all of us, I mean myself, the late Pak Koentjaraningrat, the late Harsja Bachtiar, were invited to a meeting by the late Pak Selo Soemardjan in the offices of Vice President Hamengku Buwono IX. This was in 1974. I was director of LEKNAS LIPI at the time. We discussed whether we should set up a social scientists association, although we did not have a specific name in mind then. We talked and finally decided to invite more people to a meeting. I knew that there happened to be a number of people from the regions in town for a meeting on oral history. There were some from West Sumatra, Ujung Pandang and from other regions. This was an opportunity so we held a meeting in the LIPI offices in Cik Ditiro. Because I was the host, I also chaired the meeting. There were quite a few present, perhaps 30 people.

Pak Selo straight away proposed that I be the interim head of the association. Then we had an exercise to find a name for the group. There were a few ideas, if I am not mistaken, but we decided on *Himpunan* (Association). But we wanted something broad, so we made it the Indonesian Association for the Development of Social Sciences. This way we could embrace more people. Anybody could join who wanted to advance the social sciences. Then we planned a seminar. I began to lobby for money. I got some money from the Ministry of Education and Culture, the Minister was Pak Sjarif Tayeb, I think. Anyway, we got money from there. Then I went to Padang, and lobbied the governor. The governor then was Harun Zain. The decision was finally to have a seminar and congress together. The seminar was called 'Social Sciences for Development', because development had to be associated with everything. Later, we decided on 'The Role of the Social Sciences in Development'. Then we had things on development in the regions, specifically Aceh.

The money for HIPIIS's first activities came from the Ministry of Education and Culture, and the host of its first congress was a governor. Taufik's story also shows that the social glue for this was the loyalty of underlings to their superiors. Taufik also stated that people participated in this as individuals, not necessarily representing their institutions. This was to avoid people being pigeon-holed according to their institutions.[9] Mukti Ali, the Minister of Religion, and Awaloedin Jamin, the national police chief, both attended in their individual capacity, that is, as laypersons. Taufik even asked Awaloedin Jamin to attend the seminar in civilian dress and not in uniform. Taufik then ensured that HIPIIS kept its distance from BAPPENAS and the government. He envisaged a situation where HIPIIS would promote alternative ideas on development:

At the Cik Ditiro meeting, HIPIIS was not yet formed, it was still being planned and I was just the interim chairperson. I asked the late Abdulrahman Surjomiharjo and Mely G Tan to help. They were LEKNAS people, I was their director, so they followed what their boss said. So I became the interim chair because I was the only person affiliated to an institution. In the university, they were mostly students and that could prove difficult. LIPI had more freedom to move. The seminar was held in Bukit Tinggi and I received help from the Governor as he had been with LEKNAS also. Harun Zain had been a consultant to LEKNAS before moving to Padang. And Bu Mely and others also did a lot of pioneering work. So we held the 'Role of the Social Sciences in Development' seminar there. There were many papers, and some were published. Then there was a congress, and at the congress it was decided to establish the *Himpunan Ilmu Sosial*. Well, this is development, and development plans are made by BAPPENAS. We in HIPIIS must be able to provide some alternative ideas.

HIPIIS then networked with the YIIS, which was headed up by Pak Selo Soemardjan. So, YIIS became an institution that carried out programs devised or proposed by HIPIIS. But HIPIIS was an open organization. There were no membership cards and such things. All of the ideas from HIPIIS were refined and implemented by

---

[9]   It appears that this pigeon-holing had already taken place among the economists. According to Dibyo Prabowo one of ISEI's goals was to get rid of this. "The idea was," he said, "to go try to get UI and UGM to unite. The 'split' between UGM and UI at that time led to the formation of the Indonesian Agro Economics Association (*Perhimpunan Ekonomi Pertanian Indonesia* – PERHEPI). PERHEPI was an association of economists who had less faith in liberalism and macro economics. They believed more in micro-economics, such as peasant [economics]. ISEI did not talk about peasants, but about finances, banking, macro issues. So, in reality, PERHEPI was a reaction against ISEI's characteristics, which was too macro. So the entry of UGM people into ISEI would help make relations between UI and UGM not so harsh. And I think that happened. When *Pak* Sadli came to Yogya he didn't bring this UGM thing, even though he was a UI man, though a graduate of UGM. But he was more UI than UGM. But with me there, I as able to embrace them so that many UI people wanted to come to UGM again, weren't uncomfortable, and neither was I when I went to UI. Previously the causes were off the record."

YIIS. It was YIIS, for example, that ran the Training Center for Social Science Research [*Pusat Latihan Penelitian Ilmu-ilmu Sosial* – PLPIS] training centers in Aceh (and) Ujung Pandang. As director of LEKNAS, I provided YIIS's first office at LEKNAS. So there was LEKNAS, there was HIPIIS and there was YIIS.

Taufik Abdullah led HIPIIS from his position as director of LEKNAS. Leading social sciences figures, such as Soedjatmoko and Makagiansar, although not members of the HIPIIS leadership, were also regularly invited to meetings by Taufik. For the most part, HIPIIS activities were carried out to establish "friendship" networks. For example, there was the friendship between Soedjatmoko and Taufik Abdullah who formulated the idea of structural poverty.

This was how Taufik remembered the birth of HIPIIS. It differed from that of ISEI, which was conceived by central power that was focused on development planning. HIPIIS, on the other hand, emerged from the periphery of power. This peripheral power was accessed via Taufik's formal and personal networks. The one trait that the two associations did share was that they were both born of Jakarta's elite.

Second and subsequent of HIPIIS leaders and members remember a different HIPIIS. Having said that, the aim of this discussion is not to determine which image or impression of HIPIIS is the right one. Rather, we are concerned with the unstable times within which HIPIIS existed. One of the current leaders of HIPIIS and a professor of anthropology at the University of North Sumatra, Usman Pelly recounted in an interview that this instability and inconsistency as far as the image of the institution is and was concerned:

HIPISS was established in November 1975 in Bukit Tinggi. Its founders were Selo Soemardjan, Soedjatmoko, Taufik Abdullah, Koentjaraningrat, Mely G. Tan, Alfian, Harsja Bachtiar, and Umar Kayam. I had just completed training at the PLPIS in Ujung Pandang, which was conducted by Umar Kayam and Clark Cunningham. The leading figures from the HIPIIS had gathered in the YIIS, which was founded in 1974 and was the umbrella organization of the PLPIS for Ujung Pandang, Surabaya, Jakarta and Medan. YIIS was the midwife to HIPIIS. There was no dividing line between the YIIS, HIPIIS, and PLPIS. The first chairperson of the HIPIIS was Taufik Abdullah who was also in YIIS.

According to Pelly, the dividing line between YIIS, PLPIS and HIPIISS, which was very clearly defined for Taufik Abdullah, had been erased. Further, Taufik's efforts to garner the support of the governor of West Sumatra are not mentioned. Pelly witnessed the birth of HIPIIS as an alumnus of PLPIS.

On 17 June 2003, Pelly and I had a casual conversation on a bus traveling from a conference at the University of Indonesia to the Bumi Wiyata Hotel. Pelly said that when Soedharmono was Minister for the State Secretariat in the New Order Development Cabinet, HIPIIS received three million rupiah every month for overhead costs. Pelly knew this because he was an HIPIIS chairperson at the time. HIPIIS was able to survive because of this "donation". He also explained how the ISI, led by Haryono Suyono, who was head of the National Family Planning Coordination Board (*Badan Koordinasi Keluarga Berencana Nasional* – BKKBN), was also able to operate well in a similar fashion.

The founders and funders of HIPIIS were well-known leading figures who had access to various sources of funds. To illustrate how influential these persons were, they had a say in selecting suitable candidates for certain graduate studies, Pelly said:

> I met Soedjatmoko at the closing of a PLPIS course at Ujung Pandang. Umar Kayam then recommended to Soedjatmoko that I be sent to study overseas. At that time, there was a lot of money around. If Selo Soemardjan, Taufik and Harsja all said you should go overseas, then you would certainly be going. It was more or less the same for all the PLPIS colleagues. There was cooperation between PLPIS and HIPIIS. eighty percent of the graduates from PLPISS now have a doctorate. That was the contribution of Harsja and friends.

Pelly also recounted that after Mulyanto became chairperson in 1997, HIPIIS became less active. In 2002, in a bid to improve the situation, HIPIIS organized an extraordinary congress at the BKKBN's Jakarta office on Jalan Permata. It was held there because of its vacinity to inexpensive hotels. Sofyan Effendi was elected chairperson and Moeslim Abdurrahman secretary-general. Moeslim had been strongly supported by Alwi Dahlan and Malik Fajar (Chairperson IV of HIPIIS and Minister for National Education) who also were very much in agreement with the elections. There were strong hopes that Moeslim, a non-governmental person, would be able to get HIPIIS moving. Sofyan had left his position as head of the Institute of State Personnel Administration (*Badan Administrasi Kepegawaian Negara* – BAKN), but there was the possibility of his being promoted to president of Gadjah Mada University. Pelly said: "Sofyan was made chairperson because he already held the deputy chairperson position. But then I proposed Moeslim as secretary-general. All those in favor? They all agreed." That was how Pelly described the election of the HIPIIS leadership, adding in his Medan style, that is, in a loud voice: "I was the one who said who should be chairperson and secretary-general. Pak Alwi was pushing me to get Moeslim voted as secretary-general. I knew Moeslim well because I had stayed with him for three months when we were both studying in Illinois. At that time (December 1982), my scholarship had ended so I was staying with him."

Pelly makes it very clear that HIPIIS was not merely a player in the political arena, but had become a political arena in itself. Various parties, whether part of the state power apparatus or a private professional, each struggled to realize their desire for power over others and then develop relationships to facilitate that purpose.[10] However, because of the structure of HIPIIS – there is no requirement for official membership or dues – the political arena that was or is HIPIIS is a floating mass.[11] Further, it was not uncommon for members of the various associations to move from professional group to professional group seeking opportunities. Pelly was a member of both HIPIIS and ISI, an association that also emerged from circles close by to the center of power.[12] I will return to this issue in the section on organizational activities.

It should be noted here that the floating mass structure of HIPIIS is perhaps specific to organizations that are very close to the center of power. Pelly said that HIPIIS, ISEI and PII were three organizations that were targeted by the New Order for cultivation. This was not the case for other, less strategic organizations. For these, the people who established the organizations tended to be drawn from the level of ministerial directorate and/or, at the most, directorate-general of a ministry.[13] As a result, technical discourse often dominated politics and political discussions. In other words, such organizations were not considered to be politically "sexy" or savvy.

---

[10] Irwan Abdullah's idealism can illustrate this. He was chosen as head of HIPIIS Yogyakarta branch. He saw that HIPIIS had great potential to contribute to society so he became very active in it. He was very optimistic that there would be ways to avoid state hegemony over HIPIIS. He said that by joining HIPIIS, he would be able to do more to ensure that HIPIIS could be entrapped in state cooption. Instead, the state would listen to the social scientists.

[11] In the experience of Irwan Abdullah the floating aspect feels like: "local HIPIIS are rarely heard, except in Jakarta and the one in Yogyakarta. Every congress the participants change except for the central figures that never change, such as Usman Pelly in Medan. From the time I joined the HIPIIS committee in Yogyakarta in 1990 through to the meeting in Medan, he has been a leading figure. I don't see that there is any Usman Pelly new generation who have become members of the HIPIIS. It is always the same people. If Selo Soemardjan was still alive, he would be there again also."

[12] Sunyoto Usman, UGM sociology lecturer, coordinator of the HIPIIS Yogyakarta, as with other leading figures, was also a leader of ISI. He told how Selo Soemardjan, Umar Kayam, Koetjaraningrat, Harsja Bachtiar, Sutandyo Wignyosubroto, Usman Pelly, Mely G Tan had also been in ISK. From Yogyakarta, there was Nasikun and Cipto and Sunyoto himself. ISI was established in the early 1990s in Bandung. The membership was loose and open like HIPIIS and most of its activity centered around its chairperson Haryono Suyono who was also Minister for Population and was renowned for getting government projects so that he was made chairperson again and again until at last he was replaced with Sediono Tjondronegoro a retired IPB lecturer. It was from the time of this transition that Usman Pelly and Sunyoto Usman say that its activities stopped.

[13] For example, the AAI is headed by Budi Santoso who is at the moment Director General of History and Traditional Values under the Directorate General of Culture.

The Indonesian Researchers Association (*Assosiasi Peniliti Indonesia* – API), for example, has developed as an organization based on constituents. Their leaders are accountable to their members. Its members have rights and obligations set out in a constitution. Every member pays a membership fee and dues, and pays for attendance at the congress. API was established about nine years ago as a specialist organization for members of IAAI. When the idea of forming API was first raised within the IAAI, there were those for and against it. Those who were against asked why it was necessary to form another professional organization when a larger one already existed. API has members from several different organizations connected with archaeology, such as paleontology and geology. However, membership by virtue of affiliation was not automatic. One has to first register with the API secretariat. An analogy was drawn with the medical profession with its different areas of specialization. So, too, with archaeology; there were pre-historians (chaired by R.P. Soejono) and also epigraphists. API is headquartered in Jakarta and is divided into three Districts: District I (West Java, Jakarta and Sumatra), District II (Yogyakarta and Central Java) and District III (East Java, Bali and the other areas in Eastern Indonesia).[14] According to one of its senior members, Sumijati, academic disciplines do not stand alone, because they have to be able to help solve problems that other disciplines are also trying to solve. Each discipline helps the other. The ideal is that everyone works together like ants.

Since it was established, API has had two chairpersons, held two congresses and colloquiums, in 1995 and 2000. The congress was opened by the Director-General of Culture who was, incidentally, an archaeologist. The congress sessions usually take place in the evenings. Colloquiums are held during the day and the focus is to discuss the various discoveries of its members. The outcome of the seminar is forwarded to the Director General of Culture and followed up by API headquarters in Jakarta. There are usually one or two international participants alongside the 100 or so domestic participants. A suggestion that API network with the members of the Indo-Pacific Prehistory Association has been implemented.

According to Sumijati, the personal benefit gained from membership in API includes the chance to exchange research results as well as to increase emotional ties between members. According to a younger member, Jajang Sonjaya, API is not a vehicle for entry into the top levels of the bureaucracy.

---

[14] API has mobilised young people to discuss and write at the district level. For example before the Second Congress on Yogyakarta in 2000, API District II in Yogyakarta organised a series of discussions in the Faculty of Letters at UGM, SPSP Central Java, SPSP Yogyakarta, the Archeology Center and the Benteng Museum. Since then such activities have decreased.

Another organization, which is also not deemed politically "sexy", is the AAI. In terms of the bureaucratic ladder, the highest any member of leader of the AAI has been is the head of a directorate. According to its former chairperson, the desire to keep away from the bureaucracy is as strong as the attraction of becoming dependent on it. When Kartini Panjaitan was at its helm, AAI wanted to implement an independent membership system similar to that of API. The Association was able to publish a book about Koentajaraningrat entitled *Koentajaraningrat and Anthropology in Indonesia*, edited by E.K.M Masinambow (1997). There was also a congress in 1996 in Jakarta where a discussion took place that had a significant impact on the curricula of anthropology departments in Indonesia. Membership cards were introduced and an independent office was established. Unfortunately, the association has had difficulty in collecting dues from members and actively involving them in its activities. As a result, the association is now stagnant.

There were great hopes for the AAI. Budi Santoso stated during an interview at the time:

> The AAI should have been making relevant statements for the period. Thinking about national education, terrorism, and so on. Our *reformasi* is providing many openings to reform, to build a new form. We fight among ourselves and forget the main target. AAI should also speak out on this. AAI should be raising real issues, looking at things through clear eyes and with a healthy analysis to show society that anthropology can contribute something to social life. We can provide a multicultural perspective from our studies of ethnicity – which is a major problem today.

These hopes proved too ambitious and idealistic. Without monetary funding and political backing, there was little chance that the AAI could bring about any change in the intellectual/political arena.

The truth of the matter is that all professional organizations have political agendas, whether or not they choose to announce otherwise. In this respect, ISEI is the only association that was open and transparent about its political leanings. ISEI openly walks hand in hand with state and capital. The following are excerpts from an interview that was broadcast on the Lativi[15] talk show. The interviewees were: Burhanudin Harahap – ISEI Chair (2003-2006) and Bank Indonesia Governor; Rizal Ramli – economist and cabinet minister during former President Abdurrahman Wahid's time; and Abdul Latief – businessman and former cabinet minister. These

---

[15] Wednesday, 16 July 2003, 22.00 hours Western Indonesian Time, Lativi, on the program *Wacana* hosted by Adolf Pasumah from Lativi. The first section of this talk show discussed the role of ISEI.

excerpts, along with relevant quotes from Dibyo Prabowo, highlight the interconnections between the state, professional scholars and capitalists:

Presenter:
What is ISEI's role in influencing government policy?

Chairperson of ISEI, Burhanudin Harahap:
ISEI as an intellectual organization, I think that what we say is the product of deep and conscious thought. Now the product of this thinking process will be put forward and discussed, opened to public discussion and then presented to the stakeholders. One of its (ISEI) stakeholders is the government and I think the private sector will also make use of these ideas.

Presenter:
Pak Latief, as a resource person here, isn't it very possible that the membership composition of ISEI, of which I am a member, is mainly bureaucrats and intellectuals, but we rarely see businessmen. Are businessmen interested in becoming members, and what are the benefits and relevance to businessmen?

Abdul Latief:
I used to be in ISEI, too, you know, and then we set up an Indonesia forum for activities that would help interaction between government and the private sector.

In the same interview, Dibyo Prabowo told the story of ISEI as follows:

ISEI allotted research to the regions. So there was a center, and then there were the regions. Secretariats and branches. When the branches attended congress they were obliged to present papers based on the results of their research. But ISEI could provide no money. There was no money. So the idea arose of setting up what was called the Indonesia Forum Foundation (YIF). The YIF would provide the funding, as a service, to ISEI. The Foundation needed start-up capital. That capital was obtained from the conglomerates that were present...The Foundation comprised three components: the academics/universities, the business component and the government component. Whenever business wanted to have a dialogue with the government, they always found that there were enormous difficulties. There was the Chamber of Commerce and Industry (KADIN), but that was very formal. The YIF operated informally. You could find ministers there, businessmen, people from the universities, and there would be informal discussions about our economic problems. So the essence of the forum was informal dialogue. In 1993, Pak Marlin, as minister for finance, asked the conglomerates, who were affluent at the time, for money. He got some 3.1 billion.

After his term as Second Chair of ISEI, Dibyo Prabowo, became the executive director of the Indonesia Forum:

My task in YIF was to fund the congresses and conferences. A congress could swallow up 800 million to 1 billion rupiah. So then YIF also provided funds to whoever wanted to carry out research, they did not need to be members of ISEI. We also gave scholarships to those who needed them, for example to help students complete their MA and Ph.D programs and for other studies, even for students from Uganda. I don't think that there are many social organizations that have foundations. If the various associations and organizations want to hold a congress, they never know where to get the money from, even today. ISEI was not like that because we invested the money so that when I completed my term as director we had 6 billion.

ACTIVITIES

The main activities of these professional organizations include organizing national seminars, congresses and, from time to time, publishing. Only ISEI was capable of supporting research and training. The Surabaya branch of ISEI, for example, operated an ISEI Business Research and Development Center, which held leadership training, training of Masters of Ceremony and protocol training. It also carried out basic training in management for its partner company, Pelabuhan III Pty Ltd amongst others. Most other organizations did not get beyond seminars and congresses. In this section, I will review the themes of discussion at the various seminars and congresses and why these themes were chosen. I will also review the relationship between these themes and the various organizations' positions in the political arena.

There is, of course, no one answer that applies to all organizations. Here, I want to concentrate on the case of HIPIIS and its metamorphosis. This is not an easy task as it is difficult to obtain the comprehensive documentation of HIPIIS activities needed to reconstruct them, let alone deconstruct them. The key figure behind the early HIPIIS seminars was Taufik Abdullah, HIPIIS chairperson for the first two terms. In thinking through these national seminars, he told me in an interview that his own thinking had to be systematic:

So in the first seminar (in Bukit Tinggi) we had said that the social sciences should contribute to development. The next question was how to develop the social sciences themselves. So the second seminar was 'Strategies for the Development of the Social Sciences' held in Rawamangun in Jakarta. My thinking was that if we had already said that the social sciences could be part of development, then naturally the social sciences should also be able to be developed. If they are to be developed, on what ethical basis? You can have excellent social sciences but it gets used for the purposes of power. Society can be manipulated. That is why I received help from Pak Sjarief Tayeb. I remember exactly, I was given 7 million rupiah. So the next seminar, entitled 'The Ethics of Scholarship and Raising Standards' was held in Medan. I can say it was as if we were writing a book: here was Chapter I, here Chapter II and this was Chapter III.

The seminar in Bukittinggi was in 1975. In 1977, the second congress was held in Manado and many people attended. Governor Worang opened it. The theme ... ah, I forget. But the more important thing was the discussion panel, which indeed was my plan, namely 'The Political System and Social Justice', but the title was vague. There was also a discussion on 'Religious Tolerance in North Sulawesi'. Then HIPIIS was able to organize an international congress, yes, yes, I received money again from BAPPENAS. The phenomenon that was the main issue in the international congress was migration. Participants came from the Philippines, Malaysia, Thailand and so on. That was the only international HIPIIS congress held in Yogyakarta. We became more and more focused with time. We went from the large to the small. We narrowed down our themes. First: The Social Sciences for Development. Second: Strategies for Developing the Social Sciences. Third: The Ethics of Social Science and Raising Standards. And in Manado and Malang, it was narrowed down further to 'Structural Poverty'. So, the conference completed the 'book', so to speak...the structural poverty book was monumental because it was quoted by so many people. That was where it was said that if one was born poor and brought up poor, one grew old poor and died poor. (Even though, at that time, the bureaucracy was allergic to the issue of poverty.) Because of Selo Soemardjan's lobbying, it was possible to say that HIPIIS was a non-partisan organization. In 1983, after the Makassar congress, the government took notice of HIPIIS. For the first time, the Minister for Home Affairs attended the congress, and the State Secretary, Soedharmono, read out a speech from the president.

These were some of Taufik Abdullah's recollections of the early years of HIPIIS. Its activities had been thematically organized in accordance with his personal objectives to develop the social sciences so that it could respond to development. These themes were clearly chosen to address the internal weaknesses of the social sciences in the face of the challenge posed by the political and economic development macro constellation promoted by the state. The decision to focus the third theme on ethics indicates the serious political burden that had to be borne by an association whose name included a reference to the development of the social sciences. It appears that HIPIIS was unable, even in the beginning, to distance itself from the ruling state power, because it was 100 percent dependent on the "generosity" of the government apparatus. HIPIIS had to "pay" for this in the form of statements that it was non-partisan. This position was of course very problematic, especially when HIPIIS chose to discuss structural poverty in a national seminar in Malang. Although the social scientists claim that the results were monumental because they had defied the national taboo on speaking about poverty, the partisanship of HIPIIS in siding with the peoples' desire for a way out of poverty was a failure.

Maruli Tobing and Emanuel Subangun (1998) launched very apt criticisms of the 3rd HIPIIS Congress in Malang based on their observations at the congress. They said that theory alone does not make poverty disappear. The two of them saw poverty through the fact of the tension and conflict between the discussion of poverty, and reality. The scholars discussed poverty as a problem that was intertwined with other things, always overlapping, finally to be formulated in the (scientific) concept of "structural poverty". All the scholars interviewed for this study described the results of the congress, which devised the term, as phenomenal. Yet, these discussions also concealed another reality of poverty namely reality as experience. According to Tobing and Subangun (1998: 41), the scholars at this congress in Malang avoided at all costs the conflict between the structural poverty of their concept and poverty as something truly experienced. It was the following incident that provided the basis for Tobing and Subangun pointing to a kind of eternal conflict between poverty as a concept and poverty as an experience:

A participant from the Teacher's College in Yogyakarta (IKIP Yogya) came to the front. In a steady voice he said: "When we chewed on the delicious food served to the participants of this congress, a group of poor children looked at us sadly. They were waiting for any leftovers, they were hungry. But we, who were chewing on our delicious food, were not moved at all to pay them any heed. Then we walked in and started out discussion on poverty and equity. Meanwhile those who are hungry and wait for leftovers breathed even less certainly.

Tobing and Subangun 1998: 143

In the experience of an activist who works alongside street children, the reality of poverty is described even more poignantly:

> Socio-culturally, they (street children) are always positioned as an object of the feelings of superiority of those in power. Academicians see them more as the object of study. Social organizations position them as objects of charity. The police see them as criminal objects. The mass media sees them as the object of reporting. Students see them as the object of demonstrations. Even religious leaders see them as an object of their worship. This kind of treatment will increasingly marginalize them. They are more and more consolidated as a group that is not worthy of having any part of a ruling grouping because of how the dark character that has stuck to them has been so very carefully maintained in order to safeguard the pure image of the privileged.
>
> Dananto 1999: 101-102

The footnote to this paragraph provides an outstanding conclusion because of the depth and universal implications of these discrepancies between academics and real life:

> I take the meaning of these phenomena to be:
> 1. We truly desire a social hierarchy, which positions one social group as half human or as an incomplete human. That is the reason why whenever a ruling group carries out some dark act, the perpetrators are always described only as 'elements' in order to guard the pure image of the rulers.
> 2. A human rights perspective only operates to the extent that it does not disturb the security and well being of those in power. That is why whenever a group suffering human right violations is a group that threatens our well being, we do not hear much about these violations.
>
> ibid.: 106

The position offered by Dananto is:

> The problem of the street child is located more with "Me" than with the children themselves. While I (we) am (are) absorbed in comforting ourselves with the perfection of the ruling group, as long as the social hierarchy is being reproduced, the production of street children (and such like) will also be sustained...no matter how much money is released, there will be no lightening of the burden of the street children (and such like) while ever comforting "myself" as being a member of the ruling group is what has hold of my mind. (ibid.: 102-103)

If the words "street children" are replaced with "poverty", and the words "I", "we" or "myself" replaced with "HIPIIS", this would imply, according to Dananto, that the issue of structural poverty lies with the HIPIIS and not with poverty itself. No matter what concepts or words are forged for the experience of poverty, the problem will never be solved if HIPIIS continues to be an instrument of state power.

Meanwhile, a criticism from the head of state himself shook the scholars from their state of uncertainty in dealing with the issues of development and poverty that were all around them. At the following congress in Makassar in 1998, Soeharto said: "In developing the exact sciences, perhaps we have to orientate ourselves to the West. Well, OK. But for the social sciences our orientation should be here, to the home country."

This is perhaps ironic. Usman Pelly said:

The most impressive congress was the Makassar congress.[16] That was the peak of the friendship between HIPIIS and the bureaucrats. At the conference, the *camat* (sub-district heads) were also ordered to attend. The delegation from Aceh left by ship. Those of us from Medan also joined the same ship, and then so did the delegations from Jakarta and Surabaya. We continued our discussions on board the ship. We called this the Ocean Seminar and it was used to prepare all the papers and strategies. By the time we arrived in Makassar, we were all exhausted. The participants from Jayapura were feeling the same. So there was this story: There was a friend, a doctor, who was ill. This was reported to Mualim. Mualim went down to the passenger cabins and asked: "How many doctors here?" The answer came: "Four". "So what are all these doctors doing (leaving somebody sick by themselves)?" "Attending a seminar," said one of them. Mualim then uttered: "No wonder you are in fourth class." Remember then that everybody was paying his or her own way.

Pelly's story clearly states his position, a position that was opposite to that which Taufik Abdullah tried to establish from the outset. Taufik was almost obsessed with maintaining a distance from the bureaucrats, whereas Pelly celebrated that which Taufik wanted to reject, namely the intimacy between the scholars and the bureaucrats that climaxed at the Makassar congress. This is not a question of who is right or wrong, but an illustration of how each stand – that is, that of Taufik and Pelly respectively – was in reality a form of political strategizing.

---

[16] There were approximately 1500 people at the Makassar congress; approximately 1000 at the Medan congress. The extraordinary congress in Jakarta had about 100 people present.

THE EFFICACY OF THE POLITICAL STRATEGIES OF PROFESSIONAL ORGANIZATIONS

Let us listen to how Taufik Abdullah explains his experiences:

At that time, I said to Soedjatmoko that for the meeting in Manado, let's have Adam Malik speak again. Pak Alamsyah from the Supreme Advisory Council (*Dewan Pertimbangan Agung* – DPA) can open the congress and then there can be a special speech from the House of Representatives (DPR), Adam Malik.

Soedjatmoko: "Oh, ya, good, good. Do you know Adam Malik?" "Not yet" I answered. Two days later, we met at Taman Ismail Marzuki. Soedjatmoko said: "Oh, ya, Bung Adam, this is Bung Taufik." It seems he knew of me, but we had never met. Then I said to Adam Malik, and Soedjatmoko had already spoken to him also: "The HIPIIS Chairperson is going to invite you." "Well take me to meet him then..." said Pak Adam. Adam Malik and Soedjatmoko were very close. A few days later I came to Soedjatmoko's office: "What is it that we hope for from Adam Malik?" "He can write about the role of the social sciences in helping the Parliament," said Soedjatmoko. Soedjatmoko had been Ambassador to the U.S., and he knew that parliamentary members needed expert staff, and that Adam Malik as Chairperson needed expert staff. I then wrote as carefully and as critically as I could, and Adam Malik knew that it was written by me. I was chairing, as HIPIIS chairperson, when he made the presentation. After speaking, Adam Malik whispered to me: "I added a little." He had added some quite harsh sentences. "Where can the poor find justice?" Those were not my words. What I had written did not talk about how the poor had no place to take their complaints.

When Alamsyah spoke, I was sitting next to Soedjatmoko. Alamsyah's speech was very critical. When he heard Alamsyah's speech, Soedjatmoko said that he was committing political suicide. The next day Alamsyah's and Adam Malik's speeches made the headlines in the papers. Adam Malik's voice was that of the DPR, it was different with Alamsyah. The word was that Soeharto was offended and he summonsed Alamsyah. Alamsyah had been close to Soeharto during the New Order. He was offered an ambassadorship but refused. He made strong speeches in the DPA. Then he was appointed again as Minister for Religion. Then he changed his mind and sponsored political prayers.

Taufik Abdullah explained that after he finished his terms as chairperson, HIPIIS experienced internal tensions because there was not enough cooperation among the executive. Alwi Dahlan was nominated by Taufik Abdullah and his colleagues to become the chairperson of HIPIIS. So they had a congress in Palembang in 1884 to elect Alwi Dahlan as chair. "That was the first time that HIPIIS was not an alternative but a part of the government. At the next congress in Makassar, Alwi invited Soedharmono who had become Vice-President. And later in Medan, Soeharto himself opened the congress."

We can sum up the strategy, explained by the former chair of HIPIIS, as follows: First, HIPIIS used the development perspective, as did the government, but HIPIIS adopted a non-partisan position. From this position, HIPIIS attempted to develop alternatives to the government's plans. In order to do this, national figures from outside of the government bureaucracy were involved to amplify its voice and mediate national socio-political issues, and in this case, the issue of poverty. Poverty was raised rhetorically through the concept of structural poverty, although the actual experience of poverty escaped unresolved. HIPIIS was formally recognized by the government in 1983, with the result that both the Minister for Home Affairs and the State Secretary attended the Makassar congress. More than a thousand participants, many of them bureaucrats, attended the congress. Some scholars saw the Makassar congress as the peak of cooperation between HIPIIS and the bureaucracy. Although he did not attend, the President sent a message for the first time, urging the scholars to have a stronger orientation to the homeland.

The metamorphosis of HIPIIS from an organization that started off keeping its distance from the government but which ended up a part of the government is not unique. ISEI itself positioned itself as independent from the beginning. This position brought forth much criticism but those active in the organization have remained proud and confident even up to now. During the Lativi talkshow interview, for example, the ISEI Chairperson and Bank Indonesia Governor, Burhanudin Harahap, responded to the issue of criticisms of Bank Indonesia from friends in ISEI as follows: "We will be very pleased to open up these issues and we will be very happy if there are criticisms from the friends in ISEI. ISEI should be an independent organization, with high integrity, and of course they must also be professional, just as with the BI."

As Taufik Abdullah has recounted, according to Usman Pelly[17], the politicization of HIPIIS took place after the Makassar congress. Its chairperson was Alwi Dahlan who was also, at that time, secretary to Emil Salim, the minister in charge of the Body for the Coordination of the Environment (*Badan Koordinasi Lingkungan*

---

[17] Usman Pelly was HIPIIS Coordinator for West Indonesia (1985-1993) while also holding the position of Chairperson II. The Chairperson was Alwi Dahlan. Sofyan Effendi was Chairperson I, Malik Fajar (the current Minister for National Education) was Chairperson IV. Mulyanto was the Deputy Chairperson and the Secretary-general was Mochtar Pabottinggi. Since 1994 Usman Pelly has been the chairperson of the North Sumatra HIPIIS.

Hidup – BKLH). Pelly said he was very concerned with how research projects were being distributed through the Ministry for the Environment because we were very active then on environmental questions and how to raise tolerance between ethnic groups and prosperity in general. Our team even produced the AMDAL social indicators. Usman Pelly said:

> OK then, President Soeharto had said this and that, but HIPIIS was providing a lot of assistance to Pak Emil Salim [Minister for the Environment], it was the brain trust of a minister of state. Then ISI emerged in Bandung. I was called by Kusnaka [a lecturer at Padjadjaran University]. I joined and became Chairperson III under Kusnaka. Pak Selo also joined because its chairperson, Haryono Suyono, was the head of BKKBN.[18] He was from the Ministry of the Environment and connected up with ISI even though Haryono Suyono was said to be hostile to Alwi Dahlan. He joined because of the pressure from Peter Weldon from the Ford Foundation who had helped him earlier with a scholarship to go overseas via BKKBN.

Usman Pelly was sent to study in America on the condition that he studied demography. BKKBN meetings were supported thereafter by ISI. His successes resulted in Haryono Suyono being made Minister for Population. If there is any party that contributed to Haryono Suyono's appointment as Minister, it was ISI, said Pelly. For example, the meeting to decide on how to classify poor villages was held at Jalan Permata Halim, the BKKBN office. At that time, district heads did not want their regencies to be labeled as poor. The issue was discussed in ISI. One of the participants came up with another term. Such villages would be called *desa tertinggal* "lagging villages". Suyono took this term to the palace, and Haryono became a minister because of that term. It is not important whether or not this analysis or version of the facts is true, because the fact is that Haryono Suyono did become minister as a result. This example illustrates how questionable the efficacy of an organization's activities became. This was reinforced by personal experience, such as that of Usman Pelly. He said that he became very busy with a project for housing for the poor in North Sumatra. According to Pelly:

> Haryono Suyono once telephoned me and said: "Tomorrow in Jakarta, there is to be a swearing in of the Bengkulu ISI." But, there is a problem. The Governor and his friends are waiting in the airport expecting to be received by Suyono. Instead, it was I who received them. I was taken to the governor's office to swear

---

[18]   There were close personal ties between Haryono and Selo Soemardjan.

in the ISI executive. The Governor reported: "I have ordered all the district heads to attend." I was very nervous.

According to Pelly, when there was a cabinet reshuffle and Haryono became minister, Alwi was defeated and shifted to the BP7 in 1996. He was also made a P4 Manggala at the Bogor palace. He had his gold *manggala* pinned on by Soeharto. After the Medan congress, three months before Soeharto stepped down, Alwi became minister for information. After Soeharto stepped down, HIPIIS was shaken and did not know what to do. Sofyan Effendi, who had just stepped down from BAKN, was elected as HIPIIS chairperson and Moeslim Abdurrahman became Secretary-General. Meanwhile, at the Malang congress of ISI, Tjondronegoro (a retired professor from IPB) was made chairperson with Usman Pelly as advisor.

As to who was making use of whom (bureaucrat or researcher), Pelly's answer pointed very clearly to the fact that they were making use of each other and gaining mutual political advantage:

At that time, there were many things we considered important for society that we could do by working through the government. I learned from how Widjojo Nitisastro had cooperated in early times with the military. Perhaps this is what Mochtar Lubis was referring to as intellectual betrayal ... Six months before the People's Consultative Assembly, HIPIIS was busy trying to make sure that its ideas got into the Broad Outlines of the Nation's Directions (*Garis-garis Besar Haluan Negara* – GBHN). HIPIIS had a need for real power. A very symbiotic relationship was at work here. There would be a legal form to our concepts, even if the reality were different. This was where Taufik Abdullah severely criticized Alwi Dahlan who he considered to be too ready to accommodate the wishes of the bureaucracy. But Taufik could not really say clearly what was wrong. Taufik himself was in a tragic situation because he had been dismissed from LIPI and nobody was paying him any heed.

At the HIPIIS Medan congress in 1997, Soeharto criticized the social scientists:

In studying the steps needed to prepare a professional community in Indonesia, the social scientists must not forget to look to themselves. Scholars and observers of social issues must develop their own professional capabilities. Although I am not a scholar, let alone a social scientist, I often observe those observing social developments. One result of my observations is that I often have many questions about this professionalism.[19]   Medan 1997: 3

This was a paradox. At a time when HIPIIS was binding itself with the bureaucrats in what it saw as a symbiotic relationship, the supreme wielder of power in the New Order questioned their professionalism. This was the problem that Moeslim Abdurrahman experienced when he tried to steer the social sciences and other professional associations in Indonesia towards becoming a major part of a genuine civil society. These associations had failed to seize any part of an alternative hegemony because of the absence of basic principles that provided for voluntary activity, which could guarantee autonomy and independence. The existing associations, he said, still reflected a false civil society. They always kept one foot in the camp of those in power, and we have seen in fact that the scholars were often dominated by state power through the mechanism of development projects. As a result, these associations were not in reality forums for the discussion of research results.[20]

The case of the Indonesian Historians Community (*Masyarakat Sejarawan Indonesia* – MSI), as recounted by Bambang Purwanto, can add clarity here. He said that the MSI congress was purely ceremonial and had been opened by Soeharto as well as Vice President Try Sutrisno. Since 1970, MSI had not carried out any serious scholarly discussions on history. He said: "...people just presented their papers, racing for time and oblivious to all the issues. There were many papers that were distributed but never discussed in depth." Yet even so, according to Bambang Purwanto, there were those that saw MSI as being different from HIPIIS in that MSI's activities at the local level included regular discussions every three months as well as the publication of the journal *Lembaran Sejarah*. In Bambang's view, headquartering MSI in Jakarta was in itself a problem. It was this that made the organization impotent, being too close to power.

Moeslim Abdurrahman and his colleagues had also been involved in API, the only social science association that openly distanced itself from state power. Most of its members were young researchers operating outside the state, in non-governmental organizations or NGOs. They wanted to establish a transformative social sciences, that is, a social sciences capable of change and which operates independently of state hegemony; a social sciences that is inspired by liberation theology, critical social sciences, and participatory methodology and community development (see Ganie-Rochman and Rochman, this volume). This association has since dissolved but its alumni are to be found now mainly in NGOs taking part

---

[19] This last sentence, according to one informant in Soeharto's circle at that time, was meant to say that the social scientists were only good at talking.

[20] Moeslim Abdurrahman in an interview with Ons Untoro quoted the American Anthropological Association as a good model. Members registered and paid their own way. He also said that the social sciences can never be fully professional because they involved a moral and intellectual commitment to develop society.

in training and research activities. As a result of continuing internal squabble, the API was eventually dissolved. If this association had been able to overcome its internal bureaucratic problems and maintained its presence, then perhaps an arena of scholarship free of state power might have been established. In addition, the social sciences in Indonesia might have developed to a stage where its professionalism was not brought into question.

One member of the Yogyakarta HIPIIS executive stated clearly that experience had shown that HIPIIS was not important in establishing an intellectual network or arena:

> I have more social sciences-related discussions with my friends in the NGOs. I have more discussions with them about nationalism, women and so on than with any of my colleagues in the social sciences profession, And even though the social sciences are supposed to be inter-disciplinary, I have never heard of there being any cooperation.
>
> Tri Subagyo's interview with Bambang Purwanto on 19 June 2003

CONCLUSION

This chapter has illustrated quite clearly the unstable character of organizations and associations such as HIPIIS and ISEI. Their political strategies varied and changed from time to time. Even their missions and visions changed under internal (funding) pressure and the macro political constellation. These associations were active in and advanced through politics, although the academic community, who were allergic to a dialectical approach, was absent from this. "Academic activity", in the true sense of the term, existed outside of the mainstream and existed only in organizations that operated away from the development bureaucracy at the center of state power in Jakarta. The consequence has been a delay in the advancement of the social sciences and learning.

BIBLIOGRAPHY

Bourdieu, Pierre (1994) *In Other Words: Essays Towards a Reflexive Sociology*, Cambridge: Polity Press.

Dananto, Didid Adi (1999) "Om, kasihan om": bunyi misterius kemiskinan anak jalanan" in Muhamad Hidayat Rahz *Menuju masyarakat terbuka lacak jejak pembaruan sosial di indonesia*, Yogyakarta: Ashoka Indonesia and Insist Press.

Dhakidae, Daniel (2003) *Cendekiawan dan kekuasaan dalam negara Orde Baru*, Jakarta: Gramedia.

Freire, Paulo (1999) *Politik Pendidikan: kebudayaan, kekuasaan, dan pembebasan*, Yogyakarta: Pustaka Pelajar and ReaD.

HIPIIS (1997) *Kumpulan makalah seminar nasional dan kongres HIPIIS VII*, Medan:HIPIIS.

Masinambow, E.K.M. (1997) *Koentjaraningrat dan antropologi di Indonesia*, Jakarta: Yayasan Obor.

Sarup, Madan (1993) *An Introductory Guide to Post Structuralism and Postmodernism*, Athens (OH): Ohio University Press, second edition.

Soemardjan, Selo (1984) "Kemiskinan struktural dan pembangunan: kata pengantar," in Selo Soemardjan, Alfian and Mely G. Tan (eds) *Kemiskinan struktural*, Jakarta: PT Sangkala Pulsar.

Tobing, Maruli and Subangun, Emanuel (1998) *Kegalauan ekonomi politik ORBA*, Bandung: Forum Komunikasi Masyarakat.

-10-

HISTORY, NATIONALISM, AND POWER

Asvi Warman Adam

The word "nationalism" has many definitions. One of these is that provided by Hans Kohn in a book that was translated into Indonesian in 1958: "Nationalism is a concept that holds that the highest loyalty of an individual must be to the nation-state" (Kohn 1976: 11).

History can be viewed as a form of knowledge that both teaches (cognitive function) as well as imbues (affective function) loyalty to the nation-state. History teaches or tells of a past that can be used to move through the present in the process of reaching a better future. In this context, people often quote from Soekarno's ideas on the various "eras", ideas he often put forward before independence. According to Soekarno, there is a historical trilogy – some use the terms *trimurti* or *trimatra*: *the glorious past, the dark present* and *the promising future* or *the golden future*. This trilogy was adopted by the New Order as part of their brand of governance, dividing modern Indonesian history into the "Old Order" and the "New Order".

Before the European colonizers arrived, the various regions of Nusantara were traditional kingdom-states, such as Sriwijaya, Majapahit, Banten, Aceh, Mataram and Tidore. The sense of "us" among the subjects of these kingdoms or sultanates was based on the people's position as subjects of a king or residents of a particular kingdom. According to Iwan Gardono Soedjatmiko: "The subjects or residents did not imagine a community called a nation [*The Imagined Community* of Ben Anderson], yet they lived within real communities and localities as the subjects of a particular king, sultan or governor" (Soedjatmiko 2003). This view is not entirely correct. Apart from trading and economic relations between the communities of Nusantara, a collective memory network already existed, which could be found in legends and folk tales. For example, in relation to the spread of Islam through Nusantara, the Bugis-Makassar tradition "remembered" the three *ulama* from Minangkabau; Ternate remembered Makassar and Gresik; Ambon, too, remembered Gresik; Palembang and Banjarmasin remembered Demak; the tradition of the nine saints of Java remembered the kingdom of Samudra Pasai; Minangkabau remembered Aceh, and so on (Abdullah 2001).

The Europeans came not only to trade but also to conquer this region of the archipelago. The control of this territory was also accompanied by many actions that brought pain to the sons of the soil. Their common suffering promoted the rise of a feeling of unity among them. This unity was the seed of nationality.

In his struggle for independence, Soekarno said: "Independence is a golden bridge leading to a just and prosperous society"; "the prosperous and just society" being a promising future. This was the case although the future was unclear, except for the cliché, "*gemah ripah lohjinawi, tata tentram kerta raharja*", which means "prosperous, flourishing in population, fertile, with order, peace, safety and happiness".

Symbols and rituals can help in the effort to increase the sense of nationalism. This can include the teaching of history and of national heroism, also through language, literature, theatre, film, music and national rituals such as the commemoration of important dates in history. However, all these efforts to increase national sentiment can backfire if the nationalist project is not accompanied by state policies that are truly wise. In the formation of a new nation, a state with a successful national program will win the loyalty of its citizens and in turn develop and strengthen nationalism.

The rise of nationalism constituted important capital in the struggle to win independence. In the post-colonial era, nationalism was interpreted in different ways at different times. During Soekarno's time, nationalism was connected to the awakening of the Third World and the anti-colonial spirit. Soeharto domesticated nationalism and made it accommodate to development that was based on stability and *persatuan dan kesatuan*, or political and territorial unity. In the current reformation era, after the fall of Soeharto, the idea of nationalism has been revived, albeit in the shadow of communal conflict and what is often referred to as "national disintegration". The development of nationalism is clearly described in the history texts, that is, the "standard" Indonesian National History, in curricula, in school textbooks, in museums and monuments, and in the commemoration of important historical dates including the Day of Heroes.

THE YOUTH OATH

A date of significant historical importance is 28 October 1928. It was later dubbed

"The Youth Oath" (*Sumpah Pemuda*) and took place as a result of a consensus among the leaders of the various youth and regional (ethnic) organizations. This event reflected a form of peaceful conflict with the Dutch colonizers in that the youth were symbolically "negating" the presence of the Dutch colonizers who themselves were still symbolically representing the various native groups as parts of a territory subordinate to the Dutch. At that time, Indonesian society was divided into three groups: the Dutch and Europeans, Orientals, and Natives. The word "we" in the Youth Oath pointed to the existence of another party and at the same time constituted a proclamation of a "battle of concepts" against the Dutch.

The 1928 Youth Oath, as stated in the article by Soedjatmiko quoted above, can be read as a "Proclamation of the Indonesian Nation" and as reflecting a major socio-political change in the world of ideas and thought. The "spirit" and "soul" of the Indonesian nation was given "life" in the form of the Youth Oath, read out to the accompaniment of Soepratman's national anthem, *Indonesia Raya,* at Kramat Raya No. 106 on 28 October 1928. This spirit was then fused with the "body" of Indonesia when the independent nation was born on 17 August 1945 in the midst of a struggle against Japanese fascism and Dutch colonialism.

Before the Youth Oath, there were violent conflicts at the local level fired by a hatred for the Dutch invaders. This was the turning point in Indonesia's history as her people fought the Dutch for Indonesia, rather than for local interests.

At the time of the Youth Oath, ethnic and regional sentiments were defeated by the sense of nationality. Those who came bearing regional and religious banners (including *Jong Java, Jong Soematera, Jong Islamieten Bond, Jong Celebes, Pemoeda Kaoem Betawi,* etc.) agreed to think and act as one nation. For the sake of the nation, they were prepared to put aside regional, ethnic and religious organizational interests.

There are two kinds of history. There is history as comprised of events that have taken place in the past and there is history as recounted. We cannot take issue with history as reality, as the events have already passed. But history, as it is being narrated, keeps changing, in accordance with the perspectives of those doing the narrating. So the Youth Oath, which is looked upon as one of the pillars of Indonesian nationality, continues to be commemorated annually.

However, it was not the Youth Oath that President Soekarno celebrated in 1949 but the *Indonesia Raya* anthem composed by Soepratman on 28 October 1928. Twenty-six years later, on 28 October 1954, the Second Indonesian Language Congress was held in Medan, the first such congress after Independence. Mohamed Yamin, a prominent nationalist, chose Medan because it was a multi-ethnic city. All Medanese spoke Bahasa Indonesia, which was dubbed the "language of unity".

In 1956, when separatist movements arose, Soekarno spoke about "moving away from the 1928 Youth Oath". It was in 1957, when the situation became critical, and the regional rebellions took place, that large-scale commemorations of the Youth Oath began (Foulcher 2000). There was a need for a symbol of unity and the Youth Oath declaration provided this.

After the regional rebellions were overcome, the Youth Oath was connected to the Political Manifesto (*Manifesto Politik* – MANIPOL) and in the following years, it became a part of the slogans connected to the campaign to win the hearts and votes of the people of West Papua. During the New Order, the values connected with the Youth Oath were linked to the efforts to consolidate a basis for national development. Now that Soeharto is no longer in power, there has been more talk of diversity, something that was rarely mentioned during his time or under earlier governments. Today the Youth Oath is seen not only as a symbol of unity, but also as an acknowledgement of national pluralism.

HISTORICAL DECOLONIZATION

After independence, there was a strongly felt need for historical works written by Indonesians themselves. History books from the colonial period were written by the Dutch and were about Dutch society, either in the colony or at home in Europe. Holland, as the metropolitan center of Europe, was the focus of their attention. When they did write about the colonies, it was with a European perspective or, as van Leur put it, it was history told from the "ship's deck". Therefore, the time had come for history to be written by Indonesians, from within Indonesia.

In the Dutch textbooks about the colonial wars, conclusions were always the same, that is, there was always a "happy ending". Conflicts with the locals were resolved, resistance crushed, and *Pax Nederlandica* established. At the beginning of the 20th century, the Commission of Popular Reading, for example, published stories of the experiences of Dutch soldiers in Aceh. These were also published in Javanese to encourage a wider readership, particularly among the locals (van Gent 1921).

The need for Indonesian language history books was only recognized during the Japanese period because of the ban on the use of Dutch. Sanusi Pane wrote the book *Pengantar Sejarah* (Introduction to History), which was an adaptation of a Dutch work. After Independence, there was a "decolonization", so to speak, of history. There was a strong desire to replace books written by the Dutch. Because this was not a task that could be carried out quickly, it was enough at first to adapt the Dutch works by simply reversing the historical subjects. For example, in the original Dutch version, Diponegoro might have been a villainous rebel, but in an Indonesian book he was a hero. The same applied to Dutch historical figures.

Muhammad Yamin played the leading role in aggressively de-colonizing history, even if his approach was less than scholarly at times. He wrote passionately about the glories of Sriwijaya and Majapahit[1] and about the 6000 years of *Sang Merah Putih*, the red-and-white flag (Yamin, n.d.).[2]

Sejarah Indonesia untuk sekolah menengah (Indonesian History for High School) by Anwar Sanusi was published in September 1948. It appears that at this time, there was not yet any knowledge of Buddhism as the book was divided into the following chapters: (a) ancient times; (b) the Hindu period; (c) the transition period (meaning transition to Islam); (d) the colonial period, and so on. Of particular interest are the words from the preface of this book:

> In preparing this book, every attempt has been made to depict reality truthfully. That which is false has not been justified and that which is true has been not claimed to be false or been depicted in a confused manner through emotions gone astray. In this way, students will be taught to look for the reality and there will be no depictions that will confuse them.

The book states firmly that there was no falsification of history and that it was written "to depict reality truthfully." What is false will be stated as false, and what is true will be affirmed as the truth. It is unclear if this book was a progressive piece of work and ahead of its time or if Anwar Sanusi had actually anticipated a time when history would indeed be falsified and manipulated.

This book was reprinted for the seventh time in 1954. It was used in schools until 1965. It was not used after 1965 because Anwar Sanusi was thought to be a member of the Central Committee of the Indonesian Communist Party (CCPKI). The unfortunate truth is that it was a different person with the same name who was a member of the CCPKI.

There was no intervention in history textbooks between 1945 and 1950 because

---

[1] This view was adopted more than ten years later when Nazaruddin Syamsudin announced in his inaugural professorial lecture that the Republic of Indonesia was the "third republic" after Sriwijaya and Majapahit.

[2] On my copy of Yamin's book there is no year of publication, although there is a preface dated 10 January, 1951 in Geneva. Yamin speculated that 6,000 years ago "there was a migration of Ancient-Indonesians from Southeast Asia through the Sumatran peninsular and Philippines-Sulawesi. These people respected the Red-Sun and White-Moon colors." These two colors were then connected to life elements. Red was the color of blood, so vital for humans. White was the color of sap, so vital for plants and trees. While people would have known the colors of red and white at that time, it does not mean that they used them as symbols of state as happened on 17 August 1945. It might make more sense if we were to say that the colors of the flag came from the Dutch flag of red, white and blue, but minus the blue.

it was the period of the physical revolution. The political aspects were felt after 1960. M. Ali (1963: 114-115) in the book, *Pengantar Ilmu Sejarah Indonesia,* stated that the primary tasks of Indonesian history were to show the Indonesian nation that: (a) it was equal to the white nations; (b) it had held a respected position during its golden age; (c) its period of triumph was equal to that of any other nation; and (d) its fall as a great nation was a result of the trickery, deceit, and cunning of the Dutch and their divide-and-rule policy. As mentioned earlier, during the period of guided democracy, nationalism was directed against colonialism and geared towards instilling pride and the belief that the Indonesian nation was equal to other nations in the world.

Later, this decolonization of history deteriorated into a regionalization, with the Java-centric approach, something that Resink (1968) had warned about.[3] Most of the material discussed was about Java. Most of the national heroes came from Java (this will be discussed below in the section, "The Hero Industry").

As 1965 approached, more courses on revolution were developed. In 1964, the Team for Historical Assistance for the National Movement of the Central Leadership of the National Front, under the leadership of Ali Sastroamodjojo, prepared the *Sejarah Pergerakan Nasional (1908-1964) Berdasarkan Kuliah-Kuliah Sejarah Pergerakan Nasional. Kursus Kader Revolusi, Angkatan Dwikora* (History of the National Movement [1908-1964] based on lectures on the History of the National Movement). On page 7 of the Course for Cadres of the Revolution, Dwikora Generation, it is stated: "The history of the national movement is a part of the history of the movement of the world's people. The history of the national movement is an instrument of the revolution within the framework of completing the Indonesian revolution."[4] Before this, in 1961, Sutjipto Wirjopranoto was appointed as professor at the University of Indonesia. He delivered his inaugural lecture entitled: "Pancasila MANIPOL USDEK as the Basis for the Interpretation of History". According to him, the study of history should not only be for scholarly purposes, but it must also dedicate itself to the Indonesian Revolution; it must not just study the past, but must also be able to point the way to the future "Indonesian Socialist State".

Some left wing ideas made their way into state speeches as a result of the PKI's closeness to Soekarno, through, amongst others, one of the president's speechwriters,

---

[3] Resink wrote that there were three approaches to history: *Europocentric, Regiocentric* and *Indocentric.* Europocentric should become Indonesiacentric.

[4] The chapters in this book also illustrate the trimantra of glory-suffering-bright future, i.e. Chapter II, Indonesia before the 20th Century; Chapter III – The Period of National Triumph; Chapter IV – Imperialism in Indonesia; Chapter V – History of the National Movement and Chapter VI – Towards a New World Comprising the Prosperous and Just Society.

namely Njoto. According to Ruth McVey (1979): "From the point of view of communist leaders, history becomes too important to be left to the historians." It is difficult to name with certainty any PKI figure who specifically dealt with history and the teaching of history, but the PKI did have a history institute, although it was party history that was the subject of research. The PKI also opened a History Academy for the public called the "*Ranggawarsita* Academy". There were also history teachers and writers among PKI members, such as Supardo and Ir Rutgers. Sumardjo, the Minister for Education and Culture in the "cabinet of a 100 ministers", was also a member of the Indonesian Scholars Association (*Himpunan Sarjana Indonesia* – HSI) and a B2 graduate in history from Yogyakarta.[5]

THE NATIONAL MONUMENT BEFORE AND AFTER 1965[6]

The use and abuse of history for political purposes is not a new phenomenon. It was just that the Old Order regime was not able to do this very successfully. The New Order, however, was able to do so through various media including film[7], museums[8], monuments[9] as well as the commemoration of historically important dates[10]. This manipulative use of history was not totally dependent on Nugroho Notosusanto, Head of the Armed Forces History Center, either. After Nugroho died in 1985, Benny Moerdani established the Waspada Purba Wisesa, a museum dedicated to extolling the dangers of Islam and the extreme right. Three years later, Soeharto himself opened the PKI Betrayal museum at Lubang Buaya.

---

[5] The information in this paragraph was obtained from Hersri Setiawan, a leader of the Peoples Cultural Institute (*Lembaga Kebudayaan Rakyat* – LEKRA) who now lives in the Netherlands.

[6] This section substantially relies on material in Katharine Elizabeth McGregor (2002).

[7] Films produced for this purpose include "Pengkhianatan G30S/PKI" and "Serangan Fajar".

[8] The first museum of struggle established by Nugroho Notosusanto was the Satriamandala Museum. Notosusanto had wanted to build this at the Cipanas Palace or the Bogor Palace. But Soeharto decided that it should be built at the former Yasso Wisma, which had been the last place of exile of Bung Karno. This symbolized that President Soekarno had been replaced by the military. There were two more Armed Forces museums built after Notosusanto died in 1985. One was the Waspada Purbawisesa – a project of General Benny Moerdani – opened at the Armed Forces History center complex on 10 November 1987 as a reminder of the danger of the extreme Islamic right. The other was the PKI Betrayal Museum opened at Lubang Buaya on October 1, 1990 to remind people of the latent danger of the PKI. These two museums warned of the danger of EKA (*ekstrim kanan* – extreme right) and EKI (*ekstrim kiri* – extreme left). There was also a National Soldiery Museum (*Museum Keprajuritan Nasional*) in the Taman Mini Indonesia Indah.

[9] In Yogyakarta there are two monuments to Soeharto's heroism in the General Attack of 1 March, 1949. In Blitar there is the Trisula Monument to commemorate the 1968 military operation against the remnants of the 30 September Movement.

[10] The New Order abolished two days of commemoration. May Day commemorations were stopped in 1967 and that of the Birth of Pancasila Day (1 June) was ended in 1970. It added new days of commemoration, including the Day of Kesaktian [Power/Holiness] of Pancasila (since 1 October 1966) and the National Social Solidarity Day commemorated on 20 December. It was on this date in 1948 that the army entered Yogya and joined the people to "expel the foreign power from our region".

In 1964, a design plan for a diorama in the National Monument (MONAS) was commissioned to Saptoto and Edhi Soenarso, artists from Yogyakarta. However, this plan was delayed because of the transition of power that took place after 1965. The MONAS diorama was eventually completed in 1970 but not without some changes to the original plan designed in 1964.

For one thing, the scene entitled "Soekarno Before The Colonial Court" was removed. Second, the scene "The 1926-27 Rebellion" was replaced with "Digul 1927". The purpose of the "Digul 1927" diorama was to show that it was not only the communists who were detained in Digul, but also people of many different outlooks and political inclinations. The original "1926-27 Rebellion" scene was based on the people's attack on Glodok prison in 1926, which, some have pointed out, compares with the storming of the Bastille in Paris on 14 July 1789 during the French Revolution.

The "Presidential Decree" and "Ganefo" scenes were also removed in the final piece. An interesting development was the replacement of the "Birth of Pancasila" scene with an "Adoption of Pancasila and 1945 Constitution" scene. This change was ordered by Nugroho Notosusanto. He had been appointed by Soeharto to supervise matters relating to the diorama.

Some totally new scenes were also added. These included "The Guerilla War in the War of Independence, 1945-1949", "Commander-in-Chief Sudirman leads the guerillas in 1948", "Pancasila Kesaktian Day", and "Letter of Orders, 11 March 1966" (also known as "Supersemar Day").

The Supersemar diorama was made in 1976 after Soeharto's house in Agus Salim Street was reconstructed. The reconstruction was personally attended to by President Soeharto, General Amir Machmud, General Yusuf and Nugroho Notosusanto. According to the artists who made the diorama, there was a discussion as to whether Soeharto should appear in full military uniform or in pajamas. The question was raised because 11 March 1966 was the day that Soeharto did not attend cabinet. He had taken ill. But for him to appear in pajamas would not have been good for his image of authority. A decision was made to have Soeharto lying in bed with the three generals sitting on chairs at his bedside. The scene was devised to highlight Soeharto's passivity, and that he did not lust after power (McGregor 2002: 117).

INDONESIAN NATIONAL HISTORY

According to historian A.B. Lapian[11], the Dutch had plans for a reference book on Indonesian history since the Dutch colonial era. These plans were interrupted by

---

[11] In his speech before the meeting to prepare for the Indonesian National History held in Cisarua, 2003.

the Pacific war. As far as history written by sons of the soil is concerned, Indonesia was slower off the mark than Malaysia. In Malaya (as it was known at the time), Abdul Hadi bin Haji Hasan wrote *Sejarah Alam Melayu* (A Natural History of Malaya) in 1925. It was only in 1938 that there appeared the book, *Ringkasan Sejarah Indonesia* (A Short Indonesian History) written by two unknown youths. During the Japanese period, Sanusi Pane's *Sejarah Indonesia* (Indonesian History) was published. According to Sutjipto Wiryo Suparto: "This was a quality scholarly work because he took his materials from the works of Dr N.J. Korn and P.J. Veth."

As Taufik Abdullah (1957) explains: "In 1952, a committee was formed to write a book on national history, but the committee produced nothing." A similar effort in 1957 also failed. It was only in the 1970s that progress was made. The writing of the book *Indonesian National History* (*Sejarah Nasional Indonesia* – SNI) began with discussions at the Second National History Seminar held in Yogyakarta in 1970. After the seminar, the government formed the Committee for the Compilation of a Standard Book on National History (*Panitia Penyusunan Buku Standar Sejarah Nasional* – PPBSN). The committee was headed by Sartono Kartodirdjo, Marwati Djoenoed Poesponegoro and Nugroho Notosusanto. This SNI book was to be used as the textbook in tertiary institutions as well as a reference for the writing of books for use in primary and high schools.

This book comprised six volumes, each written by four or five people. Volume I covered pre-history and was edited by R.P. Suroso. Volume II covered ancient history and was edited by Mochtar Buchori. Volume III covered the growth and development of the Islamic kingdoms (1600-1800) and was edited by Uka Tjandrasasmita. Volume IV chronicled the events between 1800 and 1900 and was edited by Sutjipto Atmodjo. Volume V covered 1900-1942 and was coordinated by Abdurrachman Surjomihardjo. And Volume VI covered 1942-1965 and was edited by Nugroho Notosusanto.[12]

After four years of research, including comparative studies conducted in the United States at the University of Berkeley and the Netherlands at Leiden University, the six volumes of the SNI were published, generating some controversy. It appears

---

[12] Chapter V on the New Order comprised the following sections (A) The crushing of the G30S/PKI; (B) The 11 March Letter; (C) Stabilization of Politics [a] the 1966-67 Transition; [b] Transfer of power from president Soekarno to Provisional Peoples Consultative Assembly Decision No IX; [c] Consolidation since 1968; (D) Economic Stabilization; (E) Five Years of Development; (F) The Integration of the Armed Forces and the Increase in Dual Function; (G) Indonesian Foreign Policy; (H) Social Cultural Development; (I) The 1971 and 1977 General Elections. These chapters explained very clearly to students who was the enemy (the PKI aided by Soekarno) and who had played a positive role (Soeharto backed by the Armed Forces) and who deserved to rule because of their positive role (the Armed Forces through the Dual Function).

that there had been conflicts between members of the writing team. Nugroho Notosusanto had summoned Deliar Noer, a member of the Volume V team who had been assigned to write "The History of the Islamic Movement, 1900-1945", and asked him to withdraw. The material that Noer had written is not included in the SNI. Noer's enforced withdrawal was followed by an exodus of the entire Volume V team, including Abdurrachman Surjomihardjo, Thee Kian Wie, and Taufik Abdullah. The last to "resign" was Sartono Kartodirdjo, who objected to being held accountable for the book's contents, especially Volume VI. In the first three editions of the SNI, Sartono's name appears on the cover along with Marwati Djoened and Nugroho Notosusanto, but was removed from the fourth and subsequent editions.

THE CRITICISM OF VOLUME VI [13]

An examination of the table of contents of this volume reveals that, during the 1942-1965 period, the military aspect is very prominent. For example, diplomacy is criticized and the military struggle praised. The Emergency Government of the Republic of Indonesia, which was led by a civilian, occupies a mere sentence, while line after line of praise is written for General Sudirman. The events of 17 October 1952, which resulted in the suspension of General Nasution, are described by reference to newspaper statements made by Nasution defending his actions. The criticism here is obvious: How can a historical figure be given the chance to defend himself or clear his name in a book that is meant to be standard reference?

Nugroho Notosusanto was chief editor with editorial members comprising Saleh Djamhari, Ariwiadi, Rochmani Santoso, Emilia B. Musin Wismar and Moela Marbun. Of the books used as references for Volume VI, Notosusanto's own works constituted the largest group, 17 in all. Next were books by Nasution and Aidit, 13 and 11 respectively. Of the other authors cited, no one was cited more than three times. While this is not impermissible academically, it does give rise to the impression that the writers were more interested in presenting their own opinions than carrying out a new and comprehensive historical study, based on established facts.

This book is somewhat difficult to defend academically. "The central problem with Volume VI is the lack of clarity of its framework," said the historian Taufik Abdullah, as quoted in the Forum article. He gave the example of how there appeared to be no attention given to the time dimension, as if everything was happening at

---

[13] This section takes part of its information from a report in Forum magazine, 3 September 1992 in addition to a reading of SNI Volume VI. I have used the 1984 edition, although there is also some reference to the 1976 edition.

the same time everywhere: "Apart from that," he said, "there is also too much attention paid to events on Sumatra and Java."

Professor Sartono Kartodirdjo also took issue with the methodology of writing. According to him, history must be written in a holistic method, so that all inter-relations are visible. For example, the diplomatic route favored and taken by Soekarno and Mohamad Hatta could not be viewed separately from the surrounding events. As Kartodirdjo wrote, "Don't think that Soekarno and Hatta were simply collaborators with the Japanese. They were also supported by the people."

The book also contains elementary weaknesses. Many of the words used are more appropriate in journalism than in scholarly historical writing. For example, on page 80, we find the sentence, "...Soekarno became angry and unleashed a diatribe that more-or-less went as follows: Here is my throat, you can kill me now if you wish. I cannot surrender my responsibility as chair of the PKI. So I will ask the PKI members tomorrow." Take note of the words "more-or-less" which gives the impression that the writer is not sure what was actually said, or perhaps he is just taking the easy way out.

We find similarly inappropriate words on page 156: "It is unfortunate that the elements who were involved have not yet been put on trial." The words "it is unfortunate" show that the writer is taking sides or is being very subjective. The book also uses the term "as is known" (page 200). In well-written history books, the term "as is known" is never used. This term is used frequently in journalism.

There is often a lack of clarity in the logic – sometimes, one might say, there is no sense at all – of how sentences are structured to come to a conclusion. One example of this can be found on pages 282 and 283. I will quote the section that seems to lead to a confusing conclusion.

> ...on 16 June 1959, the Chairperson of the Indonesian National Party (PNI), Suwirjo, sent a letter to President Soekarno (who was in Japan at the time as part of a world tour) proposing that the President decree into force the 1945 Constitution and dissolve the Constituent Assembly. The secretary-general of the Central Committee of the Indonesian Communist Party (CC PKI), D.N. Aidit, sent a letter to the PKI Fraction in the Constituent Assembly that read, 'The Political Bureau of the CC PKI only approves of fraction members attending the plenary session of the Constituent Assembly if it is necessary in order to dissolve the assembly.' It was in these critical moments, when the state of constitutional affairs was endangering both political and territorial unity, when there was a rebellion behind which there was an intervention by a major foreign power, and where parties in general were showing their impotence, that President

Soekarno and the Indonesian Armed Forces emerged as a political force that could overcome the national stalemate.

This intention of this passage is very unclear. The connections between cause and effect are also difficult to understand. It could even be misinterpreted to mean that the PKI played a major role in the Indonesian nation returning to the 1945 Constitution and that, at that time, the Armed Forces had been infiltrated by the PKI. This conclusion can be drawn because of the lack of clarity about the connection between the letter from the Chair of the PNI and Aidit's letter on the one hand and, on the other, the statement that Soekarno and the Armed Forces emerged as a national force. Page 17 reads:

There were leaders among the nationalists who refused to work with the Japanese. Well-known among these were Sutan Sjahrir and Tjipto Mangunkusumo.

Tjipto's reasons were both political and personal. His health, for one, was worsening. Amir Sjarifuddin is not mentioned at all. This is only because of his involvement with the 1948 Madiun incident, which is portrayed as a devious PKI uprising.

On page 161, the PDRI (Emergency Government of the Republic of Indonesia) only gets a mention in one sentence. Sudirman, on the other hand, is praised greatly. Further, the writers contradict themselves by saying that he is seriously ill in the first instance, but leads the guerilla struggle "totally":

The government gave a mandate to Mr Sjafruddin Prawiranegara who was in Sumatra to form and lead an Emergency Government of the Republic of Indonesia. Meanwhile, although seriously ill, the Commander in Chief of the Armed Forces of the republic of Indonesia, General Sudirman, retreated to outside the capital, Jogjakarta and totally [himself] led the guerilla struggle against the Dutch. For seven months, the whole of the people relied on General Sudirman in the great struggle to sustain the life of the State of the Republic of Indonesia. In the darkest moments of the nation's struggle, Sudirman was like a torch shining light on all around him.

Daniel Dhakidae (2003), in an analysis of the interrogations of some of the participants in the G30S in October 1965, has critically shown how these interrogations were planned to prove that the PKI wanted to seize power and control the government.[14] This is also evident in the history textbook edited by Djunedi and Notosusanto. On page 375, it is written:

After the G30S/PKI incident, it was learned that the PKI had been carrying out military training for members of the *Pemuda Rakyat* and *Gerwani* at Lubang Buaya, as preparation to seize power.

On Page 387, we read:

Every communist party everywhere in the world has the same political line. Their final aim is to establish a dictatorship of the proletariat, that is, to seize government power by whatever means necessary. The political line of the PKI had been clear since the 1948 PKI Madiun rebellion and all the developments since 1950 up until the G30S/PKI.

Also on page 387:

Then it was decided by Aidit that the movement to seize power would be directly led by D.N. Aidit as the supreme leader of the movement.

There was no reference for this assertion. Later, it was learned that there was a confession several pages long written by Aidit before he was shot in Boyolali, Central Java in 1965. The authenticity of such a letter is clearly very dubious.

The editor of the book then concludes that Soekarno was involved in G30S/PKI.[15] On pages 319 and 320, it is written:

---

[14] *"Tjatatan kronologis disekitar peristiwa 'Gerakan 30 September'"*, compiled and published by the Information Section of KOTI. These notes are without date but were compiled approximately on 22 October 1965 based on a letter written by Maj.-Gen. Soeharto. It is discussed in Dhakidae (2003).

[15] In 1984 Notosusanto's book, *Pejuang and prajurit* (Freedom Fighters and Soldiers) was published by Sinar Harapan. In this book the face of Soekarno did not appear [in a picture] of the flag-raising ceremony of 17 August 1945. Only Hatta's face was visible. The historian Abdurrachman Surjomihardjo telephoned the publisher to protest this. According to Abdurrachman, this was a falsification of history. In following editions, Soekarno's face reappeared. (I have the first and third editions). This practice of removing out-of-favor figures from photos was a practice used in Russia under Stalin. I discussed these events in 2002 with Max Riberu, editor of Sinar Harapan Publishing who was involved in the process of publishing this book in 1984. According to Max, he, Aristides Katoppo and several others went to see Notosusanto who was Minister for Education and Culture at the time. Because it was the minister who had the desire to publish the book, it was the publisher who went to the minister's office to discuss the matter. They took with them several photos that they wanted to use the book and asked the Minister to choose which ones he wanted to use. Because the photo of the 1945 flag raising that he chose was small, the Minister asked that it be enlarged. In the process of enlargement, Soekarno's face was cut out. This was what Max Riberu said. I do not whose version is correct, that of Abdurrachman Surjomihardjo or Max Riberu.

Soekarno's speeches entitled *Resopim*, *Gesuri*, *Tavip* and *Takari* all clearly presented President Soekarno's political attitude, which leaned towards the PKI and encouraged the PKI to depict the Armed Forces-Army as a negative force. The climax of the PKI's activities was the G30S/PKI Rebellion."

Soekarno is clearly the "target" in Volume VI. This is reinforced again with the statement that Soekarno was making the the political situation worse (page 422). On page 122/123 it is stated:

The pious *ulama* of West Java have stated that they no longer recognize president Soekarno as president because he has violated Islamic Law and the 1945 Constitution as well as Decisions of the MPRS.

This information has been quoted directly from the *Berita Yudha* of 28 January 1967 without any questioning of the claim that he had "violated Islamic Law". Neither was there any explanation about which Islamic Laws had been violated. On page 395, there is a report of a meeting of the Dwikora cabinet held at the Bogor Palace on October 6. Soekarno's speech reads:

The President/Supreme Commander of the Armed Forces/Great Leader of the Revolution Bung Karno affirmed that he condemned the brutal killings carried out by the counter-revolutionary adventurers belonging to what has called itself the 30 September Movement. The president has also refused to give any support to what has been called the "Revolutionary Council". Only I can decommission the cabinet, not anybody else.

KOTI, *Rangkaian Pidato dan Peringatan Resmi disekitar G30S*, Jakarta, 1965: No.18

This is the same as a short column report published by *Kompas* on 7 October 1965, and not the full report of this session of the cabinet.

In 2003, President Soekarno's speeches from 1965-1967 were published (Setiyono and Triyana 2003). But there is no copy of this speech of 6 October in the archives, which came from the State Secretariat and which were then given to the National Archives. *Tempo* magazine in the *Iqra* (feature) column discussed "A piece of mysterious history", namely the record of Soekarno's aforementioned speech. Does this record show the explanation by Njoto of the G30S incident as reported by Setiadi Reksodiprodjo, one of the ministers in the Dwikora cabinet who attended that session? Page 395/396 reads:

After the publication of the President's statement condemning G30S and more facts coming to light about how the PKI was behind the G30S, the people's anger at the PKI increased further, exploding in the burning down of the main offices of the PKI in Kramat Raya street.

On page 405:

The government also formed a committee, which was given the name, the KOTI fact-finding mission, whose members were government officials and political party leaders [no names given]. The task of this commission was to gather all the facts and information and evidence relating to the G30S/PKI incident and its epilogue. The commission members were sent to the regions between 27 December 1965 and 6 January 1966. The commission's conclusion was that there was a strong desire by the people for the President/Great Leader of the revolution to take political action. The commission's findings were conveyed to the President on 10 January 1966.

So, this commission only worked for 10 days. There was no mention of the victims of the massacres in Java and Bali during 1965-1966. On page 408:

Assisted by the Cakrawibawa regiment, the State Intelligence Agency and various criminals, there were attempts to end the demonstrations [against Soekarno]. It was only with the support of the Pancasila Front and the Armed Forces that the Tritura struggle was able to continue.

Volume VI, presented as a standard reference book, puts the Presidential Cakrawibawa guards and the State Intelligence Body in the same category as "various criminals".

Further, it would not be incorrect to say that Volume VI stands in defense of the Armed Forces or the Armed Forces elite. Pages 246-247:

The 17 October Incident was preceded by a number of causal factors. As a consequence of the end of the War for Independence, Indonesia faced the following problems:
1. Political instability with the Western European (Dutch) system of liberal democracy
2. A worsening socio-economic situation and spreading corruption
3. No speedy resolution of the issue of the liberation of West Irian
4. A deterioration of the integrity and capabilities of the government apparatus,

such as conflicts among and within the parties as well as internal unrest within the Armed Forces.

After the transfer of sovereignty the leadership of the Armed Forces, especially the Chief of Staff of the Armed Forces and also the Army were striving to consolidate and motivate the Indonesian National Army (*Tentara Nasional Indonesia* – TNI). The TNI, comprising the freedom fighters armed with great spirit and strong personal ties of loyalty, was to be upgraded to the Armed Forces (*Angkatan Perang* – AP), which would have a higher technological level and would have institutionalized discipline. If these efforts succeeded the AP would become a compact social political force able to balance the political parties and the political groups in general. So there were efforts, through the pawns of the politicos, inside the Armed Forces to prevent this. The first steps were taken by a senior officer, Colonel Bambang Supeno, who approached the regional commanders and urged them to sign a statement demanding that the President replace Colonel A.H. Nasution as the Chief of Staff of the Army.

On page 412 it is written:

Three senior Army officers, Major General Basuki Rachmad (Minister for veterans Affairs), Brigadier-General M. Jusuf (Minister for Industry) and Brigadier-General Amir Machmud, who also attended the cabinet meeting, agreed to accompany President Soekarno to Bogor. Their motivation was to ensure that President Soekarno would not feel isolated and to convince him that the Armed Forces, in particular the Army, was ready and able to manage the situation as long as they were given his full trust."

This statement was intended as a response to the accusation that the process with which the 11 March Letter of Instruction (Surat Perintah 11 March or Supersemar) was issued, was actually aimed at seizing power. These three senior officers left for the Bogor Palace simply to provide company for Soekarno "so that President Soekarno would not feel isolated." On page 414:

The second action undertaken based on the SP 11 March was the issuance of presidential Instruction No. 5 of 18 March 1966 about the arrest of 15 Ministers considered to be involved in the G30S/PKI Rebellion or who had shown ill intentions with regard to the resolution of this issue.

The presidential instruction letter actually said "securing the ministers". (The letter received by Setiadi Reksodiprodjo was attached, although cannot probably be published yet. His sons do not yet want to release the letter to the public as they may launch legal action against Soeharto for "securing" them by detaining them for years. The letter bears the name of Soeharto but is not signed.)

On 23 February 1966 at 1930 hours, President Soekarno made the following announcement to his Ministers and Armed Forces Commanders from the State Palace:

Presidential Announcement

I, the President of the Republic of Indonesia/Holder of the Mandate of the MPRS/Supreme Commander of the Armed Forces am aware that the political conflict now occurring must be ended for the sake of the safety of the people, the nation and the state.

1. I, the President of the Republic of Indonesia/Holder of the Mandate of the MPRS/Supreme Commander of the Armed Forces from this day surrender governmental power to the person empowered to implement MPRS Decision no IX/1966, General Soeharto, with no lessening of the intent and spirit of the 1945 Constitution.
2. The Implementer of MPRS Decision no IX/1996 will report the implementation of this surrender of power to the President whenever deemed necessary.
3. Calls on the whole of the Indonesian people, to the leaders of society, to the whole government apparatus and the whole of the Armed Forces to strengthen unity and to guard and consolidate the revolution and give full support to the Implementer of MPRS Decision no IX/1996.
4. Delivers this announcement to the people and the MPRS with a full sense of responsibility. May the One God protect the Indonesian people in their implementation of their ideal to create a just and prosperous society based on Pancasila.

What is interesting to note is that this announcement was published in *Berita Yudha* on 23 February 1967, *before* it was actually made. This means that *Berita Yudha* already knew what was going to happen and published the announcement before it was issued. This was not a piece of everyday news, but the report of a transfer of power at the highest level of the Republic.

Volume VI draws hasty conclusions, especially when compared to the caution usually evident in the writing style of history books used as standard references. It is no surprise then that the book concludes that the PNI and Partindo were also involved in G30S/PKI. On page 370, we read:

> With this background in mind, it is not surprising that the DPP [Central Leadership of PNI] issued a statement supporting the 30 September movement on 1 October 1965 at 10:00 AM signed by PNI secretary general and former leader of the Yogyakarta CMY, Ir. Surachman!

> It was similar with the infiltration of Partindo by the PKI. The whole of the breath and voice of Partindo was dedicated to the implementation of the PKI program. This was possible because 75 percent of the central Leadership Council of Partindo were communists wearing Partindo clothes.
>
> Kopkamtib report, *Gerakan 30 September PKI (G30S/PKI)*, Jakarta, 1978: 75.

The *Sejarah Nasional Indonesia* textbooks were severely criticized by B.M.Diah in the daily newspaper *Merdeka* on 8 April 1976 and the same articles were reprinted as a series in *Merdeka* from 18 to 29 September 1985. These articles were later compiled and published as a book (Diah 1987).

On 18 March 1976, Soeharto officially received all six volumes of SNI. The president instructed that the books be used in all government schools. On page 19 of his book, B.M. Diah wrote:

> It would be best if this book was withdrawn from circulation, and revised in accordance with a true conscience (if one exists), by historians who must dedicate themselves to honesty and to the sanctity of history, so that their books do not just become fuel for some bonfire!

In the first edition of *Meluruskan sejarah, kumpulan karangan*, Diah writes:

> Indonesian historians have passed sentence on Soekarno...on instructions from President Soekarno, the PKI and its mass organizations were able to intimidate and politically terrorize its political enemies by saying that whoever opposed Nasakom, let alone oppressed the PKI, was a counter-revolutionary and anti Bung Karno.

According to Diah, Soekarno was both accused and sentenced with this, because the intimidation and terror by the PKI was carried out under instruction from President Soekarno. In the third edition printed in 1984, this section was deleted.

Based on the SNI, Nugroho Notosusanto – together with Yusmar Basri, also from the Armed Forces History Center – compiled *Sejarah Nasional Indonesia untuk SMA* (Indonesian National History for High Schools). This book was published by the Ministry of Education and Culture in cooperation with the Balai Pustaka in 1986. In Volume III, for example, we can find various kinds of New Order propaganda. On page 121, there is a photograph depicting the viciousness of the PKI Madiun rebellion. On page 129/130, it is stated that Sutan Sjahrir promoted the formation of the BP-KNIP and that the socialists supported the formation of a parliamentary cabinet under a prime minister straying from the 1945 Constitution. On page 153 it is written: "With the crushing of the PKI Madiun rebellion, the RI was saved from the threat of the extreme left."

Soekarno was also faulted in relation to the 1965 incident:

From the time of the failure of the G30S/PKI coup to 1966, the government of President Soekarno never condemned the PKI as the force which carried out the rebellion. President Soekarno only promised to find a political solution, but there were never any signs that this promise would be carried out. This created impatience among the people, because it was in conflict with their sense of justice. The situation remained in a state of confusion and was heading into a state of crisis in national confidence.

The Volume III version for junior high school students was the same as that for senior high school students, only shorter; 190 pages as compared to 214 pages respectively.

In the teaching of history, the "greatness-suffering-bright future" schema was used. We had greatness in the time of Sriwijaya and Majapahit. The Dutch and Europeans came and extracted riches from our homeland. They were able to do this through divide-and-rule tactics. So we had to unite. Indonesian nationalism united the people in order to achieve a better future.

Gde Suwitha's economic history of the 19th century exhibits the specific character of the rhetoric used by a didactic and pragmatic history as compared with an academic history:

The economy was totally in the hands of a foreign people with their huge capital in the form of tobacco, sugar, rubber and tea plantations. Our people were only coolies and were often the victims of the foreign landlords. This drainage politics had been carried out since the time of the VOC [The Dutch East India Company]. They controlled all of trade, industry, plantations, shipping and other sectors of life. Every year mullions and millions of rupiah flowed into the harbors of the Netherlands ... Forced cultivation in agriculture created billions of guilders of wealth for the Netherlands.

Details that are included in the academic history books were left out here. For example, there were native rulers, such as Mangkunegara IV, who also owned sugar plantations and mills (Ricklefs 2001: 166), and the money that was channeled into the Netherlands treasury from 1831 to 1877 totaled 832,000,000 guilders (ibid. 2001: 159). Suwitha's simplification and omission of certain facts was to ensure that students would understand the message easily, that is, that the suffering of the Indonesian people was caused by the greed of the Dutch.

THE HEROES INDUSTRY

Every nation needs heroes. "Every great nation is a nation that values its heroes," said Soekarno. There are many biographies of Indonesian heroes in circulation, including: all the heroes from pre-historical times, including characters of legend such as Diponegoro, Imam Bonjol, Pattimura, Si Singamangaraja, Teuku Umar and his wife, Cik Ditiro, Agus Salim and Tjipto (Abdullah 1975).

Heroes Day on 11 November was set by Presidential Decree in 1957 (Schreiner 1997). It is interesting to note is that all the heroes who are remembered on Heroes Day are dead. General Basuki Rachmad, one of the three senior officers who went to the Bogor Palace for Supersemar, was the quickest ever to be declared a hero after death. In fact, he was declared a hero on the very day that he died. During the Guided Democracy era, 36 of the 49 heroes were from Java. In the New Order, two left wing heroes, Alimin and Tan Malaka, were struck off the heroes list. Their names and photos are not in the *Buku Riwayat Hidup Pahlawan Nasional* (National Heroes Biographies Book) that is used in schools.

The majority of national heroes are military personnel. The Heroes Cemetery in Kalibata, Jakarta, is "home" to the graves of some 7,000 heroes; 6,000 military and 1,000 civilian heroes. Of the 6,000 military heroes buried in Kalibata, 5,000 were from the Army, with the remaining 1,000 from the Navy, Air Force and Police collectively. Of the 1,000 civilians, only 23 were proclaimed as national heroes, among them, H. Agus Salim. The remaining had been honored with hero status at the time of their death because they had died on their posts.

One hundred and twenty-five people have been elevated to the status of national hero since the term was instituted in 1959, a quarter of whom were from the military. G30S/PKI alone gave Indonesia 10 national heroes, namely the six Army Generals and one officer who were kidnapped and killed at Lubang Buaya along with the policeman, Karel Satsuit Tubun (the guard on duty at Deputy Prime Minister Leimena's residence), and two other officers, Katamso and Sugiono, who were killed in Yogyakarta. Of the five figures made national heroes in 2002, two were military personnel, namely General Nasution and General G.P.H. Jatikusumo.

Why are there so many military personnel among the heroes, particularly at The Heroes Cemetery? The answer can be found in the definition of "hero" as set out in Presidential Decision No. 33, 1964: "A hero must be (a) citizen of the Republic of Indonesia who dies in the course of a genuine struggle in the defense of nation and state; (b) a citizen of the Republic of Indonesia who has given service in defense of nation and state who, in the course of his life, has done nothing to dishonor his earlier struggle."

The first criterion refers to military servicemen, the second to civilians. There is clearly more opportunity for "hero-ship" for the military under these criteria. Moreover, civilians have to satisfy a further qualification, namely the one relating to "not dishonoring" their struggle – a condition which, apparently, aimed to preclude figures involved in rebellions such as PRRI/Permesta in the 1950s and so on.

Another condition that must be fulfilled to be buried at the Kalibata Heroes Cemetery, apart from being a national hero, is the person in question must have been awarded at least one service medal, such as the Star of the Republic of Indonesia, the Mahaputra Star, the Guerilla Star, First Star or any of the other stars including the Eka Paksi Kartika Star (Army), Utama Yalasena Bintang (Navy), Swa Bhuana Star (Air Force) and the Bayangkara Star (Police). This would explain the military's "dominance" at the Kalibata cemetery.

Towards the end of the New Order, competition was keen among the regions to have one of their own declared a hero. No efforts were spared despite the fact that a lot of money was required. However, the competition and the efforts petered out after the 1997/1998 economic crisis.

There were also conflicts over figures who had already been declared national heroes. For instance, there was disagreement over whether Kartini should have been declared a national hero. Noted social scientist Harsja Bachtiar said that Tjut Nyak Dien, who took up arms against the Dutch, was more deserving of "hero-ship". Kartini "only fought" with the pen. This statement was harshly rebutted by the historian, Abdurrachman Surjomihardjo.

Although there was no direct debate between Th. Sumarthana and Ahmad

Mansur Suryanegara, they held opposing views on the issue. Almost simultaneously they each published a book on Kartini. Sumarthana (1993) virtually deified Kartini while Suryanegara (1995) depicted her as a pious Muslim whose heart trembled at the sound of the recitation of verses from the Quran. In effect, both of them "Christianized" and "Islamized" a Javanese woman who was not pious.

An interesting event took place on 23 November 2003 when Sergeant Major (Retired) Bakri Ilyas was buried at the Kalibata Heroes Cemetery in a military ceremony. He had participated in the revolution in West Sumatra and been awarded the War of Independence Satya Lencana I medal, War of Independence Satya Lencana II medal and the Guerilla Star in 1958. He was also registered as a Veteran of the Republic of Indonesia. Prior to 1965, he graduated with a Master of Business Administration (MBA) from the University of the Philippines. While in the Philippines, he befriended progressive Filippino students. These friendships formed the grounds for his detention without trial from 1966 to 1976. According to one source, he had been a member of the Indonesian Scholars Association which was affiliated to the PKI. There is no way to confirm this now that he lies in the Kalibata Heroes Cemetery along with the Tuparev (*tujuh pahlawan revolusi* – seven heroes of the revolution) who died on 1 October 1965.

After his release in 1976, Bakri Ilyas still had to report and his identity card was labeled with the "ET" (Ex-Prisoner) code, which made it very hard for him to find work. He was active as a leader of Pakorba (*Paguyuban Korban Orde Baru*) that struggled for the rehabilitation of victims of the 1965 revolution and victims of other human rights abuses.

Bakri Ilyas is possibly the first and only former prisoner following the upheaval of 1965 to be buried at the Kalibata Heroes Cemetery. The probable reason for this is that his illustrious military career overshadowed his status as a 1965 former political prisoner.

On Heroes Day, a minute's silence is observed as a mark of respect. According to Klaus H Schreiner (1997: 277), this practice was initiated by President Soekarno in Ambon in November 1958. The government was so serious about the practice that even cars in the city were stopped to observe the silence. "National unity" was thus achieved through public participation by order of the state.

EDUCATION IN THE HISTORY OF THE NATION'S STRUGGLE

The background to the birth of te Education of History of the Nation's Struggle (*Pendidikan Sejarah Perjuangan Bangsa* – PSPB) is that President Soeharto wanted the study of history to be more than merely a transfer of knowledge. He wanted to also implant the values of the nation's struggle in the students' hearts. Soeharto's objectives in this respect can be traced back to the time when he received information from General M. Yusuf that the students at the officers' academy had only a cursory knowledge of the history of the nation's struggle.[16]

The President therefore assembled a team to look into realizing his dream of establishing the teaching of PSPB as part of the national curriculum in schools. The team comprised: State Secretary Moerdiono; Nugroho Notosusanto, Minister for Education and Culture; Hasan Walinono, Director-General of Primary and Secondary Education; Hari Soeharto, Head of the BP7; and Basuni Suryamiharja, Chairperson of the Indonesian Teachers Union (*Persatuan Guru Republik Indonesia* – PGRI).

Nugroho Notosusanto had long proposed such a course and had passed on such proposals during the Ministries of Mashuri, Sumantri Brodjonegoro, Syarif Thayeb and Daoed Joesoef (Darmiasti 2002). These Ministers had all accepted his proposals, but they were never implemented. It was only when Nugroho became Minister that he was able to implement them.

As with many of the New Order programs, Nugroho's proposals had to have a clear legal basis. As a result, MPR TAP No II/MPR/1982, that provides the Broad Outlines of State Policy (*Garis-garis Besar Haluan Negara* – GBHN), was passed. It states: "For the purposes of sustaining and developing the soul, spirit and values of 1945 among the young generation, it will be obligatory in both private and state schools to provide education in the history of the national struggle."

The difference between PSPB and other studies of history is purpose,[17] namely PSPB more strongly emphasized the appreciation of values. For example, it was hoped that accounts of the Aceh war would help students to appreciate the struggle by the Acehnese heroes against the Dutch colonizers. PSPB was taught in 1984/1985 from the kindergarten level, all the way through to primary, junior and senior high schools. Before a specific book was written and published for PSPB, the book, *30 tahun Indonesia merdeka*[18] (30 Years of Independent Indonesia), was used along with the SNI for High Schools, edited by Nugroho Notosusanto and Yusmar Basri (both of whom were historians at the Armed Forces History Center).

The instructional goals of the PSPB were: a) students would understand that the Dutch colonization was the cause of the Indonesian people's suffering; b) students would come to believe in the justice of and rationale for the struggle of the heroes to expel the Dutch; c) students would understand that it was political and territorial

---

[16] "Pelajaran sejarah nasional jangan hanya sebagai pengetahuan, tapi betul-betul untuk ditanamkan pada anak didik," *Kompas*, 27 May 1982.

[17] Keputusan Menteri Pendidikan dan Kebudayaan Republik Indonesia no 264/U/1985.

[18] This book was published by the State Secretariat in 1975 with most of its contributing writers coming from the Armed Forces History Center.

unity that brought Indonesia to the doorway of independence; d) students would understand that the Dutch were able to use the divide-and-rule tactic successfully because there was no political and territorial unity; e) students would believe that the absence of political unity and the putting of personal and group interests before national interests resulted in a government that strayed from the 1945 Constitution (material about the short-lived Federal Republic of Indonesia); f) students would believe that the PKI's unilateral actions were attempts to enforce its will in order to destroy the Unitary State of the Republic of Indonesia; g) students would believe that the actions against the PKI were driven by the courage to defend independence and justice; and h) students would believe that the New Order's primary interests were those of the state and society.[19]

The objectives were clearly political and in accordance with the interests of the ruling regime. It was stressed that "political and territorial unity" were absolute necessities, therefore the New Order was to be supported and the PKI "crushed".

In 1994, a new curriculum for schools was issued and PSPB ceased to be taught. History is now taught as an academic subject, and values and morality are taught as part of what is known as Citizenship Studies (*Pelajaran Kewarga Negaraan* – PKN). Technical reasons were given for the change. PSPB emphasized bringing about behavioral change (the affective function) but this was never achieved in practice. Criticisms of PSPB's contents were also raised by members of academia including the historian Abdurrachman Surjomiharjo.

CONCLUSION: THE MILITARIZATION OF HISTORY AND NATIONALISM

According to Marc Ferro (1985), history is very much determined by "the kitchen in which it is prepared and cooked". Histories that are written by a university, political party, church or military research institution will, inevitably, vary. History during the New Order dominated by the Armed Forces History Center.

In the last years of Soekarno's government, there was an attempt to use history for the political purpose of "reaching Indonesian socialism". But it did not have the same opportunities as the Soeharto government to monopolize historical truth. During the New Order period, history was made an instrument to further the interests of its rulers, namely to create the perception that the New Order was the loyal bearer of the mandate to implement the 1945 Constitution and Pancasila the vanguard of the development of society. This function was covered by three themes

---

[19] *Garis-garis besar program pengajaran pendidikan sejarah perjuangan bangsa untuk SMTA*, Departemen Pendidikan dan Kebudayaan, 1985.

in the rulers' interpretation of history: 1) political and territorial unity; 2) a "correct" ideological and political system; and 3) the passing on of values.

In the view of the New Order regime, history had the power to implant ethical and ideological values. Through the study of history, "society, in particular the next generation, can copy the good examples and avoid the failures of the preceding generation". History was its instrument to bring to life and maintain a vision of the nation, "to spread noble values, sustain culture, encourage national pride and mobilize political and territorial unity."

History was also used to mobilize the internal strength of the military. According to Nugroho Notosusanto, "history is the most effective vehicle" for strengthening the spirit of integration of the Armed Forces. After the 1972 Army Seminar, the New Order proclaimed the perpetuation of the values of 1945. This passing on of the values, spirit and soul of 1945, was to commemorate those who had fought in the War of Independence. According to Kharis Suhud, the 1945 values were those of "overcoming sectional perspectives and putting the general or national and state interests above personal or group interests". There were two aims in the passing on of the 1945 values. These were, internally, to strengthen the cohesiveness of the Armed Forces and, externally, to get civilian society to emulate the good examples of and to admire the heroism of the military.

The War of Independence held a special place in the historical vision of the New Order government. As set out in the dual function doctrine, it is the claim and proud boast of the military that they were the faithful fighters for independence who defended and saved the Republic created by the Proclamation of Independence. It is these claims that provided the justification for the Armed Forces to play a major role in all aspects of life outside of their military tasks.

It is for this reason that attempts have been made to revive episodes in the TNI's struggle, long forgotten by many. For example, 20 December was declared the Day of National Social Solidarity. New Order-era Minister of Social Affairs, Haryati Soebadio, explained that it was on 20 December 1948 that the army went into the villages around Yogyakarta and, together with the people, "expelled the foreign powers from our territory".

If the War of Independence was something to be proud of, this was not the case with life under liberal democracy and subsequently Guided Democracy. These experiences were seen as times that endangered the military and weakened its struggle for economic development. The period before the New Order was named the Old Order and was depicted as being full of bad things: ideological conflict, rebellions, moral decay, stagnation in economic development; in short, everything threatened the continuing existence of the nation and state.

The New Order regime reiterated the point that its consistent implementation of Pancasila and the 1945 Constitution brought political and economic stability to Indonesia. With such a reconstruction of history, the New Order was able to justify its seizure of power from the Old Order and thereby its continued presence. Nationalism was also interpreted in a way that furthered the interests of the military. The end result was the militarization of history and nationalism.

BIBLIOGRAPHY

Abdullah,Taufik (1975) "The Study of History" in Koentjaraningrat (ed.) *The Social Sciences in Indonesia*, Jakarta: Indonesian Institute of Sciences.

—— (2001) *Nasionalisme dan sejarah*, Bandung: Satya Historica.

Ali, M. (1963) *Pengantar ilmu sejarah Indonesia*, Jakarta: Bhratara.

Darmiasti (2002) *Penulisan buku pelajaran sejarah indonesia untuk sekolah menengah atas, 1964-1984: sejarah demi kekuasaan*, M.A. thesis, University of Indonesia.

Dhakidae, Daniel (2003) *Cendekiawan dan kekuasaan dalam negara Orde Baru*, Jakarta: Gramedia.

Diah, B.M. (1987) *Meluruskan sejarah, kumpulan karangan*, Jakarta: Pustaka Merdeka.

Djunedi, Pusponegoro Marwati and Nugroho Notosusanto (eds) (1984) *Sejarah nasional Indonesia*, Jakarta: Grafindo Media Pratama, Volume VI.

Ferro, Marc (1985) *L'Histoire sous surveillance*, Paris: Gallimard.

Foulcher, Keith (2000) *Sumpah pemuda, makna dan proses penciptaan atas sebuah simbol kebangkitan Indonesia*, Jakarta: Komunitas Bambu.

Kohn, Hans (1976) *Nasionalisme, arti dan sejarahnya*, Jakarta: PT Pembangunan.

McGregor, Katharine Elizabeth (2002) *Claiming History: Military Representation of the Indonesian Past in Museums, Monuments and Other Sources of Official History from Late Guided Democracy to the New Order*, Victoria: University of Melbourne Press.

McVey, Ruth (1979) "The Enchantment of the Revolution: History and Action in an Indonesian Communist Text" in Anthony Reid and David Marr (eds), *Perceptions of the Past in Southeast Asia*, Kuala Lumpur: Heinemann.

Resink, G.J. (1968) *Indonesia's History Between the Myths*, Amsterdam: The Royal Tropical Institute.

Ricklefs, M.C. (2001) *A History of Modern Indonesia Since c.1200*, Hampshire: Palgrave.

Schreiner, Klaus H. (1997) "The Making of National Heroes: Guided Democracy to New Order, 1959-1992" in Henk Schulte-Nordholt (ed.) *Outward Appearances: Dressing State and Society in Indonesia*, Leiden: KITLV Press pp. 259-290.

Setiyono, Budi and Bonnie Triyana (eds), *Revolusi belum selesai, kumpulan pidato Soekarno 30 September 1965 - pelengkap nawaksara*, Semarang: Mesiass.

Soedjatmiko, Iwan Gardono (2003) "Sumpah pemuda dan nasionalisme", *Suara Pembaruan*, 28 October.

van Gent, F.L. (1921) *Carita peperanganing Aceh*, Commissie voor de Volkslectuur.

Sumarthana, Th. (1993) *Tuhan dan agama dalam pergulatan batin Kartini.*

Suryanegara, Ahmad Mansyur (1995) *Menemukan sejarah: wacana pergerakan Islam di Indonesia.*

Yamin, Muhammad (n.d.) *Enam ribu tahun sang merah putih*, unpublished.

INDEX

www.ingramcontent.com/pod-product-compliance
Lightning Source LLC
Chambersburg PA
CBHW020338270326
41926CB00007B/233